Winds From the North

Religion in the Americas Series

Winds From the North

Canadian Contributions to the Pentecostal Movement

Edited by

Michael Wilkinson
Peter Althouse

BRILL

LEIDEN • BOSTON
2010

Cover: P2122-MCPHERSON Aimee Semple McPherson camp meeting Group in Canada, ca. 1920s. This photo is reproduced with kind permission from the collection of the Flower Pentecostal Heritage Center.

Camp meeting group in Canada,
Front: A.H. & EVA Argue, Mary Cadwalder, Watson Argue, 2 Unidentified.
2ND ROW: 4 Unidentified, Hugh Cadwalder, Aimee Semple McPherson, Walter McAlister, 4 Unidentified.
4th row: 5 unidentified, D.N. Buntain, 2 unidentified. Others Unidentified.

This book is printed on acid-free paper.

Library of Congress Cataloging-in-Publication Data

Winds from the north : Canadian contributions to the Pentecostal movement / edited by Michael Wilkinson, Peter Althouse.
    p. cm. -- (Religion in the Americas series ; v. 10)
    Includes bibliographical references and index.
    ISBN 978-90-04-18574-6 (hardback : alk. paper) 1. Pentecostalism--Canada--History--20th century. 2. Canada--Church history--20th century. I. Wilkinson, Michael, 1965- II. Althouse, Peter. III. Title. IV. Series.

    BR1644.5.C2W56 2010
    277.1'082--dc22

                        2010015154

ISBN 978 90 04 18574 6
ISSN 1542-1279

Copyright 2010 by Koninklijke Brill NV, Leiden, The Netherlands. Koninklijke Brill NV incorporates the imprints BRILL, Hotei Publishing, IDC Publishers, Martinus Nijhoff Publishers and VSP.

PRINTED IN THE NETHERLANDS

CONTENTS

vi   CONTENTS

                         CONTROVERSY

ACKNOWLEDGMENTS

The idea for this volume emerged in discussions between the editors regarding the need for scholarly work on Canadian Pentecostalism and its transnational links to the Unites States and the rest of the world. A scholarly investigation of Canadian Pentecostalism is sorely under-represented in comparison to the research emerging from the United States. This volume is an attempt to rectify this discrepancy. As with any scholarly work, however, the effort is not the product of any one person but a collaboration of many people. Therefore we want to thank the contributors in this volume who have diligently worked to produce high quality chapters. Archival resources are critical for any scholarly endeavour. A special thank you to Marilyn Stroud and Jim Craig of the Pentecostal Assemblies of Canada archives in Mississauga for their helpful willingness in locating disparate resources for the study of Canadian Pentecostalism. Also thank you to the Flower Pentecostal Heritage Center of the Assemblies of God, where many of the early documents on Canadian Pentecostals are located. At this juncture in the history of Pentecostalism, archival resources are critical in order to preserve the historical stories, sermons, theologies, and writings. Without these archives our understanding of the early history of the movement is greatly diminished.

A number of these chapters were presented and well received at the Pentecostal Consultation of the American Academy of Religion in Montreal, and the Canadian Pentecostal symposium at the Society for Pentecostal Studies in Eugene, Oregon. We would like to acknowledge a number of people who helped in different stages of this work, including student assistants, Esteban Felix and Maria Oliva. We would especially like to thank our families, for all the support of the work we do including many hours away from home. Thank you Denise, Valerie, Victoria, Ethan, Alex, and Grace.

CONTRIBUTORS

Peter Althouse, PhD (Toronto) is Associate Professor of Theology, Southeastern University.

Linda M. Ambrose, PhD (Waterloo) is Professor of History at Laurentian University in Sudbury, Ontario where she teaches women's history and gender history.

D. William Faupel, PhD (Birmingham) is Professor of History of Christianity and Director of the Library at Wesley Theological Seminary, Washington, DC.

Shane Flanagan, MA (Acadia) completed graduate work on the history of the Pentecostal movement in Atlantic Canada.

Michael Di Giacomo, PhD (Laval) is Professor of History and Chair of the Arts and Sciences Department at Valley Forge Christian College.

Randall Holm, PhD (Laval) is Associate Professor of Biblical Studies, Providence College and Seminary.

Pamela M.S. Holmes, PhD (Toronto) is Instructor in Systematic Theology and Spirituality in the departments of religious studies and theological studies at Queen's Theological College, Queen's University.

Mark Hutchinson, PhD (New South Wales) is Reader in History and Society, and Dean of Academic Advancement, Alphacrucis College, Sydney.

David Michel, STM (Boston) is a doctoral student in Theology, Ethics, and the Human Sciences at Chicago Theological Seminary.

David A. Reed, PhD (Boston) is Professor Emeritus of Pastoral Theology and Research Professor at Wycliffe College, University of Toronto.

Adam Stewart is a doctoral candidate in the Religious Studies Department, University of Waterloo.

Michael Wilkinson, PhD (Ottawa) is Associate Professor of Sociology and director of the Religion in Canada Institute, Trinity Western University.

LIKE A MIGHTY RUSHING WIND: INNOVATION AND THE TRANSNATIONAL CHARACTER OF PENTECOSTALISM

Michael Wilkinson

Peter Althouse

INTRODUCTION

Among the many metaphors used to describe the Pentecostal movement *wind* is especially insightful. Acts 2 says: "When the day of Pentecost had come, they were all together in one place. And suddenly from heaven there came a sound like the rush of a violent wind, and it filled the entire house where they were sitting ... All of them were filled with the Holy Spirit and began to speak in other languages, as the Spirit gave them the ability."[1] The 'Acts of the Apostles' is an important biblical reference for Pentecostals. Ellen Hebden made reference to 'Acts' as she described what happened in her East End Mission in Toronto in 1906 when suddenly the Holy Ghost came upon her and she spoke in tongues.[2] R.E. McAlister likewise encountered the Holy Spirit and spoke in tongues in Los Angeles after visiting the Azusa Street Mission in 1906.[3] Winnipeg was an important centre of early Pentecostal activity in Western Canada as A.H. Argue came in contact with Durham's mission in Chicago. His daughter Zelma Argue wrote: "Don't you see it? Don't you hear it? To-day there is a sound abroad in the land. It is the sound of a 'mighty, rushing wind,' the breath of God's power."[4]

There are three important ideas that shape this volume. They are religious innovation, transnationalism, and Spirit. Religious innovation generally refers to any change in religious beliefs or practices resulting in a new development, usually in tension with the previous group, society at large, or other religious groups. Sociological literature

---

[1] Acts 2.2–4, *New Revised Standard Version*.
[2] Hebden, "How Pentecost Came to Toronto," *The Promise* May 1907, 1–3.
[3] Di Giacomo, "Pentecostal and Charismatic Christianity in Canada," 18–19.
[4] Argue, "Opportunity Means Responsibility," *The Pentecostal Testimony* September 1921, 5.

has dealt with innovation and the formation of new religious groups in specific ways. Generally, sociologists have examined the formation of new groups following the idea of charisma as developed by Max Weber. Charisma, defined as extraordinary power, is rationalized and institutionalized through a series of dilemmas often resulting in a mixed blessing.[5] Other theorists have examined how people have mobilized resources in the development of a plausibility structure or worldview which sustains the new religious group.[6] Church-sect theory, likewise, has focused on new religious groups which emerge as sectarian or reactionary from the dominant religious group usually with some connection to deprivation theories.[7] Each of these views rests upon the process of innovation, yet surprisingly, there is little work to conceptualize this important idea. Bainbridge probably gives the most attention to innovation. He defines it as "a new religious culture" that spreads to other people through various processes like diffusion, migration, missionary movements, and conversion.[8] The idea of innovation is highly insightful for understanding Pentecostalism as a new religious culture which spreads across North America and throughout the world.

While there is an innovative quality among Pentecostals it can also be controversial. What was embraced by the Pentecostals was often rejected by other sectors of Christianity. Pentecostalism was said to be sectarian, describing not just their opposition to established churches but also their form as a new religious organization.[9] In a 1955 study of religious movements in Alberta, William E. Mann wrote of many new groups including the Pentecostals and different 'cults' as examples of non-conforming religious groups.[10] In an effort to keep Pentecostalism within the contours of historic Christianity, J.E. Purdie, Principal of the first Pentecostal college in Canada argued that a good theological education would serve Pentecostal ministers well. Using the metaphor of wind, he counters: "Such stalwart men and women are not easily blown from the course by the winds of false doctrine or heresy."[11]

---

[5] Weber, *The Sociology of Religion*. O'Dea developed the idea of institutionalization as a series of dilemmas. See "Five Dilemmas in the Institutionalization of Religion."

[6] Berger, *The Sacred Canopy*; Bromley and Shupe, *Strange Gods*.

[7] Wilson, *Religious Sects*. Anderson, *Vision of the Disinherited*.

[8] Bainbridge, *The Sociology of Religious Movements*, 149.

[9] See the classic study by S.D. Clark, *Church and Sect in Canada*, 1948.

[10] Mann, *Sect, Cult and Church in Alberta*, 1955.

[11] Purdie, "Principal of the Western Pentecostal Bible College for Thirteen Years," *The Pentecostal Testimony* May 1938, 18.

And so, one group's orthodoxy is another's heresy. Religious innovation in global society always carries with it a certain level of tension.[12]

The spread of this new religious culture, as controversial as it may be, is also understood in relation to the idea of transnationalism. Transnationalism has become an important idea in the social sciences and the work of Basch, Schiller, and Blanc focused on the ways in which migrants were not simply uprooted from their old countries but maintained important links or networks with their home countries.[13] The literature on the transnational life of migrants has exploded in recent years including the religious life of migrants.[14] The point here is that incorporating the Canadian story of Pentecostalism into the North American story highlights important ways in which it is a transnational movement. Pentecostalism does not simply diffuse from America to Canada or the rest of the world. There are very important links between Canada and the United States that highlight the transnational quality of Pentecostalism. Pentecostalism is characterized by a series of global flows or movements of the Spirit which travel freely across borders.[15] Pentecostal preachers cross borders on a regular basis, back and forth between home country and host country, contributing to this new culture through sermons, tracts, testimonies, and prophesies. Canadians travel to the United States while Americans come to Canada. In our view, any story of Pentecostalism in North America must capture these important links especially between the Atlantic Provinces and New England, Toronto and New York, Winnipeg and Chicago, and finally, Vancouver and Seattle, and as far south as California.

From a biblical perspective, Spirit is often associated with the elemental forces, in which the Hebrew word *ruach* has the etymological root meaning of wind, breath, and life. Beginning with Gen. 1.2, the Spirit is depicted as wind which is an active force in creation, in that "the *ruach* of God moved upon the face of the waters." The people of Israel are delivered from the bondage of slavery when a strong wind (*ruach*) divides the Red Sea. Divine wind is also an image of judgment (Ez. 13.13–14). Spirit depicted as wind, then, conveys the sense of

---

[12] Beyer, *Religions in Global Society*.
[13] Basch, Schiller, and Blanc, *Nations Unbound*.
[14] For example, see Levitt, *God Needs No Passport*; Wilkinson, *The Spirit Said Go*; Ebaugh and Chafetz, *Religion across Boundaries*.
[15] Wilkinson, "Religion and Global Flows."

divine strength. Yet *ruach* is also combined with the Hebrew word *neshamah* (also meaning breath), together implying that the Spirit is the creator and sustainer of life. Spirit breathes life into the first human (Gen. 2.7). "The *ruach* of God has made me, and the *neshamah* of the Almighty gives me life" (Job 34.4) while Ps. 104.27–31 indicates life itself comes from and is sustained by God's Spirit. One need not belabour the point, except to say that life itself is contingent solely on God's creative Spirit, depicted in the movement of air in wind and breath.[16]

Also valued by Pentecostals is the connection between Spirit and prophecy. The Spirit imparts special abilities as divine gifts, which can be extraordinary, as in the case of Joseph or Daniel's dream interpretation, but also in the non-spectacular. God fills those who made Aaron's garments with the "spirit of wisdom" and Bezaleel "with the Spirit of God, with ability, with intelligence, with knowledge, and with craftsmanship" (Ex. 28.3). The prophetic tradition in the Hebrew Scriptures is especially nuanced. Initially, the *ruach* of God is seen to take possession of the recipient in order to bring forth inspired speech. Saul, David and Samuel all prophesied in a state of ecstatic possession attributed to *ruach*. Yet in the pre-exilic and exilic periods, prophetic inspiration was not ecstatic but simply a realization that "the Lord has spoken." The prophet spoke the words of the Lord but in a calm, matter of fact way. By the time of the exile, prophetic inspiration was thought to be bound to the past in a body of prophetic literature.[17]

Stemming from the prophetic tradition is the Spirit's activity in the dawning of messianic hope, promised through the line of David. Yet whether messianic hope was found in an individual or in corporate Israel was uncertain. Was the hope of Israel to come through a coming ruler or for the whole of Israel? *Ruach* as wind or breath was now seen as the very presence of God. Thus Joel's prophecy in 2.28–29, which was the Scripture the apostle Peter preached in Acts 2 and the basis for Pentecostal theology, was the pouring out of God's Spirit.[18] The Spirit that is poured out on the day of Pentecost is none other than the Spirit poured into the Christ (Messiah), who is now pouring out the Spirit on the people of God – the hope for Israel and the nations.

In the New Testament *ruach* is translated as *pneuma*. Although one witnesses a plethora of pneumatological patterns – Spirit of the Lord

16 Heron, *The Holy Spirit*, 3–12.
17 Heron, 12–15.
18 Heron, 16–22.

(Mt. 10.20), Spirit of the Son (Gal. 4.6), Spirit of Life (Rm. 8.2), Spirit of Grace (Heb. 10.29), Paraclete (Jn. 14.16) – the bearer of the Spirit is the Messiah of God, Jesus Christ. With the coming of the Messiah, the age of the Spirit is now open; Jesus Christ is the one on whom the Spirit rests. The narrative of Acts highlights the culmination of the Spirit in Christ, whose charismatic endowment is now transferred to the people of God, the hope of the world.[19] The theophanic depiction of God's presence draws upon the varied themes of the Old Testament, in which a 'mighty rushing wind' (Spirit) and 'tongues of fire' (perhaps an allusion to the burning bush in the calling of Moses and/or the pillar of fire guiding the deliverance of Israel from Egypt), is then connected to 'speaking in many tongues.' Peter's sermon culminates in the statement "Let all the house of Israel therefore know assuredly that God has made him both Lord and Christ, this Jesus whom you crucified (Acts 2:36)." The outpouring of the Spirit not only vindicates the life and mission of the crucified Christ but the risen Lord is now pouring out the Spirit on the people whom God has chosen.[20]

Pentecostals of all variations, including those from Canada, drew upon the rich layers of meaning in the biblical narratives for their understanding and proclamation of the 'Pentecostal' Spirit. They were fond of the narrative texts in both the Old and the New Testaments. 'This is that' was shorthand for saying that the Spirit promised by Jesus Christ, was the Spirit of creation and deliverance, and in Christ, verifying his messianic mission, and the same Spirit poured out on the church at Pentecost. The activity of speaking in tongues pointed to the presence of God's Spirit. Prophecy and the charismatic gifts were given by none other than the Spirit of the living God. God's Spirit is a mighty wind, "blowing where it wishes" (Jn. 3.8).

In various ways the contributors to this volume show how Pentecostalism, as a new religious culture shaped by notions of Spirit, spreads through some important transnational links between Canada, the United States, and elsewhere in the world. Until recently, though, little was known regarding the origins and development of Pentecostalism in Canada except in scattered papers and histories. Michael Wilkinson's edited volume *Canadian Pentecostalism: Transition and Transformation* is the most scholarly to date. Popular histories of Canadian Pentecostalism written by denominational leaders

---

[19] See Stronstad, *The Charismatic Theology of St. Luke.*
[20] Heron, 39–51.

concerned with telling their stories were influenced by American stories of origin.[21] Pentecostals themselves both north and south of the
Canada-US border perpetuated the story that the Holy Spirit spontaneously and supernaturally moved in multiple locations. Outbreaks of
Pentecostal revival were reported in Charles F. Parham's Healing Home
in Topeka, Kansas, William J. Seymour's Azusa Street Mission in Los
Angeles, California, Ellen Hebden's Healing Home in Toronto, Ontario,
and Wales, Great Britain. Concerned with the 'spontaneous' explanation, historians of the movement examined the origins of Pentecostalism with the assumption that Pentecostal revivals could not have
multiple points of origin, but one point which then spread and influenced other areas. Depending on how one defines Pentecostalism,
Azusa Street or Topeka were deemed to be the beginning of the movement, which quickly spread throughout America and into the entire
globe through missionary expansion. The result has been a kind of
American-centric view of Pentecostalism and its growth worldwide.
Most recently, scholars have questioned the single point of origin in
the United States to suggest multiple origins spontaneously arising in
the world both prior to and after Azusa Street and Topeka.[22] This in no
way denies the importance the Azusa Street revival played among early
Pentecostals. What we want to highlight are some other important
'roots' of the twentieth-century Pentecostal movement which have
some important transnational links often ignored.

The chapters in this volume are organized around origins, women,
and controversy. Throughout we have attempted to highlight the various ways in which the Spirit is particularized in Canada noting how
the moving of the Spirit is not contained by modern state boundaries.
Furthermore, there is a sense of controversy when the Spirit blows
where she will. In the section on origins the contributors focus on telling the Canadian story with attention to the innovative aspects but also
the transnational links between Canada, the United States and the
world. The second section focuses on the role of women in Pentecostal
ministry. The idea that women could play such a significant role in
religion in the early twentieth century is an innovation that requires
some attention. There are also important transnational links for the

---

[21] For examples of popular histories on Canadian Pentecostals see Kulbeck, *What
God hath Wrought*; Atter, *The Third Force*; Miller, *Canadian Pentecostals*.

[22] For example, see McGee, "'Latter Rain' Falling in the East;" Anderson, *Spreading
Fires*; idem, *Introduction to Pentecostalism*; Blumhofer, "Consuming Fire;" Cerillo,
"Interpretive Approaches to the History of American Pentecostal Origins," 29–52.

women in Pentecostal ministry discussed in this section. The ambiguous role of women in ministry and its controversial nature is also considered. Finally, the last section focuses on two important innovations both early and around the middle of the twentieth century that were extremely controversial for the Pentecostal movement. The religious issues over the 'Oneness' controversy and the 'Latter Rain' movement negatively impacted North America. However, these two innovations have gone on to be embraced elsewhere in the world and in some ways have returned to North America.

The first section probes the question of origins and identity in Canadian Pentecostalism. The sheer geographical size of Canada and its close proximity to the United States makes it difficult to identify a single point of origin for Canadian Pentecostalism. Winnipeg was an important centre for Pentecostalism in Canada which was tied to William H. Durham's Chicago Mission. Leaders from each centre would travel to the other offering leadership and support. Winnipeg's ties to Chicago illustrate the transnational quality of early Pentecostalism. People travelled back and forth between these two important sites. Durham preached in Winnipeg. A.H. Argue and his family preached in the United States. Winnipeg was also a stop off point for Europeans coming to North America to experience the new Pentecost.[23] In eastern Canada, Jim and Ellen Hebden's Healing Home in Toronto is a little known and poorly understood source for Pentecostalism in Canada, which appears to have no links to the United States until after the outbreak of glossolalia. Yet the Hebdens commissioned a number of missionaries and evangelists to spread the Pentecostal blessing, including Charles Chawner who left for Africa from Toronto. Likewise, Aimee Semple McPherson, whose brief missionary ministry to China was cut short by the untimely death of her husband Robert Semple, had links to the Hebden Mission and travelled throughout Western Ontario, then to Winnipeg and Chicago, before eventually settling in Los Angeles, California. Adam Stewart begins with a chapter examining the little known outbreak of Pentecostal spirituality in Toronto simply known as the Hebden Mission. The Hebdens migrated from England and established a home for the promotion of healing, and eventually began speaking in other tongues. They opposed any type of formal organization for fear that it would quench the Spirit which

---

[23] For example, see Wakefield, *Alexander Boddy*.

ultimately resulted in their inability to socialize a second generation of Pentecostals. Stewart argues that the Hebden Mission points to polygeneous rather than monogeneous origins for global Pentecostalism which contributes to an important debate in Pentecostal historiography.

Michael Wilkinson traces one story emerging from the Hebden Mission in the person of Charles Chawner, who was commissioned by the Hebdens to travel to Africa as Canada's first Pentecostal missionary. The Chawner story is important because it illustrates some critical differences between the Hebden's view of Spirit baptism and missionary work compared with those in the United States. The missionaries sent out by the Hebdens primarily viewed Spirit baptism as an empowerment of love for world evangelism. There is no evidence that speaking in tongues was associated with preaching the gospel without the appropriate language acquisition necessary for cross-cultural work.

Although Pentecostals in the United States were composed mostly of the Holiness traditions in its early years, early Pentecostals in Canada were drawn from diverse Protestant traditions. This eclectic composition contributed to unique theological articulations of Pentecostalism in Canada. Peter Althouse explores a theological subtradition in Canadian Pentecostalism that emerged out of J.E. Purdie's Reformed Anglican considerations and is passed on to his student Charles Ratz. Both Purdie and Ratz were educators in Pentecostal Assemblies of Canada Bible Colleges (PAOC). Purdie was an Anglican priest educated at Wycliffe College, an evangelical Anglican school at the University of Toronto and an important contributor to the early theological development of PAOC ministers. His Anglican background informed a theology that saw the Pentecostal blessing as the Spirit's infilling rather than as a subsequent baptism to initiation. The influence of Purdie on Canadian Pentecostalism points to a contextual transition within the Pentecostal movement.

Randy Holm in chapter four claims that what is important about Pentecostal origins is how they are remembered. Holm argues that early Pentecostal stories function as myth and although there may be some question about the details, the importance of early Canadian Pentecostal 'remembering' is found in their performative quality as stories with meaning. Pentecostalism is primarily an oral tradition and in Canada the narrative or testimonies about Winnipeg, Calvary Temple, Western Bible College, and the return of Jesus, all work together as a powerful story to communicate something about the early Pentecostal movement.

In the second section, the chapters focus on issues surrounding the role of women in Pentecostal ministry. According to Barfoot and Sheppard, the nascent stages of a movement afford women greater opportunity to participate and lead because charisma empowers women as equal partners.[24] Yet as a movement institutionalizes clear lines of authority begin to develop, and in societies with patriarchal structures, men assume more authority. Such is the case with women in early Canadian Pentecostalism. A number of women stand out as leaders. Ellen Hebden, Aimee Semple McPherson, Zelma and Beulah Argue, Annie Cressman and Beatrice Sims are women who dared to follow God's calling on their lives. However, the leadership of women in Canadian Pentecostalism navigated some hard felt biases that restricted women from pastoral ministry but assumed callings as evangelist or missionary (even though historically women took the role of pastors in a number of churches).

In chapter five Linda Ambrose traces the lives of two Canadian sisters, Zelma Argue and Beulah Argue Smith. Ambrose maintains that their gendered roles as daughter, sister, wife and mother afforded Zelma and Beulah the opportunity to engage in public ministry, to be significant figures in the formation and development of Canadian Pentecostalism, Zelma in the role of daughter and sister, and Beulah in the role of sister and wife. Pamela Holmes continues in chapter six to flesh out the theological contribution Zelma Argue makes to Canadian Pentecostalism. Much of what became standard theology in Canadian Pentecostalism – the experience of the baptism of the Holy Spirit as both personally energizing and socially empowering for service, the gifting and fruit of the Spirit, a metaphorical use of Scripture, revivalist sentiments regarding conversion, purity and pardon – were all part of Zelma's message. Yet she also exhibited egalitarian tendencies, contingent on a latter rain understanding of the last days. The outpouring of the Spirit in which both sons and daughters were called to ministry, as the signs of the end of time, were a clarion call to Christians to be purified, commissioned and empowered to do the work of the Lord.

Aimee Semple McPherson is another Canadian woman who gained notoriety in Pentecostal circles, probably because her story easily meshed with the American story. In chapter seven, Michael Di Giacomo examines the influence of Aimee Semple McPherson's ministry on the development of early French-Canadian Pentecostalism, which

---

[24] Barfoot and Sheppard, "Prophetic vs. Priestly Religion."

contributed to the revitalization of French-Canadian evangelicalism at a time when it was experiencing negative growth. Pentecostalism was confronted by a uniquely Canadian dilemma in that Protestant evangelicalism was associated with English-speaking Canadians, while Quebec was predominantly French Catholic. McPherson's Montreal campaign transformed a predominantly anglophone movement into a francophone one through the conversion of Louis Roussy Dutand, and set on its own trajectory a distinctly French-Canadian form of Pentecostalism.

In chapter eight, David Michel argues that McPherson's brand of revivalism contributed to a reconfiguration of Methodism in America. McPherson was socialized in Canadian Methodism, but this was primarily an intellectual appropriation. Her conversion occurred within the emotional context of Pentecostalism in Canada and her ministry spanned geographical and denominational boundaries. According to Michel, McPherson reinterpreted her Methodist background through Pentecostal lenses, and appealed to her Wesleyan heritage to make sense of her Pentecostalism. Her emphasis on emotional conversion, the revivalist context of prayer and camp meetings, holiness and healing, the practice of Pentecostal baptism, and the Pentecostalization of Methodist liturgy were easily accepted by Methodist leaders and contributed to a popular form of Methodism against the backdrop of modernism.

The last section investigates the controversial aspects of the movement emerging within Canadian Pentecostalism. In chapter nine, David Reed examines one of the earliest controversies surrounding the nature of water baptism and the doctrine of the Trinity. Reed examines the role of Canadian R.E. McAlister when he preached a controversial sermon in California on 'Jesus' Name. Franklin Small developed the ideas in relation to another controversy developing in Chicago with Durham's views of Spirit baptism and sanctification. The formation of the Pentecostal Assemblies of Canada illustrates how this new doctrine divided the founders with Small leaving the PAOC to form his own Canadian denomination.

Shane Flanagan appraises the role of Wynn T. Stairs on 'Jesus Name' Pentecostalism in the Eastern provinces in chapter ten. Like many in early Canadian Pentecostalism, Stairs demonstrated an ecumenical trend by his involvement in a number of different denominations, and his overall role in brokering a merger between his own Full Gospel Pentecostal Church and the American based United Pentecostal

Church. What started out as a small Atlantic group eventually developed into a Canadian and American-Canadian denomination. However, Stair's influence is not limited to Canada as his involvement in missionary activity spread 'Jesus Name' Pentecostalism to Columbia and Jamaica as well as Spain through the missionary activity of Bill and Ruth Drost.

The final two chapters assess the origins and development of the Latter Rain, an inherently Canadian Pentecostal innovation. Pentecostalism at the turn of the century self-identified as the Latter Rain to explain the renewed outpouring of the Spirit. Using the analogy of Palestinian weather and agricultural practices, the early rains fell in the spring for the planting of crops, followed by a dry period. The latter rains, however, fell in autumn prior to the harvest of the crops. Likewise, the charismatic outpouring of the Spirit in the Acts of the Apostles was for the purpose of establishing the church, but was followed by a decline in charismatic activity. The charismatic outpouring of the Spirit in the latter days was in preparation for the final harvest prior to the coming of Christ's kingdom. The Latter Rain Revival emerged in North Battleford, Saskatchewan in 1948 in an effort to revitalize Canadian Pentecostalism during a period of institutionalization. Although tensions surmounted between classical Pentecostals and Latter Rain proponents, the heritage of the Latter Rain would be found in the Charismatic Renewal and Independent Charismatic movements rather than in classical Pentecostalism.

D. William Faupel traces the origins of the Latter Rain Revival with Herrick Holt of the International Church of the Foursquare Gospel and George Hawtin of the Pentecostal Assemblies of Canada and its spread across the continent and around the globe. The phenomenological nature of the Latter Rain was similar to classical Pentecostalism – fasting and prayer, laying on of hands, anticipation of the charismatic gifts – though with new meanings. The structure of the church started as democratic but shifted to a hierarchical authoritarian structure. Although the Latter Rain saw itself as the harbinger of unity, it deviated from classical Pentecostalism with doctrines of the 'manifested sons of God,' a remnant of 'overcomers' who would prepare the church for the second coming of Christ, and the 'restoration of all things,' which shifted from the pre-tribulation of classical Pentecostalism to post-tribulation premillennialism.

The significance of the Latter Rain did not lie in its organizational structure, but in its influence on the contemporary charismatic movement which has adopted many Latter Rain practices. The last chapter by Mark Hutchinson traces the influence of the Latter Rain as it spread into Australia and New Zealand through media communications and a host of itinerant ministers. In a process Hutchinson describes as global return, the spread of Latter Rain spirituality reconfigured Christianity in Australia and New Zealand, returning back to the United States and Canada in the megachurch phenomenon, Scripture in Song and the music of Hillsong. Pentecostalism flows back and forth across the world and is adapted and reconfigured so that while the Latter Rain no longer exists in its original form, its spirituality is manifest in various Pentecostal-Charismatic structures and styles of worship.

The story of global Pentecostalism needs to incorporate the local stories in a careful and nuanced way. There is no single global story. Rather, the global story is found within the many local ones.[25] This volume illustrates how in North America, the introduction of the Canadian story raises questions about the American story as well as other Pentecostal events throughout the world. Other contributions from elsewhere in the world can also offer insight as they highlight similarities and differences among Pentecostals throughout these regions. No doubt, important links will be observed across the world. This volume makes a small contribution to the globalization of Pentecostalism. The stories from around the world still need to be heard and brought together so we may see the ways in which the wind has blown, and continues to blow.

BIBLIOGRAPHY

Anderson, Allan. *An Introduction to Pentecostalism: Global Charismatic Christianity.* Cambridge, UK: Cambridge University Press, 2004.
——. *Spreading Fires: The Missionary Nature of Early Pentecostalism.* Maryknoll, NY: Orbis Books, 2007.
Anderson, Robert M. *Vision of the Disinherited: The Making of American Pentecostalism.* Oxford University Press, 1979.
Argue, Zelma E. "Opportunity Means Responsibility." *The Pentecostal Testimony* September 1921, 5.
Atter, Gordon. *The Third Force.* Peterborough, ON: The College Press, 1962.
Bainbridge, William Sims. *The Sociology of Religious Movements.* New York, NY: Routledge, 1997.
Barfoot, Charles H. and Gerald T. Sheppard. "Prophetic vs. Priestly Religion: The Changing Role of Women Clergy in Classical Pentecostal Churches." *Review of Religious Research* 22 (September 1980): 2–17.

---

[25] Wilkinson, "What's 'Global' about Global Pentecostalism?"

Basch, Linda, Nina Glick Schiller and Cristina Szanton Blanc. *Nations Unbound: Transnational Projects, Postcolonial Predicaments and Deterritorialized Nation-states*. Switzerland: Gordon and Breach Publishers, 1994.
Berger, Peter. *The Sacred Canopy*. New York: Anchor Books, 1967.
Beyer, Peter. *Religions in Global Society*. New York: Routledge, 2006.
Beyer, Peter and Lori Beaman, eds. *Religion, Culture, and Globalization*. Leiden, Netherlands: Brill, 2007.
Blumhofer, Edith L. "Consuming Fire: Pandita Ramabai and the Global Pentecostal Impulse" in *Interpreting Contemporary Christianity: Global Process and Local Identities*, edited by Ogbu U. Kalu and Alaine Low, 207–237. Grand Rapids: Eerdmans, 2008.
Bromley, David G. and Anson D. Shupe, Jr. *The Great American Cult Scare*. Boston, MA: Beacon Press, 1981.
Cerillo, Augustus Jr. "Interpretive Approaches to the History of American Pentecostal Origins." *Pneuma* 19 (Spring 1997): 29–52.
Clark, S.D. *Church and Sect in Canada*. Toronto: University of Toronto Press, 1948.
Di Giacomo, Michael. "Pentecostal and Charismatic Christianity in Canada: Its Origins, Development, and Distinct Culture," in *Canadian Pentecostalism: Transition and Transformation*, edited by Michael Wilkinson, 15–38. Montreal and Kingston: McGill-Queen's University Press, 2009.
Ebaugh, Helen Rose and Janet Saltsman Chafetz. *Religion across Borders: Transnational Immigrant Networks*. Walnut Creek, CA: Altamira Press, 2002.
Hebden, Ellen. "How Pentecost Came to Toronto." *The Promise* May 1907.
Heron, Alasdair I.C. *The Holy Spirit: The Holy Spirit in the Bible, the History of Christian Thought, and Recent Theology*. Philadelphia: Westminster Press, 1983.
Kulbeck, Gloria G. *What God Hath Wrought: A History of the Pentecostal Assemblies of Canada*. Toronto, ON: The Pentecostal Assemblies of Canada, 1958.
Levitt, Peggy. *God Needs No Passport: Immigrants and the Changing American Religious Landscape*. New York: New Press, 2007.
Mann, William E. *Sect, Cult and Church in Alberta*. Toronto: University of Toronto Press, 1955.
McGee, Gary B. "'Latter Rain' Falling in the East: Early-Twentieth-Century Pentecostalism in India and the Debate over Speaking in Tongues," *Church History* 68 (1999): 648–665.
Miller, Thomas William. *Canadian Pentecostals: A History of the Pentecostal Assemblies of Canada*. Edited by William A. Griffin. Mississauga, ON: Full Gospel Publishing House.
O'Dea, Thomas F. "Five Dilemmas in the Institutionalization of Religion." *Journal for the Scientific Study of Religion* (1961): 30–39.
Purdie, J.E. "Principal of the Western Pentecostal Bible College for Thirteen Years." *The Pentecostal Testimony* May 1938, 17–18.
Stronstad, Roger. *The Charismatic Theology of St. Luke*. Peabody, MA: Hendrickson Publishers, 1984.
Wakefield, Gavin. *Alexander Boddy: Pentecostal Anglican Pioneer*. London, UK: Paternoster, 2007.
Weber, Max. *The Sociology of Religion*. Boston, MA: Beacon Press, [1922] 1991.
Wilkinson, Michael. *The Spirit Said Go: Pentecostal Immigrants in Canada*. New York: Peter Lang, 2006.
——. "Religion and Global Flows," in *Religion, Culture, and Globalization*, edited by Peter Beyer and Lori Beaman, 375–389. Leiden, Netherlands: Brill, 2007.
——. "What's 'Global' about Global Pentecostalism?" *Journal of Pentecostal Theology* 17 (2008): 96–109.
Wilkinson, Michael, ed. *Canadian Pentecostalism: Transition and Transformation*. Montreal-Kingston: McGill-Queen's University Press, 2009.
Wilson, Bryan R. *Religious Sects*. New York: McGraw-Hill, 1970.

CHAPTER ONE

A CANADIAN AZUSA? THE IMPLICATIONS OF THE HEBDEN MISSION FOR PENTECOSTAL HISTORIOGRAPHY

Adam Stewart

Introduction

In almost any introductory text on the history of religion in the United States, one will likely discover a reference to the Azusa Street Mission as Pentecostalism's unique and isolated point of origination.[1] The understanding of Azusa Street as the source of all subsequent Pentecostal missions, churches, and denominations throughout the United States, and, indeed, throughout the world, is a deeply entrenched assumption among many Pentecostals, as well as historians, social-scientists, and theologians who study the movement. The historian, Joe Creech, argues that the preponderance of this 'Azusa paradigm' of Pentecostal origins is a result of the historical consciousness of the first generation of Pentecostal writers and eyewitnesses to the events of Azusa Street, which made it difficult for them to separate "historical events from their theological interpretations of them."[2] Creech explains that these early writers and eyewitnesses imposed their theology onto the historical events that they saw before them, making it extremely difficult for later scholars to differentiate between the perceptions of Azusa Street as the very powerful, yet ultimately symbolic, point of Pentecostal origins, with the actual historical beginnings of the move-ment.[3] The first generation of Pentecostal historians, such as Zelma Argue, Frank Ewart, Stanley Frodsham, Donald Gee, Gloria Kulbeck,

---

[1] Ahlstrom, *A Religious History of the American People*, 820–821; Albanese, *America*, 124; Bridges, *The American Religious Experience*, 175–180; Corrigan and Hudson, *Religion in America*, 355; Handy, *A History of the Christian Churches in The United States and Canada*, 298; Koester, *Fortress Introduction to The History of Christianity in the United States*, 142; Noll, *A History of Christianity in the United States and Canada*, 387; Williams, *America's Religions*, 279–280.

[2] Creech, "Visions of Glory," 407.

[3] Ibid., 407–408, 420–424.

and B.F. Lawrence, relied heavily on the accounts of the early writers and eyewitnesses, and uncritically incorporated their opinions and remarks into what became the first histories of the Pentecostal movement.[4] These early histories, replete with the mythical Azusa paradigm of Pentecostal beginnings, served as the basis for most subsequent Pentecostal and non-Pentecostal retellings of the movement's history-retellings that unwittingly replicated this ahistorical mythology.[5]

One of the consequences of the wide acceptance of the myth of Azusa Street has been the tendency to ignore, or at least to marginalize, the significant influence that other early Pentecostal leaders and centres have exerted on the maturing movement. Despite the ubiquitousness of the myth of Azusa Street among Pentecostal adherents and scholars alike, there exists a growing body of literature that contests the monogenetical myth of Pentecostal origins.[6] In this chapter, I support and expand on the observations of these scholars by arguing that an historically accurate understanding of the origins of the Hebden Mission in Toronto, which recognizes the mission's impetus in the Keswick movement, and, more specifically, the healing home movement in both England and Canada, rather than the Pentecostal revivals in the United States, serves as an important corrective to the ahistorical and Americentric myth of Azusa Street. Conversely, a polygenetic theory of Pentecostal origins suggests that it is best to understand Pentecostalism as a dispersed and varied movement that owes its beginnings to a multiplicity of influences in late-nineteenth and early-twentieth century Christian revivalism, as opposed to a single, uniform, and guided process, as is assumed within both the Pentecostal mythology of origins, and the dominant scholarly treatments of the subject.

---

[4] Argue, *Contending for the Faith*; Ewart, *The Phenomenon of Pentecost*; Frodsham, *With Signs Following*; Gee, *The Pentecostal Movement*; Kulbeck, *What God Hath Wrought*; Lawrence, *The Apostolic Faith Restored*.

[5] Atter, *The Third Force*; Bloch-Hoell, *The Pentecostal Movement*; Brumback, *Suddenly … From Heaven*; Conn, *Like a Mighty Army*; Goss, *Winds of God*; Kendrick, *The Promise Fulfilled*; Miller, *Canadian Pentecostals*; Nichol, *Pentecostalism*; Quebedeaux, *The New Charismatics*; Rudd, *When the Spirit Came Upon Them*; Synan, *The Holiness-Pentecostal Movement in the US*.

[6] Blumhofer, *Restoring the Faith*; Creech, "Visions of Glory;" Dayton, *Theological Roots of Pentecostalism*; Goff, *Fields White Unto Harvest*; Hollenweger, *The Pentecostals*; Jacobsen, *Thinking in the Spirit*; McGee, *This Gospel Shall Be Preached*; Wacker, *Heaven Below*; Wacker, "The Functions of Faith in Primitive Pentecostalism," 253–375.

The Origin of the Hebden Mission

The East End Mission, or as it was more commonly known, the Hebden Mission, was established on 20 May 1906 in a three-storey building at 651 Queen Street East in Toronto by recent immigrants from England, James and Ellen Hebden. The Hebdens initially intended their mission to serve as a faith healing home. This changed, however, on 17 November 1906, when Ellen became the first known person to experience the 'Pentecostal' baptism in the Holy Spirit in Canada, and subsequently transformed the mission into the first, and most important, centre of the early Pentecostal revival in Canada. Within five months, Ellen's husband, James, and between seventy and eighty others also experienced the baptism in the Holy Spirit, and by 1910 there were fourteen other Pentecostal congregations in Canada, the majority of which had some connection with the Hebden Mission.

Until very recently nearly all that was known about the lives of James and Ellen before the establishment of the mission in Toronto was contained in a small article entitled, "This is the Power of the Holy Ghost," which Ellen published in the February-March 1907 edition of William J. Seymour's journal, *The Apostolic Faith*. In 2009, however, William Sloos conducted extensive archival research in Toronto and Southwestern Ontario, that has uncovered a swath of previously unknown information, which provides a much more complete picture of both the Hebden Mission and its founders. What we learn from these sources is that James was born to Hannah and William Hebden, and was baptized in water in Mexborough, England on 16 December 1860. The Hebdens resided in the nearby town of Swinton, an important industrial centre, where William earned a living as a labourer in a local glass works factory, situating the family among the typical working-class demographic of both the area and era. Ellen's family context, however, was quite different from that of James. She was born to Ann and Alfred Wharton on 15 January 1865 in the small village of Gayton, England, very much removed from the industrial setting of Swinton. Furthermore, Ellen's father, Alfred, was a police constable, and a respected member of the community, which would have elevated the Wharton family into a solidly middle-class standing.[7]

---

[7] Sloos, "The Story of James and Ellen Hebden: The First Family of Pentecost in Canada" *Pneuma* (Forthcoming).

When Ellen was fifteen years old, she underwent both an emotive conversion and sanctification experience influenced by the Keswick movement, which, at the time, was rapidly spreading throughout England and the Anglican Church to which the Wharton family were committed members. Ellen's father, however, being a highchurchman, did not approve of Ellen's experiences. Not able to express or cultivate her newfound spirituality within the context of her own family, Ellen moved to London, England where she found solace working in the healing home of Elizabeth Baxter, an important figure in both the Keswick and healing home movements. Elizabeth took an interest in Ellen, became a mentor to the young woman, encouraged Ellen's experience of sanctification, and helped her to develop her skills as an evangelist.[8] It was here in London that Ellen would have been exposed to Baxter's very strong belief that healing and other miracles should be expected to accompany the proclamation of the gospel as evidence of the power of God.[9]

It was after Ellen left Elizabeth Baxter's healing home that she met James Hebden, a widower and father of two children, who also had a passion for evangelism, foreign missions, and divine healing. James and Ellen were married on 24 July 1893, and eventually would have four children of their own together. After ten years of living in Swinton, and a short missionary trip to Jamaica, they, and their now six children, immigrated to Toronto in December of 1904. After approximately a year and a half of financial struggles, James and Ellen acquired a former bakery at 651 Queen Street East in Toronto, where they would finally realize their vision of opening their own healing home inspired by the example of Ellen's spiritual mentor, Elizabeth Baxter. The main floor of the building was used as the meeting hall for the mission, while the Hebdens themselves lived on the second floor. At various times throughout their ministry, they used the third floor of the building to either rent out to tenants, or to provide accommodations for individuals visiting the mission, without cost. Throughout much of the mission's history, the Hebdens held morning, afternoon, and evening services on Sundays, a Bible study class on Monday evenings, and prayer meetings twice on Wednesdays and Fridays. Moreover, the Hebdens held prayer meetings every morning, and

---

[8] Hebden, "This is the Power of the Holy Ghost," 3; Sloos, "The Story of James and Ellen Hebden," (Forthcoming).
[9] Curtis, *Faith in the Great Physician*, 185.

provided accommodations for those seeking spiritual revitalization, in their home at 191 George Street, which they acquired in 1908.[10]

On the evening of Saturday 17 November 1906, six months after the establishment of the mission, Ellen experienced the 'Pentecostal' baptism in the Holy Spirit while praying alone in her room. She provides two detailed accounts of this experience. The first is found in the same brief article in the February-March 1907 issue of *The Apostolic Faith* that provides some information about the Hebdens' lives before their immigration to Canada.[11] The second report follows a few months later in May 1907 in a short article entitled, "How Pentecost Came to Toronto," from the inaugural edition of the Hebdens' own paper, *The Promise*, the title taken from Acts 2.39 which reads, "The promise is unto you, and your children, and to all."[12] Ellen explained that in the early part of the summer in 1906, she and her husband James "began to feel a lack of power, especially to heal the sick."[13] This prompted the Hebdens to devote themselves more seriously to prayer with the hope that God might grant them the power that they needed in order to carry out the work of the mission. At the end of a hard day of work, several months after deciding to dedicate herself to a more committed regiment of prayer, Ellen retired to her room for the evening. Not long after going to bed, she claimed that the Holy Spirit prompted her to get up and pray, at which point she was immediately overtaken by the power of God. She writes: "The mighty power of God took possession of my hands, clasped them tightly together, and then moved them with such rapidity that it seemed as if they were severed from my arms." She continues: "Then God began to speak to me. First, He said, 'These are your hands no more.' I exclaimed, 'Oh! thank you, Lord!' Again, my hands were raised by the power of God and pressed tightly into my right cheek; and then they were moved to the left cheek and again pressed very hard." After being possessed by the power of the Holy Spirit, Ellen then asked God what all of this meant. She writes that God, in "a very quiet yet distinct voice said, 'Tongues.'" To this Ellen replied: "'No Lord not Tongues,'" after which, "followed a moment of

---

[10] Copely, "Pentecost in Toronto," 4; Hebden, "This is the Power of the Holy Ghost," 3; Hebden, "How Pentecost Came to Toronto," 1–3; *Promise* (February 1909): 2–4, 8; Opp, *The Lord for the Body*, 122–123; Sloos, "The Story of James and Ellen Hebden," (Forthcoming).

[11] Hebden, "This is the Power of the Holy Ghost," 3.

[12] Hebden, "How Pentecost Came to Toronto," 1–3.

[13] Hebden, "This is the Power of the Holy Ghost," 3.

deathlike stillness, when the voice again uttered the word 'Tongues.' This time I felt afraid of grieving the Lord and I said, 'Tongues, or anything that will please Thee and bring glory to Thy name.' One unknown word was repeated several times and I thought that must be Tongues." Eventually, Ellen explains that "the power of God seemed to be lifted from me," and that she was then able to go back to sleep for the night.[14]

Ellen awoke the next morning convinced that she had "received the Baptism of the Holy Ghost," and eagerly shared her experience with her husband. She recounts that during the Sunday morning meeting at the mission, "the Holy Spirit manifested His power in such a wonderful manner that everyone present saw that it was God. During the whole of that meeting the power was upon me."[15] Later that day Ellen went to the mission's afternoon meeting where she intended to sit "quietly by the organ, intending to say nothing of my new experience." However, she claimed that the Holy Spirit again came upon her causing her to shout aloud to those gathered at the meeting: "This is the power of the Holy Ghost; this is the day of Pentecost."[16] As a result of her public outburst during the Sunday afternoon meeting, Ellen records that she decided not to attend the mission's evening service in favour of spending some time alone with God in order to try and make sense of everything that she had experienced over the past two days. While alone in her apartment on the second floor of the mission, she asked God for a second time "'what all of this meant,'" to which He replied: "'He was wounded for our transgressions, He was bruised for our iniquities; the chastisement of our peace was upon Him, and with His stripes we are healed.'" After this happened, Ellen rushed downstairs to the meeting where, just after her arrival, the speaker repeated the very same passage that Ellen had just moments before received from the Holy Spirit. It was at that point, she writes: "The Spirit, through me, repeated these words after the speaker in such a loud voice that the people present declared that it did not sound at all like me speaking." It was at this moment that Ellen "knew the time had come when God wanted me to declare to the people what He had done. Stepping upon the platform, and realizing all the time that the power of God was upon me mightily, I testified to all that … I had received the baptism of the

---

[14] Hebden, "How Pentecost Came to Toronto," 1–2.
[15] Ibid., 2.
[16] Hebden, "This is the Power of the Holy Ghost," 3.

Holy Ghost according to the Bible." Ellen wrote that the next day she "began to sing very quietly but to my amazement I was singing *in another language*. I said eagerly, 'Is this Tongues?' and then another verse burst from my lips, and for two or three hours I sang in an unknown language." Later that same day Ellen reports that she attended the Monday evening meeting at the mission where again, "the Spirit sang, through me, four verse[s] in an unknown tongue," and at which point, "the Spirit spoke in power three times through me in a tongue and in English, 'This is the power of the Holy Ghost; this is the day of Pentecost.'"[17] Ellen concluded her testimony in *The Promise* by mentioning that God has given her "twenty-two languages" and that she was also "able to write in all the languages that God has spoken through me." Ellen also reported that within a month of her initial experience with the Holy Spirit, her husband James also received the baptism in the Holy Spirit, and that within five months, between 70 and 80 others had also shared in the same experience.[18]

The two accounts of Ellen's baptism in the Holy Spirit from *The Apostolic Faith* and *The Promise* differ somewhat over the details of her experience. For instance, in her first account from *The Apostolic Faith*, she records that her baptism in the Holy Spirit took place on an otherwise ordinary day during which she "toiled very hard, scrubbing the stairways, etc., and retired quite weary about 11 o'clock."[19] However, in her second account in *The Promise*, she makes it quite clear that Saturday 17 November 1906, even before her experience with the Holy Spirit, was an extraordinary day because on "that very night the last two tenants moved out of the building, and the peace of God filled the place." Also, instead of going to bed exhausted from the mundane labour of scrubbing stairways at an approximate time, she explains in her second account that after spending the day having "done quite a lot of visiting in connection with the mission, and, being very tired, I retired at 10.10 p.m."[20] In her second account Ellen is careful to ensure that her readers are aware of the fact that the day on which she received the baptism in the Holy Spirit was certainly not just any other day that she spent doing ordinary work, and the profundity of the experience

---

[17] Hebden, "How Pentecost Came to Toronto," 2–3; Hebden, "This is the Power of the Holy Ghost," 3.

[18] Hebden, "In Toronto, Canada," 1; Hebden, "How Pentecost Came to Toronto," 3.

[19] Hebden, "This is the Power of the Holy Ghost," 3.

[20] Hebden, "How Pentecost Came to Toronto," 2.

requires that she remembers the precise time of the events being described. Furthermore, Ellen's two accounts also differ in terms of the more embroidered or dramatic rhetoric that she employed in the second account. For instance, in her first account, she explains very simply that on the night of her experience she "had scarcely lain down when the Holy Spirit prompted me to arise and pray. I obeyed. Soon the power of God fell upon me."[21] Conversely, in her second account she describes the same experience by writing: "Suddenly the Holy Ghost fell upon me and I exclaimed aloud, 'Oh Jesus! Thou art a real living person! Thou art lovely beyond description!' My whole being seemed to be filled with praise and adoration such as I had never realized before."[22] The more succinct account found in *The Apostolic Faith*, which exhibits a more matter-of-fact approach, inattention to detail, and prosaic language, contrasts quite substantially with the much longer account found in *The Promise* with its emphasis on a more spiritualized tenor, precision of detail, and dramatic language. In short, Ellen's second article bears the accretions and additions that are common to any story, or in this case, testimony, that has undergone numerous retellings and reformulations. Regardless of these minor differences, the two accounts agree on the basic narrative of Ellen's experience, making her the first historically confirmed individual to have received the baptism in the Holy Spirit in Canada.[23]

What is most interesting about the origin of the Hebden Mission is that there is no historical evidence to suggest that Ellen had any previous knowledge of what was happening at Seymour's Azusa Street at the time of her baptism in the Holy Spirit in November 1906. Additionally, a contemporary of Ellen's, and early Canadian Pentecostal leader, Gordon F. Atter, exclaims that her experience with the Holy Spirit "was totally independent. She heard of the Los Angeles outpouring following her own experience."[24] An examination of the historical material available reveals that the Hebden Mission in Toronto originated independently of any influence from the Azusa Street Mission in Los Angeles, or indeed, from any other centre or individual associated with the Pentecostal revival.

---

[21] Hebden, "This is the Power of the Holy Ghost," 3.
[22] Hebden, "How Pentecost Came to Toronto," 2.
[23] Miller, "The Canadian 'Azusa.'" 5–6.
[24] Ibid., 26.

The Influence of the Hebden Mission

It did not take long for word of what happened at the Hebden Mission to spread across the city of Toronto. When Charles Chambers, a Mennonite Brethren in Christ pastor, heard about what took place at the Hebden Mission, located just six blocks from his own church, he warned the members of his congregation not to attend the fanatic meetings. Despite these warnings, members from Chambers's congregation began to attend the mission hoping to receive the baptism in the Holy Spirit. While attending a Mennonite Brethren in Christ convention in Berlin (now Kitchener), Ontario, Chambers heard former Christian and Missionary Alliance pastor, A.G. Ward, who had previously received the baptism in the Holy Spirit, preach a message on the topic of the Holy Spirit. As a consequence, Chambers changed his attitude regarding the Hebden Mission.[25] Chambers writes that the Holy Spirit "set fire to the Convention and created a holy uproar" and that "people were saved, healed and filled with the Holy Ghost." Upon returning to Toronto, Chambers reports that he "began to attend the services at the Hebden Mission," and that "the first thing I did was to apologize to Mrs. Hebden for the unkind things that I had said about them, and about the work of the Spirit that I had previously opposed."[26] When the leaders of the Mennonite Brethren in Christ Church ordered Chambers to cease his preaching on the baptism in the Holy Spirit, and suspended him from his church, he, along with eight other Mennonite Brethren in Christ ministers, joined the disparate Pentecostal movement.[27]

Of course, news of the Hebden Mission was not limited to the city of Toronto. Within five months of Ellen's baptism in the Holy Spirit she indicated in both *The Apostolic Faith* and the first issue of *The Promise*, that four evangelists, Mr. and Mrs. John E. Marrs, Mr. Bliss Secord, and Mr. Herbert Randall, had been sent out from the mission to other communities across Ontario, including Simcoe, Wingham, and Stratford, in order to "preach the full Gospel," referring, of course, to the preaching of the new doctrine of the baptism in the Holy Spirit.[28] In the subsequent four extant issues of *The Promise*, it is alleged that other

---

[25] Spaetzel, *History of the Kitchener Gospel Temple*, 5–16.
[26] Chambers, *Fifty Years in the Service of the King*, 12–13.
[27] Ibid., 13–14.
[28] Hebden, "In Toronto, Canada," 1; *Promise* May, 1907, 3.

communities across Ontario, such as Norwich, Bouck's Hill, Woodstock, Abington, Sarnia, London, Ingersoll, and Hartford were also experiencing outpourings of the Holy Spirit. Many of these events were the result of either evangelists being sent out directly from the Hebden Mission, or people from these communities visiting the mission, and then returning home with the new Pentecostal experience.[29] The March 1910 edition of *The Promise* includes a letter from a Lutheran, S.T. Odegard, from Brownlee, Saskatchewan, who reports that he heard of what was happening at the Hebden Mission from a tract that he received, which prompted him to visit the mission in Toronto on 17 July 1907. Odegard writes that "About two days after being baptized in water, God, in his infinite grace and through the sufferings and shed blood of His Holy Son, Jesus Christ, poured out upon me the Spirit, the Holy Ghost and fire until I spake in new tongues as the Spirit gave me utterance."[30] After leaving the Hebdens in Toronto, Odegard began a Pentecostal mission in Moose Jaw, Saskatchewan.[31]

In addition to the many Canadians, there was also a steady stream of Americans who made their way to Toronto in order to witness what was happening at the Hebden Mission. George Chambers recollects that during the time he spent at the Hebden Mission he "met workers from all over the world who had come to see and experience what God was doing for hundreds of others."[32] For instance, in the December 1906 issue of *The Apostolic Faith*, an O. Adams from Monrovia, California reported that at 782 Queen Street, Toronto, Canada, "a number there are seeking the Pentecostal baptism, and one sister has been baptized with the Holy Ghost and to her great surprise began speaking in tongues."[33] While the paper states that this happened at 782 Queen Street, it is most likely that either Adams supplied, or the journal printed, the wrong address, as there is no record of any other Pentecostal mission existing this early in the city of Toronto, nor at this location. Also in December, an A.S. Copley from Cambridge, Ohio made the trip to Toronto to visit the Hebden Mission and published his account in an Ohio journal entitled, *Way of Faith*; the account

---

[29] *Promise*, June, 1907, 3–4; *Promise* February, 1909, 1–3, 6–8; *Promise* March, 1910, 2, 6–7.

[30] Odegard, *Promise* March, 1910, 8.

[31] PAOC, *Songs of the Reaper*, 75.

[32] Chamber, "Fifty Years Ago," 6.

[33] *Apostolic Faith* December 1906, 3.

subsequently reprinted in the January 1907 edition of *The Apostolic Faith*. After attending two services at the mission, Copley wrote: "Here God is pouring out His spirit. Several have been definitely baptized with the Holy Ghost and speak with tongues ... Pentecost has begun in Toronto."[34] The Hebdens also held a series of three Pentecostal Workers' Conventions at their mission in 1908, 1909, and 1910, which also drew several Pentecostal evangelists and missionaries, as well as seekers and sceptics, from across Canada and the United States.[35] The speaker for the third convention held in January 1910 was the famous Pentecostal evangelist, William H. Durham, pastor of the North Avenue Mission in Chicago, whose own mission would eventually rival that of Azusa Street.[36] Also present at the third Pentecostal Workers' Convention were Robert and Aimee Semple, who left the convention in Toronto directly to embark on a missionary trip to China, the same fateful trip on which Robert became ill and later died.[37] In addition to Durham, other important Americans also visited the Hebden Mission including Frank Bartleman, and the Pentecostal evangelist, Daniel Awrey.[38] Ellen also reports in *The Promise* that several missionaries had been both sent out and funded directly from the Hebden Mission to places such as South Africa, North Africa, China, Japan, India, Mongolia, as well as the Six Nations Indian Reserve in Hartford, Ontario.[39]

The most enduring influence that the Hebden Mission had on the development of the early Pentecostal movement is irrefutably the role that it played as a centre from which the Pentecostal message was spread throughout Ontario. The early evangelists sent out from the mission were responsible for establishing some of the first Pentecostal churches in Canada, some of which still exist to this day. While the influence of the Hebden Mission was largely limited to Eastern Canada, it also played a formative role in the development of the ministries of some more significant missionaries and evangelists. One such example

---

[34] Copely, 4.
[35] Miller, *Canadian Pentecostals*, 43; *Promise* October, 1909, 2; *Promise* March, 1910, 1–2.
[36] Anderson, *An Introduction to Pentecostalism*, 45–46; Chambers, "Fifty Years Ago," 6; *Promise* March, 1910, 1, 2; Robeck, *The Azusa Street Mission and Revival*, 116; Wacker, *Heaven Below*, 262.
[37] Blumhofer, *Aimee Semple McPherson*, 91–96; McPherson, *In the Service of the King*, 102; *Promise* March, 1910, 1.
[38] Chambers, "Fifty Years Ago," 6.
[39] *Promise* February, 1909, 3–5, 7; *Promise* March, 1910, 2, 5–6.

is the first Canadian Pentecostal missionary, Charles Chawner.[40] In 1908, Chawner left his wife and two children behind in order to bring the Pentecostal message to South Africa.[41] Eventually Chawner's wife and children joined him, and his son, Austin, would go on to establish the first Pentecostal Bible colleges in South Africa and Mozambique, as well as a Pentecostal publishing house that translated and distributed Pentecostal literature throughout Africa.[42] It is difficult to overestimate the role that the Chawners played in the dissemination of Pentecostalism on the African continent, none of which would have been possible without Charles being baptized in the Holy Spirit, and called to the mission field while at the Hebden Mission in Toronto (see chapter two in this volume).

The Hebden Mission also played a crucial role in the development of one of the most important American evangelists of the twentieth century, Aimee Semple McPherson, founder of the International Church of the Foursquare Gospel. On 7 March 1907, Herbert Randall, a missionary to Egypt on furlough in Canada, received the baptism in the Holy Spirit while visiting the Hebden Mission. Sometime before May 1907, the Hebdens sent Randall to hold meetings and establish Pentecostal missions throughout several small towns in Southwestern Ontario, including the town of Ingersoll, just seven kilometres from Aimee's family farm in Salford, Ontario.[43] It was to the Pentecostal mission in Ingersoll that the Hebdens subsequently sent Robert Semple, a young Irish evangelist who had been visiting the Hebdens in Toronto, to hold meetings in late 1907.[44] In December 1907, Aimee visited the Pentecostal mission in Ingersoll, where she was captivated by Robert's emotional and earnest preaching. Within two months of this experience she herself was baptized in the Holy Spirit, and just seven months after this, was married to Robert, who introduced Aimee to a life of international evangelism and missionary work.[45] So important to her future work as an evangelist was Aimee's early encounter and

[40] Miller, *Canadian Pentecostals*, 220.
[41] Chawner, "A Cry from the Dark Continent," 4–5.
[42] Chawner, "Correspondence," 6; Chawner and Chawner, *Called To Zululand*; Griffin, "Unless a Seed," 11, 28; Kulbeck, "C.W. Chawner," 9; Miller, "Austin and Ingrid Chawner," 10–11, 24; Upton, *The Miracle of Mozambique*.
[43] Blumhofer, *Aimee Semple McPherson*, 61; *Promise* May, 1907, 3; Randall, "The Comforter Has Come to Herbert E. Randall," 1–2.
[44] Blumhofer, *Aimee Semple McPherson*, 75,–76; Miller, *Canadian Pentecostals*, 52.
[45] Blumhofer, *Aimee Semple McPherson*, 60–94; Semple McPherson, *In the Service of the King*, 75–130.

relationship with Robert Semple that Edith Blumhofer claims: "The three years during which she allowed Robert Semple to give her life its meaning became a watershed, the hinge on which everything else turned. Robert awakened her emotions, defined her spirituality, and took her off the farm and around the world, all before she was twenty years old."[46] There is little doubt that without the role that the Hebdens had in establishing the Pentecostal mission in Ingersoll, and subsequently sending Robert Semple to hold meetings in late 1907, Aimee's life would have taken an inextricably different direction.

The Distinguishing Features of the Hebden Mission

In addition to the fact that the Hebden Mission originated independently of any influence from Seymour in Los Angeles, a survey of the mission's origin and influence reveal three other important features that serve to distinguish it from Azusa Street that are central to an understanding of the implications that the Hebden Mission has for Pentecostal historiography. First among these is the Hebdens' theology of the baptism of the Holy Spirit. A close reading of *The Apostolic Faith* and *The Promise* reveals that the Azusa Street and the Hebden Pentecostals initially had very different understandings of the primary role of the baptism of the Holy Spirit. As the first paragraph of the first issue of *The Apostolic Faith* makes apparent, the Azusa Street Pentecostals understood the primary role of the modern day Pentecost as "laying the foundation for a mighty wave of salvation among the unconverted."[47] The Hebdens, on the other hand, were equally emphatic that the primary role of the baptism of the Holy Spirit was to receive "more power to heal the sick."[48] To be clear, once regular correspondence and the traveling of members between the two missions was established, the Hebdens appeared to yield to Seymour's emphasis on the role of the baptism of the Holy Spirit for evangelism. Even after making this concession, however, the Hebdens continued to place a much higher priority, and more frequent emphasis, on the role of the baptism of the Holy Spirit in healing than Azusa Street Pentecostals.

---

[46] Blumhofer, *Aimee Semple McPherson*, 92.
[47] *Apostolic Faith* September, 1906, 1.
[48] Hebden, "How Pentecost Came to Toronto," 2.

The second feature that served to differentiate the Hebden Mission from Azusa Street was their theology of speaking in tongues. The early Azusa Street Pentecostals believed very strongly, as found in the book of Acts, that the ability to speak in tongues that followed the baptism in the Holy Spirit enabled them to evangelize to all of the nations of the world without having to actually learn the languages that these people spoke. For instance, the first issue of *The Apostolic Faith* mentions that "Brother and Sister A.G. Garr, former leaders of the Burning Bush work in Los Angeles, were powerfully baptized with the Holy Ghost and received the gift of tongues, especially the language of India and dialects. Bro. Garr was able to pray a native of India 'through' in his own language, the Bengali. Sister Garr also spoke Chinese."[49] Also, the very next issue of *The Apostolic Faith* reports that a "Sister Hutchins has been preaching the Gospel in the power of the Spirit. She has received the baptism with the Holy Ghost and the gift of the Uganda language, the language of the people to whom she is sent."[50] While Ellen Hebden is careful to mention that the Holy Spirit gave her the ability to speak and write in twenty-two languages, nowhere does she indicate that this gift is to be used for the purpose of communicating to the native speakers of these languages. In fact, a missionary sent out to Sri Lanka and India by the Hebdens reported in a letter that while on the ship from Canada to Colombo, Sri Lanka: "I have been studying the language on board. Bro. Norton thinks I shall be able to read as soon as I get a bible."[51] Later on in the same letter, this missionary writes: "Ramabia is making a new translation of the bible and was praying for the Lord to send someone who knew Greek, so I came along about two days later in answer to prayer."[52] Similarly, commenting on the work of Charles Chawner in South Africa, Ellen Hebden wrote in *The Promise*: "We with them believe it to be the mind of God that a Mission Station should be there, as a number of others are already called to Zululand, and it is very necessary to have a home for the dear ones going out to be received until the place of their future labors are made plain, or during the time they are studying the language."[53] These comments reveal the very different understanding that the Hebden

---

[49] *Apostolic Faith* September, 1906, 4.
[50] *Apostolic Faith* October, 1906, 1.
[51] *Promise* February, 1909, 7.
[52] Ibid., 7.
[53] Hebden, "Good News," 2.

Pentecostals had of the purpose of speaking in tongues as compared with the early Azusa Pentecostals, and also attest to the seriousness that the Hebden Pentecostals approached the study of languages and the translation of texts, which was not common among the early Azusa Street Pentecostals.

These comments also lead directly to the third, and possibly most important, differentiating feature of the Hebden Mission – their very different socioeconomic composition, to which the references to learning foreign languages and facility with ancient languages allude. One of the defining features of the early Azusa Street Revival has historically been its African-American leader, William J. Seymour, its African-American, as well as other ethnic minority, membership, and the lower socioeconomic status of its members. While these elements have been mythologized and revised by many groups and scholars for a wide variety of reasons, the historical record is clear that the Azusa Street Mission did indeed have an African-American leader, and there were twice as many African Americans within early American Pentecostalism than there were in the general American population.[54] The Hebden Mission, however, was quite different. While it is true that James Hebden came from a working-class family of labourers in one of England's industrial centres, it is important to note that Ellen, the mission's primary leader, was reared in a solidly middle-class household that also enjoyed the respect of the community. Furthermore, at the height of the mission's activity, James and Ellen would have certainly found themselves within the middle-class of Torontonian society, evidenced by their ability to have owned and operated both the mission at 651 Queen Street East, and their large home at 191 George Street.[55] A more important indication of the radically different socioeconomic composition of the Hebden Mission as compared with Azusa Street, is the fact that the mission was largely attended by white converts from established Christian denominations, and whose missionaries were subsequently sent out by the Hebdens, were college educated, and took the time to learn the languages of those they were going to evangelize. A reporter from the *Toronto Daily Star* who both observed the meetings and interviewed Ellen, reported in a 17 January 1907 article entitled, "The Gift of Tongues in a Queen Street Mission," that: "In the

---

[54] Wacker, *Heaven Below*, 206–207.
[55] Sloos, "The Story of James and Ellen Hebden," (Forthcoming).

audience were well-to-do business men, and the women, who were
slightly in the majority, were well-dressed, evidently intelligent, and
refined." The reporter goes on to write: "Mrs. Hebden is one of the
mildest of women, and she has a sweet smile that would make anybody
feel at home in her presence. She is kind and courteous to all, and to
the reporter she could not have been more obliging."[56] These observations differ greatly from those of the reporter sent to the Azusa Street
Mission by the *Los Angeles Daily Times*, who in an 18 April 1906 article
entitled, "Weird Babel of Tongues," described the mission as compris-
ing "colored people and a sprinkling of whites," portrays Seymour as
an "old colored exhorter," and characterizes the neighborhood surrounding the mission as "hideous" due to the "howlings of the wor-
shippers."[57] In short, James and Ellen Hebden were not the children of
recently emancipated slaves, and the building on 651 Queen Street
East was not the tumbledown shack of 312 Azusa Street attended
mostly by racialized minorities. Also, throughout the five extant editions of the Hebdens' *Promise* can be found mention of the college
graduates, doctors, and other professionals who attended their mission
in very different circumstances, and for very different reasons, than did
those who, at least initially, poured into the Azusa Street Mission. I do
not point out the very obvious socioeconomic differences, or indeed,
any of these three differentiating features, between these two missions
in order to suggest a qualitative difference between the Hebden Mission
and Azusa Street. Rather, I do so only to illustrate the rich variety that
spanned the spectrum of the early Pentecostal movement, and also to
challenge any continuing claims that may exist for a homogeneous
understanding of this very multifaceted religious movement.

MONOGENESIS VS. POLYGENESIS

The tendency to identify, and subsequently mythify, a single source of
origination for new religious movements is a common tactic in religious historiography. One of the most important reasons for this is
that it creates an uncomplicated and easily transmittable narrative for
initiates to both internalize, and to promulgate to potential converts.
In the case of Pentecostalism, however, a much more important reason

---

[56] "The Gift of Tongues in a Queen Street Mission," 15.
[57] "Weird Babel of Tongues," 1.

exists for a monogenetical myth of origination. The early Pentecostals strongly believed that the modern day outpouring of God's Spirit should follow the only other script for such an event that they knew; the coming of the Holy Spirit in the book of Acts. This meant that, just as in the book of Acts, the outpouring of the Holy Spirit had to happen at a single location, and as the largest, and single most important site of the Pentecostal revival, Azusa Street soon assumed this mythical role. The early writers and eyewitnesses to the events of Azusa Street, such as Frank Bartleman, were careful to describe what was taking place in Los Angeles with one eye on Azusa Street and the other on Acts 2. For Bartleman and others, the events that transpired at Azusa Street were simultaneously history and the realization of prophecy. As a result of this early Pentecostal historical consciousness, Azusa Street was transformed from an important site of the outpouring of the Holy Spirit, to the only site of the outpouring of the Holy Spirit, from which all other revivals found their beginning. In other words, in the minds of most Pentecostals, Los Angeles became the modern day Jerusalem, and Azusa Street the new upper room; any other revivals were merely viewed as sparks that had been scattered from their true source.[58]

To counterbalance this ahistorical myth of Pentecostal origins, Pentecostals would do well to incorporate the work of historians from other traditions who have likewise had to deal with the complexity of splintering, fragmentation, and revival, common within much of Protestantism. Anabaptist historians, for instance, have in recent decades rediscovered the diversity of historical origins within the Anabaptist movement of the sixteenth century.[59] In their influential article on the ahistoricity of the monogenetical beginnings of the Anabaptist movement, James Stayer, Werner Packull, and Klaus Deppermann write: "The history of Anabaptist origins can no longer be preoccupied with the essentially sterile question of where Anabaptism began, but must devote itself to studying the plural origins of Anabaptism and their significance for the plural character of the movement."[60] Similarly, scholars have also recognized the polygenetical origin of other revivals, such as the Connecticut River Valley Awakening,

---

[58] See Bartleman, *Azusa Street.*

[59] Snyder, "Revolution and the Swiss Brethren," 276–287; Snyder, "The Birth and Evolution of Swiss Anabaptism," 501–645; Stayer, Packull, and Deppermann, "From Monogenesis to Polygenesis," 83–121.

[60] Stayer, Packull, and Deppermann, 85.

which was long thought to have originated in the pulpit of Jonathan Edward's Northampton church. Similar to Azusa Street, Northampton was certainly the most important centre of the Connecticut River Valley Awakenings, however, it was not the only, nor necessarily the first, site of revival in Connecticut, but, rather, the most dramatic and the best publicized.[61] Like the developments in both Anabaptist and Edwardsian scholarship, Pentecostal historiography would also be greatly enriched if, rather than the current obsession with the monogenetical myth of Azusa Street, more attention was focused on uncovering and delineating the rich variety of social and historical conditions, as well as the theological and practical traditions, that contributed to the polygenetical beginnings of the Pentecostal movement.

CONCLUSION

Because so little information about the Hebden Mission has either survived or been recovered, it is impossible to determine the full extent of the mission's influence on the development of early Pentecostalism. The information that is available, however, suggests that the Hebden Mission originated independently from the Azusa Street Mission, and is better understood as an outgrowth of the Keswick and healing home movements with which the Hebdens themselves identified as the source of their spirituality and impetus for ministry. That the experience of Ellen Hebden and others in Toronto resembled that of Seymour and his followers in Los Angeles, without any evidence of a pre-existing relationship between the two missions, does not in any way warrant the conclusion that the Hebden Mission, and indeed Canadian Pentecostalism, is simply another spark that was scattered from the fire of the Azusa Street Revival. To be clear, there is no denying the significant role that Azusa Street played in the dissemination of Pentecostalism within Canada. Azusa Street, and American Pentecostalism in general, however, were clearly not the only influences at work in the development and proliferation of Pentecostalism within Canada and other global centres of the movement. These findings suggest that Pentecostalism did not begin as a homogeneous religious movement that was subsequently dispersed from an isolated geographical source of origination throughout the rest of the world. Rather, the

---

[61] Marsden, *Jonathan Edwards*.

existence of other early Pentecostal missions that predated, existed simultaneously, or emerged subsequently, but independently of the Azusa Street Mission, means that Pentecostalism is best understood as a dynamic and multifaceted movement with multiple points of origin, which challenges the traditional and mythical monogenetical conceptualizations of Pentecostal beginnings.

Bibliography

Ahlstrom, Sydney E. *A Religious History of the American People*. 2nd ed. New Haven: Yale University Press, 2004.

Albanese, Catherine L. *America: Religions and Religion*. 4th ed. Belmont, CA: Wadsworth Publishing, 2007.

Anderson, Allan. *An Introduction to Pentecostalism*. Cambridge: Cambridge University Press, 2004.

The Apostolic Faith. 1, no. 1, September 1906, 1.

——. 1, no. 2, October 1906, 1.

——. 1, no. 4, December 1906, 1–4.

Argue, Zelma. *Contending for the Faith*. 3rd ed. Winnipeg: Messenger of God Publishing House, 1928.

Atter, Gordon F. *The Third Force*. 3rd ed. Peterborough, ON: The College Press, 1970.

Bartleman, Frank. *Azusa Street*. South Plainfield, NJ: Bridge Publishing, Inc., [1925] 1980.

Bloch-Hoell, Nils. *The Pentecostal Movement*. London: Allen & Unwin, 1964.

Blumhofer, Edith L. *Aimee Semple McPherson: Everybody's Sister*. Grand Rapids, MI: Eerdmans, 1993.

——. *Restoring the Faith: The Assemblies of God, Pentecostalism, and American Culture*. Urbana: University of Illinois Press, 1993.

Bridges, Lynn. *The American Religious Experience: A Concise History*. New York: Rowman and Littlefield, 2006.

Brumback, Carl. *Suddenly ... From Heaven*. Springfield, MO: Gospel Publishing House, 1961.

Chambers, George Augustus. "Fifty Years Ago." *The Pentecostal Testimony* 37, no. 5, May 1956, 6.

——. *Fifty Years in the Service of the King: Autobiography of George Augustus Chambers*. Toronto: The Testimony Press, 1960.

Chawner, Charles. "A Cry from the Dark Continent." *The Promise* 12 February 1909, 4–5.

——. "Correspondence." *The Promise* 15 March 1910, 6.

Chawner, Charles and Emma Chawner. *Called To Zululand: A Story of God's Leading*. Toronto: n.p., 1923.

Conn, Charles. *Like a Mighty Army*. Cleveland, TN: Pathway Press, [1955] 1977.

Copley, A.S. "Pentecost in Toronto." *The Apostolic Faith* 1, no. 5, January 1907, 4.

Corrigan, John and Winthrop S. Hudson. *Religion in America*. 7th ed. Upper Saddle River, NJ: Pearson Education, 2004.

Creech, Joe. "Visions of Glory: The Place of the Azusa Street Revival in Pentecostal History." *Church History* 65, no. 3, September 1996, 405–424.

Curtis, Heather. *Faith in the Great Physician: Suffering and Divine Healing in American Culture, 1860–1900*. Baltimore: Johns Hopkins University Press, 2007.

Dayton, Donald. *Theological Roots of Pentecostalism*. Peabody, MA: Hendrickson, 1987.

Ewart, Frank. *The Phenomenon of Pentecost*. Hazelwood, MO: Word Aflame Press, [1947] 1975.

Frodsham, Stanley. *With Signs Following*. Springfield, MO: Gospel Publishing House, [1926] 1946.

Gee, Donald. *The Pentecostal Movement*. London: Elim Publishing Company, [1941] 1949.

Goff, James R. *Fields White unto Harvest: Charles F. Parham and the Missionary Origins of Pentecostalism*. Fayetteville: University of Arkansas Press, 1988.

Goss, Ethel E. *Winds of God*. Hazelwood, MO: Word Aflame Press, [1958] 1977.

Griffin, William. "Unless a Seed: The Chawner Story: 100 Years of Pentecostal. Missions." *[Pentecostal] Testimony* 89, no. 2, February-March 2008, 11, 28.

Handy, Robert T. *A History of the Christian Churches in the United States and Canada*. New York: Oxford University Press, 1977.

Hebden, Ellen K. "This is the Power of the Holy Ghost." *The Apostolic Faith* 1, no. 6, February-March 1907, 3.

——. "In Toronto, Canada." *The Apostolic Faith* 1, no. 7, April 1907, 1.

——. "How Pentecost Came to Toronto." *The Promise* 1 May 1907, 1–3.

——. "Good News." *The Promise* 15 March 1910, 2.

Hollenweger, Walter J. *The Pentecostals*. 2nd ed. Peabody, MA: Hendrickson, 1988.

Jacobsen, Douglas. *Thinking in the Spirit: Theologies of the Early Pentecostal Movement*. Bloomington, IN: Indiana University Press, 2003.

Kendrick, Klaude. *The Promise Fulfilled*. Springfield, MO: Gospel Publishing House, 1961.

Koester, Nancy. *Fortress Introduction to the History of Christianity in the United States*. Minneapolis, MN: Fortress Press, 2007.

Kulbeck, Gloria G. "C.W. Chawner: Apostle to the Zulus." *The Pentecostal Testimony* December 1959, 9, 10.

——. *What God Hath Wrought: A History of the Pentecostal Assemblies of Canada*. Toronto: PAOC, 1958.

Lawrence, B.F. *The Apostolic Faith Restored*. St. Louis, MO: Gospel Publishing House, 1916.

Marsden, George M. *Jonathan Edwards: A Life*. New Haven: Yale University Press, 2003.

McGee, Gary. *This Gospel Shall Be Preached*. Springfield MO: Gospel Publishing House, 1986, 1989.

Miller, Thomas William. "Austin and Ingrid Chawner: Pioneers in Northern Transvaal and Mozambique." *The Pentecostal Testimony* August 1988, 10–11, 24.

——. *Canadian Pentecostals: A History of the Pentecostal Assemblies of Canada*. Mississauga, ON: Full Gospel Publishing House, 1994.

——. "The Canadian 'Azusa': The Hebden Mission in Toronto." *Pneuma* 8 (Spring 1986): 5–29.

Nichol, John T. *Pentecostalism*. New York: Harper & Row, 1966.

Noll, Mark A. *A History of Christianity in the United States and Canada*. Grand Rapids, MI: Eerdmans, 1992.

Odegard, S.T. *The Promise* 15 March 1910, 8.

Opp, James. *The Lord for the Body: Religion, Medicine, and Protestant Faith Healing in Canada, 1180–1930*. Montreal & Kingston: McGill-Queen's University Press, 2005.

PAOC. *Songs of the Reaper: The Story of the Pentecostal Assemblies of Saskatchewan*. Saskatoon: PAOC Saskatchewan District, 1985.

The Promise. 1 May 1907, 1–4.

——. 2 June 1907, 1–4.

——. 12 February 1909, 1–8.

——. 14 October 1909, 1, 2, 7, 8.

——. 15 March 1910, 1–8.

Quebedeaux. Richard. *The New Charismatics*. Garden City, NY: Doubleday & Co., 1976.

Randall, Herbert E. "The Comforter has Come to Herbert E. Randall." *The Promise* 2 June 1907, 1, 2.

Robeck, Cecil M. *The Azusa Street Mission and Revival: The Birth of the Global Pentecostal Movement*. Nashville, TN: Thomas Nelson, 2006.

Rudd, Douglas. *When the Spirit Came Upon Them: Highlights from the Early Years of the Pentecostal Movement in Canada*. Mississauga, ON: PAOC, 2002.

Semple McPherson, Aimee. *In the Service of the King: The Story of My Life*. New York: Boni and Liveright. 1927.

Sloos, William. "The Story of James and Ellen Hebden: The First Family of Pentecost in Canada." *Pneuma* (Forthcoming).

Snyder, C. Arnold. "Revolution and the Swiss Brethren: The Case of Michael Sattler." *Church History* 50 (September 1981): 276–287.

——. "The Birth and Evolution of Swiss Anabaptism, 1520–1530." *The Mennonite Quarterly Review* 80 (October 2006): 501–645.

Spaetzel, Roy Clifford. *History of the Kitchener Gospel Temple, 1909–1974*. Kitchener, ON: n.p., 1974.

Stayer, James M., Werner O. Packull, and Klaus Deppermann. "From Monogenesis to Polygenesis: The Historical Discussion of Anabaptist Origins." *The Mennonite Quarterly Review* 49 (April 1975): 83–121.

Synan, Vinson. *The Holiness-Pentecostal Movement in the United States*. Grand Rapids, MI: Eerdmans, 1971.

"The Gift of Tongues in a Queen Street Mission." *The Toronto Daily Star*, 17 January 1907, 15.

Upton, George R. *The Miracle of Mozambique*. Clearbrook, BC: A. Olfert & Sons Ltd., 1980.

Wacker, Grant. *Heaven Below: Early Pentecostals and American Culture*. Cambridge, MA: Harvard University Press, 2001.

——. "The Functions of Faith in Primitive Pentecostalism." *Harvard Theological Review* 77 (1984): 253–375.

"Weird Babel of Tongues." *Los Angeles Daily Times*, 18 April 1906, 1.

Williams, Peter W. *America's Religions: From Their Origins to the Twenty-First Century*. Urbana: University of Illinois Press, 2008.

CHAPTER TWO

CHARLES W. CHAWNER AND THE MISSIONARY IMPULSE OF THE HEBDEN MISSION

Michael Wilkinson

INTRODUCTION

In February 1909 the Hebden Mission reported on the work of Charles W. Chawner in South Africa in their official newsletter, *The Promise*.[1] In the article, "A Cry from the Dark Continent," Chawner states:

> The dear Lord baptized me in His Holy Spirit the beginning of Feb., 1907, and at that same time gave me a very definite call to be His witness in a far off land. From time to time as I could bear it He made it plain that I should leave all and follow Him to Zululand, and having drawn me aside one day He told me it was time to go (sic) He led Bro. Hebden in such a way that he secured the ticket much more reasonable than we expected, and so laid it on the hearts of the friends of the Mission that sufficient money was contributed, most of it in one night, all of it within about a month, to supply me with some needed clothes, pay the passage over the water, and railways right to Weenen, Natal, S.A.[2]

This chapter traces the life of Charles W. Chawner, his wife Emma, and family as they came in contact with the Hebden Mission and were sent to South Africa as Canada's first Pentecostal missionaries. Charles and Emma served in Africa from 1907 to 1949. In particular, it pays attention to the character of the Hebden Mission as a missionary sending agency and the role of Spirit baptism, visions, Spirit leading, and signs and wonders. Attention will also be given to offering a social scientific explanation for understanding the relationship between Pentecostalism and early mission activities as well as offering a description of the work of Charles W. Chawner.

---

[1] I want to acknowledge the assistance of Marilyn Stroud and Jim Craig from the Pentecostal Assemblies of Canada Archives for this research.
[2] Chawner, "A Cry from the Dark Continent," 4.

EARLY PENTECOSTALISM AND THE MISSIONARY MOVEMENT
IN CANADA

The relationship between Pentecostal mission activity and other missionary developments in Canada needs some discussion for contextual reasons. Canada was first a colony of France and then Britain and so missionary activities are related to the view of Canada as a mission field for Europeans. The primary missionary activity revolved around the aboriginal inhabitants of various cultural and language groups spread throughout the North American continent. John Webster Grant provides a developed historical study of the encounter between Europeans and the 'natives' of Canada since 1534.[3] Grant examines the aims and activities of missionaries from all denominations and the responses of the aboriginal population highlighting the positive and negative of this encounter. The adoption of Christianity with an accompanying decline in 'native' spirituality during the nineteenth century is highlighted, especially in relation to the work of the Presbyterians, Anglicans, and Methodists.[4] Catholic missions among aboriginal peoples are also significant not just in Quebec but throughout the North and West of Canada.[5] Grant counters the view that missionary activity declines during the twentieth century and highlights the activities of Pentecostals among aboriginal peoples noting how the spirit world of the 'natives' and the Pentecostals combines to facilitate much growth.[6]

Canadian missionary activity, however, is not limited to work within the country. Canadians are also going as missionaries, as did Americans and Europeans, to South America, Asia and Africa.[7] One such Canadian is the Methodist Robert Hardie.[8] Hardie was born in Caledonia, Ontario 11 June 1865. He graduated from the University of Toronto medical school in 1890 and spent the next eight years as a medical missionary in Korea. In 1900 he was ordained and became responsible for

---

[3] Grant, *Moon of Wintertime*.
[4] See the following for a discussion about the role of Christianity among aboriginal peoples in Canada. Murphy and Perin, *A Concise History of Christianity in Canada*; Semple, *The Lord's Dominion*, 127–178, 275–305.
[5] Choquette, *The Oblate Assault on Canada's Northwest*; Murphy and Perin, *A Concise History of Christianity in Canada*.
[6] Grant, *Moon of Wintertime*, 201–202. For an assessment of mission work among West Coast aboriginals in Canada, see Burkinshaw, "Native Pentecostalism in British Columbia," 142–170.
[7] Semple, *The Lord's Dominon*, 306–333.
[8] Warrick, "Hardie, Robert Alexander," 148–149.

the Wonson circuit leading large scale revivals. In 1903 Hardie had an experience he described as a baptism of the Holy Spirit and he became a leader in the early Pentecostal movement in Korea.[9]

The Pentecostal missionary impulse of the early-twentieth century is part of the broader missionary activity of Protestantism. Werner Ustorf characterizes the modern Protestant missionary movement as a particular phenomenon shaped by Victorian sensibilities and not the Reformation. More specifically, the modern missionary movement, which includes early Pentecostalism, is one of colonial encounter between Europeans and the rest of the world as they endeavoured to "unify the world through a twofold process involving modernization and Christianization."[10] By the middle of the twentieth century the Christendom project collapses and the missionary movement is left to redefine itself. Anderson correctly points out that in comparison, Catholic missions were shaped by the idea of the 'Missio Dei' and Protestant missions by 'obedience to the Great Commission' while Pentecostal mission is characterized by 'Spirit baptism.'[11] It is this idea of Spirit baptism that uniquely shapes early Pentecostal mission activity, albeit, in the context of colonial encounter and the modern missionary movement.

The early Pentecostal movement was characterized by a missionary impulse to spread the fire of Spirit baptism all over the world. Yet very little is known about the missionary nature of early Pentecostalism, especially the Canadian story. Scholarship focusing on American contributions is more developed but still little attention is given to the quality of Pentecostal mission activities.[12] The one exception is the ground breaking book *Spreading Fires* by Allan Anderson, which explores in detail the missionary character of early Pentecostalism and the contribution to global Pentecostalism from Africa, Asia, and Latin America. Anderson argues that "the present proliferation of Pentecostalism and indeed its inherent character result from the fact

---

[9] Anderson, *Spreading Fires*, 29.

[10] Ustorf, "Protestantism and Missions," 393.

[11] Anderson, *An Introduction to Pentecostalism*, 207. See Anderson and Tang, eds., *Asian and Pentecostal* for an examination of the development of Pentecostalism in Asia.

[12] Anderson, *Spreading Fires*, 4. For a detailed study of the history and theology of missionary work in the Assemblies of God, see McGee, *This Gospel Shall be Preached*, Vol. 1, 1986 and Vol. 2, 1989. Goff provides an analysis of Parham and the idea of "missionary tongues" among early Pentecostals in *Fields White Unto Harvest*, 1988.

that this was fundamentally a missionary movement of the Spirit from the start."[13] This chapter reflects this view and illustrates how one Canadian embodies the missionary nature of early Pentecostalism.

The early Pentecostal movement is shaped by a number of precursors including Pietist expressions of personal experience, Methodist and Holiness views of sanctification, nineteenth-century revivalism, the healing movement, and missionary fervour associated with premillennial ideas of Christ's soon return. The nineteenth century is also a period of colonial expansion with European societies moving rapidly throughout the world. All of these strands come together in the early twentieth century with ideas of Spirit baptism and speaking in tongues to animate the Pentecostal movement.[14]

Anderson demonstrates clearly how these theological ideas, practices, and colonial contexts act as a catalyst for the worldwide spread of Pentecostalism. More specifically he focuses on the ideas of premillennial eschatology and the urgent task to missionize the world before Christ returns coupled with the idea of Spirit baptism as 'missionary tongues,'[15] which characterized the missionary impulse of early Pentecostalism. However, many of these early Pentecostals, especially Americans shaped by Parham's view of 'missionary tongues' became disillusioned when they discovered that God had not given them the ability to speak the language of the people they believed they were called to evangelize. The idea that tongues was a known language was not accepted by all and was controversial to many. However, it had enough influence to motivate many early Pentecostals to leave America and go to places like China, India, and South Africa. These ecstatic utterances were not just signs of the end times. Spirit baptism was an empowering and enabling experience to evangelize the world.[16] While the early Canadian Pentecostal movement is also shaped by these views, there needs to be some qualification and historical

---

[13] Anderson, *Spreading Fires*, 5.

[14] I use the word animate in the same way Christian Smith talks about the belief systems or narratives humans use as moral orders which in turn structure the social institutions and organizations we inhabit. See Smith, *Moral, Believing Animals*, 2003.

[15] "Missionary tongues" refers to the belief that tongues were known languages. Early American Pentecostals were shaped by a view that the gift of tongues would facilitate the spread of the gospel without traditional modes of language acquisition. See Goff, *Fields White Unto Harvest*, for an analysis of Parham's contribution to the idea. Also, see Mark J. Cartledge, *Speaking in Tongues*, for an examination of the various debates about speaking in tongues.

[16] Anderson, *Spreading Fires*, 46–47.

particularization. The missionary impulse of Canadian Pentecostalism as exemplified through the Hebdens and Chawner does not fit this model exactly.

There is very little written on the missionary nature of Canadian Pentecostalism. The most extensive research was conducted by Irving Whitt for his doctoral program at Fuller Theological Seminary.[17] Whitt reviews the historical context of early Pentecostalism and the missiological nature of the Pentecostal Assemblies of Canada (PAOC). Overall, Whitt's study examines the development of a Pentecostal missiology in the PAOC and offers an important analysis highlighting some unique characteristics among Pentecostals in Canada which are distinct from those in the United States.

Specifically, Whitt examines three characteristics of early Pentecostal missions including xenolalia or the idea of 'missionary tongues,' signs and wonders, and the outpouring of the Spirit to precipitate a new wave of missionaries. While the last two ideas are evident in Canada, Whitt argues that the belief in 'missionary tongues' is not present in the literature about the Pentecostal revival in Canada. This is especially true about the Hebdens and the missionaries associated with the East End Mission.[18] The view among the Hebdens was that the experience of Spirit baptism was characterized as an encounter with the divine love of God, a deepening relationship with Christ, and an empowerment for service. In my reading of *The Promise* glossolalia occurs at the East End Mission but its relationship to missionary work as 'missionary tongues' is not explicit. What is clear among the Hebdens is the view of 'tongues' as a sign of God's work. Chawner never spoke of 'missionary tongues' and often wrote about using translators for preaching and learning the language to be more effective in his mission work. For example, Chawner states: "Through the kindness of a Mr. A., a Swedish missionary, I began again to study the Zulu language and went with him here and there speaking to Zulus, he interpreting."[19] Chawner also spent considerable time with Anglican missionaries studying the language during his first year in Africa.[20] Elsewhere, an unidentified reporter in *The Promise* says: "The old ship is ploughing along as fast as she can to Colombo. There are a number of missionaries on board.

---

[17] Whitt, "Developing a Pentecostal Missiology."
[18] Whitt, "Developing a Pentecostal Missiology," 160.
[19] Chawner, *Called to Zululand*, 23.
[20] Chawner, *Called to Zululand*.

It looks as though God was going to do something for India. I have
been studying the language on board. Bro. Norton thinks I shall be able
to read as soon as I get a bible."[21] Elsewhere, it is reported: "News from
Brother Hill. He is studying the language and expects soon to be able
to preach the Word to those around him in their own tongue."[22] The
main views associated with the Hebden Mission, according to Whitt,
centred on ideas of the Spirit as guide, a baptism of love, signs and
wonders, empowerment for service, and the restoration of spiritual
gifts.[23] These same qualities exemplify the missionary work of Charles
Chawner.

From Faith Home to Global Pentecostal Mission

The emphasis on mission activity, especially cross cultural mission
work, was not the early focus among the Hebdens. 'Mission' for the
Hebdens was defined in the context of an inner city work but not necessarily towards the poor and homeless either. Rather, the Hebden
Mission was a place for healing and spiritual renewal among fellow
Christians and workers for the gospel. These types of mission homes
or faith homes were common among the Methodist and Holiness
churches and their networks in the late-nineteenth and early-twentieth
century and became important centres for the early Pentecostal movement in Canada as well.[24]

Ellen Hebden states clearly in *The Promise*: "From the first we
intended taking the whole building and opening it as a Faith Home."[25]
She also talks about the amount of work that went into opening the
home and feeling very tired but desiring more power in healing. She
says: "For some months I had been seeking earnestly for more power
to heal the sick, and with this desire still in my heart I began to pray."[26]
Faith homes highlight the important role of women and healing during this time. James Opp examines this important relationship between
faith homes, healing, and women in Victorian Canada.[27] Opp accounts

---

[21] "Items from Letters Received," *Promise* February 1909, 7.
[22] Hebden, "Good News," 2.
[23] Whitt, "Developing a Pentecostal Missiology," 163–167.
[24] Dayton, "The Rise of the Evangelical Healing Movement in Nineteenth Century
America." Wacker, *Heaven Below*. Riss, "Faith Homes." Curtis, "Houses of Healing."
[25] Hebden, "How Pentecost came to Toronto," 1.
[26] Hebden, "How Pentecost came to Toronto," 2.
[27] Opp, *The Lord for the Body*, 58–63.

for the connection between the domestic environment of faith healing and the home as a spiritual space set apart from the public world of men, politics, and industry. Women served in these faith homes as guardians of spiritual and physical health. Often healing narratives by women went to great lengths to describe their thoughts and feelings about sickness and health. Devotional works, testimonies, letters, prayer, intimate conversations all took place within the faith home as a domestic space for healing. Opp says: "For middle-class Victorians, the house was commonly viewed as an extension of the body, and it is not surprising to find a close association between the concept of the sacred home and the practice of faith healing."[28] As well, these faith homes offered women leadership roles precisely because of the domestic nature of the ministry. Furthermore, says Opp: "The cultivation of a faith sufficient for the procurement of healing demanded a merging of the sacred and the domestic, the ideal environment for Victorian notions of spirituality to flourish."[29]

By the time Ellen Hebden had established her faith home in 1905, there were already numerous models in England, Toronto, Buffalo, and New York. Bethany House, for example, was founded in Toronto by Rebecca Fletcher in 1890 after her Methodist pastor informed her miracles had ceased during the apostolic age. Fletcher suffered from a tumour and prayed earnestly for a cure.[30] Faith homes were not without their controversy, however, as critics saw them in opposition to the institutionalized spaces of hospitals for healing. Women were also criticized for the role they played with some claiming they were destroying homes, influencing women to leave their husbands, exercising religious authority, and engaging in work beyond domestic duties.[31]

In this context the Chawner family came in contact with Ellen Hebden and the East End Mission. The Chawners described themselves as religious people who were not fully committed to God but became increasingly so through the ministry of the Hebdens. Emma Chawner writes about a renewed commitment to God in February 1905. In November 1905 she described a healing she experienced through the ministry of Ellen Hebden and by 1906 they were actively involved in the ministry of the East End Mission. Later that year in

---

[28] Opp, *The Lord for the Body*, 58.
[29] Opp, *The Lord for the Body*, 59.
[30] Opp, *The Lord for the Body*, 59.
[31] Opp, *The Lord for the Body*, 60.

1906 Ellen Hebden spoke in tongues after seeking God for more power
in her healing ministry. While her experience was controversial for
some at the mission, the Chawners sought God throughout the early
period and in February 1907 Charles Chawner had a vision and call to
Africa. Emma did not speak of Spirit baptism in any way for herself,
but what she did account for was the difficulty of her husband's vision
for her and the family when in 1908 he prepared to leave for Africa
without Emma and their children.[32] She says: "Then came the heart-
searching, for when the Holy Spirit spoke through my husband while
we were in prayer together, first in tongues, then with the interpretation, I tried to steel myself against it. But when I would look to Father
for help, there would steal over me a quietness, and listening, it seemed
as if I heard Father say, 'You haven't given up all.' In a very small space
of time I was brought to a place of full trust in God and willing to *let
go*, that His will might be done."[33] And so the missionary work of
Charles Chawner begins.

THE VISION, LEADING SPIRIT, AND SIGNS AND WONDERS

There are three important qualities or characteristics that define the
mission work of Charles Chawner. These include his vision and call to
Africa, a view of the Holy Spirit as guide, and signs and wonders to
validate his call. Throughout this section, I will highlight these important aspects of the early nature of Canadian Pentecostal mission work
with influences from the Hebdens. Chawner's mission work also
impacted his son Austin who became known as one of the most successful PAOC missionaries and further shaped the missionary ethos of
the denomination.[34]

Charles Chawner was born in 1861 in England and while he
described his conversion occurring at a young age, he grew cold in his
relationship with God until a renewal of faith in 1903.[35] Soon after, he

---

[32] See Aileen Chawner, "Called to Dark Africa," 5 for an account of the journey by
the daughter of Charles and Emma.

[33] Emma Chawner, "Forward" in *Called to Zululand*, 6.

[34] Miller, *Canadian Pentecostals*, 334–335; Upton, *The Miracle of Mozambique*.

[35] There is some question about the exact date of his birth. I was not able to confirm
the actual date though I searched many of the early periodicals. However, the PAOC
archive has a poster of early Canadian Pentecostal missionaries which estimated his
birth to be in 1861. Charles would have been 47 years of age in 1908 when he left for
Africa.

and Emma began to attend the East End Mission and by 1905 they were actively involved in the work. Chawner described his encounter of Spirit baptism as follows: "About 2nd of February, 1907, as I was in prayer, I felt a shock go through me that shook me like a leaf. I was made to laugh and cry by turns, to feel myself under a mighty power, shaking different parts of my body, sometimes the whole frame, at the same time feeling such an inexpressible joy that I was dealt with thus; on the third day I saw in a vision numbers of dark faces on the hillside and I among them, and through my own lips a message was given to me that I should be among them, bidding me not to tarry long in one place, that there was much land to be possessed, and Jesus was return-ing soon." Of note here are two aspects of his experience which included the bodily effect of Spirit baptism upon Chawner so that he expressed a range of emotion, laughing, crying, and shaking. Second, he spoke about a vision which became the motivating and sustaining force behind his going to Africa. However, while his vision and call occurred in early 1907, he did not leave for Africa until a year later in 1908. His family did not join him until 1909.

The delay was related to several factors including the doubts of Emma Chawner about the call and the Hebdens as well who were not convinced until the funding was secured through the support of those who attended the East End Mission. In early 1908 Emma and Charles had set aside three days to pray and to discern God's direction. Charles wrote about the time he spent in prayer with his wife, praying for God to provide the funds and to take care of his family. On Monday Febru-ary 10 he spoke with the Hebdens about going and although they still expressed some doubt, Mr. Hebden placed a deposit on Saturday for a trip to Cape Town. Later, Chawner believed it was a sign from God because the early deposit guaranteed a cheap passage. On the evening of February 10, the Hebdens asked those in attendance at the Mission if they believed God was calling the Chawners to Africa that they would financially support him and $160 was collected in an offering. By Wednesday February 12, Charles boarded a train for New York City after saying good-bye to his wife and children and the Hebdens. On Saturday February 15 he boarded the *Lucania* and sailed to England arriving in Liverpool on February 22. While in England he visited his father who he had not seen in twenty-six years and by 22 March 1908 he arrived in Cape Town with only the name of someone's relative from Toronto and a letter introducing him to them. While the vision and call motivated him to go, it is his sense of the Spirit's leading

that shaped his missionary journey. The Hebden Mission supported
Charles Chawner and sent him as the first Canadian Pentecostal
missionary.[36]

Throughout his story, Chawner continuously accounted for his decisions to travel in certain directions or to specific places and whether to
stay or continue on, as the 'Spirit led.' By this, Chawner showed how
the early Pentecostals relied upon the direct leading of the Spirit. For
example, he said: "I remained with the brother, having sweet fellowship together and witnessing to him of the baptism of the Holy Spirit.
Then through my lips the orders came: "Farther on, child; take train,
De Arr, to-morrow. Poor people, perishing. So, in glad obedience, I
bade good-by, entraining March 27th."[37] As he began his travel, he did
not know where he was going and said: "Seeking for a quiet place to
meditate, I found my way to the riverside, and the dear Lord came in
power upon me, bidding me go farther on: "Go to Mona." I had heard
of De Arr and Ladysmith through the Boer War; but I knew nothing of
this place, did not know it existed, and it was with much trepidation
that I consulted a pocket-map of the Natal railways, and found it was a
small place on a branch line, so, praising God for his guidance, I took
train to Estcourt Junction, and then, the next day to Mona. ...
Wonderful my Lord's care!"[38]

While Chawner relied upon the guidance of the Spirit he also referenced the Boer War and the great Trek as metaphors for his journey
numerous times. For example he says: "I 'trecked' along the road; it
became very hot, but Father gave me Ps. 121:6 and a breeze to cool my
brow..."[39] Elsewhere, he says "Oh what joy He poured into me as I
'trecked' along the road never trodden by my feet before and then,

---

[36] Other than the Chawners, the Hebden Mission was responsible for sending
numerous missionaries including the Hindles to Mongolia, Robert and Aimee Semple
to China, the Atters to China, Grace Fordham to Mongolia, Edgar Scurrah, South
Africa, the Slagers to China, the Lawlers to North China, and Bro. Randall to Egypt.
See Miller, *Canadian Pentecostals*, 219 and Atter, *The Third Force*, 37. The Hebdens
published a similar list in October 1909 in *Promise* of the following missionaries who
had some affiliation with the East End Mission including Charles and Emma Chawner,
James Chapman, Pirjairn, Du Cerrefour, North Africa, Thomas and Louise Hindle,
China, Edwin and Margaret Hill, China, Grace Fordham, China, Edgar W. Scurrah,
Toronto, Geordy Bowie, Jersey City, Mr. and Mrs. Hitch, Japan, Mrs. J. Norton, India,
Mr. and Mrs. Atter, China, W.H. Burns, China, and Samuel Grier, S. Africa. The
Hebdens do not include Bro. Randall who was most likely already a missionary who
experienced Pentecostal renewal while home from Egypt in Toronto.
[37] Chawner, *Called to Zululand*, 12.
[38] Chawner, *Called to Zululand*, 12–13.
[39] Chawner, *Called to Zululand*, 13.

when coming down the mountainside, I looked across the landscape and saw Zululand in the distance, the country my Lord told me in Toronto I should see and walk upon."[40] Throughout his story, the idea of a sojourner making his way from place to place, finally arriving in Zululand, is supported by his vision and reliance upon the Spirit's leading. But, Chawner also told his story in such a way that emphasized the role of signs and wonders which in turn validated his vision and call to Africa.

Signs and wonders are used throughout his story to authenticate the vision and his message as well as justify leaving behind his family during 1908. While this must have been a difficult decision, which his wife's comments demonstrated, the development of an early Pentecostal narrative revolving around the missionary became a powerful discourse for ongoing support of the work. It further justified the sacrifice the Chawners made to move to Africa at a later stage of life with their three children, Roberta, already a teenager, Austin, and Aileen. Throughout his ministry, God's provision of places for rest, food, conversion, healing, and direction are all signs and wonders. For example, Chawner writes about falling into quicksand "and had to cry mightily for help to Him. He answered and lifted my feet out of the miry clay, set them upon a rock, and established my goings (Ps. 40:2, 3)."[41] Chawner concluded about his year away by saying: "Later, guided by His, I reached home, having been away almost a year. To His glory be it written, I never needed a place to rest. He went before to prepare! Never needed a meal I cared to eat, He always arranged it. All the journey through His presence was most blessed. Though travelling over roads and paths I had never seen nor walk on, yet I had never need to ask the way; He was true to His word; He guided; and more than once when I reached a fork on the way, or cross-roads I looked up and said, 'Master, which way?' the word would come so sweetly 'This is the way' (Isaiah 30:21), and I would be led aright."[42]

Charles Chawner returned to Africa in May 1909 with his family and rarely returned to Canada. When he did, he travelled from church to church telling the story of his vision and call, the Spirit's leading, and stories of signs and wonders.[43] Chawner did not shy away from telling

---

[40] Chawner, *Called to Zululand*, 15.
[41] Chawner, *Called to Zululand*, 15.
[42] Chawner, *Called to Zululand*, 19.
[43] See Chawner, "Kinburn," 8; Chawner, "Be Ye Thankful," 2.

of the difficulties either. He spoke often of those who opposed his work, storms, drought, and eventually the death of his wife which must have affected him deeply. While away during one of his mission trips, Emma Chawner died 15 March 1933 at the age of sixty-six.[44] Charles heard about her illness through a letter but by the time he arrived home she was already dead and buried.[45] After a lengthy missionary career the first Canadian Pentecostal missionary, Charles Chawner died in 1949 and was buried in Komatipoort, South Africa.[46]

Conceptualizing the Missionary Impulse

There is very little social scientific literature on missionaries. Most anthropological literature treats missionaries and their work in a derogatory fashion. One exception, however, is the book *In the Way: A Study of Christian Missionary Endeavours* by the anthropologist Kenelm Burridge. Burridge writes about the tension between missionaries and anthropologists and argues that anthropology should treat its subjects, including missionaries, in the same way: with an openness to learn something about who they are, what they do, and why.[47] So begins his examination of the missionary enterprise which he describes as an attempt to navigate between metaculture (faith of Christianity) and culture (sociocultural structure of a people).[48] Burridge accurately describes the tension of mission work between devotion to faith and commitment to the world or ways of life of the newly adopted culture. Missionaries are interstitial figures, agents of change, preaching a message of metanoia.[49] Dedicated to their work missionaries experience particular problems of enculturating a transcultural faith while at the same time trying not to affect the local culture. The difficulties of such a task lead to other kinds of ambiguities in mission work especially as they revolve around the dialectic of God and the world. Some

---

[44] Austin Chawner, "Historical Sketch of the Beginnings," (1955): 8 [PAOC Archives]. Marion Parkinson requested information from the PAOC about Austin Chawner's work in Africa. His response included about twenty typed pages describing the story of his journey to Africa with his parents followed by an account of his own work.

[45] Chawner, "In Journeyings Often." 14.

[46] I. Chawner, "A Great Man Hath Fallen." 7, 14; Kulbeck, "C.W. Chawner: Apostle to the Zulus." 10.

[47] Burridge, *In the Way*, 1–27.

[48] Burridge, *In the Way*, 42–49.

[49] Burridge, *In the Way*, 149–161.

missionaries are successful. Others are not. The Chawners exemplify the missionary enterprise as they dedicate themselves to their work. However, they also illustrate the particular ways in which early Pentecostalism engages cross-cultural work through a theological framework shaped by Spirit baptism.

Missionaries have a variety of reasons or motivations for doing what they do. There is the mandate of the metaculture or the faith itself: to love God and to love the world; to go into the world and preach the good news of the Kingdom of God. There is also something of the belief, especially among Euro-American missionaries that the missionary is doing something good for the people whether through development, education, or commerce. Missionaries tend to rationalize what they do by citing the gospels or some other passage of scripture. Biblical authority, notes Burridge, is a central impulse for missionary activity. Secondly, there is the sense of vocation or calling into service. Missionaries, according to Burridge, place a high priority on this sense of vocation often accompanied with a renewed faith or commitment following times of prayer, study, personal trouble, or scepticism leading to faith, conviction, and commitment.[50] For Pentecostals, and especially Charles Chawner, it is his charismatic vision of Africa which motivates and shapes his calling and ministry. Early Pentecostals often told stories of some divine encounter which served to facilitate the call. Certainly, for these early Canadian missionaries, Spirit baptism empowered them.

Robert L. Montgomery in *Introduction to the Sociology of Missions* offers an analysis of missionary movements from a sociological position which gives insight into a wide range of issues. Montgomery highlights the need for sociologists to take seriously the role of mission activities, especially in the sociology of religion which has not given missions much attention. He also addresses the relationship between missionaries and social change offering a theory of religion and diffusion to account for the spread and adaptation of religious beliefs from one culture to another. Missionaries, argues the author, have played an important role in cultural change that is relatively under researched as change agents.

Montgomery argues that research on individual missionaries is lacking and what is needed is scholarship that explores the role of missionaries as change agents, the factors that contribute to the ability to bring

---

[50] Burridge, *In the Way*, 72–73.

about change including strategies, orientation of clients, role of empathy, communication, contact, and perception of clients towards missionaries. Together, they point to a complex set of factors which explain the tension of religious adaptation. A further important aspect is authority in relation to missionaries, especially charismatic authority, which helps to explain how mission work is conducted with effectiveness.[51] This too is true of early Pentecostal missionaries and the need for social science to take seriously their work including the ways in which they engaged in mission work but also the ways in which they influenced cultural change and contributed to innovative beliefs and practices.

Finally, Allan Anderson in his book *Spreading Fires*, highlights some important aspects of Pentecostal missionizing.[52] The uniqueness of Pentecostal missionary activity is not just the way in which it contrasts with Catholic missions and the 'missio dei' or Protestant missions and 'obedience to the Great Commission.' Rather, the Pentecostal missionary impulse is radically shaped by a view of the *Spirit*. Pentecostal mission work is animated by a pneumatology that emphasizes the calling and empowering of the Spirit, the ongoing leading of the Spirit, and signs and wonders to authenticate the work of the Spirit.

Research of Pentecostal mission activity and the early Pentecostal pioneers must pay attention to these ideas as they are central to Pentecostals and the uniqueness of their mission activity. The rapid worldwide spread and growth of Pentecostalism needs to be understood as a movement that is motivated and empowered by Spirit baptism. Many scholars ask why Pentecostalism is accepted by the poor and disenfranchised of the world and argue that Pentecostalism is appealing precisely because it meets the needs of those who lack materially. The focus is often upon those who receive the Pentecostal message. However, what is often missed is the basis for understanding the motivation for those who spread the message. While Pentecostalism may be appealing to the marginalized it must be understood in relationship with the Spirit empowered missionary who delivers the message. The relationship between the missionaries and their audience is reflexive and dynamic. Religious communication is always in social context, which includes the dynamic of a message in relation to those who deliver it and those who respond.[53]

[51] Montgomery, *Introduction to the Sociology of Missions*, 47–57.
[52] Anderson, *Spreading Fires*, 206–217.
[53] Beyer, *Religions in Global Society*, 10–11.

In conclusion, a social scientific understanding of Pentecostal missionary work must pay attention to these dynamic aspects of religious communication. Together, Burridge, Montgomery, and Anderson, offer a framework which accounts for the story of Charles Chawner's missionary activities including the role of the Hebden Mission, his vision of Africa, the role of the Holy Spirit in leading him, and signs and wonders to authenticate his calling and his work.

Bibliography

Anderson, Allan. *An Introduction to Pentecostalism: Global Charismatic Christianity.* Cambridge, UK: Cambridge University Press, 2004.
——. *Spreading Fires: The Missionary Nature of Early Pentecostalism.* Maryknoll, NY: Orbis Books, 2007.
Anderson, Allan and Edmond Tang, eds. *Asian and Pentecostal: The Charismatic Face of Christianity in Asia.* Oxford: APTS Press, 2005.
Atter, Gordon F. *The Third Force.* Peterborough, Ontario: The College Press, 1962.
Beyer, Peter. *Religions in Global Society.* New York, NY: Routledge, 2006.
Burkinshaw, Robert K. "Native Pentecostalism in British Columbia," in *Canadian Pentecostalism: Transition and Transformation,* edited by Michael Wilkinson, 142–170. Montreal-Kingston: McGill-Queen's University Press, 2009.
Burridge, Kenelm. *In the Way: A Study of Christian Missionary Endeavours.* Vancouver: University of British Columbia Press, 1991.
Cartledge, Mark J. ed. *Speaking in Tongues: Multi-Disciplinary Perspectives.* Milton Keynes, UK: Paternoster, 2006.
Chawner, Aileen. "Called to Dark Africa." *The Pentecostal Testimony* May 1929, 5.
Chawner, Austin. "Historical Sketch of the Beginnings," (1955): 8 [PAOC Archives].
Chawner, Charles. W. "A Cry from the Dark Continent." *The Promise* 12, February 1909, 4–5.
Chawner, Charles W. and Emma Chawner. *Called to Zululand: A Story of God's Leading.* Toronto: Self published, n.d.
——. "Kinburn." *The Pentecostal Testimony* January 1924, 8.
Chawner, Charles W. "Be Ye Thankful." *The Pentecostal Testimony* January 1925, 2.
——. "In Journeyings Often." *The Pentecostal Testimony* August 1938, 12–14.
Chawner, Ingrid. "A Great Man Hath Fallen in Israel." *The Pentecostal Testimony* 15 March 1949, 7, 14.
Choqette, Robert. *The Oblate Assault on Canada's Northwest.* Ottawa, Ontario: University of Ottawa Press, 1995.
Curtis, Heather D. "Houses of Healing: Sacred Space, Spiritual Practice, and the Transformation of Female Suffering in the Faith Cure Movement, 1870–90." *Church History* 3 (2006) 598–611.
Dayton, Donald. "The Rise of the Evangelical Healing Movement in Nineteenth-century America." 4 *Pneuma* (1982) 1–18.
Goff, James R. *Fields White Unto Harvest: Charles F. Parham and the Missionary Origins of Pentecostalism.* Fayetteville, Arkansas: The University of Arkansas Press, 1988.
Grant, John Webster. *Moon of Wintertime: Missionaries and the Indians of Canada in Encounter since 1534.* Toronto: University of Toronto Press, 1984.
Hebden, Ellen R. "Good News." *The Promise* March 1910, 2–3.
——. "How Pentecost Came to Toronto." *The Promise* 15 March, 1910: 2
"Items from Letters Received," *The Promise* February 1909.

Kulbeck, Gloria G. *What God Hath Wrought: A History of the Pentecostal Assemblies of Canada*. Toronto, Ontario: The Pentecostal Assemblies of Canada, 1958.

——. "C.W. Chawner: Apostle to the Zulus." *The Pentecostal Testimony* December 1959, 10.

McGee, Gary B. *This Gospel Shall Be Preached: A History and Theology of Assemblies of God Foreign Missions to 1959*. Springfield, MO: Gospel Publishing House, 1986, 1989.

Miller, Thomas William. "The Canadian Azusa: The Hebden Mission in Toronto." *Pneuma* Spring (1986) 5–29.

——. *Canadian Pentecostals: A History of the Pentecostal Assemblies of Canada*. Edited by William A. Griffin. Mississauga, Ontario: Full Gospel Publishing House, 1994.

Montgomery, Robert L. *Introduction to the Sociology of Missions*. Westport, CT: Praeger Publishers, 1999.

Murphy, Terrence and Roberto Perin, eds. *A Concise History of Christianity in Canada*. Toronto: Oxford University Press, 1996.

Opp, James. *The Lord for the Body: Religion, Medicine, & Protestant Faith Healing in Canada, 1880–1930*. Montreal & Kingston: McGill-Queen's University Press, 2005.

Riss, R.M. "Faith Homes," in *New International Dictionary of Pentecostal and Charismatic Movements*, edited by Stanley M. Burgess and Eduard M. Van Der Maas, 630–632. Grand Rapids, MI: Zondervan, 2002.

Semple, Neil. *The Lord's Dominion: The History of Canadian Methodism*. Montreal and Kingston: McGill-Queen's University Press, 1996.

Smith, Christian. *Moral, Believing Animals: Human Personhood and Culture*. New York, NY: Oxford University Press, 2003.

Upton, George R. *The Miracle of Mozambique*. Toronto, ON: The Pentecostal Assemblies of Canada, 1980.

Ustorf, Werner. "Protestantism and Missions," in *The Blackwell Companion to Protestantism*, edited by Alister E. McGrath and Darren C. Marks, 392–402. Malden, MA: Blackwell Publishing, 2007.

Wacker, Grant. *Heaven Below: Early Pentecostals and American Culture*. Cambridge, MA: Harvard University Press, 2001.

Warrick, Susan E. "Hardie, Robert Alexander," in *Historical Dictionary of Methodism*, 2nd ed, edited by Charles Yrigoen and Susan E. Warrick, 148–149. Scarecrow Press, 2005.

Whitt, Irving Alfred. "Developing a Pentecostal Missiology in the Canadian Context (1867–1944): The Pentecostal Assemblies of Canada." Fuller Theological Seminary, Dissertation, D. Miss, 1994.

CHAPTER THREE

THE ECUMENICAL SIGNIFICANCE OF
CANADIAN PENTECOSTALISM

Peter Althouse

INTRODUCTION

Unlike its American counterpart, the Pentecostal Assemblies of Canada (PAOC)[1] has been more open to Christian history and tradition, and therefore better positioned for an ecumenically sophisticated understanding of its theology. The preamble to the PAOC's *Statement of Fundamental and Essential Truths* reads, "The Pentecostal Assemblies of Canada stands firmly in the mainstream of historic Christianity. It takes the Bible as its all sufficient source of faith and practice and *subscribes to the historic creeds of the universal church*."[2] In *What We Believe*, Canadian Pentecostal educator J.E. Purdie compiled and explained the theological positions of the denomination:

> 'What is the doctrinal position of the Pentecostal Movement?' The answer can be given that the Movement believes the *same basic doctrines as are contained in the teaching of historic Christianity as set forth in three Ancient Creeds of the early Church known as the Apostles, the Nicene, and the Athanasian; and also the Confessions of the Fathers drawn up at the time of the Reformation by the Reformed Churches of the sixteenth and seventeenth centuries. These Creeds and Confessions are not considered* to teach anything above or beyond the Scriptures, but only set forth in a systematic form the truths contained within the Holy Scriptures. *Thus the Pentecostal Movement is an orthodox, spiritual Church holding and teaching what the historic Evangelical Church has held and taught since Apostolic days.*[3]

Immediately obvious is the fact that the PAOC saw itself in continuity with historic Christianity in its affirmation of the Creeds and Protestant

---

[1] I want to acknowledge the assistance of Marilyn Stroud and Jim Craig from the Pentecostal Assemblies of Canada Archives for this research.

[2] *Statement of Fundamental and Essential* Truths, 2, italics mine.

[3] Purdie, *What We Believe*, 2–3, italics mine.

Confessions, rather than in conflict with the catholicity of the church. Charles Ratz, one of Purdie's students and subsequently an important educator in Eastern Ontario, commented that Purdie distinguished between the external organization and the internal organism. "He spoke of the external church, the internal church. He had another term for it, churches as an organization [sic], churches as an organism [sic]. When he spoke of the Historic Church, he believed that the Pentecostal people were a continuation of the internal or historical organism. Not so much…with the outward church or organization."[4] What is less obvious is the implication this openness to the 'organic' catholicity of historic Christianity has on the Pentecostal doctrine of Spirit baptism and its corollary of initial evidence. Indeed, Spirit baptism may not even be an appropriate expression, in that a sub-tradition in the PAOC preferred the terminology of 'infilling of the Spirit.'

The question I wish to explore then is how does this emphasis on historic catholicity in Canadian Pentecostalism shape its theological identity, specifically its understanding of the Pentecostal distinctive of Spirit baptism? The nomenclature of Spirit baptism has become so ensconced in Pentecostal theology, that it has become shorthand for defining Pentecostalism in North America. However, the terminology of Spirit baptism as a subsequent act to the initiation of faith creates both biblical and theological difficulties. According to the Apostle Paul: "There is one body and one Spirit – just as you were called to one hope when you were called – one Lord, one faith, one baptism, one God and Father of all (Eph. 4.4–7 NIV)," and "For we were all baptized by one Spirit into one body – whether Jews or Greeks, slave or free – and we were all given the one Spirit to drink (I Cor. 12:13)." Yet, this seems incongruent with the Lucan account of the activity of the Spirit as depicted in Acts. Although the event of Pentecost and subsequent activities of the Spirit are images of reconciliation and unity between ethnic and class divisions, the promise of Jesus Christ is that "in a few days you will be baptized with the Holy Spirit" (Acts 1.5b), so that "you will receive power when the Holy Spirit comes on you (Acts 1.8a)" and "All of them were filled with the Holy Spirit and began to speak in other tongues as the Spirit enabled them" (Acts 2.4). At the risk of oversimplification, however, North American Pentecostals generally make a distinction between Spirit baptism in the initiation of faith that occurs

---

[4] Ratz, 1996.

in one's calling and regeneration. This is qualitatively distinct from the baptism in the Spirit that occurs as a subsequent act, evidenced by speaking in unknown tongues, and transformative in both personal (trans)formation and efficacy of witness. How one articulates these doctrines vary, but generally Pentecostals in North America articulate this dual baptism as two separate crisis experiences. The preference of some Canadian Pentecostals to use the terminology of Spirit infilling over Spirit baptism points to an attempt to synthesize the Pauline and Lucan witness in Scripture, but also to remain within the parameters of historic Christianity in which the catholicity of the church is defined in its apostolic witness and ecumenical Creeds as one faith, one baptism.

There is thus a sub-tradition in Canadian Pentecostalism, particularly in the PAOC, that prefers the terminology of the infilling of the Spirit over baptized in the Spirit, because it is more ecumenically viable and meshes better with historic Christianity. This sub-tradition is rooted in the influence that J. Eustace Purdie, an Anglican priest who was the principal of the first Canadian Pentecostal Bible College, had on a generation of leaders in the PAOC, as well as one of Purdie's students who later became an important educator for the denomination, Charles A. Ratz. Furthermore, it is an important factor in the origins and identity of Canadian Pentecostalism.

Biblical Tensions

J.R. Williams has noted the interplay of expressions in the Acts of the Apostles, and the difficulty this creates for Pentecostals and an appropriate terminology to describe their experiences of the Spirit. The favourite expression of many Pentecostals is 'baptism' in the Spirit, but baptism is not found in the Bible. "Baptized in the Holy Spirit" occurs only twice in Acts (Acts 11.16; 10.44–46). However, other expressions are used to describe the work of the Spirit on the early church. The expression 'filled' is also used. They were all filled with the Holy Spirit on the Day of Pentecost, according to Acts 2.4. Acts 9.17 states that Saul was "filled with the Holy Spirit." Thus some Pentecostals will speak of the 'infilling' of the Spirit, but once again this term is not found in Scripture. Thus while Scripture tells us that Jesus informed his disciples that they would be baptized in the Spirit, on the Day of Pentecost they were filled. Although one could argue 'baptize' and 'filled' are synonymous in that the former connotes submergence in the Spirit and

the latter an inner penetration, I will argue that the terminology of
'filled' better places the Canadian Pentecostal movement within the
context of historic Christianity. One could also point to other terms
found in Acts and used by Pentecostals: 'outpouring,' 'the falling of the
Spirit,' the Spirit 'comes on you.' Regardless, none of these terms suggest that one has more of the Spirit when one is filled, but that one has
received the Spirit from the onset of faith and is now completely
claimed by the Spirit.[5] From a biblical perspective then both 'baptized'
and 'filled' are legitimate expressions of the Spirit's further activity in
the believer. However, I wish to argue that the terminology of infilling
bypasses some of the ecumenical difficulties embodied in the term
baptism.

The tension between the pneumatology of Luke and Paul has been
an acute problem in Pentecostal-Charismatic scholarship, especially in
writers who are uncomfortable with the doctrine of subsequence, i.e.,
that the Spirit's baptism in initiation is followed by another event of the
Spirit's baptism with glossolalic activity. J.D. Dunn's classic work
Baptism in the Holy Spirit was a critical but sympathetic discussion of
the Pentecostal doctrine of Spirit baptism, and a clarion call to
Pentecostal scholars. Dunn argues that although Pentecostals should
be commended for their enthusiasm in emphasizing the Spirit's activity in the life of the believer, they misread the biblical account of Spirit
baptism. Preferring a Pauline reading, under which Luke's account
must be subsumed, Dunn argues that baptism in the Spirit is an expression related to the initiation of faith – being baptized in the Spirit is an
expression of the event of regeneration. The Pentecostal expression of
Spirit baptism as a subsequent act of faith for the purposes of Christian
formation and social transformation is not biblical. Pentecostals make
two fatal errors: Pentecostals have followed the catholic tradition of
separating conversion-initiation (represented in water baptism) from a
gift of the Spirit which follows after conversion. Curiously, Dunn suggests a correspondence in the Pentecostal doctrine of subsequence and
the catholic doctrine of confirmation. Secondly, Pentecostals mistak-
enly follow the Protestant separation between faith and water baptism,
where the Spirit has already engendered faith in the believer and water
baptism becomes a mere confession of this commitment. In the NT
water baptism itself is the act of faith and repentance.[6]

---

[5] Williams, "Baptism in the Holy Spirit," 355–356.
[6] Dunn, *Baptism in the Spirit*, 227.

Pentecostal scholar Gordon Fee agrees with Dunn. Fee argues that the Pentecostal doctrine of subsequence – that the baptism in the Holy Spirit is a subsequent and separate act of grace following initiation – is not biblical. Although he fails to support his argument, Fee claims that the rejection of subsequence has little bearing on the Pentecostal doctrine of Spirit baptism.[7] Other Pentecostal biblical scholars have since responded to Dunn's criticism using the biblical methodology of redaction criticism. Starting with *The Charismatic Theology of St. Luke*, Canadian Pentecostal Roger Stronstad argues that Luke's writings employ a distinct theological agenda and therefore makes the complementary themes of salvation history and the charismatic activity of the Spirit theologically significant.[8] This work was followed by Robert P. Menzies' *Empowered for Witness: The Spirit in Luke-Acts*. Agreeing with Stronstad, that one must read Luke as a theologian with a distinctive and differing theological agenda from Paul, Menzies' argues for a distinction between the soteriological pneumatology of Paul and charismatic pneumatology of Luke.[9] Other Pentecostal scholars have followed suit, using variations of redaction and literary criticism to argue that the narrative of Luke-Acts offers a theological account of the gospel, and therefore offers the church theologically specific data.[10] The charismatic activity of the Spirit, whether it be Spirit baptism, infilling, missionary service, or endurance of suffering is afforded doctrinal credibility. A mediating position is suggested by Max Turner, a sympathetic scholar but critical especially of Menzies dichotomy between Luke's Jewish view of the Spirit of prophecy, and Paul's soteriological view of the Spirit. Instead, and I agree with Turner's criticism on this point, Paul's theology (as well as John's) is a logical extension of the Spirit of prophecy, and "Luke's 'Spirit of prophecy' is much more strongly soteriologically oriented."[11] Not only is the separation of the charismatic from the soteriological problematic from a biblical standpoint, but theologically salvation includes the charismatic spectrum in terms of the ongoing eschatological vision and the ecclesial mission of the church.

---

[7] Fee, *Gospel and Spirit*, 105–119.

[8] Stronstad, *The Charismatic Theology of St. Luke*.

[9] Menzies, *Empowered for Witness*, 232–43.

[10] Penney, *The Missionary Emphasis of Lukan Pneumatology*; Wenk, *Community-Forming Power*; Middelstadt, *The Spirit and Suffering in Luke-Acts*.

[11] Turner, *Power from on High*, 13.

Theological-Historical Background

From a theological perspective the teaching of Spirit baptism emerged
in a specific historical context of Wesleyan Holiness. In the United
States both Charles F. Parham, the architect of the Spirit baptism doctrine, and William J. Seymour, the African American preacher who
emphasized the experiential characteristic of the Azusa Street Mission,
were from within the Methodist Holiness camp. In this context, the
Wesleyan theology of perfection or entire sanctification played a critical role. Wesley's doctrine of sanctification sought to compliment the
forensic theme of justification with an emphasis on the life of holiness.
Salvation, for Wesley, was not merely an ontological change with little
bearing on this life, but an existential change, a divine reordering of
our fallen human condition so that we may be restored to the image of
God. Christian perfection was the goal of the Christian life, in which
one struggled to overcome voluntary transgression of God's law.[12]
However, Wesley's theology of perfection morphed into multiple directions after his death. Of concern here is how the Holiness movement
shifted emphases: First of all, entire sanctification shifted from being
viewed as the telos of a lifelong struggle to a crisis moment that became
an entry point into higher Christian living; secondly, it shifted from
the language of forgiveness and cleansing from sin, to the language of
power for service and witness; and finally the terminology of baptism
in the Holy Ghost quickly became associated with entire sanctification
(even though Wesley resisted this description), until finally the span
of the Christian life was to include three crisis moments: conversion-
initiation, second blessing of entire sanctification, and baptism in the
Holy Ghost for power.[13] When Parham started to ask the question at
the beginning of the twentieth century – what is the 'Bible evidence'
that one has been baptized in the Holy Ghost – he already had a prior
understanding of three works of grace (conversion, entire sanctification and endument of power). By looking at Luke-Acts he came to the
conclusion that speaking in unknown tongues was the 'Bible evidence'
of Spirit baptism.

The point is that the context in which American Pentecostalism
emerged was one in which the issue of subsequent and separate acts of

---

[12] Dayton, *Theological Roots of Pentecostalism*, 45–47.
[13] I need not go into detail regarding this historical development of this transition
other than to commend Donald Dayton's excellent work in the area.

grace were already at play. In the context of the Holiness movement, Wesley's *ordo salutis* was already parsed out into distinct stages of the Christian life, so that when Pentecostalism emerged Spirit baptism as a subsequent act of grace was presupposed rather than a point of theological reflection.

The Canadian context however is somewhat different. True, the Holiness movement was influential in many parts of Canada. Holiness advocate Phoebe Palmer, who articulated the 'shorter way' to Holiness as an act of faith rather than through 'tarrying' on God, held meetings in Hamilton, Eastern Ontario and the Maritime provinces. The Palmers claimed to have a hundred conversions and ninety people experience 'entire sanctification.'[14] Likewise, Ralph C. Horner was a leading Holiness evangelist in Eastern Canada. His Holiness claims, which started to shift towards a three works of grace position, were opposed by other Methodists in Ontario. Later in his ministry Horner insisted on a third experience after justification and entire sanctification, as "'soul-winning power' after 'perfected love made me groan for power to reach the perishing masses and lead them to Jesus.'"[15] A number of 'Hornerites' were among the first to respond to the Pentecostal message in Ontario, notably Robert E. McAlister. All in all, numerous early Pentecostal leaders in Canada emerged from the Holiness camps, including McAlister, Ellen Hebden, Andrew H. Argue, Alfred. G. Ward, Reuben. E. Sternall, D. Jack Saunders, Daniel N. Buntain and Aimee Semple McPherson.[16]

Yet Reformed theology played a significant part in Canadian Pentecostalism through the Revivalist tradition. The theology of prominent American Revivalists Jonathan Edwards and 'New Light' theology of Charles Finney had its Canadian counterparts in Henry Alline (1748–1784) and Donald McDonald (1783–1867). Alline emigrated from New England and spread 'New Light' Calvinism throughout the Maritime Provinces. McDonald was a Scottish Presbyterian who preached 'new birth' revival in Nova Scotia. Miller makes the unsubstantiated claim that J.E. Purdie was 'probably' influenced by this tradition;[17] however I have made the argument that Purdie needs to be understood within the context of his own Reformed Anglican

---

[14] Miller, *Canadian Pentecostals*, 24–25.
[15] Dayton, 99.
[16] Miller, 25–25.
[17] Miller, 23–24. Also see Rawlyk, *The Canada Fire*.

tradition.[18] Charles A. Ratz, a student of Purdie who taught at Eastern Pentecostal Bible College, stated that Purdie "saved him from the Holiness error."[19]

Purdie, however, represents a third stream in Canadian Pentecostalism that is linked to the Reformed Anglican tradition. Purdie was an Anglican priest who graduated from Wycliffe College, Toronto, an Anglican school that emphasized the Reformed Anglican position and low-church ecclesiology. Between 1907 and 1925 he served in parishes in Manitoba, New Brunswick and Saskatchewan, and in 1919 was filled with the Holy Spirit. In 1925 he was invited by the executive of the Pentecostal Assemblies of Canada to become the founding principal of the first denominational school, Canadian Pentecostal Bible College, Winnipeg, a position he held with minor interuption until 1950. According to Purdie, he modeled the college curriculum after Wycliffe College, to emphasize "a thorough understanding of doctrine and emphasizing church history along with biblical studies."[20] Perhaps this emphasis contributes to the openness the PAOC has to the Creeds and traditions of historic Christianity.

On the surface, the PAOC appears simply to follow its American counterpart in describing the link between Spirit baptism and speaking in tongues through the doctrine of initial evidence; that, is the first instance of speaking in tongues is evidence that one has been baptized in the Spirit. I will leave the whole question of initial evidence until later, but for now there are nuances to that doctrine in both the American and Canadian contexts that can be missed by too casual a reading. For the moment, however, I would like to explore the Canadian reading of the Pentecostal doctrine, a reading that uses infilling as the preferred term. *The Statement of Fundamental and Essential Truths* states:

> The Baptism in the Holy Spirit is an experience in which the believer yields control of himself to the Holy Spirit. Through this he comes to know Christ in a more intimate way, and receives power to witness and

---

[18] Althouse, "The Influence of Dr. J.E. Purdie's Reformed Anglican Theology," 3–28.

[19] Charles Ratz made this statement to me following my presentation on J.E. Purdie at the Society for Pentecostal Studies meeting in March 1996.

[20] Kydd, "Purdie, James Eustace," 1013; also see Guenther, "Pentecostal Theological Education," 99–122. A comparison between the courses offered by Wycliffe College and the courses offered by Canadian Bible College does not support Purdie's claim. Althouse, 26–28.

grow spiritually. ... The initial evidence of the Baptism in the Holy Spirit is speaking in other tongues as the Spirit gives utterance. This experience is distinct from, and subsequent to, the experience of new birth.[21]

On the surface, the PAOC appears to tow the line of the Assemblies of God, its sister organization in the United States.[22] However, if one scratches below the surface, one starts to see the emergence of a sub-tradition in the PAOC that prefers the terminology of infilling. In *What We Believe*, Purdie refuses to use the expression baptism in the Spirit. Statement No. 14, "The Infilling of the Holy Spirit," states:

> 'Now if any man have not the Spirit of Christ, he is none of His.' On the other hand every believer is not necessarily *filled* with the Spirit according to Lu. 24:49; Acts 1:8 and 2:4. Therefore the purpose of the Infilling is to give us additional power in order that we may be more useful to the Lord and bring greater glory to His name. ... There is no evidence whatsoever in the New Testament that the power and Infilling of the Spirit has ever been withdrawn from the church.[23]

Indeed the terminology of Spirit baptism is conspicuously absent from the entire document. Moreover, Purdie seems to imply that not all believers are "necessarily *filled* with the Spirit," but that this experience leads to a deeper Christian life for some.

In *Concerning the Faith* Purdie likewise emphasizes the terminology of infilling though he concedes at one point that "the 'Infilling of the Holy Spirit' [is] sometimes called the 'Baptism of the Spirit.'" Question after question develops an understanding of the Infilling: "What is the Infilling of the Holy Spirit?" "Who may receive the Infilling of the Holy Spirit?" "What are the evidences of the Infilling of the Holy Spirit?" and so on.[24] Purdie resists the temptation to parse off the Spirit's activity in the initiation of faith and the filling of the Spirit for Christian

---

[21] *Statement of Fundamental and Essential Truths*, 5.

[22] After the PAOC assumed a more formal relationship with the AG in the US, it adopted nearly word for word the doctrines of the AG, despite the fact that it had existed for seven years without an official doctrinal statement. In 1926 the PAOC adopted the terminology of "Consummation of the Baptism of the Holy Spirit" for the title and "Initial Physical Sign" as the doctrine. "Pentecostal Assemblies of Canada," *Pentecostal Testimony*, February 1926, 2–3. In 1928 the PAOC followed the AG and changed the title simply to "The Evidence" but kept the doctrine the same. "Constitution and By-Laws of the Pentecostal Assemblies of Canada," 17. See discussion later in this chapter.

[23] Purdie, *What We Believe*, 22–23.

[24] Purdie, *Concerning the Faith*, 44–46.

service into two distinct acts of grace, but rather wants to highlight the interconnection between the two, that the infilling is a "measure" of the Spirit we already have:

Q. 253 What is the Infilling of the Holy Spirit?
A.   The Infilling of the Holy Spirit means that the believer who already has a measure of the Spirit, is now filled and empowered for service according to Acts 1:8 and 2:4.[25]

In fact, in distinguishing the infilling of the Spirit from sanctification Purdie explicitly rejects the notion that the infilling (or sanctification for that matter) is a second work of grace:

Q. 268 Can it be said that either the Infilling of the Holy Spirit or Sanctification is doctrinally what is termed a 'second work of grace' performed by God?
A.   No. God does not need to accomplish any new act of grace when He fills one with the Spirit or gives him the victory and the cleansing that the New Testament terms Sanctification.[26]

Q. 270 What would be involved if we taught that doctrinally there is such a thing as a second work of grace?
A.   It would limit the completeness and finality of God's work on Calvary and also interfere with the completeness of His work in Justification, thus leaving the faithful and sincere believer in an unsettled condition, wondering from day to day if all were well with him spiritually.[27]

Yet at the same time he does suggest that the infilling is logically distinct from initiation because he resists integrating the infilling with regeneration (a move, for instance, the Assemblies of God theologian Frank Macchia makes in *Baptized in the Spirit*). Purdie states, "To be regenerated or born again by the Holy Spirit and have a measure of His presence is one thing; to be FILLED with the same Spirit is something additional."[28] Purdie stands in line, however, with the Reformed Revivalist and Keswick traditions of evangelicalism to argue that the

[25] Purdie, *Concerning the Faith*, 44.
[26] Purdie, *Concerning the Faith*, 46.
[27] Purdie, *Concerning the Faith*, 46.
[28] Purdie, *Concerning the Faith*, 45.

purpose of the infilling is empowerment for Christian service and witness:[29]

> Q. 255 What is the purpose of the Infilling of the Holy Spirit?
> A.   It means that God gives us additional power and liberty for service enabling us to freely and efficiently witness for Christ – Acts 1:8.[30]

In both *Concerning the Faith* and *What We Believe*, publications endorsed by the PAOC, Purdie definitely prefers the terminology of infilling.

Yet the issue is not quite so clear. In a doctrinal series for the *Pentecostal Testimony*, Purdie uses the terminology of 'Baptism of the Holy Ghost,' 'infilling' and 'filled with the Spirit' interchangeably.[31] Originally I thought that this was probably an editorial change.[32] However, I have since discovered that Purdie appears to prefer the terminology of baptism in his Lecture Notes on the Baptism of the Holy Spirit. In the Introduction, Purdie claims that "the Baptism of the Holy Spirit is felt to be the distinctive testimony of this movement."[33] He begins by arguing that the Pentecostal baptism is not regeneration: "There is abundant evidence that the Scriptures plainly teach the Baptism in the Holy Spirit to be a definite experience, apart, and subsequent to regeneration. As Calvary preceded Pentecost, so the New Birth precedes the Baptism in the Holy Spirit."[34] Moreover, baptism in the Spirit is not sanctification. Sanctification "separates the believer from the self life, conforming him to the image of Christ," whereas Spirit baptism "is the coming of the Third Person of the Trinity, in, and upon, the believer." Sanctification "separates the soul to God," while Spirit baptism "fills the soul WITH God." Sanctification relates to "our oneness with Christ in His death and resurrection," whereas baptism "has to do with our enduement of power from on high."[35] Purdie then engages a point by point discussion of the baptism of the Holy Spirit, the biblical sign that one has received the baptism, and the consequences of receiving the baptism.

---

[29] Althouse, 17–18.
[30] Purdie, *Concerning the Faith*, 44.
[31] Purdie, "Great truths of the Word of God, Part V," 5–6.
[32] Althouse, 16–17.
[33] Purdie, "Lecture Notes," 1.
[34] Purdie, "Lecture Notes," 2.
[35] Purdie, "Lecture Notes," 3.

Why this stark difference? His Lecture Notes consistently use variations of the terminology of Spirit baptism while his doctrinal publications consistently use the terminology of infilling. His Lecture Notes
are probably historically prior. *Concerning the Faith* and *What We
Believe* were published shortly after his retirement in 1950. Does this
depict a shift in his thinking? Did he use the terms interchangeably
throughout his life? Did he feel freer to use his preferred terms after his
retirement? We do not really know. What we do know is that the PAOC
endorsed and approved his doctrinal views. Minimally, this suggests
that the terminology of infilling represents a sub-tradition in Canadian
Pentecostalism. This sub-tradition was continued by one of Purdie's
students, Charles A. Ratz.

Ratz, articulating a similar position on the Pentecostal blessing
easily shifts between baptism in the Spirit and infilling, but prefers
infilling. He claims, "I said we need to perpetuate [the] Pentecostal
distinctive, being filled with the Holy Spirit."[36] In a student handbook
titled *The Holy Spirit: An Outlined Bible Study for Personal or Class Use*,
Ratz delineates between 'the baptism with the Spirit' and 'the Infilling
of the Spirit.' "The Word exhorts all believers to 'be filled with the Spirit'
(Eph. 5:18). Whether we call this Pentecostal experience 'The Baptism
in the Spirit' or 'The Infilling of the Spirit' does not matter. Perhaps for
clarity, when speaking to others who oppose, it is better to speak of
'The Infilling of the Spirit.'"[37] Although ambiguous regarding those
"who oppose" (possibly he is referring to the Wesleyan Holiness critics
that ascribe to entire sanctification and/or the Reformed tradition of
cessationism), his discussion of meanings and distinctions in baptism
suggest he is referring to those who believe that Spirit baptism comes
in the initiation of faith. Perhaps he is being more ecumenically
minded, reserving the terminology of Spirit baptism for Christian initiation. He distinguishes 'ritual baptism,' which is a symbolic representation but with no saving grace in itself, and 'real baptism,' which is
"one of the unifying graces"[38] of the Spirit that places the believer into
the body of Christ. The one baptism referred to in Eph. 4:5 is real and
by the Spirit. "... [T]he baptism of the Holy Spirit into one body engen-
ders the most vital and perfect union that could be formed among

---

[36] Ratz easily shifts between these terms in both conversation and his writing. Ratz,
1996.
[37] Ratz, *The Holy Spirit*, 97.
[38] Ratz, *The Holy Spirit*, 95.

men. Ritual baptism does not tend to unify believers.... The one baptism in Eph. 4:5 is speaking of the Spirit baptism concerning the organism called 'the body of Christ.'"[39]

Ratz argues for a distinction between the potential and the experiential. "Potentially all believers are placed into the body of Christ by the Spirit on the Day of Pentecost. Experientially all believers are placed into the body of Christ by the Spirit at regeneration. ... This baptism is 'by the Spirit,' that is we were placed into the body by means of the Spirit."[40] "Since this baptism refers to the believer's position in the body of Christ at conversion, the believer is not exhorted to seek this baptism, however, is commanded to be filled with the Spirit."[41] Baptism in the Spirit is reserved to mean the activity of the Spirit in initiation of faith and, in divergence from Purdie, is linked to regeneration. Yet "All believers receive the Spirit at regeneration but all are not filled with the Spirit."[42] Later he distinguishes between the positional and the experiential in a slightly different way. "The positional aspect refers to the believer being placed into the body of Christ. The experiential has reference to the infilling of the Holy Spirit in I Corinthians 12:13. The disciples and followers of the Lord were both placed in the body of Christ and filled with the Spirit."[43] Ratz draws a closer connection between the Lucan and Pauline traditions, suggesting that 'to be filled' is not only related to the activity of glossolalia, but to the Pauline discussion of charismatic gifts. Clearly, the infilling of the Spirit with the evidence of unknown tongues is the preferred terminology over baptism in the Spirit, despite his claim to the use of either.

In section 4, "The Twofold Meaning of being Baptized by the Spirit," Ratz makes a distinction between Spirit baptism as the believer's position in Christ, and the infilling of the Spirit as the charismatic fullness of the future:

a) *The Believer's Position* – 'For by one Spirit are we all baptized into the body.. [sic]' I Cor. 12:13a. This takes place at the time of regeneration or salvation. All believers are then baptized by the Spirit into the body of Christ.

---

[39] Ratz, *Holy Spirit*, 89.
[40] Ratz, *Holy Spirit*, 94.
[41] Ratz, *Holy Spirit*, 94.
[42] Ratz, *Holy Spirit*, 94.
[43] Ratz, *Holy Spirit*, 97.

b) *The Infilling of the Holy Spirit* – 'And have been all made to drink into one Spirit' I Cor. 12:13b. This is the charismatic fullness of the Spirit which is evidenced by speaking 'with other tongues, as the Spirit gives utterance' Acts 2:4.[44]

"Many people, immediately upon receiving salvation, reach out in faith and, yielding to the Spirit's power, are filled with the Spirit. Many who have been saved and enjoy the presence of the Holy Spirit within have not been filled."[45] While there is still a sense that the infilling is experientially subsequent to the baptism of the Spirit in initiation, Ratz is unwilling to make an ontological separation between two distinct acts of grace.

EVIDENCES OF THE SPIRIT

The assumption among many North American Pentecostals is the doctrine of 'initial evidence,' the belief that speaking in tongues is the first indication that a person has been baptized in the Spirit, is critical in defining baptism in the Spirit. Certainly the question of evidence of the Spirit's activity in the life of the believer was an important concern for early Pentecostals, with discussions that span back into the Holiness and Revivalist movements. Assemblies of God historian Gary McGee proclaims: "For many early Pentecostals, the force of the biblical data compelled them to believe that of all the Pentecostal phenomena, tongues alone was purposefully given to authenticate Spirit baptism."[46]

However, a closer examination of the early movement reveals sophisticated nuances in the doctrine that are too easily overlooked. Distinctions can be observed among various Pentecostal personalities and bodies, in both the United States and Canada. According to McGee, the terminology of 'initial' first appeared in the Assemblies of God's Statement of Fundamental Truths (1916), though the terminology of 'evidence' was not used. In 1917, a distinction was made between the reception of tongues in the baptism in the Spirit, and the gift of tongues described by the Apostle Paul in I Corinthians.[47] A debate quickly ensued between Daniel W. Kerr and F.F. Bosworth, the latter claiming

---

[44] Ratz, *Holy Spirit*, 96.
[45] Ratz, *Holy Spirit*, 98.
[46] McGee, "Early Pentecostal Hermeneutics," 103.
[47] "Minutes of the General Council of the Assemblies of God," 1917, 21.

that any of the charismatic gifts could indicate Spirit baptism. Daniel Kerr rebutted that the initial instance of tongues is what indicates baptism and that this experience is expected of all believers. Bosworth willingly withdrew from the Assemblies to avoid controversy.[48]

A perusal of the "Minutes of the General Council of the Assemblies of God in the United States, Canada and Foreign Lands" reveals that the original 1916 doctrinal statement on Spirit baptism did not even use the terminology of evidence. Under the heading, "The Full Consummation of the Baptism in the Holy Spirit," the statement reads:

> The full consummation of the baptism of believers in the Holy Spirit and fire, is indicated by the initial sign of speaking in tongues, as the Spirit of God gives utterance: Acts 2:4. This wonderful experience is distinct from and subsequent to the new birth. Acts 10:44–46; 11:14–16; 15:3, 9.[49]

The following year, the Council corrected the statement to include the word "physical," because "By an oversight last year, the word 'physical' got left out before the word 'sign'...."[50] This wording remained stable until 1927, when the word 'evidence' was inserted into the heading, to read: "The Evidence of the Baptism in the Holy Spirit." However, 'initial' was not used in relation to 'evidence,' and the doctrine itself remained the same.[51]

It was not until 1977 that the terminology of 'initial evidence' started to be used, not in relation to the doctrine itself, but as a requirement for the ordination of ministers. In 1947, the requirement for Pentecostal ministry was that the applicant "must give testimony to having received the Baptism in the Holy Spirit according to Acts 2:4,"[52] and in 1969, ministers were required to show evidence of the 'Spirit-filled life' in accordance to Acts 2:4,[53] but not until 1977 was a resolution put forth to change the 'Spirit-filled life' to 'initial physical evidence.' Now the ministerial candidate had to provide "Testimony to having received the baptism in the Holy Spirit with the initial physical evidence of

---

[48] McGee, 110.

[49] "Minutes of the General Council of the Assemblies of God," 1916," 11.

[50] "Minutes of the General Council of the Assemblies of God," 1917," 21.

[51] "Constitution and By-Laws of the General Council of the Assemblies of God," 1927, 10.

[52] "Constitution and Bylaws: The General Council of the Assemblies of God," 1947, 18.

[53] "Minutes of the Thirty-Third General Council of the Assemblies of God," 1969, 112.

speaking in other tongues according to Acts 2:4."[54] Finally, in 1983 the
transition was completed when a resolution was made to change the
heading of the doctrine to "The Initial Physical Evidence of the Baptism
in the Holy Spirit." Yet the doctrine itself remains "initial physical
sign."[55]

Why this fundamental revision of a basic Pentecostal doctrine, with
a concerted effort to read 'initial evidence' back into the history of the
Assemblies of God? The differing nuances are interesting. By emphasizing 'initial physical sign' space was provided to allow for other 'non-
physical' indicators such as abiding love or possibly non-physical
charismatic gifts, but tongues was the phenomenological indicator of
Spirit baptism. The use of 'Spirit-filled' or the statement the 'Baptism in
the Holy Spirit according to Act 2:4' hints at more openness as to how
to interpret the Acts 2:4 narrative and its implications for Pentecostal
theology and ministry. The use of the word 'consummation' in its early
years is suggestive of an eschatological understanding, which sees the
completion or fulfilment of the baptism in the Spirit as fundamentally
connected to its inauguration in the coming of the Spirit in the baptism of water and the initiation of faith. The use of the word 'evidence'
without the terminology of 'initial,' beginning in 1927, suggests an
understanding of the doctrine more resonate with the early Pentecostal
movement, than with its later revisions.

The first decade of early Pentecostalism was more concerned with
the 'Bible evidence' of Spirit baptism. At a New Year's Eve service in
1901 Parham asked that question, "What is the *Bible evidence* of the
baptism of the Spirit?" His conclusion was, "speaking in tongues as the
Spirit gives utterance."[56] For Parham, speaking in tongues was not glossolalia but xenolalia. In other words, Parham believed that one who
was baptized in the Spirit was given the supernatural ability to speak in
other earthly languages. Its purpose was a supernatural enduement for
missionary work in anticipation of the coming of Christ.

William Seymour's view was different. Initially he adopted Parham's
understanding of missionary tongues, but quickly evolved his understanding. Seymour firmly believed that speaking in tongues was the

[54] "Minutes of the Thirty-Seventh Session of the General Council of the Assemblies of God," 1977, 81.
[55] "Minutes, Revised Constitution and Bylaws: The General Council of the Assemblies of God," 1983, 69.
[56] Parham, *The Life of Charles F. Parham*, 58–59.

'Bible evidence' of Spirit baptism as an enduement of power of the sanctified life. In 1915 Seymour wrote: "The Baptism with the Holy Ghost is a gift of power upon the sanctified life; so when we get it we have the same evidence as the Disciples received on the Day of Pentecost (Acts 2:3, 4), in speaking new tongues."[57] In mid 1907, Seymour appropriated Parham's view and argued "the ability to speak in tongues was *the evidence*, 'the Bible evidence,' of the baptism with the Holy Spirit." However, in September 1917, perhaps due to his break with Parham, Seymour argued that *"Tongues are one of the signs that go with every [Spirit-] baptized person...but it is not the real evidence of baptism in the everyday life."*[58] He soon expanded the question of evidence to include love, the fruit of the Spirit, the life of prayer, healing the sick and love for the unsaved. Seymour asks, "What is the real evidence that a man or woman has received the baptism with the Holy Ghost?"

> Divine love, which is charity. Charity is the Spirit of Jesus. They will have the fruits of the Spirit. Gal. 5:22 "The fruit of the Spirit is love, joy, peace, longsuffering, gentleness, goodness, meekness, faith, temperance; against such there is no law. And they that are Christ's had crucified the flesh with the affections and lusts." This is the real Bible evidence in their daily walk and conversation; and the outward manifestations; speaking tongues and the signs following; casting out devils, laying hands on the sick and the sick being healed, and the love of God for souls increasing in their hearts.[59]

In fact, Seymour believed that to be one in the Spirit included racial reconciliation. He thought that the believer was empowered by the Spirit to live in unity with the whole family of God, without prejudices, suggesting an understanding of Spirit baptism that included notions of social justice.[60] One could argue that Seymour's position developed later and that one should look back to Parham's view. Yet by that same logic one could also argue that the 'initial evidence' doctrine is a later development. Pentecostalism, both in its early stages and even today, is an extremely diverse movement with a multiplicity of views as Pentecostals try to articulate their experiences of the Spirit.

In turning to the Canadian scene what becomes immediately obvious is that the Purdie-Ratz tradition was engaging the debate in terms

---

[57] Robeck, "William J. Seymour and 'The Bible Evidence,'" 77.
[58] Robeck, "William J. Seymour," 80–81.
[59] Robeck, "William J. Seymour," 81.
[60] Seymour, "The Doctrines and Disciplines of the Azusa Street," 1915, 12–13.

of 'Bible evidence' rather than 'initial evidence.' Admittedly, the PAOC's *Statement of Fundamental and Essential Truths* affirms the doctrine of initial evidence. Article VI.3 (5) states:

> The Baptism in the Holy Spirit is an experience in which the believer yields control of himself to the Holy Spirit. Through this he comes to know Christ in a more intimate way, and receives power to witness and grow spiritually. Believers should earnestly seek the Baptism in the Holy Spirit according to the command of our Lord Jesus Christ. The initial evidence of the Baptism in the Holy Spirit is speaking in other tongues as the Spirit gives utterance. This experience is distinct from, and subsequent to the experience of the new birth.[61]

The statement appears to accept *carte blanche* the doctrine of 'initial evidence,' but is distinct from the Assemblies of God position of 'initial physical sign.' However both Purdie and Ratz offer a different position. In *What We Believe*, Purdie articulates multiple evidences:

> The question is often asked, "What is the evidence that one is filled with the Holy Spirit?" The *Biblical evidence* that one is filled with the Holy Spirit is that he speaks supernaturally in a tongue he has never learned (Acts 2:4).... A further evidence of the Infilling of the Holy Spirit is that one receives power for witnessing, which every believer needs (Acts 4:33); a much greater passion for souls; a greater reverence for the Word of God, and a greater love toward all true Christian people, as well as the deepening of the prayer life.... Those who have received the Infilling of the Spirit are marked off in the world by their earnestness to help others, and also their fresh zeal to study the Word of God.[62]

In *Concerning the Faith*, Purdie makes a distinction between the 'supernatural evidence' which is physical in its demonstration and the 'practical evidences' in the formation of the believer. He asks:

> Q. 256 What are the evidences of the Infilling of the Holy Spirit?
> A.   They are:
>   1. The physical evidence of speaking in other tongues –
>   Acts 2:4; 10:44–46; 11:15; 19:6.
>   2. Following the supernatural evidence of the Infilling of
>   the Holy Spirit, there are practical evidences, such as
>   power for witnessing – Acts 4:33; passion for souls; a
>   greater love for the Word of God, and towards all true
>   Christian people.[63]

---

[61] *Statement of Fundamental and Essential Truths*, 5.
[62] Purdie, *What We Believe*, 22–24.
[63] Purdie, *Concerning the Faith*, 44.

Obviously, Purdie believed that there were multiple 'Bible evidences' of the infilling of the Spirit, including speaking in tongues, but also love for God and the other as well as power for witness. Except for his statement "Following the supernatural evidence of the Infilling of the Holy Spirit," what is curiously absent is any discussion of 'initial evidence' and a distinct separation between initiation and subsequent 'fillings' of the Spirit.

Once again though, Purdie takes a different stance in his Lecture Notes. His language changes as he asks, "WHAT IS THE SCRIPTURAL SIGN THAT ONE HAS RECEIVED THE BAPTISM OF THE HOLY SPIRIT?" to which he responds, "I believe 'The Baptism of believers in the Holy Ghost is indicated by the *initial physical sign* of speaking with other tongues as the Spirit gives them utterance.'"[64] This change in language seems to be taken from the Assemblies of God's "Statement of Fundamental Truths." Is this why he puts the statement in italics? But then he continues in the section on the results of Spirit baptism, "While supernatural utterance is the *pre-eminent initial, physical sign* of the full Pentecostal Baptism, *it is by no means the most important* [italics mine]." He then lists in the discussion: "The burning zeal of Pentecost," "The white heated love and sacrifice," "The passion for souls," "Wholehearted separation from the world," "The pilgrim character," "Panting for the coming of Christ," "The Spirit of prayer and intercession," "Love for, and illumination of the Word of God," "Power to witness for Christ," "And boldness to face opposition in His name."[65] It appears that experiencing glossolalia (or even other ecstatic experiences) was not an end in itself but the point of entry into greater love, formation and service. What is not so clear is why he changed his language in describing the connection between tongues and the Pentecostal blessing of the Spirit. Was he borrowing from American sources, which had become part of the PAOC's doctrinal formulation?

When one turns to Ratz, that language of initial evidence is almost completely absent. In a rather unclear statement Ratz states, "Not only is the believer baptized into the body of Christ but he is filled with the Spirit. The initial infilling of the Spirit is always accompanied by the one who is filled speaking in other tongues as the Spirit gives utterance [sic]."[66] However, Ratz says that the infilling of the Spirit is "the

---

[64] Purdie, "Lecture Notes, 6, italics mine.
[65] Purdie, "Lecture Notes," 8–9.
[66] Ratz, *Holy Spirit*, 97.

charismatic fullness of the Spirit which is evidenced by the speaking with other tongues, as the Spirit gives utterance."[67] Yet Ratz does not engage in the discussion of evidence in this document, mostly discerning the relationship between the Spirit in the initiation of faith and the Spirit's infilling as a subsequent experience.[68]

It appears from this brief discussion of the Purdie-Ratz tradition that they were attempting to engage the full spectrum of the early Pentecostal debates concerning the Pentecostal blessing. Both Purdie and Ratz appear to have looked to an earlier tradition that searched for 'biblical evidence' of the Spirit's infilling rather than distilling it down into a doctrinal statement of 'initial evidence.' However, Purdie also engaged the language of 'initial physical sign' in his Lecture Notes, a curious distinction from his published works. What is unclear is why Purdie would make one argument in his Lecture Notes, which he presumably taught a generation of Canadian Pentecostal ministers, and a substantially different argument in his official publications, which were endorsed by the PAOC. Perhaps Purdie, and to a lesser extent Ratz, were attempting to navigate the tensions within Canadian Pentecostalism.

ECUMENICAL SIGNIFICANCE OF CANADIAN PENTECOSTALISM

At the beginning of this chapter I asserted that a sub-tradition that preferred to use the terminology of 'infilling of the Holy Spirit' in Canadian Pentecostalism offers a theology that has ecumenical potential. This sub-tradition is, I believe, ecumenically significant on two fronts: the internal debates in the contemporary Pentecostal movement regarding 'initial evidence,' and the external debates with the broader Christian community that is hesitant in delineating two baptisms in the journey of the Christian life. Of late, the internal debates in North American Pentecostalism have revolved around the question of 'initial evidence.' My perusal of the historical development of the doctrine in the "Minutes of the General Council of the Assemblies of God" reveals doctrinal revision in which the terminology of 'initial evidence' is a relative late-comer. As well, a concerted effort by the former General Executive of Thomas E. Trask and James K. Bridges

---

[67] Ratz, *Holy Spirit*, 96.
[68] Ratz, *Holy Spirit*, 97.

attempted to redefine 'initial physical sign' by inserting 'immediate.' In other words, the phenomenon of speaking in tongues is 'immediate evidence' that one has received Spirit baptism. Although this was often the case experientially in the history of the movement, it was certainly not absolute. For instance, Assemblies of God leader J. Roswell Flower and British Pentecostal Donald Gee claimed to have received the baptism in the Spirit but did not speak in tongues until weeks or even months later.[69] Current debates surrounding 'initial evidence' have come from contemporary Pentecostal scholars, but especially Frank Macchia who argues that the connection between Spirit baptism and speaking in tongues is sacramental, the sign of the Spirit's presence in the believer. He also wants to integrate Spirit baptism with regeneration to argue that baptism in the Spirit is connected to being born of the Spirit.[70]

In Canada, as I have argued, the doctrine of 'initial evidence' is opened up to include broader meanings, as long as one sees an integral connection between speaking in tongues and the Pentecostal blessing of the Spirit. One of the reasons for this openness is the Purdie-Ratz sub-tradition, which was hesitant to make 'initial evidence' too explicit. Both Purdie and Ratz preferred to go back to the older Pentecostal tradition of 'Bible evidence.' Purdie noted multiple evidences of the Spirit, including but not limited to speaking in tongues, power for witness, love of Scripture, greater love and a deepening prayer life. Tongues were physical and supernatural, while the other evidences were practical in the growth of the Christian life. Ratz spoke of 'initial infilling' and 'charismatic fullness' that is evidenced by tongues, but appears to be engaging the older 'Bible evidence' tradition. Perhaps Pentecostals in the PAOC were not truncated by a propositional doctrinal formulation, but were more open to theological diversity in how the activity of the Spirit was to be understood in relation to Scripture and Christian experience.

On the second front, the question of two baptisms as separate acts of grace seems to be open to interpretation. One of the issues in the liturgical traditions of the charismatic renewal is that while glossolalia is

---

[69] Robeck, "An Emerging Magesterium," 193–197. For a rhetorical response see James K. Bridges, "The Full Comsummation of the Baptism in the Holy Spirit," http://enrichmentjournal.ag.org/200004/092_full_consummation.cfm. [accessed November 18, 2009].

[70] Machia, *Baptized in the Spirit*.

further experience of the Spirit in the Christian journey, it is not quite accurate to call it a baptism of the Spirit. The Spirit is received in water baptism as the one baptism of faith. This position would resonate with the criticism of Dunn and Fee, who want to reserve Spirit baptism as an event of initiation. Indeed one of the criticisms of the Pentecostal doctrine is that it argues for two (or three) distinct modes of grace. Unhinging baptism in the Spirit (with tongues) from the reception of the Spirit in the baptism of faith contravenes the one faith, one Lord, one baptism credo of Gal. 4. I would like to propose that the Purdie-Ratz sub-tradition of the PAOC offers an alternative expression of the Pentecostal blessing that overcomes the Lucan-Pauline tensions and stands in line with the creedal position. To be filled with the Spirit marks a point, and perhaps multiple points, in the Christian path where the believer is empowered and gifted by the Spirit for inward and outward transformation. According to Purdie, even though the infilling is logically distinct from initiation, this is not a separate act of grace but a continuation of the work already accomplished in the cross. For Ratz, baptism in the Spirit specifically refers to the initiation of salvation when the believer is placed into the body of Christ. Yet the Christian is also encouraged to be filled with the Spirit throughout her journey, in a way that incorporates the Lucan and Pauline understandings of the charisma of the Spirit. In other words, the charismatic life is not parsed into a second act of grace that involves speaking in tongues and the demonstration of charismatic gifts in the Pauline sense, but all are incorporated under the rubric 'to be filled with the Spirit.' Consequently, the Canadian tradition of Pentecostalism is more resonate with ecumenical concerns.

Bibliography

Althouse, Peter. "The Influence of Dr. J.E. Purdie's Reformed Anglican Theology on the Formation and Development of the Pentecostal Assemblies of Canada." *Pneuma* 1 (1997): 3–28.

Bridges, James K. "The Full Consummation of the Baptism in the Holy Spirit." http://enrichmentjournal.ag.org/200004/092_full_consummation.cfm (accessed November 18, 2009).

"Constitution and Bylaws: The General Council of the Assemblies of God, 1947." Flower Pentecostal Heritage Center. http://ifphc.org/DigitalPublications/USA/Assemblies%20of%20God%20USA/Minutes%20General%20Council/Unregistered/1947/FPHC/1947%20Constitution.pdf (accessed November 2009).

"Constitution and By-Laws of the Pentecostal Assemblies of Canada Including Essential Resolutions and Other Information." 1928. Pentecostal Assemblies of Canada Archives.

Dayton, Donald W. *Theological Roots of Pentecostalism*. Metuchen, NJ: Scarecrow Press, 1987.

Dunn, James D.G. *Baptism in the Spirit*. Philadelphia: Westminster Press, 1970.

Fee, Gordon D. *Gospel and Spirit: Issues in New Testament hermeneutics*. Peabody, MA: Hendrickson, 1991.

Guenther, Bruce. "Pentecostal Theological Education: A Case Study of Western Bible College, 1925–1950," in *Canadian Pentecostalism: Transition and Transformation*, edited by Michael Wilkinson, 99–118. Montreal & Kingston: McGill-Queen's Press, 2009.

Macchia, Frank D. *Baptized in the Spirit: A Global Pentecostal Theology*. Grand Rapids, MI: Zondervan, 2006.

McGee, Gary B. "Early Pentecostal Hermeneutics: Tongues as Evidence in the Book of Acts," in *Initial Evidence: Historical and Biblical Perspectives on the Pentecostal Doctrine of Spirit Baptism*, edited by Gary B. McGee, 96–118. Peabody, MA: Hendrickson, 1991.

Menzies, Robert P. *Empowered for Witness: The Spirit in Luke-Acts*. Sheffield: Sheffield Academic Press, 1991.

Middelstadt, Martin William. *The Spirit and Suffering in Luke-Acts: Implications for a Pentecostal Pneumatology*. London: T & T Clark, 2004.

Miller, Thomas William. *Canadian Pentecostals: A History of the Pentecostal Assemblies of Canada*. Mississauga, ON: Full Gospel Publishing House, 1994.

"Minutes of the General Council of the Assemblies of God in the United States, Canada and Foreign Lands, 1916." Flower Pentecostal Heritage Center. http://ifphc .org/DigitalPublications/USA/Assemblies%20of%20God%20USA/Minutes %20General%20Council/Unregistered/1916/FPHC/1916.pdf (accessed November, 2009).

"Minutes of the General Council of the Assemblies of God in the United States, Canada and Foreign Lands, 1917." Flower Pentecostal Heritage Center. http://ifphc .org/DigitalPublications/USA/Assemblies%20of%20God%20USA/Minutes %20General%20Council/Unregistered/1917/FPHC/1917.pdf (accessed November, 2009).

"Minutes of the Thirty-Third General Council of the Assemblies of God, 1969." Flower Pentecostal Heritage Center. http://ifphc.org/DigitalPublications/USA/Assemblies %20of%20God%20USA/Minutes%20General%20Council/Unregistered/1969/ FPHC/1969.pdf (accessed November, 2009).

"Minutes of the Thirty-Seventh Session of the General Council of the Assemblies of God, 1977." Flower Pentecostal Heritage Center. http://ifphc.org/DigitalPublications/ USA/Assemblies%20of%20God%20USA/Minutes%20General%20Council/ Unregistered/1977/FPHC/1977.pdf (accessed November, 2009).

"Minutes, Revised Constitution and Bylaws: The General Council of the Assemblies of God, 1983." Flower Pentecostal Heritage Center. http://ifphc.org/DigitalPublications/ USA/Assemblies%20of%20God%20USA/Minutes%20General%20Council/ Unregistered/1983/FPHC/1983.pdf (accessed November, 2009).

Parham, Sarah E. *The Life of Charles F. Parham, Founder of the Apostolic Faith Movement*. Reprint. The 'Higher Christian Life": Sources for the Study of the Holiness, Pentecostal and Keswick Movements, 35. Edited by Donald W. Dayton. NY: Garland Publishing, 1985.

Penney, John Michael. *The Missionary Emphasis of Lukan Pneumatology*. Sheffield: Sheffield Academic Press, 1997.

"Pentecostal Assemblies of Canada." *Pentecostal Testimony* 5, February 1926, 2–3.

Purdie, J.E. "Lecture Notes." n.d.

——. *Concerning the Faith*. Toronto, ON: Full Gospel Publishing House, 1951.

——. *What We Believe*. Canada: Full Gospel Publishing House, 1954.

——. "Great Truths of the Word of God, Part V." *Pentecostal Testimony* February, 1956, 5–6.

Ratz, Charles A. *The Holy Spirit: An Outlined Bible Study for Personal or Class Use.*
Peterborough, ON: College Press, [1963?].
——. Interviewed by author. Toronto, ON. April, 1996.
Rawlyk, George A. *The Canada Fire: Radical Evangelicalism in British North America,
1775–1812.* Kingston, ON: McGill-Queen's University Press, 1994.
Robeck, Cecil M., Jr. "An Emerging Magesterium: The Case of the Assemblies of God."
Pneuma 2 (2003): 164–215.
——. "William J. Seymour and 'The Bible Evidence,'" in *Initial Evidence: Historical and
Biblical Perspectives on the Pentecostal Doctrine of Spirit Baptism*, edited by Gary B.
McGee, 72–95. Peabody, Massachusetts: Hendrickson Publishers, 1991.
Seymour, W.J. "The Doctrines and Disciplines of the Azusa Street Apostolic Faith
Mission of Los Angeles, Cal," (1915). Assemblies of God Archives.
Statement of Fundamental & Essential Truths. Toronto, Ontario: The Pentecostal
Assemblies of Canada, 1980.
Stronstad, Roger. *The Charismatic Theology of St. Luke.* Peabody, Massachusetts:
Hendrickson Publishers, 1984.
Turner, Max. *Power from on High: The Spirit in Israel's Restoration and Witness in Luke-
Acts.* Sheffield: Sheffield Academic Press, 2000.
Wenk, Matthias. *Community-forming Power: The Socio-Ethical Role of the Spirit in
Luke-Acts.* Sheffield: Sheffield Academic Press, 2000.

CHAPTER FOUR

THE FUNCTION OF MYTH AND REMEMBRANCE AMONG PENTECOSTALS IN THE CANADIAN MID-WEST

Randall Holm

INTRODUCTION

In 1919 the Pentecostal Assemblies of Canada (PAOC) was incorporated as a religious denomination with Toronto as its epicentre. While its name was associated with national pretensions, in truth it was a regional entity with a jurisdiction that stopped short of moving further west than the Province of Ontario. In Western Canada, Pentecostalism followed a different path with its own set of leaders and geographical centre. The fact that there were links between the two regions in promoting evangelists who traveled should not obfuscate the dangerous assumption of 'Pentecostal homogeneity' in the development of Canadian Pentecostalism. It was not until 1925, almost twenty years after the first Pentecostal stirrings in Canada, that a conference held in Winnipeg merged the East and the West and the PAOC became a true national religious organization.[1]

This chapter examines the contribution of Canada's Western origins for Pentecostalism, namely the city of Winnipeg. Our focus is the family of A.H. Argue beginning in the year 1907, an assessment of the first Canadian Pentecostal flagship church, Calvary Temple, the first

---

[1] The story has yet to be written how the divide between the East and West continues to be an Achilles heel in the development of the PAOC. The divide is most clearly felt in the biennial General Conferences that are alternatively held in the West and East. Resolutions that are defeated in one region with a weighted number of credential holders from that region may be passed at the next General Conference when the credential ratio is reversed. The divide has been spread along theological, practical and ecclesiological lines. See the discussion on Divorce and Remarriage in, Holm, "A Paradigmatic Analysis of Authority within Pentecostalism."

Canadian Pentecostal Bible training institute,[2] and finally, some observations about Pentecostal views of eschatology.[3]

THE PLACE OF WINNIPEG IN THE CANADIAN PENTECOSTAL STORY

Winnipeg, with its vast plains, is the geographical centre of Canada. In the early part of the twentieth century, next to Toronto and Montreal, Winnipeg quickly became the third largest city in Canada, a remarkable feat given its inhospitable climate. But while there is little one can do about weather, Winnipeg demonstrated its hospitability by welcoming immigration from a congested Europe seeking new land to till at affordable prices. Taking advantage of an expanding railway line, its central location vis á vis the rest of Canada, and its capacity for harvesting large amounts of grain, the population of Manitoba increased between 1891 and 1921 from about 150,000 to 620,000.[4] Yet Manitoba has never been for the faint-hearted. Its harsh winter not only guarantees a certain hardy disposition, but it prompts its citizens to ban together for the greater good. Perhaps in part this accounts for a sense of fair play and social consciousness that has defined Manitoba's history. In 1919 Winnipeg was the scene of a general strike of more than 35,000 union employees and unorganized labourers in response to labour inequities. Winnipeg was also home to Reverend James Woodworth, who stepped out from behind his Methodist pulpit and helped organize the General Strike and other political social reform. In time, Woodworth's work led to the formation of the Co-operative Commonwealth Federation (CCF), which was a precursor to the establishment of Canada's National Democratic Party (NDP).[5] It should not surprise anyone that Pentecostalism in the West developed asymmetrically from the East.

---

[2] The school was initially known as Central Canadian Bible Institute (1925), later changed its name to Western Bible College (1931), until it finally closed its doors in 1950 and merged with Bethel Bible Institute in Saskatoon. Guenther, "Pentecostal Theological Education," 100–103.

[3] Special mention should also be given to Frank Small. A Winnipeger and close friend of A.H. Argue, Small becomes significantly instrumental in the beginnings of a strain of Pentecostalism that will develop under the nomenclature, Jesus Name or Oneness Pentecostalism. Largely an indigenous movement to Pentecostalism, Oneness reworks the orthodox understanding of the Trinity. For a detailed history of that development see the chapter by David Reed in this volume.

[4] How Stuff Works, "History of Manitoba," n.p.,

[5] See Gutkin and Gutkin, *Profiles in Dissent*, 251–298.

Defining a religious movement, in particular one as new and diverse as Pentecostalism, is not an easy task. Any historical study on early Pentecostalism must contend with the issue that its message was slanted towards an oral rather than a written tradition. Pentecostal stories were spoken, and if written, were in the form of periodicals, college year books, self-published books and tracts, none of which were written with the intent of historical preservation. Appropriately, the national publication of the PAOC is titled *Testimony*.[6] Unfortunately for the modern scholar 'testimony' is frequently considered a poor cousin to those who are more familiar with discourse rooted in a written tradition.

Pentecostals were not against recording their stories, but they were not interested in preserving them for posterity. The stories were told, be it in written or in oral form, to evangelize, to edify and when necessary to instruct.[7] In time, a second wave of inquiry developed in the PAOC which paid more attention to such things as the geographical place of origin, and the mapping of its stories in relation to its culture, society and other religious groups. In keeping with its oral tradition, though, memories were largely uncritical and wide-eyed.[8]

Today, over a hundred years after its introduction into Canada, Pentecostalism has not only survived but it has now caught the attention of what could be identified as a third wave of historical investigation with academia jumping into the fray to explore, among other things, the geographical, social and economic contexts of the movement.[9] For the faithful, scholarly exposure can appear threatening. For some, at stake is the providential basis of their own religious story. Growing up in the Pentecostal tradition I am not unsympathetic to such fears, but would contend that these developments are also signs

---

[6] Initially titled "*Canadian Pentecostal Testimony*," its current name is simply *Testimony*. Since its first issue in 1920 it has served as the official publication of the PAOC.

[7] In addition to the aforementioned "Pentecostal Testimony, see Argue, *Contending for the Faith*; and "The Apostolic Messenger," a newspaper like periodical personally published by A.H. Argue.

[8] See Kulbeck, *What God hath Wrought*; Rudd, *When the Spirit Came Upon Them*; Miller, *Canadian Pentecostals*.

[9] This trend was nudged forward with the 1979 publication of Robert Mapes Anderson book, *Vision of the Disinherited*. It was significantly accelerated with Harvey Cox's 1996 contribution, *Fire From Heaven*. In Canada perhaps the first uniquely Canadian volume to fulfill this recent shift would be Wilkinson, *Canadian Pentecostalism*.

of maturity, with the benefits of scholarly inquiry outweighing potential pitfalls.

An examination into the origins of the Canadian Pentecostal story is
an exercise in this third wave of historicity. My interest is not so much
in what happened, but the perception of what happened for the insid-
ers most affected, and the impact of that perception on the continued
growth of Pentecostalism. Specifically I am interested in the stories,
people, places and events that have been carried into the future in the
fluid form of myths, which exist cautiously in a perpetual state of
renegotiation.[10]

To help me in this regard I am indebted to the work of philosopher
J.L. Austin and his seminal work on 'speech act theory.' Austin divides
speech into two principle categories: constative and performative.
Constative speech states, describes, and responds to the question, what
does this mean? Performative speech performs and responds to the
question, what does this speech do? In this regard performative is more
adept at capturing the spirit of oral communication. Written traditions,
on the one hand, are given to language that states, describes and can be
judged as either true or false. Testimony, on the other hand, whether in
oral or written form is better explained as performative language. Its
power does not lie in its capacity toward analytical persuasion but in its
ability to change one's imagination and perception of events.[11]

I offer one last caveat before proceeding further. I must distinguish
between how I employ the words 'myth' and 'fact.' With fact, we ask
what happened while we seek to verify the data with collaborative evidence. But facts themselves are relatively sterile. Why did they happen?
What impact they have had on other developments is a question left
unanswered. In time some facts graduate into durable stories. At this
point we might even call them myths. Myths belong to performative
language. They are fluid and generally find the category of true or false
potentially misleading. Sometimes the myth aligns itself with what we
know as the facts and we might even conclude it is an accurate por-
trayal of events. But more often than not, and with the passage of time,
we are no longer in a position to determine what the facts are, if we
ever were. However, we would never call myth fictive in this usage. We
might better ask if the myth is weak or strong. In other words, how

---

[10] For an example of how myths work in this usage see Buckner, "'Limited Identities'
Revisted," 4–15.

[11] See Austin, *How to Do Things with Words*.

does it perform or play out in public consciousness? In exploring the impact of Winnipeg I draw attention to four denominationally shaping Winnipegan 'myths.' In no particular order they are A.H. Argue, Calvary Temple, J.E. Purdie and Western Bible College, and the return of Christ.

A.H. Argue

The story of Pentecostalism in Winnipeg begins with Andrew Harvey Argue. Born in 1868 in Ontario, A.H. Argue and his growing family[12] made their way to Winnipeg in 1906, where he began a successful real estate business with two of his brothers. In his spare time when not selling real estate, Argue showed considerable acumen working as a lay preacher within the Methodist tradition. In the course of his evangelistic travels, Argue heard reports of an outbreak of religious enthusiasm in Los Angeles and Chicago where people reportedly were speaking in other tongues. Curious and hungry for deeper expressions of spirituality, Argue took a train to Chicago, the scene of William H. Durham's Mission. As the story goes, Argue 'tarried' at the mission for twenty-one days before receiving the gift of 'speaking in tongues' or the ability to speak in another tongue other than his native language. Upon receiving this gift, Argue returned home and immediately began holding prayer meetings in his home at 299 St. John's Ave. The year was April 1907, just months after similar outbreaks in Toronto and Los Angeles.

Similar to the stories of what happened elsewhere among early Pentecostal meetings, Argue's home became too small a venue for those who were drawn to this new religious fervour. Subsequently, Argue and his growing congregation purchased successively larger venues to accommodate the crowds. They eventually settled in present day Calvary Temple located in the heart of downtown Winnipeg. The story of A.H. Argue has been amply chronicled elsewhere.[13] Arguably his influence on the beginnings of the Pentecostal story in Canada is perhaps without parallel. He had a significant influence on other Canadian Pentecostal pioneers such as Frank Small, D.N. Buntain, A.G. Ward, and Walter and Robert McAlister. With his publication of

---

[12] With his wife Eva, the Argues had six children, Harvey, Zelma, Beulah, Eva, Watson and Edwin.

[13] See Miller, "The Significance of A.H. Argue for Pentecostal Historiography," 120–158.

the periodical, "The Apostolic Messenger" which eventually attained a distribution of 40,000 copies, Argue has a secure place in any future Canadian Pentecostal 'Hall of Fame.'

My concern is not about Argue's achievements. Rather, I want to entertain the force of his 'name sake' as a contemporary myth. Or to put it into other words, how is Argue remembered? How is his memory evoked? De facto he was a founding father of the Pentecostal movement in Canada. He opened a church in Winnipeg that went on to become the largest Pentecostal church in Canada. His sons and daughters carried his work into subsequent generations, all of which factor into his legacy. I submit, however, that the myth that has become Argue is his twenty-one days at the Chicago North Avenue Mission. Reminiscing on his Pentecostal experience, Argue said:

> Being hungry for God's best, I went to Chicago to witness what was taking place. Here I saw numbers being filled with the Spirit, which continued to deepen my hunger. I waited on God for twenty-one days. (Later I remembered that Daniel had waited on God for twenty-one days.) During this time I had a wonderful vision of Jesus. His countenance was so radiant that as I lifted my hand before Him, it became transparent. At the end of the twenty-one days I was filled with the Holy Ghost, speaking with other tongues as the Spirit gave utterance.[14]

In a prairie worldview where nothing happens quickly and everything has a season, the movement from one season to the next is usually fraught with hard work and discipline. In the big picture, twenty-one days is the least one should expect for something as valuable as the infilling of the Holy Ghost. And here my point is not to debate the veracity of twenty-one days, but to examine the place of this story in contemporary Pentecostal testimony.

The record will show that it would not be long before Pentecostals abandoned the idea of tarrying for the gift of the Holy Spirit. Whether tarrying was too much discipline, too much a part of the prairie ethos, theologically too difficult to synthesize with the idea of gift and tarrying together in the same sentence, or whether the pace and impatience of society at large took over, the practice of tarrying quickly waned in favour of more intense and immediate results.[15] Nonetheless

---

[14] Argue, "Azusa Street Revival Reaches Winnipeg," 9.

[15] As a Pentecostal growing up in the church I remember many an altar service where people prayed for the baptism of the Holy Spirit with the gift of speaking in tongues. The idea of tarrying was an hour at the end of the service or if one really was blessed it might have gone late into the evening, but no one ever thought about twenty-one days.

twenty-one days of tarrying elevates the mythic place of Argue and his continued influence in Canadian Pentecostalism. Symbolically, waiting draws on the biblical narrative of Jesus' forty days in the 'wilderness' or the disciples waiting forty days in Jerusalem for the advent of the Holy Spirit.

Beulah Smith, one of Argue's children who later became an evangelist in her own right, recalled what her mother told her concerning the return of her father from Chicago following his twenty-one day experience.

> At the end of the 21 days my Mother received a telegram and the telegram said, "Have been filled with the Holy Spirit and will be home on the first train." Now in those days you didn't have cars to go to the station to meet your loved ones coming in. So dad took the street-car up and my mother was so concerned about my father returning home and now being filled with the Holy Spirit. I can remember them telling me how my mother prayed and she said, 'Lord, help me that I may know how I should greet my husband. Should I give him a kiss or not, a holy man filled with the Holy Spirit?" And how my mother got all the children back. She said, "Children, all stay back because your father is coming home and he has been filled with the Holy Spirit." Of course I don't remember that (Beulah Smith would have been about a year old at the time) it was just told me.[16]

Argue and in particular his twenty-one day 'tarry' is a perfectly mythic story for Pentecostals. It has grail-like qualities because it calls into question any smugness of contemporary Pentecostals who claim immediately accessible spiritual experiences. How can one compete with such a narrative? You could perhaps if you were the wife of A.H. Argue. Despite living now with a 'Holy Spirit-filled man' Eva Argue was initially unsure if her husband should actually surrender his real estate business and become a full time evangelist. In the end she too embraced his calling by her own tarrying. "We always felt that if we missed a meeting we would miss seeing someone come through with whom we had been tarrying."[17] Eventually Eva would tarry herself in order to receive the baptism in the Holy Spirit.

> I asked that I might know a little what His (Christ) suffering in Gethsemane meant. I do not advise this for everyone; He surely took me at my word. I felt His power come into my body. Such a weight of burden

---

[16] Smith, "Thomas Miller Interviews Beulah Smith & Eva Robinson."
[17] Argue, *A Vision and a Vow*, 41.

came upon me - groanings, suffering and sorrow - till at one time the
breath seemed to leave my body.

When this burden lifted I felt so light. As the power of the Lord
came upon me, I trembled and shook. It seemed my body lifted off the
floor, ready to go up. The only weight was my wedding ring. Dimly I
could hear a voice of another language, and listening I found it was
myself speaking. The Lord had baptized me with His precious Holy
Spirit.[18]

Eva Argue was 'lifted up' that day. Her tarrying was fruitful but she still
had to bear the burden of her wedding vows. In practical terms it meant
carrying an extra load of family responsibilities as her husband traveled
across the continent evangelizing. Alas, such was perhaps the calling of
her own personal Pentecost.

Invariably in light of such accounts, present day experiences generally seem pale in comparison. That is the way myth works. Over the
course of time some stories gain potency even at the expense of facts.
The facts in this case represent the total picture. A.H. Argue was committed to the Pentecostal message and for that he is rightly mythologized but by all accounts he was not the model family man – a fact that
in today's world might tarnish one's image as a true pioneer. Perhaps
we see this qualified picture of A.H. Argue in Beulah Smith's interview
late in her life with Pentecostal historian Thomas Miller. When Miller
asked Smith, "why do you think the sense of … (sic) and the power of
conviction seems to have been so much stronger in the services than
we seem to see in our meetings today?"[19] We already see the effect and
power of the myth at work. For Miller it was not "do you think?" it was
"why do you think" the power of conviction was stronger before than
today? But Smith's response is also informative, "Yes it was," was her
immediate response and then in a more qualified tone she added:
"Maybe it's because that I was young and I had my life before me and
this really got hold of me, the outpouring of the Spirit and I just felt
I had to do something I don't know why they don't have (sic), as
yet maybe we have emotion stirred just as much and maybe we're just
not aware of it."[20] Or maybe as a child of her father, her image of his life
was more nuanced than others.[21] Witnessing both the promise and

---

[18] Argue, *A Vision and a Vow*, 42–43.
[19] Smith, Interview.
[20] Smith, Interview.
[21] By all accounts A.H. Argue was very supportive of his daughters when they
too found themselves in vocational pastoral ministry. However, as a father he was

struggles of her father she was reluctant to fully embrace the myth that became her father and his legacy. In any event, today the myth not only lives on but in many circles is held up as a vital cog in the pursuit of yet another new Pentecost.

CALVARY TEMPLE

In the heart of the city of Winnipeg on the corner of Hargrave and Cumberland Streets stands Calvary Temple. Not only is it one of the oldest Pentecostal churches in Canada having just recently celebrated its centennial anniversary (1907–2007), it remains an iconic presence in Canadian Pentecostalism. Beginning in A.H. Argue's St John's Avenue home in April 1907,[22] the congregation made its first major purchase by moving to a 'retired' Wesley Church on the corner of William Avenue and Juno Street. The first service was held on Sunday 30 November 1919. The church also caught the attention of the colourful Aimee Semple McPherson, who two months later conducted a crusade at the church. Perhaps ironically, the affectionate name of the church in those days was the Old Wesleyan Church.[23] This would be home for the church until 1938 when the present church was purchased and the name changed to Calvary Temple. After several major renovations in subsequent years, the church achieved iconic value in the heart of Winnipeg. The average citizen on the streets of Winnipeg may not know what the PAOC is, or even what Pentecostalism is, but could probably give directions to Calvary Temple.

For many years Calvary Temple was listed as the largest church in Canadian Pentecostalism. While notable in a denomination which accords much significance to numerical growth, size is not why Calvary Temple achieved such a mythic presence. Contra the myth that has become A.H. Argue, Calvary Temple is not associated with the hyper-exuberant spirituality that has been characteristic with much of Pentecostalism, but is a statement on Pentecostal stability.

---

frequently absent and he relied heavily on his wife Eva who was given to illness to care for the family. See Chapter 5 and 6 in this volume.

[22] The church began services one year to the month after the beginning of another iconic assembly in California otherwise known as the Azusa Street Mission. However unlike Azusa, which in little over a decade would cease operations, this Winnipeg connection has remained strong and viable since its inception.

[23] A journey through the *Winnipeg Free Press* in those early days contains many ads for the Old Wesley Church, ironic given its Pentecostal namesake.

If Calvary Temple has survived as an active force it is because of its longstanding stability, its recognized presence in the community and its emphasis on missions. With any revival movement characterized by emotion, Calvary Temple has infused into the PAOC a dependable if not predictable presence. The success of Calvary Temple has been a steady leadership, with the exception of a congregational schism in 1924. Since 1937 the church has only had four lead pastors – Watson Argue, son of A.H. Argue (1937–1948), T.E. Ness (1948–1953), H.H. Barber (1953–1996) and Bruce Martin to the present time.

The church has also maintained a longstanding commitment to missions both within the inner core of the city and around the world. Within one year after beginning house meetings, the Winnipeg assembly began sending people to all parts of the world. As early as 1908, three young people were sent to Liberia and China which began a trend that continues to this day. Presently, Calvary Temple is supporting in one way or another missionaries in Rwanda, Uganda, Sudan, India, Cuba, Mexico, Columbia, and Mozambique.[24] To meet this commitment over 20% of their $2,500,000 budget in 2007 was allocated as charitable giving.[25] Finally, perhaps even more remarkable, Calvary Temple has resisted the trend of large inner city churches to move out of the core of the city and resettle in the suburbs. In a city of 650,000, Calvary Temple has not changed its downtown location or its name[26] or its policy of community presence.

In 1957, the year of its fiftieth anniversary Calvary Temple declared "the cry of our hearts is for a fresh outpouring of the Holy Spirit of God so that this generation might be worthy of the blessed heritage that is ours."[27] If Pentecostalism is defined as fresh outpourings of the Spirit in exuberant charismatic presence, then Calvary Temple is not the epitome of the Pentecostal heritage. However, if Pentecostal heritage is defined by dedication to a stable and durable mission, then both myth and fact merge in Calvary Temple.

---

[24] The official church website for Calvary Temple is http://www.ctwinnipeg.com.

[25] 2007 represents the last year of reported income expenditures for Revenue Canada.

[26] Pentecostals like to be on the cutting edge of trends. Today, many of their churches are changing their name to reflect more inclusive openness. Calvary Temple has not followed that trend with its dated name, but that has not prevented them from being in the forefront of any interchurch or civil activity within the city of Winnipeg.

[27] "A Brief History ... Outlining the early days of the Pentecostal Movement in the City of Winnipeg."

J.E. Purdie and Western Bible College

In deference to Robert Mapes Anderson's deprivation thesis, which argues that early Pentecostalism represented a revival among the disenfranchised,[28] several scholars have noted that Canadian Pentecostalism does not readily fit a disenfranchised paradigm.[29] Although A.H. Argue had only a grade six education, he was a successful business man, which permitted him the freedom to publish a journal, travel throughout North America and plant a church in Winnipeg. Likewise, many other pioneering leaders came from established church traditions where they already held credentials. But perhaps nowhere is Anderson's thesis more challenged than with the invitation to assess James Eustace Purdie,[30] an Anglican priest who came to Winnipeg to direct the first Pentecostal centre of biblical education. Sharing facilities at the Old Wesley Pentecostal church and formerly St. George's Anglican Church, Central Canadian Bible Institute opened on 16 November 1925 and began with a school enrolment of thirty-two students.[31] Within five years enrolment increased to 130 students. It was Purdie's job to direct and establish a curriculum that reflected Pentecostal values. What emerged was a modified Reformed and Keswick theology that was augmented with Pentecostal experience.[32] The core of that theology was retained for the PAOC in a catechism Purdie wrote upon retiring in 1951 called *Concerning the Faith*.

Reflecting on Purdie's place in Canadian Pentecostal historiography, former General Superintendent Tom Johnston, concluded:

> There isn't a man in all of Canada who has contributed more of a lasting nature to The Pentecostal Assemblies of Canada than J. Eustace Purdie. He has laid for us a foundation of Biblical doctrine that has paid dividends, and will continue to pay dividends so long as the Lord owns and acknowledges us as a branch of His church serving Him in this great Dominion.[33]

---

[28] Anderson, *Vision of the Disinherited*.

[29] Miller, "Significance," 153, For a review see James Craig, "Out and Out for the Lord," 19ff.

[30] Purdie held a number of degrees from different schools but it was his five years at Wycliffe that contributed to the *gestalt* of his theology.

[31] Guenther, "Pentecostal Theological Education."

[32] What is remarkable about this is Purdie's commitment to Reform theology while being surrounded by leaders who were more familiar and sympathetic to Wesleyan leanings.

[33] Tom Johnston, cited in Craig, 28.

Again my aim here is not to revisit the doctrinal and organizational contribution of J.E. Purdie,[34] but to respond to the myth that has become Purdie. Namely, in Purdie the early development of the PAOC was spared the frontier doctrinal vicissitudes typical of Pentecostal expansion in other parts of the world.

In 1930, after a promising start, the Winnipeg school was closed and relocated to Toronto. Reporting the closure on 4 October 1930, The *Winnipeg Free Press* led with the headline "Western Pentecostalist Disappointed Over School Being Shifted from Winnipeg to Toronto." The reason, the newspaper notes, is that after four graduating classes with a total of thirty-eight students only six have come from points east of the Great Lakes. The ministries of the denomination in the West absorbed most of those who had completed the program.[35] One may have wondered what the West was now expected to do in order to fulfill its future ministries, or why the East did not simply start another college. In any event the East wanted the services of J.E. Purdie and apparently that meant a relocation of existing services rather than a second school.[36]

How many students relocated from Winnipeg to Toronto is uncertain. Invariably some of them made their way to another small fledgling evangelical interdenominational Bible Institute in Winnipeg that also began in 1925. In the fall of 1930, the acting principal of Winnipeg Bible Institute (WBI) was a man named H.C. Sweet, who was also Pentecostal by experience. This presented a significant dilemma for WBI, a college with dispensational commitments. To resolve this dilemma, and in the absence of a Pentecostal college, the Board of WBI passed the following resolution in January 1931:

> In view of the fact that in the past the School has not been entirely free from criticism of tolerance of, if not acceptance of, the Pentecostal position and because of some recent manifestations in meetings held by a group of the students it is thought wise at this time to declare what position the school shall take in respect to this matter.

---

[34] For detailed reviews of Purdie's contribution see Althouse, "The Influence of Dr. J.E. Purdie's Reformed Anglican Theology," 3–28. And Craig, "Out and Out for the Lord." Also see Chapter 3.

[35] *Winnipeg Free Press* October 4, 1930.

[36] Althouse suggests that sectors in the denomination may have been trying to get rid of Purdie who was deemed to be too Calvinist. See "The Influence of Dr. J.E. Puridie's Reformed Anglican."

We believe it to be the united opinion of the board that the school is not now, nor is it intended to be Pentecostal, and we do hereby state our position - namely, that the school is opposed[37] to Pentecostalism as such, and will so declare itself publicly, feeling that it is in its best interests that this tendency to misunderstanding should be entirely cleared away.

This will involve our stating definitely the foregoing position to the student body as at present constituted, and have them agree to conform to whatever regulation shall be required regarding the conduct of the meetings, with the definite understanding that there shall be no demonstration or manifestations on the part of students in or on the school premises.

Further, that because of the past experience of the school, it is necessary at this time to take the position that students application for admission in future and having espoused the Pentecostal teaching shall not be accepted.[38]

In all ten students or one-third of the student body left the college. Where would these students and others like them go, especially if they could not make the trip to Toronto? The net result was the formation of another new Pentecostal college sponsored by D.N. Buntain the pastor of Calvary Temple with the assistance of H.C. Sweet, recently resigned from WBI. One year later, the college in Toronto failed, closed its doors, and Purdie hurried back to resume his position as principal of the college newly established by Buntain and Sweet – hardly a halcyon story of leadership or ecclesiastical stability.

But it would be unfair to lay the blame on Purdie. From all accounts Purdie was sure of his mission. He wanted to lay down an edifice of theological stability for the neophyte movement. The record suggests, however, that many other denominational leaders were less enthusiastic of Purdie's plans. Should we believe that with such success in Winnipeg, Purdie could not get a college started in Toronto? Officially, the college in Toronto folded because it was not economically viable as a result of the Great Depression. Privately, Purdie not only struggled with the relocation of the college to Toronto at the expense of closing the college in Winnipeg but he was also frustrated with leadership hostility towards education in general and his 'modified Calvinism.'[39]

---

[37] In the original notes the word "opposed" is scratched out and replaced with a hand written emendation reading "not sympathetic with."

[38] "Minutes of Meeting of the Winnipeg Bible Institute".

[39] See Craig, "Out and Out for the Lord," 38. Craig notes that during this time Purdie on two occasions contemplated returning to the Anglican church in an official capacity.

In any event, upon his return to Winnipeg Purdie remained at the helm of the Winnipeg College until he resigned in 1950, when the college subsequently closed its doors and relocated to Saskatoon where it merged with another Pentecostal Bible Institute.

In the end Purdie had substantial regional success. He was in the business of theological education. Yet, he worried about preachers "who are, but who have a zeal without knowledge. And because they lack the true understanding of what they believe, their congregations suffer."[40] Ultimately his national success came through his many graduates who went on to become college teachers and influential pastors. Purdie, however, was never really capable of overcoming the Pentecostal suspicion of intellectualism, which continues to question the necessity of formal education. There is no doubt that Purdie believed in the value of good Christian education and in the end he writes positively that his call for clear theological education was justified, or so the myth suggests.[41] A closer reading, however, raises suspicions that good education has never really been a priority of Canadian Pentecostal leaders.

Recent developments in the PAOC have once again called into question the relationship between theological education and Pentecostal spirituality.[42] In the year 2000 denominational leaders of the largest Pentecostal regional college, Eastern Pentecostal Bible College (EPBC) decided to "take their college back" and "return it to its roots."[43] If Purdie were alive he might well have asked to which roots were they looking? Did these 'roots' bear any resemblance to what Purdie was trying to achieve? In the case of EPBC 'taking back' meant returning to some idyllic vocational model of training in conjunction with local pastors in the greater Toronto area. It was suggested that faculty were out of touch with the realities of church ministry and in need of assistance. The fallout of the decision was significant. Student enrolment initially plummeted and the college struggled financially.[44] The reasons are complicated and not the concern of this chapter except to point out that the impetus for the change was to return to a vision of the past – which turns out to be a myth removed from the facts. The fact is Purdie struggled with the same prevailing tension, between the quest

---

[40] Guenther, 104.
[41] Guenther, 105.
[42] Holm, "Master's College and Seminary."
[43] Holm, "Master's College and Seminary."
[44] Since the announced changes the college has gone from the largest denominational college in the country to one that now meets in a church basement.

for charismatic exuberance against the necessity of sound biblical study, a tension that still exists today in many Pentecostal circles.

Purdie's vision for Canadian Pentecostal theological education is probably in the same place he found his efforts – purgatory, a holding place somewhere short of the Promised Land. The Purdie myth, however, works by creating a sense of security that Canadian Pentecostalism escaped the hyper-emotionalism and whims associated with any deprivation theory. The facts here bear the truth that Purdie's pursuit of a balanced theology between head and heart was as difficult for him as it has been for almost any other Pentecostal body. This does not mean Purdie was not influential in Canadian Pentecostalism, but that his vision never really took root in a manner that he hoped.

RETURN OF CHRIST

On 22 November 1909 the *Winnipeg Free Press* announced the third annual Pentecostal Convention being held just outside the city of Winnipeg, in Selkirk Manitoba. The convention ran from 26 November to 6 December with daily meetings at 10 AM, 3 PM and 8 PM. The article lists the chief points as stated by its promoters as being, "old-time repentance, sanctification and the baptism of the Holy Ghost with signs following which it is claimed are to be looked for as in the apostolic days namely speaking in other tongues, divine healing for the body and the soon coming of Jesus."[45] The convention attracted thousands. While the themes of repentance, sanctification, speaking in tongues, healing and Christ's return would define the early Pentecostal message, it was the latter theme of Christ's return that fuelled the urgency and intensity of the Pentecostal message.

When asked to describe the early meetings in Winnipeg, Beulah Smith remembered at twelve years of age the moving of the Holy Spirit and feeling

> that the Lord was coming that night and that everybody had to get saved. I would go to the back and it didn't matter. The worst old "wine – o" sitting at the back ... I would go up to him and I would say, "Do you not know the Lord is coming and maybe it's tonight and will you not give your heart to the Lord? I can remember my father preaching ... he would preach mostly about the coming of the Lord ... I can remember praying

---

[45] *Winnipeg Free Press* 22 November, 1909.

beside a trunk and saying, "Oh, Lord, don't come to-night, don't come to-night. Because I feel that I'm just not quite ready, even though I have been filled with the Holy Spirit. The conviction of sin was so very, very strong in those meetings and the emotions were very stirred up.[46]

In the early stages of twentieth-century Pentecostalism there was an indelible association between spiritual enthusiasm expressed through speaking in tongues and the message that Christ is returning. The two reinforced each other. The manifestation of tongues was the perfect harbinger for the soon return of Christ, a sign that the kingdom was imminent. What could explain this outbreak of spiritual activity? For Pentecostals it was the view that Jesus was returning soon. Preaching on the soon return of Christ kept attention on the gift of the Holy Spirit, identified as speaking in other tongues. Could one really ever be ready enough to meet the Lord? Conversely, preaching on the subject of the gift of speaking in tongues heightened an awareness that believers were living in the last days.

These were intense days for Pentecostal believers. Little wonder people lined up outside meeting places waiting to see what would happen next. Here however, 100 years later the myth stumbles. The scent for the 'return' is now cold. Any connection between the gift of the Holy Spirit and the soon return of Christ has largely been severed, and more recent attempts at revitalizing this connection with new predictions of the return have only further enhanced this separation with the general religious public.[47]

SEEING MYTHS TOGETHER

So where do we go from here? If we plot these myths together along performative and constative lines the result is instructive. The comparative grids help in part to explain the present in relation to the past, and more importantly they suggest a path to altering the future. First, we must remember that myths are not fictive. They reference real events and people and are capable of enduring the test of time. Their reality is not the issue. How they are remembered and how that memory functions is the issue. Second, myths are fluid and good myths

---

[46] Smith, 3–4.

[47] As North Americans in particular prepared for the new millennium a plethora of books announcing the return of Christ flourished until of course the millennium arrived and little had changed.

endure even if they are operating sometimes on false pretences. For example, even if the myth of the second coming has weakened with age it is still part of the official teaching. It continues to operate but I would contend that dislocated from the Argue story, both Spirit baptism and the second coming have further surrendered some truthfulness. Argue and his spiritual devotion have maintained a strong grip on the Canadian Pentecostal psyche,[48] but its force has been transformed into an unachievable grail that functions as a brace against future disappointment. In the end it cannot be duplicated because there is little will among contemporary Pentecostals to see it surpassed.

Similarly, in terms of performance I suggest the need for sound theological education is affirmed but as it develops it moves further away from the facts of history. The need is recognized, but how to implement theological education while holding to a vision of spiritual exuberance is a point of tension within Pentecostalism. Finally, Calvary Temple is a church that continues to adapt to its surroundings. Its story continues, but it no longer has the mythic strength of its past. Perhaps this is the secret to its ability to endure. As the measure of performance increases can the constative value of the event maintain its veracity? Not everyone will share my analysis. In most cases the contest of myths operates under the surface of public and scholarly discourse. In respect to the PAOC, I have attempted to raise a difficult discussion, however tentatively, to the surface. Readership response will determine if I have been successful.

BIBLIOGRAPHY

"A Brief History … Outlining the early days of the Pentecostal Movement in the City of Winnipeg." Bulletin prepared for the Golden Jubilee of Calvary Temple, Series 2, Manitoba District Church File.

Althouse, Peter. "The Influence of Dr. J.E. Purdie's Reformed Anglican Theology on the Formation and Development of the Pentecostal Assemblies of Canada." *Pneuma* 1 (1997): 3–28.

Anderson, Robert Mapes. *Vision of the Disinherited.* Peabody, MA: Hendrickson, 1992.

Argue, A.H. "Azusa Street Revival Reaches Winnipeg." *Pentecostal Testimony*, May, 1956, 9.

---

[48] My point here is not so much about Argue, who many modern Pentecostals have never heard of, but about the nagging suspicion in Pentecostal circles that things are not as spiritually intense as they were in the past. Within the PAOC there is no lack of clarion bell ringing to get back to earlier times of revival and should anyone happen on the Argue story, they quickly become convinced that "This is That."

Argue, Zelma. *A Vision and A Vow or The Vision and Vow of a Canadian Maiden: The Story of my Mother's Life*. Springfield, MO: Gospel Publishing House.
_____. *Contending for the Faith*. Winnipeg: Messenger of God Publishing House, 1928.
Austin, J.L. *How to do Things with Words*. Cambridge: Harvard University Press, 1962.
Buckner, Philip. "'Limited Identities' Revisted: Regionalism and Nationalism in Canadian History" *Acadiensis* (Autumn, 2000): 4–15.
Calvary Temple: http://www.ctwinnipeg.com.
Craig, James. "Out and Out for the Lord": James Eustace Purdie An Early Anglican Pentecostal. MA thesis, University of St. Michael's College, 1995.
Guenther, Bruce. "Pentecostal Theological Education: A Case Study of Western Bible College, 1925–1950," in *Canadian Pentecostalism: Transition and Transformation*, edited by Michael Wilkinson, 99–118. Montreal & Kingston: McGill-Queen's Press, 2009.
Gutkin, Harry and Mildred Gutkin. *Profiles in Dissent: The Shaping of Radical Thought in the Canadian West*. Edmonton, Alberta: NeWest, 1997.
Holm, Randall. "A Paradigmatic Analysis of Authority within Pentecostalism." Ph.D. diss., Laval University, 1996. http://web.mac.com/rfholm/iweb/Site/Publications.html.
_____. "Master's College and Seminary: A Case Study in a Pentecostal Integration of Faith and Learning." Paper presented at the annual meeting of the Society of Pentecostal Studies, March 2004. Accessed at http://web.mac.com/rfholm/iWeb/Site/Masters.html. How Stuff Works. "History of Manitoba." n.d., n.p. http://history.howstuffworks.com/canadian-history/history-of-manitoba.htm (accessed 1 March, 2009).
Kilbeck, Gloria. *What God Hath Wrought: A History of the Pentecostal Assemblies of Canada*. Toronto: The Pentecostal Assemblies of Canada, 1958.
Miller, Thomas William. *Canadian Pentecostals: A History of the Pentecostal Assemblies of Canada*. Mississauga, ON: Full Gospel Publishing House, 1994.
_____. "The Significance of A.H. Argue for Pentecostal Historiography." *Pneuma* (Fall, 1986): 120–158.
"Minutes of Meeting of the Winnipeg Bible Institute." 2 January 1931. Providence College, Otterburne, Manitoba.
Rudd, Douglas. *When the Spirit Came Upon Them: Highlights from the Early Years of the Pentecostal Movement in Canada*. Burlington. ON: Antioch Books, 2002.
Smith, Beulah. "Thomas Miller Interviews Beulah Smith & Eva Robinson: Daughters of the Late A.H. Argue of Winnipeg, Manitoba." Transcribed interview by Thomas W. Miller, PAOC archives, n.d.
Studebaker, Steven. *Defining Issues in Pentecostalism: Classical and Emergent*. McMaster Theological Studies. Eugene, OR: Pickwick Publications 2008.
Wilkinson, Michael, ed. *Canadian Pentecostalism: Transition and Transformation*. Montreal & Kingston: McGill-Queen's Press, 2009.
Winnipeg Free Press 22 October 1909.
Winnipeg Free Press 4 October 1930.

Women

CHAPTER FIVE

ZELMA AND BEULAH ARGUE: SISTERS IN THE CANADIAN PENTECOSTAL MOVEMENT

Linda M. Ambrose

INTRODUCTION

In April 1925, the *Pentecostal Testimony* reported that a Canadian evangelist and her sister were touring through the American Midwest. An elder from the church in Terre Haute, Indiana reported:

> Evangelist Zelma E. Argue, accompanied by her younger sister, Beulah, of the Wesley Church Assembly in Winnipeg, Man., had a most wonderful meeting in this city. After two weeks they were joined by their father, A.H. Argue, at which time the two sisters went to Jasonville, Ind., for a ten-day meeting. Already seventy-five have received the baptism of the Holy Spirit and seventy-five new members have joined with the church. The campaign will continue another week with the three members of the Argue family. We praise God for this great meeting.[1]

This chapter traces the life and work of those two Canadian sisters: Zelma Argue and Beulah Argue Smith, who traveled widely in evangelistic crusades on both sides of the Canada-US border and served in local churches in both countries. Zelma, the better known of the two in Pentecostal circles today,[2] remained single throughout her life, while Beulah, the younger of the two, married a well-known Canadian Pentecostal minister, and had four children. Based on the work of the Argue sisters as portrayed in the pages of *The Pentecostal Testimony*, (the national denominational magazine of the Pentecostal Assemblies of Canada) between 1920 and 1990, this chapter considers the gendered aspects of the Argue sisters' ministries, exploring how their lives reflected themes in the larger story of North American Pentecostal women during the first half of the twentieth century.

---

[1] "Terre Haute, Ind.," 6.
[2] For a very good overview of Zelma Argue's life and ministry, see Shearer, "Zelma Argue," 18–23.

Zelma Argue was born in 1900 in North Dakota, the eldest daughter of Andrew Harvey (A.H.) and Eva Phillips Argue. Beulah Argue was born six years later, after the family had moved back to Winnipeg, where they played a major role in the Pentecostal movement in Canada. In 1939, on the occasion of their mother's death, the *Pentecostal Testimony* made it clear that the entire Argue family, spread across the country, was heavily involved in ministry. Mrs. Argue left behind

> her husband, A.H. Argue, widely known evangelist and Bible expositor, Zelma, who has traveled with her father in recent years as an evangelist; Wilbur, who is engaged in business; Beulah, wife of Bannerman Smith, Pastor of the Ottawa Assembly of the Pentecostal Assemblies of Canada; Eva, wife of Fulton Robinson, Regina; Watson, Pastor of Calvary Temple, Winnipeg, Man., and Elwin, well-known young Canadian evangelist.[3]

Although Zelma and Beulah's lives took different paths, both sisters devoted themselves to full-time Christian ministry. The Rev. Miss Zelma Argue performed ministry work as a traveling evangelist, inspirational writer, and pastor. She died in Santa Rosa, California in January 1980. The Rev. Mrs. Beulah Argue Smith, who traveled with her sister for a few years in the mid-1920s, also taught at Bible Colleges, married a Pentecostal pastor, had four children, wrote for the denominational paper, and died in Toronto, Ontario in 1990. These two lives provide significant examples of early Canadian Pentecostal women who were active in ministry over a period spanning most of the twentieth century.

What makes the lives and works of these two women particularly interesting is the context in which they worked. The Pentecostal Assemblies of Canada (PAOC), only arrived at the decision to ordain women as ministers in 1984, so how is it that these two women were so ahead of their time? How were their very public roles of ministry legitimized? How were their lives and ministries shaped by gendered roles and considerations? This chapter argues that their family ties and the gendered nature of the female roles they occupied as daughter, sister, wife, and mother, afforded these two women opportunities to minister publicly over such an extended period.

---

[3] "A Brief Account of the Life of the Late Mrs. A.H. Argue," 12.

Historiography of Canadian Women in Pentecost

The literature on Canadian women in the church has grown significantly in recent years. In 1992 Ruth Compton Brouwer lamented the lack of attention paid to religion in English-Canadian women's history.[4] Since that time the gap in the literature has begun to be redressed by scholars who have published a variety of works, including those on women in the holiness movements and Methodism, nineteenth-century middle-class women as Protestant missionaries, and nineteenth- and early twentieth-century working-class women's place in the Salvation Army.[5] While Brouwer argued more than fifteen years ago that religion was the unacknowledged quarantine in English-Canadian women's history, I am now suggesting that in the growing literature of women in the Christian church, the neglected area is women in charismatic and Pentecostal churches. Although American scholarship has begun to emerge, there is very little Canadian scholarship on Pentecostals in general, and even less on Canadian Pentecostal women in particular.[6]

While some reference to Canadian Pentecostalism can be found in broader studies of evangelicalism, placing the movement into its broader North American context in religious history,[7] there is very little on the gendered aspects of Pentecostal experience. The lack of attention to Pentecostal women was recently highlighted by an American researcher, David Roebuck, when he called for historians to explore this neglected past.[8] This chapter comes partly in response to that call. Roebuck suggested that 'scholarly biographical work' on Pentecostal women was particularly needed and I suggest that the biographies of

---

[4] Brouwer, "Transcending the Unacknowledged Quarantine," 47–61.

[5] Whiteley, *Canadian Methodist Women*; Schmidt, *Grace Sufficient*; Brouwer, *New Women for God*; Gagan, *A Sensitive Independence*; and Marks, *Revivals and Roller Rinks*.

[6] One of the most prolific authors who deals with American Pentecostal women is Edith L. Blumhofer, whose contributions include: "Canada's Gift to the Sawdust Trail," 387–402; idem, *Restoring the Faith*; and idem, "Women in American Pentecostalism," 19–20. See also Pope-Levison, *Turn the Pulpit Loose*; and Benvenuti, "Pentecostal Women in Ministry."

[7] Stackhouse, *Canadian Evangelicalism in the Twentieth Century*; and Noll, et al., (eds). *Evangelicalism*. On Canadian Pentecostalism, see Wilkinson, *The Spirit Said Go*; and Wilkinson, ed., *Canadian Pentecostalism*.

[8] Roebuck, "Pentecostal Women in Ministry," 29–44.

the Argue sisters seem like a good place to begin that work for early Canadian Pentecostal women's history.

Zelma and Beulah Argue are just two of the many Canadian women who worked in ministry throughout North America during the early years of the Pentecostal movement. My recent search in the archives of the PAOC in Mississauga, Ontario turned up the names of approximately thirty such women.[9] Among those identified so far, it seems that marital status did not deter women from ministry, but it did determine the kinds of roles that women would play at various stages of their lives. Typically, single women tended to be evangelists and missionaries; young married women traveled with their husbands, then after children arrived, couples tended to settle into pastorates with the wives serving alongside their husbands; married couples sometimes went to the foreign mission field as well, to work alongside the more numerous single women. As we shall see, there were exceptions to this pattern and while some aspects of the Argue sisters' experiences seem typical of the group, other parts of their work defy the usual pattern.

The one role that women seemed not to play was in administration of church affairs (church government roles such as board membership, etc.). Scholars have explained this lack of involvement as a sexist, exclusionary measure on the part of men who sought to maintain power over church governance. Indeed, as the Pentecostal movement became more institutionalized, the tendency to exclude women from positions of authority seemed to grow stronger. Sociologists have noted that this trend echoes the model proposed by Max Weber who argued that the religion of the underprivileged tends to allot more equality to women, and to continue to do so until a religious movement becomes more

---

[9] My preliminary research at the PAOC Archives in Mississauga in September 2007 uncovered 30 Canadian women to explore including: Zelma Argue, Beulah (Argue) Smith, Laura (Arnold) McAlister, Jessie (Snyder) Atter, Marion Parkinson, Annie Baker, Ethel Bingeman, Rosanna (Thaler) Blair, Alice Mary Chorley, Mabel (Bromley) Cunningham, Carro Davis, Susie Davis, Margaret Day, Alice Belle Garrigus, Jessie Gillespy, Coralee Haist, Ellen Hebden, Louise Hindle, Elizabeth Jamieson, Marian (Keller Wittick) Weller, Bertha (Smiley) LeBrocq, Margaret (Brown) McAlister, Louella (Haist) Morrison, Sophia Nygaard, Annie Cressman, Jean Elizabeth Sharpe, Beatrice Sims, Lila (McAlister) Skinner, Lettie Ward, Joyce Watson, and Lillian Barbara Yeomans. Of these women, 14 served as overseas missionaries, 12 were pastors and/or pastors' wives, and 10 were evangelists. Twelve of them remained single; the rest were married. Other scholars have noted that the list of Canadian Pentecostal women is long, but has not been widely researched. See for example: Kulbeck, *What God Hath Wrought*; Atter, *The Third Force*; Miller, "The Canadian Azusa," 5–29; Miller, *Canadian Pentecostals*; Holm, "Pentecost," 27–34; Riss, "Who's Who among Women of the Word;" Rudd, *When the Spirit Came Upon Them*.

institutionalized as an established church.[10] American scholars Barfoot and Sheppard set out to test the viability of Weber's model for American Pentecostalism, and found that it does help to explain the ways in which women have been excluded from full participation in positions of authority.[11] Feminist scholars of theology such as Pamela Holmes have applied a similar analysis to the Canadian Pentecostal churches, arguing that the PAOC denomination follows the same pattern. Holmes cites numerous examples of women who, because of sexist church policies, were denied the recognition that their effective and faithful ministries deserved, despite the Pentecostal principle of equality of the sexes in matters of the Spirit. Using the historical record of business meetings at PAOC Conventions, Holmes traces how discriminatory decisions were institutionalized.[12]

GENDER HISTORY AS A PARADIGM FOR EARLY PENTECOSTAL WOMEN'S WORK

Those studies about how institutional power became concentrated in the hands of the male sex as the Pentecostal movement evolved into an institutionalized church are useful to explain the contemporary experiences of discrimination against women, but they are less helpful in explaining the early experiences of women like the Argue sisters who fulfilled a wide range of ministry activities and who seem to have experienced a remarkable degree of acceptance and authority in the church. Theological studies of Pentecostal belief systems have offered explanations about why women were central to the early movement, pointing to two key teachings, the imminent return of Christ and the outpouring of the Spirit on both sexes, to explain why Pentecostals were more welcoming to women in ministry in the first decades of the twentieth century than were other denominations. The focus of this chapter is on what two of those early women did as Pentecostal evangelists and why they were accepted in roles that women coming after them were much less likely to fill.

Gender history is a useful approach to help understand the experiences of early Pentecostal women in Canada because it considers the

---

[10] Weber, *The Sociology of Religion.*
[11] Barfoot and Sheppard. "Prophetic vs. Priestly Religion," 2–17.
[12] Holmes, "Ministering Women in the Pentecostal Assemblies of Canada," 171–194.

relationships between men and women, seeks to understand how the sexes cooperate and compete to reinforce and sometimes to challenge existing roles, and explores how power relations operate both between the sexes and within each sex. As Joy Parr and Mark Rosenfeld explained in their 1996 book *Gender and History in Canada*, "Gender is a term feminist theorists developed to explain how being male or female is not simply the result of biology but is socially constructed and reconstituted. Gender is shaped by social interaction. Gender identities – masculinity and femininity – acquire meaning in relation to one another."[13] The roles of women within Canadian Pentecostalism have obviously been reconstituted and negotiated over time, as the controversies over women's rightful place in the church attest. A gendered approach to the early women of Canadian Pentecost such as Zelma and Beulah Argue is more than a recovery mission with the goal of 'adding women' to the story. It is an exploration of how women cooperated with men to fulfill their sense of God's calling on their lives.

More than thirty years ago Natalie Davis, a pioneer of women's history, pointed out the futility of attempting to understand women's experiences in isolation from those of men when she argued, "It seems to me that we should be interested in the history of both women and men, that we should not be working only on the subjected sex any more than a historian of class can focus entirely on peasants."[14] With that directive in mind, this chapter studies the work of the Argue sisters, by placing them in the web of relationships they occupied within their family and within Pentecostal circles. To understand their work, it is important to see how they functioned in relation to the men in their lives, both their family members (father, brothers, and in Beulah's case husband), and the other men with whom they worked (mostly pastors who hosted their meetings). Relationships among women are also important to historians of gender, and therefore some attention is also given Mrs. Argue, the mother of these women, as well as other female evangelists who were role models for them.

Gender history seeks to understand people in the web of relationships and roles that they occupy. As Joy Parr has argued, gender history "entails an inherent instability in identities – that being simultaneously a worker, a Baptist, and a father, one is never solely or

---

[13] Parr and Rosenfeld, *Gender and History in Canada*, 1.
[14] Natalie Davis cited in Scott, *Gender and the Politics of History*, 29.

systematically any of these."[15] In the case of Zelma and Beulah Argue, they were not simply evangelists, but also simultaneously musicians and writers, sisters and daughters, and in Beulah's case, also wife and mother. The Argue sisters were simultaneously taking up many roles and never occupying solely one role at any given time. Placing these women back into their complex web of family and ministry relationships helps both to clarify and complicate explanations about the freedom and latitude they enjoyed in their ministry lives.

A.H. ARGUE: PROMOTING HIS DAUGHTERS' MINISTRY

As the daughters of A.H. Argue, Zelma and Beulah were well connected to people with power and authority in Canadian Pentecostal circles. Thomas Miller explains that Argue was very influential in the early Canadian movement and widely respected, not only by his own children, but by Pentecostals throughout North America.

> Zelma's admiration for her father is understandable, given her natural respect for him and her opportunities to witness his effectiveness as an evangelist; nonetheless she was no sycophant, and her pen portraits of the "grand old man" have been validated by other observers. In her comments upon his personal approach to the awesome responsibilities of the evangelist, she wrote that: "The pattern for all his ministry was to first wait much upon God in confident faith and expectation, to declare the Word and believe God then to act. Out of much wrestling with God in the secret places, came the unpredictable works of God in the public services."[16]

While the Argue children spoke highly of their father, the admiration was not limited to the family circle.

Moreover, the respect and admiration between father and daughters was mutual as A.H. commended his children, including his daughters, to the Pentecostal assemblies across the continent. There is some evidence that A.H. encouraged his children in ministry. Long before ordination was available to Canadian Pentecostal women through the PAOC, Argue encouraged Zelma to seek ordination in the United States through the Assemblies of God. In part, this fatherly support was an important affirmation of Zelma's calling and it came from an

---

[15] Parr, "Gender History and Historical Practice," 354–76.
[16] Miller, "The Significance of A.H. Argue for Pentecostal Historiography," 145. See also, Rudd, *When the Spirit Came Upon Them*, 34–41.

important source. As her father, Zelma must have found his endorse-
ment personally affirming, but it also meant he was recommending her
to the larger church body. This was more than the case of a proud father
promoting his child. This was a case of a Canadian church father, highly
respected across the country and the continent, promoting his child to
the wider body of believers.

In part however, this proud father's insistence that his daughter
should seek credentials for ordination was also a smart business move.
A.H. knew that with her ordination papers in hand, Zelma was entitled
to half-price railway fares both in the United States and in Canada.[17]
Zelma's American birth place may have worked in her favour to expe-
dite her ordination and cross-border travel because it seems that the
road was not quite as smooth for her younger sister. Preaching in
Chicago in the summer of 1927, Beulah referred to the difficulties she
had initially encountered in crossing the United States border. Her difficulties might have been because of her young age, or because she did
not have sufficient paperwork in hand to explain the purpose of her
trip, but she explained that after obtaining some form of photo identification to which a $20 fee was attached, her movement between the
two countries was eased.[18] These brief glimpses into the practical considerations that the Argue sisters faced affirms James Opp's conclusion
that by 1920, the Argue family was "in the process of transforming
themselves into professional evangelists."[19]

When A.H. endorsed his daughters' ministry work however, there
was more to it than just a proud father promoting his children, or a
smart business man helping his workers to economize on travel costs.
A.H. was fully committed to the fact that God sometimes calls women
into full-time ministry because he had worked alongside some very
well-known female evangelists. His first direct exposure to and involvement with a woman in ministry came when he was conducting crusades in the United States and he worked with American healing
evangelist Maria Woodworth-Etter. Indeed, both Zelma Argue and her
brother Watson were deeply affected by Woodworth-Etter's children's
meetings and often referred back to them as life-changing. This
occurred during a three year period when he moved his family from

---

[17] Shearer, 19, and 23, n. 11.
[18] Argue, "Three Classes of People at the Border," 9.
[19] Opp, *The Lord for the Body*, 150.

Winnipeg to California from 1913 to 1916.[20] Back home in Canada, the Argue family hosted Aimee Semple McPherson during her Winnipeg crusade in March 1920.[21] Later that year the Argues assisted in McPherson's meetings in Montreal, giving leadership to the afternoon sessions.[22] Indeed, the Argues' association with these female evangelists was very close. One source suggests Zelma Argue's ability in the Montreal crusade impressed Aimee Semple McPherson so much that McPherson tried to recruit the young woman to leave her father's ministry and join with her instead.[23] But it seems that A.H. Argue also recognized in Zelma what McPherson saw: a capable young woman with good stage presence who could be a great asset to his ministry. Because he was no stranger to the idea of women evangelists, having worked with at least two famous female evangelists by the time he launched his ministry with his daughter Zelma, A.H. encouraged his daughter to stay with him rather than join McPherson's ministry.

EVA ARGUE: AILING MOTHER AND ABSENT PARTNER

Indeed, in his own work A.H. had need of his daughter's help. Although he freely endorsed female evangelists, Argue's own wife Eva did not join him in traveling on his crusades, not because he did not want her to, but because her health did not permit it. In a tribute to Eva Argue after her death in 1939, Zelma recounted that her mother had suffered from several health problems. "In 1925, at the conclusion of Dr. Price's great campaign [in Winnipeg], in which she had been a faithful altar worker, she suffered a collapse in health."[24] This physical problem, added to the fact that she was raising six children during the busiest years of A.H. Argue's traveling years, meant that Eva did not take up

---

[20] Rudd, *When the Spirit Came Upon Them*, 34–41. See also Shearer, "Zelma Argue," 18. For a biography of Woodworth-Etter which traces the connections with the Argue family, see Warner, *Maria Woodworth-Etter*, 183, 188, 196, n. 5, 278, and 351.

[21] For press accounts of McPherson's Winnipeg crusade, see "Gifts to Evangelist," 3; "Mrs. McPherson Concludes Revival Campaign in City," 3; and "Recent Evangelistic Campaign," 6.

[22] On Aimee Semple McPherson, see Bahr, *Least of All Saints*; Blumhofer, *Aimee Semple McPherson*; Blumhofer, "That Old-Time Religion," 217–27; Blumhofer, "Canada's Gift to the Sawdust Trail," 387–402; Dicken, "Take Up Thy Bed and Walk," 137–53; Epstein, *Sister Aimee*; McGinnis, "Aimee Semple McPherson," 45–56; and Setta, "Patriarchy and Feminism in Conflict," 129–37.

[23] Shearer, "Zelma Argue," 19, citing Blumhofer, "Zelma E. Argue," 156.

[24] "A Brief Account of the Life of the Late Mrs. A.H. Argue," 12.

the role of travel companion and co-worker with her husband. Being unable to travel with her husband must have been a disappointment to Eva Argue, who had grown up Methodist, and later worked with the Salvation Army in Winnipeg. Both of those church traditions gave prominent place to women in ministry, and Eva would have been very familiar with the idea of women on the platform and wives labouring alongside their husbands.[25]

As Zelma recounted about her mother, "unable herself to go to the front of the battle, she helped others to go. Unable to be with her husband on the field, she sent her children. 'Go! Hold up his hands,' she would say."[26] So in obedience to her mother's wishes, Zelma as the eldest daughter, and her brother Watson took their places at their father's side. Here again gender history provides a useful tool to analyze the ways in which the Argue family's ministry operated because this is an example of how power was exercised within the family. Joan Wallach Scott points out that "gender is a primary way of signifying relationships of power,"[27] but it is important to remember that these power relationships are not only about power between the sexes, but also power relationships among people of the same sex. Gender historians explore how hierarchies of power operate, and when it came to this Pentecostal woman, it seems that even from her home and from her sick bed, Eva Argue exercised power over her children, urging them to take part in the work of the ministry in her absence. At Eva's insistence, A.H. Argue traveling with his son and his daughter seemed to be a fulfillment of the Joel prophecy about sons and daughters prophesying in the last days. From the first issues of the *Pentecostal Testimony* published in 1920, references to the Argue evangelistic trio abound, and the threesome was made up of father, son and daughter.

Although Eva Argue was not physically present on those tours of preaching, she nevertheless had an influence. Jean Miller Schmidt, writing about Methodist preacher's wives, cites the four-fold model created by Leonard I. Sweet, who "identified four distinct models of that role from the Protestant Reformation to the twentieth century: the Companion, who 'held up her husband's hands in his sacred calling'; the Sacrificer, who 'clasped her hands in pious resignation' and

---

[25] On Methodist women, see Schmidt, *Grace Sufficient*; and Sweet, *The Minister's Wife*. On Salvation Army women, see Marks, *Revivals and Roller Rinks* and her "The Hallelujah Lasses."

[26] "A Brief Account of the Life of the Late Mrs. A.H. Argue," 12.

[27] Scott, *Gender and the Politics of History*, 42.

'hindered him not in his work' by staying out of his way and raising her family on her own'; the Assistant, who 'became her husband's right-arm, sharing many pastoral responsibilities and functioning as an extension of his ministry'; and the Partner, who 'ministered with both her own hands' developing a 'ministry alongside her husband.'"[28] Sweet suggested that "every minister's wife probably developed her own unique strategy," and that for many women, these models "often coexisted and intermingled with older roles."[29] From what we know of the Argue family's experiences, it seems that Eva mainly occupied the role of 'sacrificer', remaining at home to raise the other children and tend to her own health needs. At the same time, she actively prayed for her husband and children, suggesting something of the 'companion' model, even in her absence.[30]

Eva's children, particularly Zelma, adopted the roles of 'assistant' and 'partner' to their father in the work of the ministry. Zelma was the one who 'ministered with both her own hands' and eventually developed 'a ministry alongside' though in this case, it was alongside her father, rather than a husband. For a historian of gender, it is interesting to see how the roles of wife and daughter were blurred in the person of Zelma. In the absence of his wife, Zelma became very much her father's assistant and partner; she brought a feminine presence to the evangelistic meetings and filled a void that her mother's absence created.

THE ARGUE SISTERS EVANGELISTIC TEAM

In 1925, a series of crises led to a major change in the Argue family's evangelistic crusades. The Calvary Temple in Winnipeg, which was the Argues' home church and home base for their traveling ministry, had recently experienced a change of leadership and Zelma's brother Watson was named as the senior pastor, with A.H. Argue serving as his associate.[31] In addition, after a successful series of meetings where

---

[28] Schmidt, *Grace Sufficient*, 3. Schmidt is citing Sweet, *The Minister's Wife*, 113–14.

[29] Schmidt, *Grace Sufficient*, 3.

[30] "Evangelists A.H. Argue, Pioneer Evangelist and Zelma Argue, Have Successful Meetings at Belleville," 19.

[31] The troubles at Wesley Church were first mentioned in the *Pentecostal Testimony* in October 1924, when A.H. Argue was named as interim pastor and Watson was serving as his assistant, working with the young people's group. "Winnipeg, Manitoba," 2; In January 1925, that working relationship was reversed when, at the annual business meeting, Watson Argue was named as senior pastor with his father as his associate. This arrangement meant that A.H. had more freedom to tend to his other responsibilities. "Winnipeg," 7.

Charles S. Price was their guest at the church in Winnipeg, Eva Argue's health collapsed, and that development, along with the added church responsibilities meant that travel for the famous Argue family trio was seriously curtailed. The solution to that situation led to a new configuration of the Argue family evangelistic team. While Watson stayed in Winnipeg to pastor the church, A.H. assisted him and stayed close to his wife during her recuperation. Zelma was free to travel but she needed a companion and the family decided to launch another member onto the evangelistic circuit in the person of Beulah, who was only nineteen years of age. The 1925 report of the sisters' meetings in Indiana, cited at the beginning of this paper is the first published account of the two sisters teaming up in this manner, and it is significant to note that those meetings were held in the spring of the year after Beulah's school term at the Bible College ended.[32]

The period of Zelma and Beulah's shared ministry as traveling evangelists was relatively short; it only lasted from 1925 to 1928 and it was concentrated in the spring and summer months. Their partnership was created due to extenuating family circumstances, further limited by the fact that Beulah was a full-time student unable to travel during the school year, and finally ended because Beulah accepted a marriage proposal. Yet while it lasted, the sisters held highly successful campaigns in several major centres in the United States including Chicago and Los Angeles. Their work produced rave reviews from the pastors that they worked with, particularly in western Canada.

This account from Alberta was typical of the kind of coverage the sisters' campaigns received:

> The Argue sisters have just come to open a campaign there [Lethbridge] and we are expecting to hear of a great time of refreshing in Lethbridge. … When we arrived home again the great campaign with the Argue sisters was in full swing. It turned out to be a great meeting. The interest grew, and the crowds came until our large hall was packed clear out on the street and many turned away. It was one of the best meetings we have yet held in Edmonton. The climax came the last night, when over a score came out to seek salvation, and many of them testified at the close that they had found the Lord.[33]

---

[32] During the month of March 1926, Zelma and Watson shared some meetings in southern Ontario, but that arrangement ended when the two sisters began traveling together after Beulah's school year ended. "Hamilton, Ont.," 12.

[33] "News from Alberta," 9.

The tour continued throughout the summer of 1926, and the positive reports continued to pour in. In August, this report appeared in the *Pentecostal Testimony*: "We ran into the swells of the revival waves left by the Argue Sisters [in Lethbridge], who had just concluded a campaign and had returned to Edmonton for a second short campaign, and I am sure there was a welcome awaiting them there. God Bless them. 'I commend unto thee Zelma and Beulah.'"[34] This pattern of travel beginning after Beulah's school year ended each spring was repeated right up to 1928. In May of that year, the sisters planned a campaign in Saskatchewan that was much anticipated.[35] Beulah remained in that province afterward, conducting a series of meetings on her own in Herschel, Saskatchewan and in Saskatoon during the month of June 1928, in the weeks leading up to her marriage.[36]

The Argue sisters were highly esteemed not because of their advanced age or wide experience but on the contrary, because of their youth. Here is a prime example of these Pentecostal women occupying two roles simultaneously: being young and being female. In the theology of Pentecost, there is room for gender equality based on the scripture from Joel: in the last days, sons and daughters will prophesy. Zelma Argue referred to this in the first issue of the *Pentecostal Testimony*, when she wrote: "In that dear familiar quotation, Acts 2:17, 18, there is a certain part which we young people can justly lay claim upon as our own. ... on the strength of this passage, divinely appointed women, handmaidens of the Lord, are conceded the right to prophecy, to minister, under the power and the guidance of the Holy Spirit." But this young handmaiden continued: "Yet there is more. Away back in the days of Joel, when this passage was first given by inspiration, it was forseen and foreordained that upon young men and young women, even upon children, the Lord would pour out of His Spirit in those last days." She obviously took that passage as a means to stake her claim of legitimacy because she herself was young and female. She continued her article by exhorting her readers, "Young people of Pentecost, get the vision! Let the fire of the Holy Ghost burn within you, melting out the dross, clarifying your vision, and making you a flame of fire. Already He is taking some of us who, not so long ago, were just Sunday

---

[34] "Continued Report of Western Trip by Chairman," 4.
[35] "Herschel, Sask.," 3.
[36] "Students from Canadian Bible College, Winnipeg, Man., working in Saskatchewan," 1; "Saskatoon, Sask.," 19.

school children, seeking Him in little children's meetings, and is send-ing us out with His message."[37]

The legitimacy of allowing women and even young women to take on this leadership role was shored up by the eschatological sense of urgency that early Pentecostals took from their conviction that they were indeed living in 'the last days.' Other authors have developed this argument, particularly for the American case.[38] The emphasis on the imminent return of Christ went a long way to lending legitimacy to young evangelists like the Argues. Pentecostal leaders appealed to the scripture about the 'fields being white unto harvest' and that one should 'pray the Lord of the harvest send out workers.' If women were willing to work, and reported a sense of God's calling on their lives, then the logic was that they should be welcomed into the evangelistic field to help with the harvest of souls.

ZELMA ARGUE: EVANGELIST AND WRITER

As the Argue brothers and sisters began to choose their life partners, the family's evangelistic team dynamic changed again. After Beulah's marriage to C.B. Smith at the end of the summer 1928, Zelma did some solo campaigns in Moose Jaw in the winter of 1929 and Watson traveled as a guest evangelist to the Smiths' church in Saskatoon.[39] Watson was working more and more with the Canadian Bible College based in Winnipeg and he was traveling to conduct campaigns throughout the West. When Watson married in June 1930, it was clear that his days of traveling with his sister Zelma were over, because his wife would be his new companion and partner in the work.[40] There are reports of Zelma traveling alone for a campaign in Carberry, Manitoba in 1931 where the local pastor and his wife were known to the Argues, having graduated from the Canadian Bible College in Winnipeg.[41] Zelma also filled in at the last minute at a convention in Saskatoon when the sched-uled speaker was ill and unable to attend. Reporting on the meeting

---

[37] Argue, "Your Sons and Your Daughters," 3.
[38] On the last days theology that legitimized the ministry of women see Barfoot and Sheppard, 9 and Roebuck, 35–37.
[39] "Saskatoon Evangelistic Campaign," 19; "Report from the Superintendent of Saskatchewan," 16–17; "Pastor C.B. Smith of Saskatoon reports a gracious revival," 19.
[40] "Wedding Bells," 20.
[41] "Carberry, Man.," 2.

afterward, the pastor (her brother-in-law, C.B. Smith) praised Zelma's performance, saying: "Sister Argue did not spare herself in helping those who were seeking as she remained in the prayer room until the small hours of the morning praying and encouraging hungry hearts." He continued: "Sister Argue spoke each evening. The meetings were all spiritual, volumes of praise and worship ascending at intervals."[42]

With two of her siblings and previous traveling companions now married and settled into new partnerships with their spouses, Zelma resumed her partnership with her father over the next few years on campaigns that took them to San Diego during the winter of 1931, on tour through southern Ontario in the spring of 1932, and then through western Canada the following year. For the next few years, frequent reports of campaigns and camp meetings held by 'Evangelist A.H. Argue and his daughter Miss Zelma Argue' filled the pages of the *Pentecostal Testimony*. Their travels took them back and forth across Canada and frequently into the United States as well, with reports from Kansas City, Missouri and Ebenezer, New York in the spring of 1934.[43]

The frenetic pace with which the father-daughter team traveled is well documented throughout the pages of the denominational magazine. In February 1936, the *Pentecostal Testimony* published news about various evangelists, and the short entry about A.H. Argue revealed: "The Argues are wintering in Florida and doing evangelistic work in that state. Our latest correspondence from them came from St. Petersburg."[44] While this was obviously a much more comfortable climate than Winnipeg could offer in the wintertime, the Florida location was only partly for the purposes of rest. Eva Argue's health had improved to the point where she could accompany her husband and daughter to winter in the south, and from that new base, A.H. and Zelma continued their evangelistic work. After that winter in Florida, the Argues spent time in various locations across the United States, including a series of meetings and return visits to California where the Argue family had maintained contacts from their days with Maria Woodworth-Etter and Aimee Semple McPherson. Those connections

[42] "Saskatchewan Convention," 2.
[43] "Fire Falls," 12; "Western New York Camp," 9. Reports abound of the work of A.H. and Zelma in this period, and one occasion that is commonly cited is the camp meeting that was held in Paris, Ontario on the occasion of the opening of Braeside Camp in the summer of 1935. See Blair, "The Braeside Camp at Paris, Ont.," 6.
[44] "The Evangelist," 2.

serve to explain Zelma's ties to that state and why she eventually took up a pastorate there.

Zelma was also concentrating on another kind of work during the winter of 1936: her writing. Since the launch of the *Pentecostal Testimony* in 1920, Zelma had been a regular contributor to the publication. But now she was publishing her work in book form as well. In February 1936, her book *Garments of Strength*, was released, and eighteen months later, the *Pentecostal Testimony* was advertising three additional titles written by her: *Strenuous Days*, *Prevailing Prayer*, and *The Beauty of the Cross*. In October 1937, the *Pentecostal Testimony* described her writings as "a devotional series with readings for everyday in the month. In this way, their value never wears out."[45] Her popular writing was said to be so much in demand that "Miss Argue's books sell themselves."[46] Apparently her books could also sell other things, and the *Pentecostal Testimony* launched a subscription campaign using her books as an incentive, promising that "it is a good time to subscribe now and thus take advantage of receiving one of Miss Argue's books ABSOLUTELY FREE."[47]

In the midst of her busy travel and preaching schedule, Zelma Argue was indeed a prolific writer. With almost 200 articles published in American Pentecostal periodicals and most of those simultaneously published in the Canadian *Pentecostal Testimony*, Shearer claims that "it is believed that [Zelma Argue] wrote more articles for the *Pentecostal Evangel* than anyone except C.M. Ward."[48] Her publications regularly appeared not only in the Canadian *Pentecostal Testimony*, but also in the American publications of the Pentecostal movement especially *The Latter Rain Evangel*, and *The Pentecostal Evangel*.

Zelma Argue, following her calling to the life of an evangelist, never did marry. Her mother died in 1939 at the relatively young age of 64, while her father lived until 1959 and reached the age of 90 years.[49]

---

[45] "Subscription not Conscription," 26.

[46] "Subscription not Conscription," 26.

[47] "Subscription not Conscription," 26.

[48] Shearer, 21 citing Muster and Gram, "Obituary of Zelma Argue." Indeed that claim is easily substantiated with an online search of the periodicals available at the Flower Pentecostal Heritage Center website: www.ifphc.org. A search for "Zelma Argue" in the online digitized periodicals reveals 202 items. A gendered analysis of her writing would be another profitable way to explore the various roles that Zelma Argue adopted.

[49] "A Brief Account of the Life of the Late Mrs. A.H. Argue," 12; and "Triumphant Home-Call," 7, 15, 26–27.

Zelma partnered with another woman, Jeanette Jones, to pastor the Trinity Gospel Tabernacle in Los Angeles, California from 1948 to 1957. After Zelma's resignation as pastor, she traveled again on crusades for seven more years, until she took her retirement in 1964 supported by a pension from the Assemblies of God.[50] While technically she never did step into the role of evangelist's or pastor's wife, during her years of travel with her father and her brother, Zelma Argue fulfilled the role of 'help mate' while at the same time firmly establishing her own individual ministry apart from either of them. Further study about her pastoral work with Jones could help to uncover whether one of the two women assumed the lead role while the other was more the 'wife' and nurturer of the pair, or whether they were equal partners in the work, complementing one another's gifts and overlapping in the roles they assumed within the ministry.

Beulah Argue Smith: Wife and Mother, Minister and Musician

In contrast to her older sister, Beulah did marry and her marriage in 1928 explains in part why her traveling ministry with Zelma was so short lived. Beulah's husband, the Rev. C.B. Smith, was an evangelist, pastor, and administrator for the PAOC denomination whom she met while they were both students in Winnipeg. Together the Smiths took up various pastorates in Saskatchewan, Ontario and British Columbia before settling in Peterborough, Ontario where C.B. assumed the presidency of the PAOC Bible College, a post he still held at the time of his death. Given that brief biographical overview, one might predict that Beulah Smith's life, particularly her married life, was very conventional. It sounds like a typical life for a woman, in keeping with the developments in the second half of the twentieth century where women married to church leaders typically took on the traditional roles of supporting and promoting their husbands' careers. But Beulah Argue Smith's married life and ministry career defy such simplified and stereotypical predictions.

Beulah Argue married Campbell Bannerman Smith on July 28, 1928 in Winnipeg after the two young people had graduated from the Winnipeg Bible College. C.B. Smith was ordained just a few weeks after

---

[50] Shearer, "Zelma Argue," 20. She cites Argue, "Memories of Fifty Years Ago," 6.

the wedding in August 1928. It was a busy summer for the newlyweds as the *Pentecostal Testimony* reported: "On August 19th Evangelist C.B. and Beulah M. Smith came to [Woodstock, Ont. to] give us a three weeks' campaign. At this writing, two weeks of the campaign have passed and God has been richly blessing their ministry."[51] In the same issue, it was reported that "Brother and Sister Smith are going to Convention in Montreal, and then to Saskatoon, Sask., to take the pastorate there."[52] The following year, the *Pentecostal Testimony* reported in February 1929: "The Assembly in Saskatoon is making splendid progress under the leadership of Brother and Sister C.B. Smith. They are looking forward to an evangelistic meeting with Brother A. Watson Argue, next February."[53] Here again, the family ties were evident, as Beulah's brother Watson was expected as the guest evangelist. The Smiths seemed destined for a conventional life in the ministry, having landed a pastoral job so early in their marriage.

However, it is somewhat surprising to read that two years later, Beulah was traveling once again to conduct evangelistic meetings – and doing so on her own. From Carman, Manitoba, Pastor H. Wesley O'Brien writes: "We praise God for a good report of the work here. In a recent campaign of three weeks, beginning January 18th, with Mrs. C.B. Smith of Saskatoon as Evangelist, many were saved, some healed and the saints built up. Sister Smith's unique sermons were also enjoyed by many people from other churches. The town was stirred as it has never been for many a day. The work among the children was grand and we have a group of them that praise God for salvation. Souls are being added to the Lord and several are tarrying for the Baptism of the Holy Spirit. Please pray that they may be filled. We pray that the Lord will send our Sister back to us at some future time for another campaign."[54] That same spring, another report from Saskatoon reminded readers that although Beulah sometimes traveled alone, the Smiths' marriage was fine and they were very much partners in ministry. The April 1931 edition of the *Pentecostal Testimony* included a "Report from Saskatchewan" with this update: "Brother and Sister C.B. Smith of Saskatoon are believing for greater things in their Assembly than ever before. The young people's [sic] work is very encouraging."[55]

---

51 "Holy Ghost Revival Hits Woodstock, Ontario," 11.
52 "Holy Ghost Revival Hits Woodstock, Ontario," 11.
53 "Report from the Superintendent of Saskatchewan," 17.
54 "Good Reports," 16.
55 "Report from Saskatchewan," 7.

As encouraging as the pastoral work was for the couple, they felt that their calling was to evangelism and at the end of the summer of 1931, the Smiths resigned from the church in Saskatoon "to take up work in other fields."[56] The other field was that of evangelism, something that was very familiar to Beulah Argue Smith. For the next two years, the Smiths followed an itinerant path to various locations holding evangelistic campaigns. Reports of their campaigns in southern Ontario were regularly featured in the pages of the *Pentecostal Testimony*. In December 1931, Pastor Atter from Westmeath, Ontario reported: "We thank God for another visitation of Pentecostal power at Westmeath. Evangelists C.B. and Beulah Smith ... gave forth the old time Pentecostal message in the power and demonstration of the Spirit, bringing great conviction and stirring the whole community."[57] The following month, reports of two more campaigns in Windsor and Wallaceburg, echoed the same kinds of successes. One recounted that during the Smith meetings, "several professed salvation, much prejudice was broken down with outsiders, and the saints were much encouraged. Sister Smith's messages on prophecy were much enjoyed."[58] The Smiths attended the graduation ceremonies of the Pentecostal Bible College in Toronto in May 1932, and in June, the *Pentecostal Testimony* reported that they had just concluded a series of meetings in Woodstock, Ontario where they had ministered four years earlier, just a few weeks after their wedding. The account of the meeting, reported: "Among those who received the Baptism were Mr. and Mrs. Yoe, who have been tarrying for four years. The work has gradually been going forward in Woodstock, and the results of these meetings will prove a blessing."[59] The Smiths also spent time in the fall of 1932 in Galt, Ontario where a new Pentecostal Temple building had recently been erected. After attending the opening of that new building, the couple remained on for three weeks of meetings. One of the outcomes of those meetings was reported to be a greater acceptance of Pentecostalism demonstrated by other church denominations. The Smiths were credited with creating that acceptance. The *Pentecostal Testimony* recounted: "Like many other places, Galt had suffered on account of the prejudice in the hearts of the city people toward the Pentecostal Movement but, praise

---

[56] "C.B. Smith and wife..." 2.
[57] "Interesting News," 2
[58] "Windsor, Ont.," and "Wallaceburg, Ont.," 17.
[59] "Woodstock, Ont.," 2.

God, through Brother and Sister Smith's ministry, the ice was broken through and several souls were saved. We knew before the church was opened that it would certainly require the blessing of the Lord in order to bring about a spiritual awakening and we believe God used Brother and Sister Smith's ministry in a wonderful way to help break through."[60]

After two years of traveling to various locations to hold crusades of varying lengths, the Smiths gave up their itinerant lifestyle for the permanency of a pastoral charge once again. The *Pentecostal Testimony* announced in May 1933: "Rev. C.B. Smith has accepted the Pastorate of the Ottawa Assembly, and is taking charge of the work there immediately."[61] Not surprisingly the news of this new permanent placement was soon followed with news of a new baby. On July 10, 1934, Beulah gave birth to a son, George Campbell Smith, who would eventually follow in his father's footsteps toward ordination and pastoral work.[62] With the young family securely settled into the leadership of a congregation in a large urban center, it seemed inevitable that Beulah's days as a traveling evangelist were over. But surprisingly, that was not the case.

Before her new baby had celebrated his first birthday, Beulah was back on the road holding meetings. As surprising as it is to find her doing this as a married woman and a new mother, it is even more surprising to realize that she was doing so on her own, and not as her husband's 'helper.' The *Pentecostal Testimony* reported in May 1935: "Bethel Tabernacle, Toronto, expects to have sister Beulah Smith, of Ottawa, with them for a campaign shortly."[63] Beulah's solo travels as a married woman with children are reminiscent of Aimee Semple McPherson's pattern, but with one important difference: Beulah Smith was happily married to her pastor husband while McPherson did not maintain a long-term marriage commitment.

Indeed, a gender history analysis points out the striking differences between Beulah and Aimee Semple McPherson and their relationships with the men in her lives. While McPherson's father was never really involved in her ministry (her mother was her main partner and organizing agent), Beulah Argue Smith worked cooperatively with her

---

[60] "Galt, Ontario," 13.
[61] "Calgary, Alta.," 2.
[62] "Birth Announcements," 12.
[63] "Across Canada," 14.

family members, both before and after her marriage. As a young single woman, she had stayed home in Winnipeg with her ailing mother while her father, brother and sister traveled as evangelists. Then, when her father and brother were needed to do pastoral work at the church in Winnipeg, Beulah joined her sister Zelma as a traveling evangelist. After her marriage, Beulah occupied the role of pastor's wife, and evangelist's wife, but she still maintained an active solo career as a popular speaker, who toured alone, without her husband. Beulah's life of ministry was complex. In her traveling ministry, she was no longer living in her father's shadow, or teaming up with him as Zelma did. Yet neither was her traveling ministry always done in partnership with her husband at this stage. She was frequently listed as the featured evangelist for campaigns in churches and at summer camps and whether her husband participated or not is unclear. It seems that most often he did not, and that his absence was due to the heavy work demands on him as the pastor of a large church, and also because of his commitments to the administrative work of the denomination. Even as a married woman and a mother of very young children, Beulah was still sought out as an evangelist.

And yet, looking a little deeper one still sees the gendered aspects of Beulah's ministry work. She was not advocating an abdication of traditional female roles, but instead, she embraced those roles in addition to her more non-traditional forays into the world of preaching and evangelism. When she took up the editorship of a children's page at the *Pentecostal Testimony* in August 1937, for example, she was still described primarily as a wife: "This month we welcome to our staff of editorial writers Mrs. C.B. Smith of Ottawa, Ont. Mrs. Smith is well known throughout Canada. As a member of the Argue family Mrs. Smith traveled many years in evangelistic work across the continent. Now the wife of one of our busiest pastors Mrs. Smith has kindly consented to edit each month the column OUR BOYS AND GIRLS. We feel sure this column will be read with interest by our many thousands of readers throughout the world."[64] There is no doubt that in addition to Beulah's family ties, her gendered status as a mother made her seem particularly suited for this work. "Mrs. Smith wants to help your boy and girl. Send your problems and questions to Mrs. C.B. Smith, 348 Waverly St., Ottawa, Ont."[65]

---

[64] "Editor's Note," 17.
[65] "Editor's Note," 17.

Beulah Smith continued this editorial work on the children's page on a monthly and then bi-weekly basis for the next three years. Her writing was very much a form of extended parenting, as she nurtured young believers in their faith and entertained them with stories, puzzles, and various features. When the May 1, 1940 issue of the *Pentecostal Testimony* announced that she was leaving the children's page, the publication reinforced the fact that Smith was occupying multiple roles in ministry in addition to her family responsibilities. As a result, the *Pentecostal Testimony* editor told her young readers: "I am sure that you will all be sorry to learn that Mrs. Beulah Argue Smith, on account of her busy life as secretary, evangelist, preacher and mother finds it impossible to continue as editor of this page."[66] Further reinforcing the fact that this editorial role was mainly a nurturing one, the editor continued by assuring his young readers: "Another kind understanding mother will be looking after your interests through this page," and instructing them that they should now direct their letters to a Toronto address on Danforth Avenue.

In fact the Smiths were moving to that same Toronto address to take up the pastorate of the Danforth Gospel Temple, but Mrs. Smith could no longer continue her editorial work. It is not surprising that this busy woman might opt out of one of her many commitments as she and her husband made the move to a new church. Indeed, one would predict that she might need to do this in order to keep up with the competing demands of family and ministry responsibilities in a new city. Yet here again, it was not that Beulah Smith was stopping her ministry work to concentrate more single-mindedly on her family commitments. Indeed, with the move to Toronto came a whole new set of work opportunities. Toronto was the site of the new Ontario Bible School, the Pentecostal training facility for the Eastern District of the PAOC, and in addition to his new church, C.B. Smith took on the new responsibility of President of this fledgling Bible school from 1940 to 1944. But Beulah also joined the teaching staff and on April 15, 1941 the *Pentecostal Testimony* announced her new position. The caption under her photograph read: "Mrs. C.B. Smith under appointment to staff of Ontario Bible School for next term." The same caption went on to announce that "pastors, workers and friends will gather from city and country at Evangel Temple, Toronto on April 24th for a

---

[66] "To the Boys and Girls," 15.

great final closing rally for the [school] year."[67] One assumes that
Beulah would have attended that occasion, though the astonishing
thing is that within four weeks of that event, she gave birth to her second son, David.[68] It was astonishing because in the 1940s, pregnant
women did not usually appear in public, and often gave up their jobs
as the due date drew near.[69] Smith's new appointment as the school's
music teacher would have to be balanced with the demands of her
infant son, who had not yet reached the age of six months when the
new term began in the fall of 1941. Two years later, David's younger
brother Robert who would continue in the family tradition of ministry,
was born.[70] Beulah Argue Smith's life was a clear example of what gender historians have noted about the concurrent and overlapping roles
that an individual often occupies. Not only was she the daughter of a
well known evangelist, the wife of a well known pastor and college
administrator, and the mother of a growing young family, but Beulah
Argue Smith was simultaneously a Pentecostal evangelist, and a college
instructor.

In 1944 C.B. Smith was promoted to the highest office in the PAOC
when he became General Superintendent for Canada. He occupied
this post for eight years and also edited the *Pentecostal Testimony*
during that time. In 1952 the Smith family moved to Victoria, B.C. to
pastor the Glad Tidings Tabernacle. They remained there for five years,
before returning in 1958 to Ontario when C.B. was called to become president of the PAOC Bible College, which had relocated from
Toronto to Peterborough and had a new name: Eastern Pentecostal
Bible College.[71] By this time, the four Smith children were mostly
grown up. Robert, the youngest at fifteen years, was still at home; David

---

[67] "Bible Schools Plan Closing Nights," 14.

[68] There was no birth announcement published in the *Pentecostal Testimony* for
David's birth, nor was Beulah's status as a pregnant woman revealed in its pages.
However, the Honourable David P. Smith went on to have an illustrious career in
Canadian politics as an active member of the Liberal Party of Canada, and at the time
of writing (Spring, 2008) he was serving as a member of the Canadian Senate, having
been appointed to the Senate by Jean Chretien in 2002. His official website at www
.parl.gc.ca reveals that he was born in Toronto on May 16, 1941. That date fell just four
weeks after his mother's appointment to the staff of the Ontario Bible School was
announced.

[69] Mitchinson, *Giving Birth in Canada*.

[70] Rev. Robert Smith is Senior Pastor of the London Gospel Temple, a PAOC church
in London, Ontario. For a brief biography of his ministry career see the church website
www.lgt.org

[71] Kulbeck, "God's Men in God's Schools," 10, 33.

was seventeen years old, and would soon begin his university studies at Carleton University in Ottawa.[72] Again Beulah took up a post as an instructor at the College, teaching music to church workers, evangelists and missionaries and assuming the title of Director of Music. Just three years after their move, C.B. Smith was killed in a tragic car accident while on his way to a preaching engagement. Tributes to the much loved pastor, administrator and family man poured in.[73] A building dedicated to his memory was constructed on the campus of the Eastern Pentecostal Bible College, and in the spring of 1965, Beulah Argue Smith cut the ribbon to officially open the facility. The C.B. Smith Memorial Building bears a plaque which simply states: "Dedicated to the Glory of God and in Loving Memory of Rev. C.B. Smith President of Our College 1940–1944 [and] 1958–1961."[74]

As a widow Beulah Argue Smith remained on the staff of the College and kept busy with her music students. Her students testified to her popularity and the impact she had on them.[75] As Director of Music, Smith gave leadership to the school choirs and "many of her former students who are in the ministry today vividly recall her leading the student body in rousing versions of 'The Word of God' and 'The Hallelujah Chorus' at countless graduation exercises."[76] She was also instrumental in hosting annual 'Schools of Missions' on the campus during the summer when missionaries who had returned from the field could come together with pastors and missions promoters for instruction and fellowship.[77] Smith continued her work at the College until the 1970s when she moved to a new retirement facility for Pentecostal workers in Toronto known as Shepherd's Lodge. The Rev. Beulah Argue Smith died in Toronto early in 1990 and her obituary in the *Pentecostal Testimony* reported that in addition to her ministry accomplishments, she "was a devoted wife, mother, sister, grandmother and great-grandmother."[78]

---

[72] Smith, "University and the Christian," 28–29.
[73] See "Rev. C.B. Smith," 11; Purdie, "A Tribute to the late Rev. C.B. Smith," 33; and Griffin, "An Appreciation of Rev. C.B. Smith," 34.
[74] "C.B. Smith Memorial Opened," 11.
[75] Flewit, "Mentors to Many," 21.
[76] *Pentecostal Testimony* March 1990, 38.
[77] Muggleton, "The School of Missions," 19.
[78] "Canadian Scene – With the Lord – Rev. Beulah Smith," 38–39.

Conclusion

Zelma and Beulah Argue were highly regarded as powerful women of influence during their lifetimes, and their legacy is commemorated and celebrated among Canadian Pentecostals. On several occasions from 1984 to 1994, articles appeared in the *Pentecostal Testimony* reminding readers of these 'pioneers of the faith.'[79] That veneration reminded late twentieth-century Pentecostals that "since the inception of the PAOC we have had some great women who were pioneers, missionaries, evangelists, pastors, teachers, and active pastors' wives."[80] That same article included a list of almost fifty such women and stated: "Next generation of women in ministry, please stand up!"

Reflecting on the lives of women such as Zelma and Beulah Argue, it is clear that gender history can help to explain how and why these early women made their contributions. Placing the Argue sisters back into the complex web of their family ties and ministry connections is an important first step in understanding the roles they played. One might argue that Zelma and Beulah Argue were exceptional because of the men to whom they were related, and that those relations gave them legitimacy. Yet it is clear that while their father's or husband's endorsements were important, they only serve as a partial explanation for their ministry successes. These sisters were heavily influenced by the women around them as well. Eva Argue played a central role in the lives of her daughters, as did Maria Woodworth-Etter and Aimee Semple McPherson, two widely known female evangelists of the early North American Pentecostal movement.

An analysis of Zelma and Beulah's own life choices around marriage and motherhood is also central to understanding their lives and ministries. Zelma's singleness afforded her extended opportunities for travel and writing and in the absence of her ailing mother, Zelma accompanied her father in his traveling ministry fulfilling the role usually occupied by a wife by bringing a feminine presence to his crusades. Beulah opted for the more traditional roles of marriage and motherhood, but surprisingly these choices did not end her ministry career.

---

[79] See for example, "Portraits of Some Pioneers," 18; "Former Women's Ministries Director Remembers," 29; Miller, "Portraits of Pentecostal Pioneers," 20–21; "Next Generation of Women in Ministry Please Stand Up!" 2; and Flewit, "Mentors to Many," 21.

[80] "Next Generation," 2.

As Mrs. Smith, she continued her involvement in evangelistic crusades, writing, and teaching. In many ways, her life defies the stereotypical pattern one might have expected it to follow.

Daughter, sister, wife, mother, preacher, evangelist, musician, teacher and writer: the Argue sisters occupied this complex and varied set of ministry roles throughout their lives. Gender history, with its attention to the context of their relationships and the complexity of simultaneously occupying several different roles, helps to explain how the ministries of these women were legitimized and why their legacies are still celebrated today.

BIBLIOGRAPHY

"A Brief Account of the Life of the Late Mrs. A.H. Argue." *Pentecostal Testimony* 15 May 1939, 12.
"A Tribute to the late Rev. C.B. Smith." *Pentecostal Testimony* March 1962, 33.
"Across Canada." *Pentecostal Testimony* May 1935, 14.
"Memories of Fifty Years Ago." *Pentecostal Evangel* 22 April 1956, 6.
Argue, Beulah. "Three Classes of People at the Border." *The Latter Rain Evangel* August 1927, 9.
Argue, Zelma. "Your Sons and Your Daughters." *Pentecostal Testimony* December, 1920, 3.
Atter, Gordon. *The Third Force*. Caledonia, ON: ACTS Books, 1962.
Bahr, Robert. *Least of All Saints: The Story of Aimee Semple McPherson*. Toronto: Prentice-Hall, 1979.
Barfoot, Charles H. and Gerald T. Sheppard. "Prophetic vs. Priestly Religion: The Changing Role of Women Clergy in Classical Pentecostal Churches." *Review of Religious Research* 22 (1980): 2–17.
Benvenuti, Sheri R. "Pentecostal Women in Ministry: Where Do We Go From Here?" *Cyberjournal for Pentecostal-Charismatic Research*. www.members.cox.net/pctiicyberj/ben.html (accessed August 4, 2007).
"Bible Schools Plan Closing Nights." *Pentecostal Testimony* April 1941, 14.
"Birth Announcements." *Pentecostal Testimony* September 1934, 12.
Blair, J.H. "The Braeside Camp at Paris, Ont." *Pentecostal Testimony*, September 1935, 6.
Blumhofer, Edith L. *Aimee Semple McPherson: Everybody's Sister*. Grand Rapids: Eerdmans, 1993.
——. "Canada's Gift to the Sawdust Trail: The Canadian Face of Aimee Semple McPherson," in *Aspects of the Canadian Evangelical Experience*, edited by G.A. Rawlyk, 387–402. Montreal and Kingston: McGill-Queen's Press, 1997.
——. *Restoring the Faith: The Assemblies of God, Pentecostalism and American Culture*. Urbana, Ill: University of Illinois Press, 1993.
——. "Women in American Pentecostalism." *Pneuma* 17 (Spring 1995): 19–20.
——. "That Old-Time Religion: Aimee Semple McPherson and Perceptions of Pentecostalism, 1918–1926." *Journal of Beliefs and Values* 25 (2004): 217–27.
Brouwer, Ruth Compton. "Transcending the Unacknowledged Quarantine: Putting Religion into English-Canadian Women's History." *Journal of Canadian Studies* 27 (1992): 47–61.

——. *New Women for God: Canadian Presbyterian Women and India Missions, 1876-1914*. Toronto: University of Toronto Press, 1990.

"Calgary, Alta." *Pentecostal Testimony* May 1933, 2.

"Canadian Scene - With the Lord - Rev. Beulah Smith." *Pentecostal Testimony* March 1990, 38-39.

"Carberry, Man.," *Pentecostal Testimony* February 1931, 2.

"C.B. Smith and wife..." *Pentecostal Testimony* August 1931, 2.

"C.B. Smith Memorial Opened." *Pentecostal Testimony* May 1965, 11.

"Continued Report of Western Trip by Chairman." *Pentecostal Testimony* August 1926, 4.

Dicken, Janice. "Take Up Thy Bed and Walk: Aimee Semple McPherson and Faith-Healing." *Canadian Bulletin of Medical History* 17 (2000): 137-53.

"Editor's Note." *Pentecostal Testimony* August 1937, 17.

Epstein, Daniel Mark. *Sister Aimee: The Life of Aimee Semple McPherson*. New York: Harcourt Brace Jovanovich, 1993.

"The Evangelist." *Pentecostal Testimony* February 1936, 2.

"Fire Falls." *Pentecostal Testimony* May 1934, 12.

Flewit, Shirley. "Mentors to Many." *Pentecostal Testimony* October 1991, 21.

"Former Women's Ministries Director Remembers." *Pentecostal Testimony* December 1984, 29.

Gagan, Rosemary R. *A Sensitive Independence: Canadian Methodist Women Missionaries in Canada and the Orient 1881-1925*. Montreal and Kingston: McGill-Queen's Press, 1992.

"Galt, Ontario." *Pentecostal Testimony* December 1932, 13.

"Gifts to Evangelist." *Manitoba Free Press* 6 March 6 1920, 3.

Griffin, George B. "An Appreciation of Rev. C. B. Smith." *Pentecostal Testimony* March 1962, 34.

"Good Reports: Carman, Man." *Pentecostal Testimony* March 1931, 16.

"Hamilton, Ont.," *Pentecostal Testimony* March 1926, 12.

"Herschel, Sask." *Pentecostal Testimony* April 1928, 3.

Holm, Randall. "Pentecost: Women's Emancipation Day?" *Eastern Journal of Practical Theology* 5 (1991): 27-34.

Holmes, Pamela M.S. "Ministering Women in the Pentecostal Assemblies of Canada: A Canadian Pentecostal Feminist Exploration," in *Canadian Pentecostalism*, edited by Michael Wilkinson, 171-194. McGill-Queen's University Press, 2009.

"Holy Ghost Revival Hits Woodstock, Ontario." *Pentecostal Testimony* September 1928, 11.

"Interesting News." *Pentecostal Testimony* December 1931, 2.

Kulbeck, Gloria. "God's Men in God's Schools." *Pentecostal Testimony* March 1961, 10, 33.

——. *What God Hath Wrought: A History of the Pentecostal Assemblies of Canada*. Toronto: The Pentecostal Assemblies of Canada, 1958.

Marks, Lynne. *Revivals and Roller Rinks: Religion, Leisure and Identity in Late Nineteenth-Century Small-Town Ontario*. Toronto: University of Toronto Press, 1996.

——. "The Hallelujah Lasses: Working-Class Women in the Salvation Army in English Canada, 1889-92," in *Gender Conflicts: New Essays in Women's History*, edited by Franca Iacovetta and Mariana Valverde, 67-117. Toronto: University of Toronto Press, 1992.

McGinnis, Janice Dicken. "Aimee Semple McPherson: Fantasizing the Fantasizer? Telling the Tale of Tale-Teller," in *Boswell's Children: The Art of the Biographer*, edited by R.B. Fleming, 45-56. Toronto: Dundurn Press, 1994.

——. "Take Up Thy Bed and Walk: Aimee Semple McPherson and Faith-Healing." *Canadian Bulletin of Medical History* 17 (2000): 137-53.

Miller, Thomas William. "The Canadian Azuza: The Hebden Mission in Toronto." *Pneuma* 8 (1986): 5–29.

——. "The Significance of A.H. Argue for Pentecostal Historiography." *Pneuma* 8 (1986): 120–158.

——. *Canadian Pentecostals: A History of the Pentecostal Assemblies of Canada.* Edited by William A. Griffin. Mississauga, ON: Full Gospel Publishing House, 1994.

——. "Portraits of Pentecostal Pioneers: A.H. Argue." *Pentecostal Testimony* April 1987, 20–21.

Mitchinson, Wendy. *Giving Birth in Canada.* Toronto: University of Toronto Press, 2002.

Muggleton, Jack. "The School of Missions." *Pentecostal Testimony* November 1963, 19.

Muster, Frederick A. and Mel Gram, "Obituary of Zelma Argue." *Christian Life Center,* 29 January 1980, n.p.

"News from Alberta." *Pentecostal Testimony* July 1926, 9.

"Next Generation of Women in Ministry Please Stand Up!" *Pentecostal Testimony* June, 1991, 2.

Noll, Mark, et al., eds. *Evangelicalism: Comparative Perspectives on Popular Protestantism.* Oxford: Oxford University Press, 1994.

Opp, James. *The Lord for the Body: Religion, Medicine, & Protestant Faith Healing in Canada, 1880–1930.* Montreal & Kingston: McGill-Queen's Press, 2005.

Parr, Joy. "Gender History and Historical Practice." *Canadian Historical Review* 76 (1995): 354–376.

Parr, Joy and Mark Rosenfeld. *Gender and History in Canada.* Toronto: Copp Clark, 1996.

"Pastor C.B. Smith of Saskatoon reports a gracious revival." *Pentecostal Testimony,* March 1929, 19.

Pope-Levison, Priscilla. *Turn the Pulpit Loose: Two Centuries of American Women Evangelists.* New York: Palgrave Macmillan, 2004.

"Portraits of Some Pioneers." *Pentecostal Testimony* July 1984, 18.

"Report from Saskatchewan." *Pentecostal Testimony* April 1931, 7.

"Report from the Superintendent of Saskatchewan." *Pentecostal Testimony* February 1929, 16–17.

"Rev. C.B. Smith." *Pentecostal Testimony* March 1962, 11.

Riss, Richard. "Who's Who among Women of the Word." *Spread the Fire* (October1997), www.christianity.ca/church/history/2004/01.000.html (accessed August 4, 2007).

Roebuck, David. "Pentecostal Women in Ministry: A Review of Selected Documents." *Perspectives in Religious Studies* 16 (2006): 29–44.

Rudd, Douglas. *When the Spirit Came Upon Them: Highlights from the Early Years of the Pentecostal Movement in Canada.* Burlington, ON: Antioch Books, 2002.

"Saskatchewan Convention." *Pentecostal Testimony* September 1931, 2.

"Saskatoon, Sask." *Pentecostal Testimony* June 1928, 19.

"Saskatoon Evangelistic Campaign." *Pentecostal Testimony* January 1929, 19.

Setta, Susan M. "Patriarchy and Feminism in Conflict: The Life and Thought of Aimee Semple McPherson." *Anima* 9 (1983): 129–37.

Schmidt, Jean Miller. *Grace Sufficient: A History of American Methodism, 1760–1939.* Nashville: Abingdon Press, 1999.

Scott, Joan Wallach. *Gender and the Politics of History.* New York, NY: Columbia University Press, 1988.

Shearer, Sheryl. "Zelma Argue: Handmaiden of the Lord." *A/G Heritage* (2002) 18–23.

Smith, David. "University and the Christian." *Pentecostal Testimony* September 1963, 28–29.

Stackhouse, John. *Canadian Evangelicalism in the Twentieth Century.* Toronto: University of Toronto Press, 1993.

"Students from Canadian Bible College, Winnipeg, Man., working in Saskatchewan," *Pentecostal Testimony* June 1928, 1.

Sweet, Leonard I. *The Minister's Wife: Her Role in Nineteenth-Century American Evangelicalism*. Philadelphia: Temple University Press, 1983.

"Subscription not Conscription." *Pentecostal Testimony* October 1937, 26.

"Terre Haute, Ind." *Pentecostal Testimony* April 1925, 6.

"To the Boys and Girls." *Pentecostal Testimony* 1 May 1940, 15.

"Triumphant Home-Call: A.H. Argue with the Lord." *Pentecostal Testimony* March 1959, 7, 15, 26–27.

"Wallaceburg, Ont." *Pentecostal Testimony* January 1932, 17.

Warner, Wayne. *Maria Woodworth-Etter: For Such a Time as This: Her Healing and Evangelistic Ministry*. Gainsville, FL: Bridge-Logos, 2004.

"Wedding Bells." *Pentecostal Testimony* July 1930, 20.

"Western New York Camp." *Pentecostal Testimony* June 1934, 9.

Whiteley, Marilyn. *Canadian Methodist Women, 1766–1925: Marys, Marthas, Mothers in Israel*. Waterloo: Wilfrid Laurier Press, 2005.

Wilkinson, Michael. *The Spirit Said Go: Pentecostal Immigrants in Canada*. New York: Peter Lang, 2006.

Wilkinson, Michael, ed. *Canadian Pentecostalism: Transition and Transformation*. Montreal & Kingston: McGill-Queen's Press, 2009.

"Windsor, Ont." *Pentecostal Testimony* January 1932, 7.

"Winnipeg," *Pentecostal Testimony* February 1925, 7.

"Winnipeg, Manitoba." *Pentecostal Testimony* October 1924, 2.

"Woodstock, Ont." *Pentecostal Testimony* June 1932, 2.

CHAPTER SIX

ZELMA ARGUE'S THEOLOGICAL CONTRIBUTION TO EARLY PENTECOSTALISM

Pamela M.S. Holmes

INTRODUCTION

Zelma Argue, born in 1900 to Andrew Harvey and Eva Argue, was closely connected to early Canadian Pentecostalism in Winnipeg, specifically to the outpouring of the Spirit in the Argue home in April 1907.[1] Similar to other Canadian Pentecostal evangelists,[2] Argue ministered faithfully to establish the Pentecostal movement in both Canada and the United States.[3] Zelma began her evangelistic work soon after completing high school,[4] and became prominent in Pentecostal circles north and south of the border, her name appearing in the first *Canadian Pentecostal Testimony* (December 1920),[5] as an evangelist in the March 1921 edition,[6] in *The Pentecostal Evangel* of the Assemblies of God (June 1920)[7] and she was recognized by the General Council of the American Assemblies of God as an "Ordained Minister in Good

---

[1] "With the Lord," 20.

[2] For example, Harvey McAlister is reported to have resigned his congregational ministry in Winnipeg, Manitoba and was holding a Bible Conference in Portland, Oregon. See *The Pentecostal Testimony*, July 1922, 1. Zelma and Beulah Argue of Winnipeg are reported to have ministered in Terre Haute and Jasonville, Indiana in *The Pentecostal Testimony*, April 1925, 6.

[3] There was so much interaction between these two nations and beyond that "A Great Unity Conference of the Pentecostal Movement of North American" was called to "Reach an Agreement on a Scriptural Method of Co-operation, and Promote a closer Bond of Fellowship, among God's Spirit-Baptized People." See *The Pentecostal Testimony* September 1922, 2. In addition, *The Pentecostal Evangel* reports on the work in Montreal "Reports From the Field," 14. *The Pentecostal Testimony* reported that at the "second Annual meeting of the Pentecostal Assemblies of Canada" in November 1920, affiliation with the American "General Council, Assemblies of God, was effected." See December 1920, 1.

[4] Zelma Argue, "The Inward, Outward and Upward Purpose of the Spirit," 18.

[5] *The Pentecostal Testimony* December 1920, 1.

[6] *The Pentecostal Testimony* March 1921, 1, 4.

[7] "Reports From the Field," 14.

Standing" as early as 1920.[8] By 1950 she was pastoring churches in California, the state where she would eventually die in 1980.[9]

Argue not only ministered alone[10] but also alongside her father, A.H. Argue,[11] her "younger sister, Beulah,"[12] and her brother, Watson.[13] Through the ministry of the Argue family, Calvary Temple in Winnipeg, and Evangel Temple in Toronto were established along with several other works.[14]

Zelma Argue contributed to early Pentecostal theology through her evangelistic crusades and publications in the *Canadian Pentecostal Testimony*, *The Pentecostal Evangel* and *The Latter Rain Evangel*. In addition she wrote four books: *What Meaneth This?* (later renamed *Contending for the Faith*), *The Vision and Vow of a Canadian Maiden*, *Garments of Strength* and *Practical Christian Living*. She is an important Canadian figure who contributed to Pentecostalism's early doctrinal teachings.[15] An examination of Argue's work will reveal an egalitarian impulse in her theology, logically coherent in her views on sanctification, the Spirit filled life and the immediacy of the

---

[8] *Combined Minutes of the General Council of the Assemblies of God*, 1920, 51. Already by 1924, she was responsible for orders for "Full Gospel Literature Boxes," a container used to hold newspapers, tracts and congregational information, giving an address in Wood River, Illinois as her contact information. "Full Gospel Literature Boxes," 8.

[9] "With the Lord," 20.

[10] See for example, "Greenfield Park, Que.,"17. Occasionally Argue was called in at the last moment to fill in for someone else who was sick. See for example, C. Smith, "Saskatchewan Convention." She willingly went, worked hard and was well received.

[11] In her early years, Zelma Argue often traveled with and assisted her father, evangelist A.H. Argue, whom she claimed had been baptized in the Spirit in "the old North Avenue Mission," affiliated with the Stone Church, Chicago. See Argue, "The Inward, Outward and Upward Purpose of the Spirit," 18; and *The Pentecostal Testimony* December 1920, 3; January 1921, 2; March 1921, 1; November 1921, 3; June 1922, 3; April 1931, 6; October 15, 1943, 9. In 1958, she and her father together wrote an article recalling their ministry together in honour of the "50th anniversary of the outpouring of the Spirit" understood to have occurred in 1907 as the group had met in Winnipeg, Manitoba in May 1957. See Zelma Argue, in collaboration with her father, Argue, "More than Half a Century of Pentecostal Grace and Glory," 8, 36.

[12] *The Pentecostal Testimony* April 1925, 6; July 1926, 9; August 1926, 4–5. For a closer look at her ministry with her sister, Beulah Argue Smith, see the chapter by Ambrose in this volume.

[13] See *The Pentecostal Testimony* December 1920, 1; March 1926, 12.

[14] P.D. Hocken, "Argue, Zelma," 331. See also, Zelma Argue, *Contending for the Faith*.

[15] She was known to make the front page of the American Assemblies of God periodical as "Zelma Argue, Winnipeg, Man., Canada." See "Emergency Ministries: 'The Time Is Short,'" 1, 10.

eschatological coming of Jesus, all of which validated her calling to the life of evangelism.

HOLINESS INFLUENCES

The holiness tradition of the late-nineteenth century emphasized women's participation in the work of ministry and Argue's theology reflects a holiness influence. Her father, A.H. Argue, was converted in the Salvation Army, and was friends with Dr. George Watson, who preached 'the deeper truths' in Winnipeg, and held meetings in Ontario with American bishop, J.H. King, of the Fire-Baptized Holiness Church.[16] In addition, Fire-Baptized Holiness "Ruling Elder" and "Ordained Evangelist," Mrs. Annie Douglas,[17] had prepared the soil in Winnipeg for holiness teachings. This chapter shall focus in particular on the theological similarities between Douglas and Zelma Argue with an eye to the egalitarian tendencies in Argue's message.

Douglas, and her husband John, were actively involved in the Methodist church in Toronto as class teachers and evangelists of holiness.[18] However, when they arrived in Winnipeg in 1892, the Methodist church in that city rejected holiness teachings.[19] Consequently, the Douglases obtained a building, the former Bethel Methodist Church not far from Grace Methodist Church, and started the Bethel Undenominational Holiness Mission, where they ministered for more than fourteen years[20] until their retirement in Vancouver.[21] While holiness proponents B.H. Irwin and Ralph Horner were described as "the two most prominent advocates of the 'third

---

[16] Miller, *Canadian Pentecostals*, 73.

[17] See the "Official List of the Fire-Baptized Holiness Association of America," in *Live Coals of Fire*, 8, where Douglas, Annie, Winnipeg, Man. is listed under "Ordained Evangelists" and "Ruling Elders." Douglas' "Personal Testimony" appears on page 7 of the same issue.

[18] Douglas, *A Mother in Israel*, 21–51.

[19] Douglas, 59.

[20] Douglas, 64, 96.

[21] Douglas, 136. During this same time, Joseph H. King, the future "General Overseer" of the Fire-Baptized Holiness Church who replaced B.H. Irwin in 1900 is listed as being in Toronto, Ontario in the "Official List of the Fire-Baptized Holiness Association of America," in *Live Coals of Fire*, 8. Also see Synan, *The Holiness-Pentecostal Tradition*, 57, 59. This is not surprising, seeing as Ralph Horner had already introduced Holiness to Canada from his Ottawa, Ontario location according to Mrs. A.E. Horner, *Ralph C. Horner, Evangelist*. Irwin had introduced the Fire-Baptized Holiness Church to both Ontario and Winnipeg by 1897.

blessing' teachings,"[22] it was Annie Douglas who actively cultivated and sowed holiness teachings and the proto-Pentecostal message in Winnipeg. Along with salvation and entire sanctification, the 'third blessing' was the baptism in the Spirit.[23] According to Pentecostal Holiness historian Vinson Synan, the Fire-Baptized movement sometimes linked the phenomenon of speaking in other tongues with receiving 'the fire,' but not in terms of 'initial evidence,' as with later Pentecostal theology.[24]

Zelma Argue did not write in any systematic fashion, but a perusal of her writing discloses important theological themes that contributed to early Pentecostal doctrine. As much as possible, Argue's own words shall be used in an attempt to represent her teachings with reasonable accuracy. What emerges is an egalitarian sensibility influenced by the egalitarian tendencies in holiness teachings, which she then passed on to the people to whom she ministered and the organizations in which she worked.

The Spirit in Sanctification

Annie Douglas focused on the attainment of holiness through the experience of the Holy Spirit, sometimes in the form of the 'Holy Spirit and glory,' sometimes in relationship to the 'Holy Spirit and fire' and sometimes the Holy Spirit alone.[25] In a three works of grace pattern, a person was first converted through the conviction of sin. A person would then need to receive sanctification by the Spirit, and then be filled with the Spirit.[26] The Spirit actively poured out, "fell," convicted, "anointed," "filled ... to overflowing," "melted," "lifted," and "preached through" people.[27] Similarly, Argue based her theology on the work and role of the Holy Spirit. As far as Argue was concerned, the Spirit worked from conviction to glorification. "Every blessing of the soul is brought to us by the ministry of the blessed Holy Spirit. From the first heart wooing of conviction, to the final triumph. ..."[28] As an "earnest of

---

22 Dayton, *Theological Roots of Pentecostalism*, 100.
23 Synan, 50.
24 Synan, 55–56.
25 Douglas, 63.
26 Douglas, 66–67.
27 Douglas, 35, 63, 66, 87.
28 Argue, "The Threefold Purpose," 7.

our inheritance,"[29] the Spirit served to preserve and quicken, as an identifying feature which placed a sign upon those who were the property of Jesus guaranteeing those so sealed that they will be kept "until the day of redemption."[30]

The baptism of the Spirit, for Argue, provided the believer with a "little bit of glory within" and the power to witness.[31] The "secret … of soul-winning is the power of the Holy Ghost." Although she had only been to "Bible School a few weeks at a time,"[32] the "Spirit of truth" rather than logical arguments convicted people of sin and convinced them that the Word of God was sound and that salvation was necessary.[33]

Argue preached that the "test of a genuine revival is the presence or absence of old-time conviction of sin" accompanied by the "burning tears of repentance." She contended that "deep, heart-searching, piercing arrows of conviction, bringing sorrow and remorse for sin, always mark heaven-born revivals."[34] The 'blessings' that then followed such conviction and repentance included "the sweetest smile of heaven … upon their faces, and the sweetest, most gentle adoration rising to the Lord" as "full salvation" was received.[35] The baptism in the Spirit was a deepening commitment and resulted in a "greater love for and power with the souls of those he laboured to see saved."[36]

The Sanctification Controversy

With William H. Durham's declaration that sanctification is found in the 'finished work of Calvary,' leadership for the Pentecostal movement in the United States shifted from Azusa Street, California to Durham's North Avenue Mission in Chicago, Illinois. Zelma Argue's father had received his baptism of the Holy Spirit while he tarried on the Spirit in Chicago,[37] and Zelma later ministered in that city. The 'finished work'

---

[29] Argue, "The Inward, Outward and Upward Purpose of the Spirit," 19.
[30] Argue, "The Threefold Purpose," 7.
[31] Argue, "The Threefold Purpose," 7.
[32] Beulah Argue seems to have had more Bible College training than Zelma, at least in the early years. A picture of the "Canadian Pentecostal Bible Institute," shows Beulah and indicates that she was in her second year. *Pentecostal Testimony* April 1927.
[33] Argue, "Honoring the Power of the Holy Spirit in a Revival," 17, 20.
[34] Argue, "Conviction," 2–3.
[35] Argue, "Conviction," 2–3.
[36] Argue, "How Moody Used the Power," 2.
[37] Synan, 132–132.

claimed that sanctification was a gradual process[38] that began at conversion as an outflow of the work of Christ on Calvary, rather than something that could be attained in an experience of entire sanctification.[39] Durham's views caused a great deal of anguish and fragmentation in the early Pentecostal movement.

While Argue was recognized as an evangelist within the PAOC and an ordained minister within the AG, her understanding of sanctification was closer to that of Douglas' holiness understanding[40] than either of the two Pentecostal organizations. The AG took a solid stand against the crisis sanctification experience of the holiness movement when it formed in 1914 and insisted that "'entire sanctification' should be 'earnestly pursued' as a 'progressive' rather than an instantaneous experience."[41] Similarly, in Canada the PAOC's early constitution stated:[42]

> Entire sanctification is the will of God for all believers, and should be earnestly pursued by walking in obedience to God's Word … In experience this is both instantaneous and progressive. It is wrought out in the life of the believer by his appropriation of the power of Christ's blood and risen life through the person of the Holy Spirit, as set forth in the Word.

Like Douglas, Argue taught that the baptism of the Spirit was a one time event subsequent to a personal salvation experience given in response to the prayers of Christians who sought assistance.[43] Spirit baptism was not to be confused with sanctification which precedes it according to both Douglas and Argue.[44] Argue believed that God had entrusted Christians with the "Baptism in the Holy Ghost and fire."[45] The "fire of the Holy Spirit" was that which burns within a person "melting out the dross."[46] She cited as proof that baptism is separate from sanctification with an example from the last supper where Jesus instructs the disciples: "Now are ye clean through the word which I have spoken unto you." As it was not until weeks later that the day of Pentecost occurred, both the method (clean through the word) and the

---

[38] Synan 133.

[39] Synan, 150.

[40] Douglas, 82.

[41] Synan, 155.

[42] Kulbeck, *What God Hath Wrought*, 345.

[43] See Argue, "How Moody Used the Power," 2; Argue, "The Threefold Purpose," 7; Argue, "Honoring the Power of the Holy Spirit in a Revival," 18. See also "Tapping the Resources of God," 1, 10, 11.

[44] Argue, "The Threefold Purpose," 7. Douglas, 66–67.

[45] Argue, "How Moody Used the Power," 2.

[46] *Pentecostal Testimony* December 1920, 3.

timing were different for the two experiences.[47] She illustrated from her own care for her trombone which she played in her evangelistic meetings[48] that before any "instrument" can be used, it must be "washed and cleansed." Then the "precious oil of the Holy Spirit" can be poured out in abundance upon it.[49]

However, Douglas also encouraged believers to remain close to God and to receive continuing experiences, which were necessary in order to remain cleansed and renewed.[50] Similarly, and perhaps as a nod to the finished work, Argue taught that "God has placed in the church the different gifts, wisdom and knowledge, faith, gifts of healing, etc."[51] Along with the gifts of the Spirit, Argue maintained that the fruit of the Spirit, as "graces" be recognized.[52] These fruits "adorned" Christians as "covering anointing of the Holy Spirit" that allowed them to be "beautiful, truly representing Him whom we love!"[53] Mediating the dispute which offended many holiness Pentecostals, Argue did not label sanctification a "fictitious experience."[54] Rather, Argue insisted that sanctification was required first and then transformation towards Christ likeness or 'graces' continued after being baptized in the Holy Spirit.

EGALITARIANISM AND THE MINISTRY OF WOMEN

Annie Douglas was accustomed both in practice and in principle to the work of women in ministry. Phoebe Palmer, who was significant in the formation of the holiness revival in Methodism, had in 1859, five years after Douglas' birth,[55] developed an understanding of sanctification which included a defence for ministering women based on Joel and Acts 2, especially in *The Promise of the Father* and "Neglected Speciality in the Last Days."[56] Curiously, Palmer used the same Joel-Acts narrative that Pentecostal's later employed to validate women in

---

[47] Argue, "The Threefold Purpose," 7.
[48] See for example, "Reports From the Field," 14.
[49] Argue, "The Threefold Purpose," 7.
[50] Douglas, 1ff.
[51] Argue, "Honoring the Power of the Holy Spirit in the Revival," 17–20.
[52] Argue, "Adorning the Gospel," 4.
[53] Argue, "Adorning the Gospel," 4.
[54] Synan, 150–151.
[55] Douglas, 15.
[56] Dayton, 88–89, 108 quoting Phoebe, *The Promise of the Father*, 191ff. Other writings linking Pentecostal and ministering women included *Hulda A. Rees, the Pentecostal Prophetess* in 1898, 91, 109.

ministry. Douglas had found Palmer's ministry inspiring.[57] Echoing
Palmer's position, she attributed her own preaching and praying
directly to the Holy Spirit.[58] She also accepted and worked alongside
many women, including Martha Hisey, Emma Hostetler and Lillian B.
Yeoman, who later ministered with the PAOC, albeit as unordained
workers.[59] When Douglas left Winnipeg, she had turned the work over
to a Mennonite Mission led by, among others, Hisey and Hostetler.[60]
A.G. Ward, a Christian and Missionary Alliance minister who eventually worked with A.H. Argue and the PAOC shared a meeting hall with
these Mennonite women when he started his mission in Winnipeg.[61]

Argue was directly influenced by female preachers one of whom was
Maria Woodworth-Etter, who provided for Argue a transition between
holiness and Pentecostalism.[62] Woodworth-Etter planted churches
which spread Holiness teaching in the nineteenth century and Pentecostal teaching in the twentieth century. Estimates suggest that up to
500 people a week were converted under her ministry in 1885 alone.[63]
While in California with her family, Argue was affected by Woodworth-
Etter.[64]

Argue's Spirit focused and Christ centred theology, possessed an
egalitarian impulse. Both men and women have a responsibility to be
actively involved in ministry and evangelistic efforts,[65] legitimated by
"that dear familiar quotation, Acts 2:17, 18" upon which "young people can justly lay claim" as their own.[66] God was taking those "who, not
so long ago, were seeking Him in little children's meetings" and sending them "out with His message."[67] Additionally, women were "conceded the right to prophesy, to minister, under the power of the Holy
Spirit" on the basis that the promise was "for each individual, for it was

[57] Douglas, 23, 34.
[58] Douglas, 26.
[59] Douglas, 96–97, 106–107 cf. Holmes, "Ministering Women in the Pentecostal
Assemblies of Canada."
[60] Douglas, 96–97.
[61] Miller, 71.
[62] Such as Aimee Semple MacPherson, founder of the International Church of the
Four Square Gospel, born in southwestern Ontario to a Salvation Army mother and
Methodist father. For her story see Blumhofer, *Aimee Semple McPherson.*
[63] Warner, "Woodworth-Etter, Maria Beulah (1844–1924)," 1211–1213.
[64] Argue, "Act Your Faith," 8–9.
[65] Argue, "The Inward, Outward and Upward Purpose of the Spirit," 18.
[66] Argue, "Your Sons and Your Daughters," 3.
[67] Argue, "Your Sons and Your Daughters," 3.

to those afar off, even to as many as the Lord should call."[68] Such "abnormal" occurrences as "an army of 'handmaiden' witnesses who have mysteriously appeared, lifting their voices to witness that Jesus is coming soon" was clearly prophesied in Joel 2.28 and a "necessary sign of the coming of the Lord."[69] Even children were granted the right to minister based on the prophetic words of Joel where the Acts passage was "first given by inspiration ... foreseen and foreordained."[70]

Argue appealed to youth, women and children to be active in ministry, by using examples of women from the Scriptures to underscore her point. For example, she taught women to resist the temptation to duplicate the disobedience of Eve "that brought SIN to the world, and with it sorrow, suffering and death." In contrast, Mary was a positive model for all to emulate. Mary's choices resulted in "the SAVIOUR" being brought "into the world, and with him Joy, Peace and Eternal Life." Mary's decision to "tarry until" with "the disciples *and the other women*" (emphasis mine) resulted in the reception of the "promised endument of power, the incoming of the Holy Spirit."[71]

Argue's egalitarian theology appears to have been positively received as she continued to preach and write in both the United States and Canada. In this sense she must have been reflecting an impulse in keeping with the theological tenor of her audience even as she promoted an egalitarian model of ministry which was not the norm in many of the Christian churches of her time. However, while Douglas and Woodworth-Etter had furthered the cause of ordained, ministering women long before the 1920 women's suffrage movement, and Argue during, the PAOC and AG were both unable to maintain this momentum,[72] despite her own ability to continue in ministry.

According to Barfoot and Sheppard, early Pentecostalism afforded women the right to preach because they were recognized as called by God in their prophetic anointing. They relied on the theory of Max Weber, who argued that women were allotted equality in the inauguration of religious movements, specifically as prophetesses with

---

[68] Argue, "Your Sons and Your Daughters," 3.

[69] Argue, "Emergency Ministries," 1, 10.

[70] Argue, "Your Sons and Your Daughters," 3.

[71] Argue, "Your Sons and Your Daughters," 3, She also wrote a book about her mother entitled, *A Vision and A Vow or The Vision and Vow of a Canadian Maiden*.

[72] See Holmes, 171ff. For a discussion of the AG's approach to its ministering women see Cavaness, "God Calling," 49–62 and "Factors Influencing the Decrease in the Number of single Women in the Assemblies of God World Missions."

charisma. However, after a short time men monopolized the priestly functions and eventually excluded women from positions of power. In the early stages of Pentecostalism (1901–1920), what Barfoot and Sheppard called Prophetic Pentecostalism, women were recognized by their calling, the confirmation of their calling through charisma and a latter rain reading of eschatology that claims from Joel 2.28 that "your sons and daughters shall prophesy" (see below). Prophecy is equated with preaching, and the employment of the charisma of prophecy legitimated a woman's authority in the community. Yet in the subtle development of hierarchy, women were restricted from positions of authority. What this meant in early Pentecostalism is that women were granted the right to preach and to be ordained, but were eventually restricted to the role of evangelism or missions.[73] Zelma Argue deviated from this exclusionary pattern by serving as a pastor in California after the 1950s and as an evangelist in Canada and the United States.

Women and the Evangelistic Impulse

A Spirit empowered egalitarian impulse in Argue's ministry provided strength for evangelistic efforts. Like Douglas, Argue stressed Spirit empowered evangelism.[74] For Douglas, the fire of the Holy Spirit melted individuals "into liquid love" – a love that became a "fire for souls."[75] Argue maintained that "Evangelism outside the message of the power of the Holy Ghost, is in a deplorable condition today." Even though God had "raised up noble and stalwart witnesses to the infallibility of the Bible" such a "learned and literal witness to the authenticity of the Scriptures" was not sufficient. A second "supernatural witness" was evident in "men and women from the highways and the byways of life, some of whom have not spent years in great universities" who have been called by God. These folk depend on God rather than their own understanding. They have the "burning message of the Gospel, of the power of Jesus' blood to wash away sins, of power through faith for the sick to be healed" and have discovered that God is faithful in working

---

[73] Barfoot and Sheppard, "Prophetic vs. Priestly Religion," 2–17.
[74] Argue, "'The Next Towns Also,'" 2–3; "Preach the Word," 1, 4; "The Streets of Winnipeg," 5–6; "He Beheld the City, and Wept Over It," 16–17; "Showing God's Strength to a Troubled Generation," 4–5; "Another Plea for Evangelism," 4–5; "He Saw The Multitudes," 4–5.
[75] Douglas, 36.

with them, "confirming the Word with signs and wonders." As a result, the Holy Spirit was working in "supernatural measure," similar to that of the early church, and people were responding in faith and belief.[76]

While it was the Holy Spirit who gave the Christian both the motivation and power to evangelize, it was the individual's responsibility to respond.[77] In an appeal to young people, Argue highlighted the example of David, who was anointed with oil and then declared that "the oil of the anointing is upon us." However, while anointing resulted in purification, it was not to be selfishly hoarded. Rather, the oil was constantly replenished as it is poured out in service to others.[78] This response is effective, she assured:

> When we, in the power of the Spirit, confidently lift up Jesus before the people, presenting Him in all assurance as mighty to deliver, and assuredly as Saviour, as Baptizer, as Healer, the normal consequence will be for the faith of the hearers to be quickened to appropriate His abundant provisions. This is not a negative dealing with non-productive theories, but presenting a mighty Christ, who is even now, in all His various capacities, the power of God, for every need – for every hunger.[79]

EGALITARIAN SIGNIFICANCE OF ESCHATOLOGY

Finally, like Douglas,[80] Argue's teaching was eschatological. The egalitarian impulse noted in Argue's work was premised on the belief that the world was soon going to end and that these were the 'last days' where the need was great, the labourers few, and the time short.[81] In Argue's eschatology, God was "moving in history ... in a mysterious way towards the accomplishment of His wonders."[82] In 1920, Argue claimed that the "wonderful outpouring of the Latter Rain" had been "falling the last fourteen or more years." This outpouring was "a sign of the last days just as truly as modern inventions, or the troublous times, or the return of the Jews."[83] The term 'latter rain' was drawn from Joel.

---

[76] Argue, "Conviction," 2.
[77] Argue, "The Inward, Outward and Upward Purpose of the Spirit," 18.
[78] Argue, "Purified But Self-Centered," 2.
[79] Argue, "The Towel of Serving," 1, 6, 7.
[80] Douglas, 97.
[81] Argue, "Your Sons and Your Daughters," 3.
[82] Argue, "Now!" 6.
[83] Argue, "Your Sons and Your Daughters," 3.

D. William Faupel argues that five models vied for dominance in the
early Pentecostal movement: The Full Gospel, The Latter Rain, The
Apostolic Faith, Pentecostal, and the Everlasting Gospel. The Full
Gospel was doctrinal and operated around the theological themes of
justification by faith, physical healing through the atonement, the coming of Jesus Christ, the baptism of the Holy Spirit with speaking in
tongues, and, from the holiness tradition, sanctification as a second
work of grace. This was known as the fourfold or fivefold gospel
depending on whether or not one adopted a holiness perspective. The
Latter Rain was a worldview which informed the Pentecostal understanding of history, especially speaking to the reason why charismatic
gifting diminished after the apostolic period but were arising once
again in the twentieth century. This model allowed early Pentecostals
to interpret their doctrines historically in light of the emergence of the
Latter Rain Covenant. The Apostolic model was restorationist in orientation, arguing that the church fell into apostasy after the
Constantinianization of the church, but that the Reformation restored
cardinal doctrines, and the restoration of the church was continuing
with the charismatic gifts, signs and wonders and the ascension ministries of Apostles, Prophets, Evangelists, Pastors and Teachers. The
Pentecostal model was experiential and looked to the Acts 2 narrative
as the inauguration of a new era of divine power. The dawn of
Pentecostalism was seen as a second Pentecost ushering the church
into the age to come. The Everlasting Gospel (or sometimes called The
Gospel of the Kingdom) was eschatological in orientation focusing on
the imminent, premillennial return of Christ, a motivating impetus for
evangelism and missionary work.[84] The Full Gospel and Latter Rain
models can be discerned in Argue's theology. Her theology clearly
reflects the historical reading of the latter rain, in that Joel prophesied
about the early and the latter rain. Christians in the early church as
depicted in Acts witnessed the early rain, while the latter rain was the
Pentecostal outpouring of the twentieth century. The latter rain was in
preparation for a worldwide evangelistic campaign.[85] While there were
two 'rains' or 'outpourings' of the Spirit, the same characteristics
accompanied both. First, "the presence of the Holy Ghost" filled and
anointed the followers of Christ. Second, people's hearts were stirred

---

[84] Faupel, "The Function of 'Models' in the Interpretation of Pentecostal Thought,"
51–71 and The Everlasting Gospel, 45–82.
[85] Argue, "Conviction," 2; "Finishing Our Course," 3.

and they cried out to God.[86] These features, contended Argue, were a "last witness before the tribulation to an 'apostate' church and a God-rejecting generation" in order to melt hearts "that learned dissertation on the Scriptures" failed to sway.[87]

While Argue herself was a pacifist,[88] she argued in apocalyptic fashion that fighting would truly end only when Christ returned to the earth. Wars themselves were attributed to "the lusts of unregenerate men" and the "fact of a personal devil with hosts of evil forces at his command as the unseen directors."[89] In Argue's contextual analysis, the two World Wars were proof that the eschatological end was near "as the nations, nearing their time of travail, move to take each one its position as scripturally indicated, for the approaching Armageddon."[90] She declared that the time will come when "the cities of the nations will fall" (Rev. 16.19). The third part of men will be killed "by fire, and by smoke and by brimstone" (Rev. 9.18). It will require "seven years to cleanse the land after Armageddon (Ezek. 39.9). Men will stop their noses (Ezek. 39.11). Men will blaspheme God because of the plagues (Rev. 16)."

Other signs pointed to the last days. Modernism was one which she asserted was really "as old as the hills" proclaiming that humanity was capable of improving itself on its own. For Argue, this was the essence of apostasy, summed up in the statements, "*I* am the master of my fate, *I* am the captain of my soul, My head is bloody, but unbowed."[91] Modernism was only the latest form of an age old conflict between those in submission to God and those who opposed God. She taught that conflict was occurring in the unseen world with terrific pressure on all social spheres.[92]

Argue wrote that Satan was "bitter in his hatred of God and of righteousness and faith," and planned to "get the minds of people in his

---

[86] Argue, "Conviction," 2.
[87] Argue, "Conviction," 2.
[88] As can be illustrated by the words she selected for an article, "We want a warless world because Christ hates war." Argue, "The Outlook of an Unregenerate World," 2. The ambivalent attitude towards war as something which Christians should not desire because Christ hates it yet at the same time as serving as proof that these were indeed the last days may help to explain why the original pacifist impulse within Pentecostalism during the First World War was eclipsed by the nationalistic militarism of the Second. For an excellent discussion see Beaman, *Pentecostal Pacifism*.
[89] Argue, "The Outlook of an Unregenerate World," 2.
[90] Argue, "Emergency Ministries," 1, 10.
[91] Argue, "Embracing Apostasy," 9.
[92] Argue, 3.

power" as he knew that "his time is short." The mind was "the entrance to the spirit of man," where "the powers of spiritual darkness" would work through a range of channels to deceive, not only the "great and brilliant" but also the "very elect." When people "yield" their "minds to the spirit of this age, the ruler of the course of this world implants … the spirit of this age," that is, "the spirit of apostasy" which may then "ripen, develop, and mature" and thus "bring in the Antichrist, the ruler of the powers of this world"[93] whom "the world is preparing to receive and worship … at the end of this age." This Antichrist would possess two characteristics. "He would *exalt himself, magnify himself, lift himself up*" (emphasis hers) and, according to "Revelation … his number will be six, six, six." Selfishness is significant because it led to the downfall of "Lucifer, son of the morning" who "first raised his will in rebellion against the will of the Creator, Sustainer, and Governor of the universe." Through this act "discord in the universe was born." In comparison, Christ humbled Himself to the will of God and "became obedient unto death, even the death of the cross'" and was, therefore, exalted by God."[94]

Along with the Antichrist, Argue taught that a Beast would appear based on Revelation 14. Many would "worship the Beast and his image, and receive his mark in his forehead, or in his hand" thus incurring the "wrath of God." This wrath involved being "tormented with fire and brimstone in the presence of the holy angels, and in the presence of the Lamb … for ever and ever."[95]

She denounced modernism and everything associated with it, including evolution.[96] In addition, she urged Christians to guard their minds by claiming the blood of Christ in faith over their minds analogous to the way in which the Hebrew people enslaved in Egypt sprinkled blood on their doorposts to avoid the angel of death during the time of Pharaoh's rebellion against the command of God to free His people. The minds of Christians would then be protected by the "power of the Blood."[97]

---

[93] This is accomplished by breaking "down faith in the Cross" and "in the Blood of the everlasting covenant" and "in the Word of God" and results in blatant "rebellion against God." Argue, "Embracing Apostasy," 3.

[94] Argue, "Up? Or Down!" 6.

[95] Argue, "Embracing Apostasy," 9.

[96] Argue, "Up? Or Down!" 6. In denying "the Fall" and ignoring the "problem of sin" modernism had demonstrated itself to be against the Gospel. Argue, 9.

[97] Argue, "Up? Or Down!" 6.

Christians were to be "Spirit-warned and scripturally-warned" as their salvation was soon coming.[98] They were to be assured as they looked at their "troubled world, that a new era" was dawning. They should also "listen, listen, listen, for the accents of His voice" as God is "speaking to those who have ears to hear. ... That the advent of His Holy King is at the doors."[99] Christians should wait patiently and expectantly for Christ's immanent return which would come suddenly.[100]

This immanent return would include being "caught up to meet the Lord in the air," the "final triumph" for Christians.[101] The rapture was to precede a tribulation period, a time when God's wrath and judgement was to fall upon an unbelieving generation followed by a peaceful and abundant millennial reign of Christ shared in by believers.[102] During this reign, the Holy City, the "new Jerusalem" would be established by God on earth after having descended from heaven. Taking the words of Revelation quite literally, Argue described this city as having "jasmine walls ... twelve gates of pearl ... lying foursquare," with "twelve foundations," a "river," the "tree of life, "yielding ... twelve manner of fruit, each according to its month, for the healing of the nations." There would be "no more curse." Within the city was to be found the "Throne of God and of the Lamb" along with "His servants" who not only "serve Him" but also "see His face" and have "His Name ... in their foreheads." The "glory of God" lights this city and the "Lamb is the light" so there is no need for sun and moon.[103]

Of particular significance to Argue was this city's *transparency ... like unto clear glass ... clear as crystal ... transparent glass*" (emphasis hers). The value of this transparency was that it allowed "the light to shine through." Using coal and diamonds as analogies, she points out that it is through "pressure" that nuggets of coal have, "... lost their soft black character, and have crystallized into marvellous purity and beauty. No longer do they show forth their own character, of earth's substance, but instead constantly reflect, with great beauty, the many colored rays of the light from the sun, according as the stone is cut."[104]

---

[98] Argue, "Emergency Ministries," 1.
[99] Argue, 6.
[100] Argue, "Lest Coming Suddenly!" 8, 31, 33.
[101] Argue, "The Threefold Purpose," 7.
[102] Argue, "Conviction," 3; Argue, "Strange Disappearance," 8.
[103] Argue, "A City Like Glass," 2.
[104] Argue, 2.

Similarly, and very creatively, Argue compares Christians living in
the world who, in keeping themselves "guileless, blameless in character, separated from all works of darkness," show through the light of
Christ once they too have become transparent through being "purified
in the refiner's fire until the face of the Refiner is accurately reflected
therein." This transparency and reflection benefited Christians but was
not for them alone. Rather, it is for the sake of others "to show forth to
the nations the glory of God."[105] While the 'Bride' was keen to be found
pure when the 'Bridegroom' returned to bring her to Himself, separation from the world was not to be achieved at the cost of avoidance of
the fields of ministry. The belief that Christ would soon return
demanded active evangelism.[106] That was why the Spirit had been sent,
as a sign that these were the last days and to empower believers for
evangelism.

Argue was careful not to let any Christian off the hook when it came
to their evangelistic duty. Whether they liked it or not, being called to
Christ meant everyone was a witness to the gospel. As servants of God,
imitators of Jesus' servant hood, the question was not whether or not
you were involved in evangelism but the quality of witness.[107] As she
explained, "We are the representatives of God's grace. Prospective cus-
tomers judge the stock by the quality of the samples presented." She
then urged, "What kind of advertisements do we make? Attractive, or
repelling? Convincing, or misleading?"[108]

Argue particularly honed in on young women. She wrote that "young
women of 'Pentecost'" were to be a biblical standard worthy of those
who were "Spirit-filled and consecrated to God." Such women were not
to adopt the "standards" and "ideals" of the "world ... ripening for
Anti-Christ" but rather conform to the "unchanging Word of God"
which was understood to have taught "simplicity" and "purity." She
wrote that women were to "think, speak, dress, act, and live as becometh
women professing godliness." To underscore her point, she listed several passages of Scriptures which spoke of godly women and wrote that
if women started to "conform to the world in personal appearance, or

---

[105] Argue, 2.

[106] Argue, "Purified But Self-Centered," 2.

[107] Argue, "Towel of Serving," 7. Argue published material to assist and encourage
Christians to be good witnesses. See *Garments of Strength* and *Practical Christian
Living*.

[108] Argue, "Adorning the Gospel," 4.

in action" they would "lose out on the sweetness and power of God."[109] In her eschatology, Argue tied together the themes of sanctification and evangelism as an important role for women, who had been purified and called to the work of ministry.

Christian living involved a "victorious and joyous walk" which made for both "powerful Christians" and a "strong life" capable of casting "off defeat" and overcoming "circumstances or surroundings." Argue said that "fretting, murmuring and defeat, have to go as we commence rejoicing in the Lord."[110] Christians were to "pray without ceasing" "through the Holy Ghost," which, in conjunction with "praise," placed one on a solid footing. In addition, a grateful attitude was encouraged.[111] And the Spirit was not to be quenched as "He is a gentle Dove, and easily grieved. A careless word or prayerless attitude that breaks the spirit then becomes a serious thing."[112] Prophesying was to be affirmed and not despised for "Christ Himself is called Prophet, Priest and King." The gift of prophecy was considered "an important gift of the Holy Spirit, placed by God in the Church." Such prophesying often accompanied the "incoming of the Holy Spirit," in Argue's opinion, based on Acts 19. The current "outpouring of the Latter Rain" was reported by Argue as being accompanied by a strong wave of prophecy to the effect that Jesus is coming soon, the judgments of God are coming upon the earth, and the exhortation to be ready ... witnessed in many parts of the earth."[113]

Notably, this prophesying was sometimes of a very specific nature. Argue told of "different spiritual Christians of financial means" who were "distinctly impressed of the Lord to unload a considerable portion of their holdings in favor of God's work" before the 1929 stock market crash. It was not until afterwards that they understood why. In addition, Argue claimed that a prophetic word was given during a meeting led by Sister Woodworth-Etter which warned of the coming First World War. This prophecy had the effect, Argue claimed, that, "God has spoken to this nation" using "the mouths of His servants and witnesses. Now He is about to speak at the mouth of the cannon." Finally, Argue related a story told to her by her father of a "prophecy

---

[109] Argue, "Two Types of Women Described in the Bible," 2–3.
[110] Argue, "Despise Not Prophesyings," 3.
[111] Argue, 3.
[112] Argue, 3.
[113] Argue, 3.

given by a little Jewish girl" before the War who said, "Woe to the inhabitants of this earth! Woe to this generation!" Argue then reminded her readers that "in Old Testament days true prophecy was carefully safeguarded … In the New Testament it is likewise fully guarded." Therefore, prophesying, although requiring evidence, should not be despised. "In our zeal to weed out the false, let us not also weed out the true," Argue warned.[114]

Argue ominously declared, "In the Old Testament days, the world rejected God the Father. In the New Testament days, the world rejected and crucified Jesus Christ the Son. In the church age, the world is rejecting the Holy Ghost, whose call is to repentance and faith" before going on to give a stern warning. While "Jesus tells us that sins against the Son of man may be forgiven," those "who sin against the Holy Spirit hath not forgiveness, neither in this world, nor in the world to come." She then explained the nature of such a sin. "Hebrews 6:6 speaks of a falling away for which there is no repentance." According to Argue, this "falling away" involves, "those who deny the Eternal Son, who deny His power to save, who, having had the glorious light of the gospel, sin wilfully" in denying its power of salvation, and in definitely and finally turning from the offer of grace presented by the Holy Spirit, and definitely embrace the spirit and teachings of apostasy. For real apostasy is 'the great falling away.' Who is the Lord Jesus Christ? In answering that question a man may seal his destiny."[115]

Argue cited the story of those who claimed that Jesus had "an unclean spirit" as proof for her assertion. Jesus "called this sin the sin against the Holy Ghost" in this story where, for the only time, "Jesus speaks of the unforgivable sin." It is a "sin against the Holy Ghost," Argue explained "because it is the mission of the Holy Ghost to reveal … Jesus." "All may know, through the Word and the Spirit, who Jesus really is. If then we refuse this knowledge, we refuse and cut off our only way of salvation," Argue claimed.[116]

CONCLUSION

The preceding has been an overview of one Canadian's theological contribution to early Pentecostalism in North America as she ministered

---

[114] Argue, 3.
[115] Argue, "Embracing Apostasy," 3.
[116] Argue, "Embracing Apostasy," 3.

in Canada and the United States. Zelma Argue died in Santa Rosa, California on 29 January 1980.[117] During her lifetime, Argue's efforts in establishing Pentecostalism were instrumental in the growth and establishment of this young movement, particularly in its infancy, as she gave her life to the ministry to which God had called her in her preaching and teaching. The egalitarian emphasis of Argue's theology was rooted in a biblical reading that saw the Spirit as instrumental in purifying. Preparing and equipping women for ministry was urgent because the eschatological day was dawning. Everyone, including women, were being called to labour for the harvest. In the process, she was both influenced by and contributed to the development of early Pentecostalism in Canada and the United States.

The Fire-Baptized Holiness Church "served as an important link in the chain that later produced the modern Pentecostal movement" by way of its "teaching that the baptism of the Holy Ghost was an experience separate from and subsequent to sanctification."[118] Douglas' affiliation with the Fire-Baptized Holiness group is important in the role that it played in preparing the people of Winnipeg and the surrounding area for the Pentecostal message, the locale from which Zelma and the whole Argue family appropriated and proclaimed their theology. By 1906, when the Hebden Mission was beginning in Toronto and the Azusa Revival in Los Angeles, California, Douglas and her husband were in the process of retiring in Vancouver.[119] The Pentecostal message was about to be planted in Winnipeg by the Argue family with influences from Durham's mission in Chicago and the holiness teaching of Douglas.[120] While Douglas' printed material was limited,[121] Argue's writings were much larger thereby extending her influence beyond her evangelistic meetings and spreading a holiness-Pentecostal message throughout North America. The theology she propagated was biblical, pneumatological, eschatological, evangelistic and egalitarian, all of which reflected holiness influence and serve as an archetype of Pentecostal teaching.

---

[117] "With the Lord," 20.
[118] Synan, 59. It also influenced Seymour and Azusa Street by way of Charles Parham.
[119] Douglas, 136.
[120] Miller, 71ff.
[121] Along with the sources cited here, Douglas mentions that she was invited by "Dr. Dumble" to write articles for the Toronto based publication entitled the *Berean*. Douglas, 92–93.

148   CHAPTER SIX

BIBLIOGRAPHY

Argue, Zelma. "Your Sons and Your Daughters." *The Pentecostal Testimony* December 1920. 3.
——."Purified but Self-Centered." *The Pentecostal Testimony* March 1921, 2.
——. "Communion with Jesus." *The Pentecostal Evangel* 1 October 1921, 5.
——. "The Outlook of an Unregenerate World." *The Pentecostal Testimony* January 1922, 2.
——. "Adorning the Gospel." *The Pentecostal Testimony* June 1922, 4.
——. "This Bread." *The Pentecostal Evangel* 10 June 1922, 7.
——. "Two Types of Women Described in the Bible." *The Pentecostal Testimony* July 1922, 2–3.
——. *Contending for the Faith*. Winnipeg, Canada: The Messenger of God Publishing House, 1923, [1928].
——. "Conviction." *The Pentecostal Evangel* 15 May 1926, 2–3.
——. "Strange Disappearance." *The Pentecostal Evangel* 17 July 1926, 8.
——."The Inward, Outward and Upward Purpose of the Spirit." *The Latter Rain Evangel* August 1926, n.p.
——."The Threefold Purpose." *The Pentecostal Evangel* 6 November 1926, 7.
——. "Honoring the Power of the Holy Spirit in the Revival." *The Latter Rain Evangel* December 1927, 17–20.
——. "Up? Or Down!" *The Pentecostal Evangel* 22 March 1930, 6.
——."The Good Hand of God Upon Him." *The Pentecostal Evangel* 31 May 1930, 2.
——. "Embracing Apostasy." *The Pentecostal Evangel* 23 August 1930, 3, 9.
——. "A City Like Glass." *The Pentecostal Evangel* 7 March 1931, n.p.
——."Sham Rock or Solid Rock." *The Pentecostal Evangel* 4 April 1931, 7.
——."Wine Mixed With Water (Isaiah 1:22)" *The Pentecostal Evangel* 23 May 1931, 4.
——. "My Beloved Is White and Ruddy." *The Pentecostal Evangel* 5 September 1931, 12.
——. "Despise Not Prophesyings." *The Pentecostal Testimony* November 1932, 3.
——. "Now!" *The Pentecostal Evangel* 7 January 1933, 6.
——."The Courage of Joshua." *The Pentecostal Evangel* 13 May 1933, 1.
——. " Finishing Our Course." *The Pentecostal Evangel* 16 June 1934, 1, 3, 8.
——."The Cost and Value of Jeremiah's Ministry." *The Pentecostal Evangel* 21 July 1934, 4–5.
——. "The Towel of Serving." *The Pentecostal Testimony* 6 October 1934, 1, 6–7.
——. *Garments of Strength*. Springfield, MO: Gospel Publishing House, 1935.
——. "Judge Nothing Before the Time." *The Pentecostal Evangel* 3 March 1935, 2.
——. "God's Method of Announcing an Approaching Crisis." *The Pentecostal Evangel* 14 December 1935, 6–7.
——. "God Works!" *The Pentecostal Evangel* 23 August 1936, 2.
——. "Revival through Unity of Prayer." *The Pentecostal Evangel* 28 November 1936, 2–3.
——. *Practical Christian Living: Choice Thoughts for Daily Meditation*. The Garnered Grain Series. Compiled by Zelma Argue. Grand Rapids, Michigan: Zondervan Publishing House, 1937.
——. "'The Next Towns Also': A Plea for Fresh Efforts at Direct Evangelism." *The Pentecostal Evangel* July 1937, 2–3.
——. "Tapping the Resources of God." *The Pentecostal Evangel* 7 May 1938, 1, 10–11.
——. "God – Our Reward, and Our Rewarder." *The Pentecostal Evangel* 5 November 1938, 5.
——. "Preach the Word." *The Pentecostal Evangel* 17 June 1939, 1, 4.
——. "Emergency Ministries: 'The Time is Short." *The Pentecostal Evangel* 2 December 1939, 1, 10.

——. "The Streets of Winnipeg." *The Pentecostal Testimony* 15 July 1940, 5–6.
——. "Showing God's Strength to a Troubled Generation." *The Pentecostal Testimony* 1 July 1941, 4–5.
——. "Wings at Christmas." *The Pentecostal Testimony* 15 December 1941, 4.
——. "Another Plea for Evangelism." *The Pentecostal Testimony* 5 July 1943, 4–5.
——. "A Coronation Day at Brantford, Ontario." *The Pentecostal Testimony* 15 April 1944, 15.
——. "A Well Watered Garden: (Isaiah 58:10–14)." *The Pentecostal Testimony* 15 May 1944, 16.
——. "He Beheld the City, and Wept Over It." *The Pentecostal Testimony* 1 June 1944, 16–17.
——. "He Saw The Multitudes." *The Pentecostal Testimony* 15 November 1944, 4–5.
——. "Be of Good Comfort." *The Pentecostal Testimony* 1 March 1948, 8.
——."Coronation Meditations." *The Pentecostal Testimony* June 1953, 4–5.
——. "Act Your Faith." *Pentecostal Evangel* 19 July 1959, 8–9.
——. "Lest Coming Suddenly!" *The Pentecostal Testimony* April 1967, 8, 31, 33.
——. *A Vision and A Vow or The Vision and Vow of a Canadian Maiden: The Story of my Mother's Life*. Springfield, MO: Gospel Publishing House, n.d.
Argue, Zelma and A.H. Argue. "More than Half a Century of Pentecostal Grace and Glory." *The Pentecostal Testimony* October 1958, 8, 36.
Barfoot, Charles H., and Gerald T. Sheppard. "Prophetic vs. Priestly Religion: The Changing Role of Women Clergy in Classical Pentecostal Churches." *Review of Religious Research* 22 (September 1980): 2–17.
Beaman, Jay. *Pentecostal Pacifism*. Hillsboro, Kansas: Center for Mennonite Brethren Studies, 1989.
Benjamin,Walter. *The Origins of German Tragic Drama*. Translated by John Osborne. London: NLB, 1977.
Blumhofer, Edith L. *Aimee Semple McPherson: Everybody's Sister*. Grand Rapids, MI: Eerdmans, 1993.
Burgess, Stanley M. and Eduard M. Van Der Maas, eds. *The New International Dictionary of Pentecostal Charismatic Movements*. Grand Rapids, MI: Zondervan, 2002.
Cavaness, Barbara. "Factors Influencing the Decrease in the Number of Single Women in the Assemblies of God World Missions." Ph.D. Dissertation, Fuller Theological Seminary, 2002.
——. "God Calling: Women in Assemblies of God Mission." *Pneuma* 16 (Spring): 49–62.
Combined Minutes of the General Council of the Assemblies of God, 1920.
Dayton, Donald W. *Theological Roots of Pentecostalism*. Peabody, MA: Hendrickson, 1987.
Douglas, Annie. *A Mother in Israel: The Life Story of Mrs. Annie Douglas and a Tribute by Rev. J. McD. Kerr. Toronto, Canada*. Edited by Rev. G.S. Hunt, Seattle, Wash. Oklahoma City, Oklahoma: Charles Edwin Jones, 1909, Reprinted 2002.
——. "Personal Testimony." *Live Coals of Fire*. Lincoln, Nebraska 1 no. 2 (13 October 1899): 7.
Faupel, D. William. "The Everlasting Gospel: The Significance of Eschatology in the Development of Pentecostal Thought." Ph.D. Dissertation, University of Birmingham, 1989.
——."The Function of 'Models' in the Interpretation of Pentecostal Thought." *Pneuma* 1 (1980): 51–71.
Hocken, P.D. "Argue, Zelma," in *The New International Dictionary of Pentecostal and Charismatic Movements*, eds. Stanley M. Eduard M. Burgess and Van der Maas, 331. Grand Rapids, MI: Zondervan Publishing House, 2002.
Holmes, Pamela. "Ministering Women in the Pentecostal Assemblies of Canada: A Feminist Exploration," in *Canadian Pentecostalism*, edited by Michael Wilkinson, 171–194. Montreal-Kingston: McGill-Queen's University Press, 2009.

Horner, Mrs. A.E. *Ralph C. Horner, Evangelist: Reminiscences from His Own Pen Also Reports of Five Typical Sermons*. Brockville, Canada: The Standard Church Book Room, n.d.

Jay, Martin. *The Dialectical Imagination: A History of the Frankfurt School and the Institute of Social Research 1923–1950*. Boston and Toronto: Little, Brown and Company, 1973.

Kulbeck, Gloria G. *What God Hath Wrought: A History of the Pentecostal Assemblies of Canada*. Toronto, Canada: The Pentecostal Assemblies of Canada, 1958.

Miller, Thomas. *Canadian Pentecostals: A History of the Pentecostal Assemblies of Canada*. Mississauga, Ontario: Full Gospel Publishing House, 1994.

"Official List of the Fire-Baptized Holiness Association of America." *Live Coals of Fire*. (Lincoln, Nebraska) 1, no. 2 (13 October 1899): 8.

Palmer, Phoebe. *The Promise of the Father*. Boston: H.V. Degen, 1859.

Rees, Byron J. *Hulda A. Rees, The Pentecostal Prophetess*. Philadelphia: Christian Standard, 1898.

"Reports from the Field." *The Pentecostal Evangel* 12 June 1920, 14.

Synan, Vinson. *The Holiness-Pentecostal Tradition: Charismatic Movements in the Twentieth Century*. Grand Rapids: Eerdmans, 1971.

Warner, W.E. "Woodworth-Etter, Maria Beulah (1844–1924)," in *The New International Dictionary of Pentecostal and Charismatic Movements*, edited by Stanley M. Burgess, and Eduard M. van der Maas, 1211–1213. Grand Rapids, MI: Zondervan, 2002.

Wiggershaus, Rolf. *The Frankfurt School: Its History, Theories and Political Significance*. Translated by Michael Robertson. Cambridge and Oxford: Polity Press, 1994.

"With the Lord." *The Pentecostal Testimony* April 1980, 20.

CHAPTER SEVEN

AIMEE SEMPLE MCPHERSON: 'SHOT IN THE ARM' FOR FRENCH-CANADIAN PROTESTANTISM

Michael Di Giacomo

INTRODUCTION

This chapter focuses on one small segment of Canadian Pentecostal evangelist Aimee Semple McPherson's long, influential, and controversial ministry that merited little more than a paragraph in Edith Blumhofer's biography – the series of meetings in Montreal in December 1920 and the role this event played in the context of francophone Protestantism in Canadian history.[1] The early Pentecostal movement in North America was essentially borderless. Canadians like Robert E. McAlister, Andrew H. Argue, and Aimee Semple McPherson were early pioneers of the Pentecostal movement that were influential on both sides of the Canada-US border. McPherson became an American cultural and religious icon and could easily have been described (although she was not) as America's sweetheart. That description was already taken to describe Gladys Louise Smith, better known as Mary Pickford, another Canadian. McPherson travelled widely from the 1920s through to the 1940s attracting thousands upon thousands of followers. She was based in the United States but she never forgot her Canadian roots. This chapter describes her role as catalyst to the fledgling French-Canadian Pentecostal movement in Quebec. Her meetings in Montreal were an historical highlight that not only gave wings to the movement in Quebec but reversed the tide of the dying French-Canadian evangelical movement to make it one

---

[1] Blumhofer, *Aimee Semple McPherson*, 154. Another well-received biography is Epstein, *Sister Aimee*. The two preceding books spend much time with McPherson's early life. Matthew Avery Sutton's *Aimee Semple McPherson and the Resurrection of Christian America* on the other hand focuses on the evangelist's last fifteen years, especially her status as an American cultural icon and religious celebrity. Sutton explores her role in converging religion, entertainment, and patriotism and argues specifically that she began the melding of patriotism, American culture, and Pentecostalism.

that has experienced continual growth ever since. The social and historical context of francophone Protestants in Canada will be presented after which the reasons for the decline of francophone Protestantism at the beginning of this century will be outlined. Subsequently, the argument put forth here is that Aimee Semple McPherson's meetings in 1920 should be considered a major turning point for it not only contributed to the expansion of the Pentecostal movement in Quebec, it also breathed new life into a dying francophone evangelical movement in Canada.

THE THREE WAVES OF FRENCH-CANADIAN PROTESTANT EXPANSION

Scholars of French-Canadian Protestantism have hypothesized about and referred to three different waves of French-Canadian Protestant expansion in Canadian history.[2] The first wave was the Huguenot presence in the founding of New France. The social and political context of the time as well as Roman Catholic hegemony did not permit Protestant expansion by any other means but by immigration. The total number of French Protestants right up until 1760, the time of the British Conquest, was probably no greater than 1000 and even this small number was not reached without difficulty because of opposition from Catholic clergy.[3]

The second wave of French-Canadian Protestant expansion began with the arrival of Swiss missionaries Henriette Feller and Louis Roussy who founded the *Grande Ligne* Mission in 1835, the first permanent mission whose objective was the evangelization of francophones in North America.[4] This wave includes the evangelizing efforts of the French-Canadian Missionary Society, an interdenominational body begun in 1839.[5] The Presbyterians had already formed a

---

[2] Smith, ed. *Histoire du protestantisme au Québec depuis 1960* and "Towards a Contextual Praxis for the Urban French World," 80–87. For further study into francophone Protestantism in Canada a good place to start is Lalonde's *Des loups dans la bergeri*. It provides an overview of French-speaking Protestant history in Quebec and includes much of recent scholarship on the subject. A brief overview of the available scholarship on the subject can also be found in my article "FLITE," 49–88.

[3] See Bédard, *Les protestants en Nouvelle France* and Larin, *Brève histoire des protestants en Nouvelle-France et au Québec.*

[4] Strout *The Latter Years of the Board of French Evangelization of the Presbyterian Church in Canada*, 2.

[5] Strout, 8.

French-Canadian Protestant mission in 1841. On 10 October 1851, the
Church of England in Canada (not the Anglican Synod in Canada for
it did not want jurisdiction) also began a French-Canadian evangelization program with the Montreal Association in Aid of Colonial Church
and School Society. It seems that Canadian Anglicans were never very
interested in evangelizing the French Canadians.[6] In 1870 the
Presbyterian Church established a French evangelization program
among the French, the Presbyterian Board of French Evangelization,
which seems to have made a substantial impact in French-Canadian
Society.[7] Richard Strout writes:

> It is to the Presbyterian Church in Canada through its Board of French
> Evangelization that belongs the honor of having developed the largest
> network of Franco-Protestant parish schools across Quebec. They edu-
> cated more pupils than any other single Protestant body. The number of
> communities served by Presbyterian mission schools – no less than
> eighty – equals that of all the other Protestant churches combined [...]
> The high point as concerns the operation of parish schools had come in
> 1887 when twenty-six were in existence with a total enrollment of at least
> 599 pupils [...] The highest number of enrollments was in 1897, 540 stu-
> dents in twenty-four schools.[8]

In terms of members and adherents under the care of the Board's missionaries, the number ranged from 1,890 in 1903 to 2,476 in 1911.[9]

The Rev. Charles Chiniquy, former Catholic priest and 'Apostle of
Temperance' converted to Protestantism, played a significant role in
the evangelization of French Canadians in the last quarter of the nineteenth century, with the greatest results in the 1875–1877 period.
According to historians Richard Lougheed and Wesley Peach, Chiniquy
and the Presbyterians were particularly successful in converting French
Canadians to Protestantism,[10] although Chiniquy's success has been
questioned by historians Linteau, Durocher, Robert, and Ricard.[11] We
must qualify these figures further. There are no precise numbers of
French-Canadian converts in the nineteenth century. There were thousands of abjurations between 1875 and 1877, however. The fact that

---

[6] Strout, 10.
[7] Strout, 8.
[8] Strout, 29.
[9] Strout, 33.
[10] Lougheed, "The Controversial Conversion of Charles Chiniquy," 368–370; Peach,
"Evangelism – Distinctly Quebec," 156.
[11] Linteau, et al, *Histoire du Québec contemporain*, 258.

many moved to the United States makes the exact number of converts difficult to estimate.[12] It has been estimated that from the 1830s to the beginning of the twentieth century anywhere from 30,000 to 45,000 French-Canadian Catholics converted to Protestantism through the efforts of all Protestant denominations[13] with approximately a hundred French Protestant churches established by the turn of the century.[14] The third wave of French-Canadian Protestant growth was observed especially in the 1970s and 1980s. Mainly applicable to the evangelical sector of Protestantism, growth during this time period was in large measure the result of the deep cultural transformation undergone by Quebec commonly known as the Quiet Revolution.[15]

DECLINE IN FRENCH-CANADIAN PROTESTANTISM AT THE TURN OF THE 20ᵀᴴ CENTURY

By the turn of the century, French-Canadian Protestantism was already in a state of decline for which several reasons have been evoked. First, the different denominations began to question the focus of their mission to French Canadians, i.e., evangelistic activity vs. education.[16] Second, demographic changes at the time, especially the growing population in western Canada, most of which were non-British or non-American, led to a re-orientation in home missionary work. The Presbyterian Church, for example, replaced the evangelization of French Canadians with that of immigrants settling in western Canada, mainly because evangelizing the latter was easier and less costly. The Presbyterian Church of Canada asked itself in its 1917 General Assembly "whether it is good business to spend in Quebec unless we are prepared to spend in the other districts where two dollars worth of energy will accomplish more than ten in that community where the Roman Catholic Church has a grip upon politics and

---

[12] Lougheed, letter to Di Giacomo.
[13] Lougheed, *The Controversial Conversion*, 368; Peach, 156.
[14] Smith, "Towards a Contextual Praxis," 80.
[15] Di Giacomo, "Quebec Pentecostals, 1966–1995; Lewis, "Evangelical Renewal in French Canada," 3–14; Smith, *Histoire du protestantisme au Québec depuis 1960*; Remon, ed. *L'identité des protestants francophones au Québec*; Scorgie, "Twentieth-Century Evangelistic Renewal in French Canada;" Peach, "Evangelism," 153–176; Smith, "The History of French Protestantism in Quebec," 16–22; *Faith Today* November 1977.
[16] Strout, "The Latter Years," 4–7.

people absolutely impossible in the freer democracy of the other provinces."[17]

Another reason for the decline of French-Canadian evangelization was that influential members of the Board of French Evangelization were dying. Those who were most influential in keeping the Presbyterian Church of Canada focused on French Canada were no longer there to fan the flame. The passing away of Charles Chiniquy was another factor which allowed the fervency of French Canada Missions to die. Furthermore, an indigenous French-Canadian leadership, absolutely necessary to conserve the results and continue the work of French evangelization, was not developed, with many francophones joining the anglophone community.[18] Patriotism was also no longer a motivating factor in evangelizing the French Canadians at the turn of the century, with religious prejudices having declined, or at least shifted. There were increasing doubts as to the advisability of evangelizing Roman Catholics. The political situation was also something of a factor, although hard to measure. In the wake of the Riel case and the tensions surrounding the separate school question in Ontario, New Brunswick and Manitoba, politicians did what they could to lessen the religious tensions. By the turn of the century religion was becoming less of an issue in politics as Canada became increasingly secularized.[19]

Probably the greatest reason was the inroads made by liberal and modernist theology. There was also a decrease in emphasis on a personal conversion experience.[20] By and by, the social gospel, and therefore social activism, which was usually promoted by theological liberals, replaced evangelism.[21] Darwinism and higher criticism began to infiltrate North America in the last quarter of the nineteenth century. In the 1880s Canadian scholars trained in Higher (historical) Criticism found positions in Canadian universities. The new perspectives, methods, and conclusions of exegesis caused controversy and led to the modernist-fundamentalist polemic which was especially strong in the United States. British evangelical reaction to the new theology and higher criticism, in contrast to the Americans, took on more of a

---

[17] Acts and Proceedings of the General Assembly of the Presbyterian Church in Canada, 15 as quoted in Strout, *The Latter Years*, footnote no. 1, 77.
[18] Strout, 62.
[19] Strout, 60–76.
[20] Strout, 64.
[21] Strout, 40–59.

critical-accommodating tone.[22] In Canada, it seems, though not void of controversy,[23] ministers were more easily assimilated into liberal theology than their American counterparts.[24]

The transformation of Protestantism must be seen as a part of a wider societal cultural change. The turn of the century was a prosperous time for Canada, a time of peace yet great social change: innovations in technology, the arrival of big business in Canada, the rise of the white-collar worker, urbanization, and population movements from the country to the cities. Social evils accompanied prosperity, including the deterioration of the inner city and a rising suicide rate. With the great widespread social, technological, and intellectual changes as a backdrop, the turn of the century was the beginning of the end of the evangelical consensus.[25]

Nonetheless, religious activity proliferated at this time: social work, evangelistic crusades, women's unions or Deaconess Orders such as the Women's Christian Temperance Union. The idea of women venturing out into the public arena was first seen as inappropriate by some, but this gave way to the idea that women should actually be given the right to vote in order to defeat intransigent politicians suspected to be tied to "liquor interests." The Lord's Day Alliance formed to lobby against the industrialization of the Lord's Day and uninterrupted work, which eventually led to the passing of the Lord's Day Act. Involvement in social reform movements soon led to the belief that evangelism and social reform were inseparable.[26] But even though many Protestants embraced the new ideas in sociology, science, and psychology, adapting them to religion and church work, others favoured a more traditional approach and therefore resisted cultural change. Eventually a rift took place and widened between Protestants who wanted to remain loyal to past traditions and concepts and those who advocated a more progressive approach.[27] Out of this division in Protestantism grew new organizational patterns, new leaders, and new institutions.[28]

---

[22] See Noll, *Between Faith and Criticism*, 11–61.
[23] Airhart, "Ordering a New Nation and Reordering Protestantism, 1867–1914," 111–112.
[24] Strout, "The Latter Years," 60–76.
[25] Airhart, 114–117.
[26] Airhart, 117–123.
[27] Airhart, 114–117.
[28] Airhart, 125.

On the Canadian cultural scene, a growing rift between anglophones and francophones occurred due to a series of issues. The Louis Riel uprising, the disputes over French-language rights outside Quebec, the Boer war, WWI and WWII aggravated the split in Canada along French-English ethnic lines.[29] Historian Mason Wade described the widening cultural divide of the late-nineteenth and early-twentieth century in Canada as interplay between English-Canadian imperialism and French-Canadian nationalism. Referring especially to Manitoba politician Clifford Sifton's anti-French sentiments in the Manitoba school question, he writes: "[Henri] Bourassa's nationalism was not merely a reaction against imperialism; it was a reaction against the attempt of certain English Canadians since 1885 to make Canada a land of one tongue and one culture, and to treat the French Canadians as foreigners in their own country."[30]

In June of 1902, Napoléon Garceau organized in Drummondville the first mass nationalist rally, which ended in pledges of allegiance to the French-Canadian nationality and to its constituent elements of faith, language, laws, and traditions, and to the British Crown.[31] Abbé Lionel Groulx, Abbé Émile Chartier and Père Hermas Lalande began a religious movement that soon took on political overtones, the *Association catholique de la Jeunesse canadienne-française*, which also contributed to rising French-Canadian nationalism.[32] Anti-conscription riots in Quebec City in March 1918 put down by the military, also fuelled nationalist and separatist movements.[33]

The first two decades of the twentieth century was then an era of theological controversy within Protestantism, set in the context of wide-spread social change, including a growing rift between French and English Canada. It is within this context that Rev. Charles Baker, the pastor of the Drummond Street Pentecostal Church invited evangelist Aimee Semple McPherson to hold an evangelistic campaign in Montreal. The meetings, primarily aimed at English Canadians, held in a Protestant Church (St. Andrew's Presbyterian) whose 2000-seat capacity proved inadequate to accommodate the throngs that desired to attend, without the benefit of translation for

[29] Wade, "Political Trends," 145–146.
[30] Wade, 147.
[31] Wade, 149.
[32] Wade, 149–150.
[33] Wade, 159.

francophones,[34] served as the catalyst that would spark Pentecostal growth among French Canadians. There were a few French-Canadian Pentecostals before the Aimee Semple McPherson meetings, but it was subsequent to these meetings, and especially because of the conversion of Baptist pastor Louis Roussy Dutaud to Pentecostalism, that French-Canadian Pentecostalism was able to expand rapidly.[35]

THE GENESIS OF FRENCH-CANADIAN PENTECOSTALISM

Pentecostalism came to Quebec by way of Ontario and found receptive hearts at first among English-speaking Quebecers.[36] Pastor and Mrs. Charles Baker from Ottawa crossed the Ottawa River into Quebec on 23 August 1913 to hold a series of evangelistic meetings at McBean in the Gatineau area.[37] Twenty-eight people were converted and baptized following the week of meetings. At around the same time in Montreal, Kydd Byrne supervised home prayer meetings, which were later moved to a hall on Van Horne Street. Not much is known about Kydd Byrne nor is it clear if his group began and evolved independently or in association with the fledgling Pentecostal movement. On 25 November 1916 Pastor Baker and his wife came to Montreal to preach at the mission on Van Horne Street.[38] It is not clear whether the Van Horne Street mission became Pentecostal subsequent to or prior to Baker's visit, nor if it ever became a Pentecostal group. Possibly, only a few members might have embraced the Pentecostal message after which they became associated with Baker. We do know that in Byrne's meetings a young British Methodist minister and immigrant of French ancestry, Philip LeBrocq, received the experience Pentecostals call the baptism of the Holy Spirit with accompanying glossolalia.[39] Lebrocq's significance lies in the fact that he would be the first leader of a distinctly

---

[34] See Rudd, "The Great Montreal Revival," 8–9; Baker, "Canada's Largest City is Visited with Floods of the 'Latter Rain,'" 2.

[35] See my article "FLITE" for statistics on Pentecostal expansion in Canada from 1921–1991 as well as my article "La vieille capitale," 79–94 for a brief commentary on statistics based on the 2001 Canadian Census.

[36] Kulbeck, *What God Hath Wrought*, 100.

[37] Rust, "Les premières églises pentecôtistes françaises à Montréal," 5.

[38] Cressman and Gagnon, *Le Mouvement de Pentecôte au Québec*, 4. This booklet is a translation and adaptation of Cressman, "A Half Century of Pentecost in Quebec," 4–7, 33; Rust, "Les premières églises," 3.

[39] Cressman and Gagnon, 5.

francophone Pentecostal group begun within a larger anglophone congregation led by Charles Baker. Because of his ability to speak French, Philippe LeBrocq was eventually called upon by Charles Baker to give leadership to a small group of francophones who had requested prayer meetings and services in their own language. And so in 1919, Pentecostal meetings were begun in the French language under the direct supervision of Philip LeBrocq, who by now was a deacon in Pastor Baker's church.[40]

Charles Baker was certainly the undisputed leader of the whole Pentecostal movement in Quebec. Formerly a Methodist lay preacher and men's clothing businessman in Ottawa, he brought his wife to Pentecostal meetings hoping to see her cured of cancer. The Pentecostal movement had arrived in Ottawa in 1907 through the efforts of Methodist holiness minister Robert E. McAlister, who had received his Pentecostal experience at the Azusa Street mission in Los Angeles and had returned to Canada to become one of the pioneers in the Canadian Pentecostal movement. It was McAlister who organized the evangelistic meetings attended by the Bakers. The guest speaker during the Ottawa evangelistic campaign was A.H. Argue, another pioneer of the Canadian Pentecostal movement who had received his Pentecostal experience at William Durham's North Avenue Mission in Chicago.[41] Argue prayed for Mrs. Baker who was miraculously healed.[42] Subsequent to this miracle, the Bakers went into full-time Pentecostal ministry, and consistent with the missionary impulse and zeal of the early Pentecostals traveled to Montreal to preach the Gospel and to establish one of the most important and influential churches of the Canadian Pentecostal movement. Various moves became necessary to accommodate the growth in numbers, first to McGill College Avenue, then to the Empire Cinema on Stanley Street, and then back again to McGill College Avenue, and finally the growing congregation – Evangel Pentecostal Church – settled across from the old Montreal Forum, the home of the Montreal Canadiens professional hockey team.[43]

---

[40] Cressman, 4.
[41] See Miller, "The Significance of A.H. Argue for Pentecostal Historiography," 120–158.
[42] Miller, *Canadian Pentecostals*, 62–67.
[43] Kulbeck, 101.

AIMEE SEMPLE MCPHERSON

In the autumn of 1920, Baker's Pentecostal congregation welcomed evangelist Aimee Semple McPherson for a series of evangelistic meetings at St. Andrew's Church. For three weeks, from 17 November to 6 December, McPherson preached the gospel and prayed for the sick. The campaign was duly reported by the Pentecostal 'press' as well as the secular press. There were eight reports of the meetings in *The Montreal Gazette*[44] and one in *The Montreal Daily Star*.[45] Interestingly, news reports or announcements in the major French-language newspapers *Le Devoir* and *La Presse* are nowhere to be found. This silence in the French-Canadian press is attributable, no doubt, as much to the Canadian phenomenon of the "two solitudes" between English and French communities as to the highly polemical context of the time between Catholic (usually francophone) and Protestant (usually anglophone).

The reports in the *Montreal Gazette* were even-handed, void of any scepticism. The reporter objectively reported the great number of healings he observed, at times even giving the name and address of the persons healed. His reporting is quite a contrast to the report of the meetings by Pastor Charles Baker in the denomination's publication, *The Pentecostal Testimony*. The latter was oriented towards faith edification and avoided any discussion of a lack of healing. On the contrary, the evangelistic campaign was described as a glorious event characterized by revival fervour. Pastor Baker emphasized the healing of people, transformed lives, the great crowds, and the powerful preaching of the evangelist.[46]

The reporter, on the other hand, did not have spiritual edification on his mind, as he described what he saw. Notwithstanding, there is no evidence of criticism. He reported that many were healed, especially deaf people. At times the reporter would personally investigate the healings. He reported that healings were at times instantaneous, at times gradual, at times spectacular, and at times, no healing was forthcoming for those who received prayer. One case caused a sensation,

---

[44] 18 November 1920, 9; 19 November 1920, 11; 27 November 1920, 4; 1 December 1920, 4; 3 December 1920, 4; 4 December 1920, 4; 6 December 1920, 4; 8 December 1920, 5.
[45] 6 December 1920, 22.
[46] Baker, 2.

the case of twenty-two year old Esther James. A seriously sick person, on the verge of death according to her doctor, enjoyed healing for two days before relapsing into an even worse state. Before the end of the crusade, it was reported in the paper that she had died. However, there was no criticism leveled at the evangelist. On the contrary, it was reported that the woman in question had received a spiritual blessing that prepared her for death.[47] The newspaper reports made mention of Catholics attending the meetings. One woman even presented to McPherson a letter from her parish priest authorizing her to attend the meetings and receive prayer from the evangelist.[48] The whole tone of the reports is quite astonishing for a reader living in today's cynical and highly critical world.

The hall was filled to capacity on several occasions. For at least one meeting a very long line-up of people waited for the religious service to begin. And still hundreds had to be turned away. The police were brought in to control the crowds and traffic. The final meeting lasted eight hours, starting at two o'clock in the afternoon, with a one-hour supper break, and resuming at eight o'clock. Even though McPherson formally concluded the meeting at 10:45 pm, she continued to pray for the many waiting in line seeking prayer while the hall emptied.[49]

There is nothing to suggest that the meetings in Montreal were significantly different from any other of McPherson's gospel campaigns throughout North America. That McPherson had an amazing appeal, a sense of the dramatic, and a talent for preaching in an entertaining style is substantiated by accounts of her numerous other campaigns. She easily rivalled the popularity of Billy Sunday (the press labelled her often as the female Billy Sunday) and D.L. Moody.[50] McPherson had a more personable, simple, and gentle way of addressing her hearer, in contrast to the denunciatory style of Billy Sunday. And there is nothing to suggest that her Montreal campaign was marked by any excess emotionalism or controversy. The *Montreal Gazette*'s first article on the meetings reported that McPherson's:

> address was on the subject of the baptism of the Holy Spirit, and it was
> delivered with a readiness and command of language and an earnestness

---

[47] "Cure Not Lasting, Patient Relapsed," 4; "Esther James, Who Rose From Bed in Church, is Dead," 5.
[48] "Priest Sent Note to Woman Healer," 4.
[49] "Eight Hour Line of the Afflicted," 4.
[50] Blumhofer, *Aimee Semple McPherson*, 13.

of manner that carried the audience by its very vehemence. There was no criticism of churches and no denunciation of the world at large, but just a presentation of the truth as she read the Scriptures, to which was added personal experiences and convictions.[51]

As Edith Blumhofer points out, reporters were actually surprised by the emotional restraint and orderliness of her meetings and at times underscored the 'saneness' of the meetings and the 'common sense' of the evangelist.[52] The *Montreal Gazette* highlighted that her address was followed "without any undue pressure or over-coaxing."[53] However, to the evangelist's chagrin, journalists did tend to put too much emphasis on her healing ministry even though McPherson did not claim to heal and regretted the media's emphasis on healing. Nevertheless, it seems that many hundreds and even thousands received genuine healings in the course of her ministry.[54] From all accounts, McPherson's Montreal campaign was just as successful as her numerous other meetings in North America in terms of crowds that gathered, conversions to Christ, number of healings, and transformed lives. The long-term impact, however, in spurring a fledgling Pentecostal movement to greater expansion while at the same time reviving a dying evangelical move-ment makes McPherson's campaign especially significant in the Canadian context. It would be the beginning of a continuously expand-ing religious movement that would eventually reach its greatest impact on Quebec society in the 1970s in the wake of Quebec's Quiet Revolution.[55]

The impact of her Montreal campaign for francophone Pentecostal and evangelical expansion is undeniable. During the campaign, a seri-ously ill French-Canadian wife of a Baptist pastor, suffering from tuberculosis, a cancerous rib, and infection in her limbs, insisted over her husband's objections on being taken to the McPherson meetings. She was totally and miraculously healed, so much so that her husband, Louis Roussy Dutaud, sceptical though he was, had to confess after his wife's healing and transformed life that God was indubitably present

---

[51] "Woman Missioner Drew Penitents," 9.
[52] Blumhofer, 220–221.
[53] "Woman Missioner Drew Penitents," 9.
[54] Blumhofer, 135–180.
[55] The growth of Pentecostals in Quebec is as follows. 1921, 374; 1931, 1,214; 1941, 2,420; 1951, 4,025; 1961, 5,730; 1971, 8,535; 1981, 17,420; 1991, 28,955. See www.stat-can.ca for details about religious identity in Canada. Also, see Di Giacomo, appendix A in "Flight" for figures.

and at work in McPherson's Pentecostal meetings. Subsequently, Rev. and Mrs. Dutaud received the Pentecostal experience, the baptism of the Holy Spirit. Although other French Canadians were converted during the McPherson meetings, it was Dutaud who was destined to become the first French Canadian pastor to take the reins of the fledgling francophone Pentecostal group, take it out of Baker's anglophone church and transform it into a distinctly francophone movement. The son of parents who had been converted to Christ through the ministry of Madame Feller and Louis Roussy of the *Grande Ligne* Mission (the second wave of francophone Protestantism as previously discussed), Dutaud studied for the ministry at the Feller Institute and at Woodstock College in Massachusetts and subsequently became pastor of the *Grande Ligne* Mission. Because of his thirty years of pastoral experience Dutaud was asked by Baker to take charge (Philip LeBrocq had left Montreal during this time to pastor in Ontario)[56] of the newly converted French Canadians who spoke little or no English.[57]

Consequently, on 20 April 1921, the doors of the first French-speaking Pentecostal Church officially opened in the north end of Montreal. Unsurprisingly, it was named "*La première église de pentecôte française*."[58] It is not known exactly how large the meeting hall was. We do know that it consisted of two rooms, and that the Dutauds' son, Gérald, had to play his saxophone in the closet to leave room for all who wanted to attend the meetings. At its peak in the early 1940s the number of adherents may have reached about 300 people, quite large for a francophone Protestant church in the fiefdom of the socially-powerful Catholic church of that day.[59] Dutaud continued his ministry for the next ten years (never paid more than $23.00/week[60]), preaching in Montreal and holding evangelistic meetings in Trois-Rivières and Quebec City.[61] He finally passed away on 3 February 1931, at the age of sixty-seven,[62] but his death did not mean the death of the French-Canadian Pentecostal movement, which continued to experience growth.

---

[56] Rust, 11–12.
[57] Kulbeck, 93.
[58] Rust, 13.
[59] Rust, 15.
[60] Rust, 14.
[61] Kulbeck, 94–95.
[62] Rust, 15.

North American Pentecostalism was cross-cultural and international so that Canadian and American Pentecostalism influenced each
other. English-speaking ministers from outside Quebec contributed
significantly to the growth of the French sector of the Pentecostal
movement. Francophone Pentecostalism was spawned and grew within
an anglophone environment. Subsequent to the McPherson meetings
and the conversion to Pentecostalism of Louis Roussy Dutaud in 1920,
French-Canadian Pentecostalism gathered momentum and began its
own distinct development. Further expansion resulted in the planting
of up to eighteen francophone churches by 1960, a retirement home,
the founding of a French-language ministerial training institute, Berea
Bible Institute (*Institut biblique Bérée*), and during the 1940s and 1950s
a day school, the Montreal Christian Academy (*Académie chrétienne
de Montréal*), a Gospel radio program,[63] a television program,[64] and the
French Conference (*La Conférence française*), which was the consolidation in 1949 of the francophone Churches into a distinct grouping
within the PAOC. Interestingly, as the French-Canadian Pentecostal
movement grew, consolidated, and structured, those who gave leadership, such as Emile Lassègues and Walter Bouchard, albeit of French
origin with French names, were actually anglophone Americans.[65]
Lassègues hailed from California and Bouchard from Rhode Island.
Philippe LeBrocq, who had left the francophone group to pastor elsewhere, returned to become pastor of *La première église de pentecôte
française* following Dutaud's death. He was British, as previously mentioned. It was not until 1962 that the first French Canadian born in
Quebec became Superintendent of the *Conférence française*, namely,
Roland Bergeron.[66]

CONCLUSION

Scholars have hypothesized that French-Canadian Protestant history
can be described in terms of three distinct groups or waves: the first
being the French Protestants of New France whose presence was a
result of immigration, the second being the evangelization of French-
Canadians in the nineteenth century as a result of the ministries of

---

[63] Called *La Bonne Nouvelle*. See Cressman, "Pentecost in Quebec."
[64] Called *Message de Vie*. André Gagnon.
[65] Marie-Paule Gagnon; Rust, 21.
[66] Cressman and Gagnon, 23.

Henriette Feller, Louis Roussy, and Charles Chiniquy, and various Home Missionary organizations created for the purpose of evangelizing the French Canadians, and the third being the revival and very rapid growth of francophone evangelicalism in the 1970s and 1980s in the wake of Quebec's Quiet Revolution. In this version of history, francophone Protestantism was on a downward trend, dying, and losing ground by the time of the First World War. This is certainly substantiated by available records that show indeed that of the one hundred francophone evangelical churches at the turn of the century, only sixty were left by the beginning of the 1960s with an average attendance of thirty-five.[67]

However, while it is true that overall the francophone Protestant community did experience a steady decline from the turn of the twentieth century until the early 1970s, the numbers would have been worse without the slow, albeit relatively steady growth of the francophone Pentecostal movement. The three-wave version does not recognize that within a steadily declining francophone Protestant community there was a dynamic and growing Pentecostal movement. The three-wave version completely ignores the fact that the Pentecostal movement slowed the downward trend of francophone Protestantism. It can furthermore be argued that the stagnation of the Pentecostal movement in French Canada in the 1960s was a temporary slowdown, not a downward trend. By the 1970s Pentecostalism became without a doubt the largest sector of francophone evangelicalism.

Finally, the three-wave version of francophone Protestant history does not give due recognition to the events and historical figures that reversed the downward, dying trend of the francophone Protestant community in Canada. A number of people need to be credited with the introduction and revival of French-Canadian Protestantism in Quebec of the early-twentieth century. R.E. McAlister and A.H. Argue were both Canadian Pentecostal leaders who owe their Pentecostal experience to missions in the United States: the Azusa Street Mission and the North Avenue Mission, respectively. Both were instrumental in the healing of Mrs. Charles Baker who subsequently, with her husband, entered Pentecostal ministry and introduced the Pentecostal message to Quebec. Philippe LeBrocq was the first to give leadership to a distinct francophone group although within an English church.

---

[67] Smith, "Towards a Contextual Praxis," 87.

Canadian Pentecostal evangelist Aimee Semple McPherson was introduced to Pentecostalism through her first husband who experienced Spirit baptism at the Hebden Mission in Toronto. McPherson was also instrumental in the healing of Mme Louis Dutaud who subsequently with her Baptist husband entered Pentecostal ministry and contributed to the expansion of a distinctly French-Canadian Pentecostalism in Quebec. McPherson can therefore be credited with being the catalyst that gave dynamism to the Pentecostal sector of francophone Protestantism. If francophone Pentecostalism was given a 'jump start' or a 'shot in the arm' by McPherson, then due recognition needs to be accorded to her Montreal campaign of 1920. Because of the arrival of the Pentecostals and particularly McPherson, consideration should be given to adding another wave of expansion among francophone Protestants in the Protestant religious history of Quebec.

BIBLIOGRAPHY

Airhart, Phyllis D. "Ordering a New Nation and Reordering Protestantism, 1867–1914," in *The Canadian Protestant Experience 1760–1990*, edited by George Rawlyk, 98–138. Montreal-Kingston: McGill-Queen's University Press, 1990.

Baker, C.E. "Canada's Largest City is Visited with Floods of the 'Latter Rain.'" *The Pentecostal Testimony* January 1921, 2.

Bédard, Marc-André, *Les protestants en Nouvelle France*, Québec: Société Historique de Québec, 1978, (*Cahiers d'Histoire* 31).

Blumhofer, Edith L. *Aimee Semple McPherson: Everybody's Sister*. Grand Rapids: Eerdmans, 1993.

Cressman, Salome, "A Half Century of Pentecost in Quebec." *The Pentecostal Testimony*, September 1964): 4–7, 33.

Cressman, Salome and Gilles Gagnon. *Le Mouvement de Pentecôte au Québec: Bref aperçu historique*. Centre Évangélique, 1455 Ave. Papineau, Montréal, n.d.

_____. "Pentecost in Quebec." Pamphlet produced and distributed by the Missionary Department of the Pentecostal Assemblies of Canada. Mississauga, ON.

"Cure Not Lasting, Patient Relapsed." *The Montreal Gazette* 1 December 1920.

Di Giacomo, Michael. "Quebec Pentecostals, 1966–1995: The Making of a Revival." Ph.D. dissertation, Université Laval, 1999.

_____. "La vieille capitale: son importance pour la croissance du pentecôtisme canadien-français," *Etudes d'histoire religieuse* 70 (2004): 79–94.

_____. "FLITE: Religious Entrepreneurship in Quebec in the 1970s and 1980s," *Journal of the Canadian Church Historical Society*. 1 (Spring 2004): 49–88.

"Eight Hour Line of the Afflicted." *The Montreal Gazette* 6 December 1920.

Epstein, Daniel Mark. *Sister Aimee: The Life of Aimee Semple McPherson*. New York: Harcourt Brace, 1993.

"Esther James, Who Rose from Bed in Church, is Dead." *The Montreal Gazette* 8 December 1920.

Gagnon, André. Audio-taped interview, November 20 & 27, 1996.

Gagnon, Marie-Paule. Audio-taped interview, June 19, 1996.

Kulbeck, Gloria G. *What God Hath Wrought: A History of the Pentecostal Assemblies of Canada*. Toronto, Ontario: The Pentecostal Assemblies of Canada, 1958.

Lalonde, Jean-Louis. *Des loups dans la bergerie: les protestants de langue française au Québec, 1534–2000*. Montréal: Fides, 2002.

Larin, Robert. *Brève histoire des protestants en Nouvelle-France et au Québec: XVIᵉ - XIXᵉ siècles*. Saint-Alphonse-de-Granby, Québec: Éditions de la Paix, *Patrimoine 2*, 1998.

Lewis, Don. "Evangelical Renewal in French Canada." *His Dominion: A bulletin of the Canadian Theological Seminary*, 9 (1983): 3–14.

Linteau, Paul-André, René Durocher, Jean-Claude Robert, François Richard. *Histoire du Québec contemporain: De la Confédération à la crise (1867–1929)*. Montréal: Boréal, 1989.

Lougheed, Richard. "The Controversial Conversion of Charles Chiniquy." Ph.D. dissertation, University of Montreal, 1994.

Mark A. Noll. *Between Faith and Criticism: Evangelicals, Scholarship, and the Bible in America*. Grand Rapids: Baker, 1991.

Miller, Thomas. "The Significance of A.H. Argue for Pentecostal Historiography." *Pneuma* 8 (1986): 120–158.

_____. *Canadian Pentecostals: A History of the Pentecostal Assemblies of Canada*. Mississauga: Full Gospel Publishing House, 1994.

Peach, Wesley. "Evangelism – Distinctly Quebec," in *Reclaiming a Nation*, editedy by A. Motz, 153–176. Richmond: Church Leadership Library, 1990.

"Priest Sent Note to Woman Healer." *The Montreal Gazette* 27 November 1920.

Remon, Denis, ed. *L'identité des protestants francophones au Québec: 1834–1997*. Les cahiers scientifiques 94, 65e congrès de l'Associations canadienne-française pour l'avancement des sciences, Université du Québec à Trois-Rivières, 14–15 May 1997.

Rudd, Douglas. "The Great Montreal Revival." *The Pentecostal Testimony* February, 1995, 8–9.

Rust, Ronald. "Les premières églises pentecôtistes françaises à Montréal." Unpublished paper. Faculté de théologie évangélique, 1998.

Scorgie, Glen G. "Twentieth-Century Evangelistic Renewal in French Canada." Vancouver: Regent College, 1980.

Smith, Glenn. "Towards a Contextual Praxis for the Urban French World: A Case Study to Engage Christian Direction, Inc. with Montreal, Quebec." D.Min. dissertation, Lombard, Illinois: Northwestern Baptist Theological Seminary, 1991.

_____. "The History of French Protestantism in Quebec." *Ecumenism* 120 (1995): 16–22.

_____. ed. *Histoire du protestantisme au Québec depuis 1960*. Québec: Les editions La Clairière, 1999.

Strout Richard E. "The Latter Years of the Board of French Evangelization of the Presbyterian Church in Canada: 1895–1912." M.A. thesis, Lennoxville, Quebec: Bishop's University, 1986.

Sutton, Matthew Avery, *Aimee Semple McPherson and the Resurrection of Christian America*. Harvard University Press, 2007.

Wade, H. Mason, "Political Trends." In *Essais sur le Québec contemporain (Essays on Contemporary Quebec)*, edited by Jean-Charles Falardeau, 145–146. Québec: Presses de l'Université Laval, 1953.

"Woman Missioner Drew Penitents." *The Montreal Gazette* 18 November 1920.

CHAPTER EIGHT

AIMEE SEMPLE MCPHERSON AND THE RECONFIGURATION OF METHODISM IN AMERICA, 1916-1922

David Michel

INTRODUCTION

Aimee Semple McPherson was one of the most important religious figures of twentieth-century America. Despite her ministerial work as healing evangelist and denominational leader, her impact on mainline Christianity has remained obscure. Scholars of American religious history have wrongly assumed that all early Pentecostals maintained an adversarial or dismissive attitude toward other Christians and vice versa. Generally, the historiographic trend has been to claim that Pentecostalism was rejected by the majority of the Protestant churches. In 1979 Robert M. Anderson argued that "the old-line denominations were little affected by the Pentecostal movement" and that there was no "identifiable Pentecostal faction within any."[1] Anderson implies that early Pentecostals were much ignored by the more established churches. Though Matthew A. Sutton has recently argued that McPherson impacted the emerging fundamentalist movement, historical scholarship since the publication of Anderson's work has not focused on the linkages between McPherson and liberal churches.[2]

In this chapter I re-examine the interactions between McPherson and ministers belonging to the Methodist Episcopal Church (MEC), the MEC South (MECS), and related bodies. In doing so, I go against the thrust of previous historical scholarship by arguing that McPherson made significant contributions to early twentieth-century Methodism by incarnating a practice of camp meeting spirituality that strengthened the MEC evangelistic push, offering individuals an alternative way of being Methodist through faith healing and Spirit baptism, and reforming congregational liturgy. Both Methodism and Pentecostalism

---

[1] Anderson, *Vision of the Disinherited*, 141.
[2] Sutton, *Aimee Semple McPherson and the Resurrection of Christian America*.

were reconfigured through the ministry of this Canadian-born evangelist. First, I will sketch a survey of McPherson's early ministry followed by a discussion of the importance of her Canadian roots and Wesleyan heritage, and her contributions to American Methodism. Last, I will propose that the findings of this chapter call for a reorientation of research on Methodism, the Holiness movement, Fundamentalism, and Pentecostalism in the United States.[3]

SURVEY OF MCPHERSON'S EARLY MINISTRY

Aimee Kennedy (1890–1944) was born near Ingersoll, a town located in the Province of Ontario, Canada. In 1908 she married Robert Semple who earlier came into contact with Pentecostalism through the Hebden Mission in Toronto. The couple were later granted ministerial credentials by William Durham from Chicago. They lived in Canada and the United States before starting missionary work in China in 1910. After the death of her husband, the young widow returned to America, married Harold McPherson, and developed an evangelistic ministry. In 1919 McPherson was licensed as an evangelist by the Assemblies of God (AG), which she left after two years. "Sister Aimee" preached in more than 100 cities between 1917 and 1923 and achieved legendary status during her lifetime. She published a paper, *The Bridal Call*, and settled in Los Angeles, where she organized the Echo Park Evangelistic Association. She later founded her own congregation (1923), a radio station, and a new denomination, the Church of the Foursquare Gospel (CFG). By 1933 the CFG reported 520 ministers and 278 churches.[4]

---

[3] The focus of this chapter is on the Methodist Episcopal Church [North], although mention is also made of the Methodist Episcopal Church South and the Methodist Protestant Church. In 1830 a dissident group formed the Methodist Protestant Church over issues of lay representation. In 1844 a significant number of southerners supporting slaveholding left the Methodist Episcopal Church. The northern branch was later referred to as the Methodist Episcopal Church (MEC) or the Methodist Episcopal Church North; the southern branch became the Methodist Episcopal Church South (MECS).

[4] See Blumhofer, *Aimee Semple McPherson*; Sutton, *Aimee Semple McPherson*. Aimee Semple McPherson is referred to as 'McPherson,' 'Aimee,' and 'Sister Aimee' throughout the paper. The chapter's main source of biographical information on McPherson is her autobiography, *This is That*. Generally, data taken from this source are not referenced throughout this study in order to reduce the number of citations. Sources for data on McPherson that are not taken from the 1923 edition of *This Is That* are properly referenced. Interpretive comments that are not attributed are from this writer.

McPherson did more than preach the gospel south of the Canadian border; she also contributed to the reshaping of Methodism, which was becoming more formal or 'mainline.' Sister Aimee preached in at least eleven Methodist churches in five states and the District of Columbia between 1916 and 1922. The location of churches she preached in are as follows: Corona (1916) and New York City, New York (1918 and 1919); Baltimore (1919); Washington, D.C. (1920); Alton, Illinois (1920); Philadelphia, Pennsylvania (1920); Normal Heights and San Diego, California (1921); Rochester (1921 and 1922).[5] Methodists who attended McPherson campaigns in non-Methodist locales in Denver (1921 and 1922) and St. Louis (1921) were also influenced by this female evangelist. Sister Aimee spoke in tongues, baptized new converts by immersion, and did not antagonize her mainline followers. Pastors Charles Shreve from the District of Columbia and Louis Carter from Missouri were impressed that Aimee pointed people, even the sick, to Jesus Christ and not to herself.[6] However, there was more to Aimee's wide appeal among Methodists in America.

HER CANADIAN ROOTS AND PENTECOSTAL IDENTITY

McPherson received a lot of preparation for her ministry among American Methodists thanks to her Wesleyan heritage and the early support given her by Methodists or former Methodists in Canada. This in turn would lead her to reinterpret Pentecostalism as a version of Methodism. Both her father, James Kennedy, and her mother, Minnie, came from a long line of Methodists going all the way back to the time of John Wesley. In Ontario, her father directed a local choir and taught the young girl about acts of power in past Methodism. Minnie also

---

[5] See McPherson, "In the John Street Methodist Episcopal Church," and *The Story of My Life*; Feidler, "Mrs. McPherson's Meetings in Baltimore, MD"; Leech, "Personal Testimony." The names of the churches in which McPherson held meetings are: Corona: The Swedish MEC (1916); New York City: John Street MEC (1918 and 1919); Baltimore: an unnamed Methodist church and St. Paul Methodist Protestant Church; Washington: McKendree MEC; Alton: First Methodist MEC (1920); Philadelphia: Hancock Memorial MEC and Mt. Airy MEC (1920); Normal Heights: Normal Heights MEC; San Diego: First MEC (1921); and Rochester: Asbury MEC (1921 and 1922). At times McPherson held meetings in several locations in the same city during the same campaign. She would preach once or twice in local churches while holding larger meetings in other venues in the same town. McPherson did not report meetings in congregations affiliated to the MECS during the period under consideration.

[6] Carter, "Days of Miracles Not Passed."

made sure that her daughter was rooted in the history of the Salvation Army, an offshoot of British Methodism. Mrs. Kennedy had been raised by a mother who shared with her how people used to be 'slain in the Spirit' during the time of Wesley.[7] McPherson's mother later joined the Army, and had her infant daughter dedicated in a Salvationist service. Minnie also shared contemporary stories of how people were falling under the power in Salvationist circles. Her daughter attended the Army barracks, which led the young girl to claim a Salvationist identity.

By observing women, like her mother and the Brigadier's wife leading prayer services and testimony meetings, Aimee learned a lot that she would put to use in her own evangelistic ministry. She later stopped attending the local barracks and attended the Salford Methodist Church. Methodism provided her plenty of opportunities to be exposed to revivalism because experiential religion had remained the norm among Methodists in late nineteenth-century Ontario. Furthermore, emotionalism must have been more pronounced in the rural area where the Kennedys lived. In fact, once a revivalist unsuccessfully begged Aimee to come to the altar for salvation.[8]

Through listening to her parents, attending Sunday school, and reading Wesley's writings, McPherson learned much about the history of Methodism before leaving Ontario. Yet McPherson's actual knowledge of the Methodism was only intellectual, because she was never converted under Methodist auspices in Canada. In 1907 she finally experienced Christian conversion, and the following year, received the baptism of the Holy Spirit through the ministry of Pentecostal evangelist Semple, her future husband.[9] Aimee's debt to Methodism increased

---

[7] The terms 'to be slain in the Spirit' or 'to fall under the power' usually refer to a mystical experience wherein someone under the influence of the Holy Spirit falls and remains motionless, lying as if dead for a period of time. 'Wesleyan heritage,' here, refers to Aimee's descent from parents affiliated with Wesleyan groups and her upbringing in the Salvation Army and the Methodist Church in Canada. In Aimee's mind the Salvation Army was part of Methodism and her understanding of her Wesleyan heritage would include her familiarity with the Salvation Army. In the three editions of *This Is That* (1919, 1921, 1923) she claimed that a Salvationist minister was in her parents' home when she returned converted, while she later reported that the minister was a Methodist in *Story of My Life*.

[8] Blumhofer, *Aimee Semple McPherson*; Semple, *The Lord's Dominion*.

[9] Charles F. Parham was the first to link the baptism of the Holy Spirit with speaking in tongues. As a revivalist and founder of the Pentecostal movement, he widely promoted his new ideas throughout the South and Midwest. William J. Seymour, a former follower of Parham, led the Azusa Mission in spreading the Pentecostal movement

due to the early support that people with a Wesleyan affiliation extended to her first husband. In London, Ontario William H. Wortman, a Methodist class leader welcomed the holding of meetings in his home by Durham and the Semples.[10] Later, after claiming the divine healing of a dislocated ankle, McPherson 'submitted' to God and discovered her calling to healing ministry in an Ontario service led by Lemuel Hall, a former southern Methodist and the pastor of the North Avenue Mission in Chicago.[11]

McPherson's strong awareness of her Wesleyan heritage led her to first link Methodism to Pentecostalism as a young Pentecostal convert living under her parents' roof in 1908. Awaiting a disappointed Minnie coming to pick her up right after she [Aimee] had been slain in the Spirit, the young girl rationalized that the emotional experience she went through resembled reported phenomena that had occurred in past Salvationist and Methodist history. I take this to mean that the young convert concluded that the baptism of the Holy Spirit must be 'normal' since respectable Wesleyans were open to similar manifestations. In a way McPherson was already recasting Pentecostalism via the doctrine of Spirit baptism as a version of old-fashioned Methodism. She was probably the only Pentecostal to appeal to Wesley and Methodism in order to explicate the phenomenon of glossolalic baptism. Her appeal to ecclesiastical history to justify the current practice of Pentecostal baptism was rare within Pentecostalism. Pentecostals were biblical primitivists and felt that the New Testament alone should serve as a canon for their doctrinal distinctives.

McPherson's appreciation of ecclesiastical tradition also stemmed from her roots in Canada, where unity among Protestant groups was

---

throughout the United States and overseas. From the beginning Pentecostalism claimed that speaking in tongues was the 'Bible evidence' of the baptism of the Holy Spirit and strongly promoted faith healing, a practice that had already been popularized before 1900, along with the right of women to preach. William Durham, who was based in Chicago, received the baptism of the Holy Spirit at Azusa, and later conferred ministerial credentials on Robert and Aimee Semple. 'Baptism of the Holy Spirit,' 'baptism of the Spirit,' 'baptism of the Holy Ghost,' 'Spirit baptism,' and 'Pentecostal baptism' all refer to the same phenomenon. The word 'Pentecostal' derives from Pentecost, a Jewish feast that was being celebrated when the Spirit of God fell on the early Christians, according to Acts 2 (Robeck 2006). Members of the Holiness movement consider those who are sanctified or baptized in the Spirit (without speaking in tongues) to be Spirit-filled. Likewise, Pentecostals claim that those who have received the baptism of the Spirit and speak in tongues are Spirit-filled. The terminology 'Spirit-filled' is used by both groups.

[10] McPherson, "Methodism and Pentecost;" Blumhofer, *Aimee Semple McPherson*.
[11] Blumhofer.

cultivated.[12] After receiving a warm welcome by Wortman and Hall, Aimee was further persuaded that Methodists were receptive to Pentecostalism and continued to hold that the biblical concept of Spirit baptism was a Methodist doctrine that needed to be rediscovered. In Philadelphia she so excelled at convincing others of the Methodist character of Pentecostalism that a district superintendent issued her an exhorter's license during a revival in the Mt. Airy MEC in 1920.[13] This Pentecostal evangelist flaunted her Methodist credentials, even after she was ordained to the Pentecostal ministry by the AG. It was this self-consciousness and self-presentation as a Pentecostal Methodist that set the stage for Sister Aimee to make major contributions to American Methodism.

McPherson's Contributions to American Methodism

As a preacher Sister Aimee was profoundly shaped by the religious training she received in her home country. There, she learned that conversion was experiential, that one's worship of God could be emotional and that women could lead prayer meetings and do altar work. Initially, she claimed to have found no female preachers in Canada who could serve as models, except Evangeline Booth, a Salvation Army commander (1896–1906). Eventually, her first husband shared with her about the important ministry of Ellen Hebden, a female pioneer of Pentecostalism in Canada.[14] In America McPherson's ministry was reaffirmed by her acquaintance with female evangelists Maria Woodworth-Etter and Carrie Judd Montgomery in Indianapolis (1917) and Oakland (1918), respectively.[15] Influenced by her Wesleyan heritage, Sister Aimee was poised to impact the Methodist culture of various Christians south of the Great Lakes.

Aimee made three major contributions to American Methodism. One major and complex contribution McPherson made was the promotion of what I call 'camp meeting spirituality,' which embraced emotional worship, experiential conversion, public testimonies, and revivalism. Kenneth O. Brown argues in *Holy Ground* that Methodists

---

[12] Blumhofer.

[13] McPherson, "Methodism and Pentecost;" Sutton, "'Between the Refrigerator and the Wildfire.'"

[14] McPherson, *The Story of My Life*; Miller, "The Canadian 'Azusa.'"

[15] McPherson, *This is That*, 1919; McPherson, *The Story of My Life*.

in Georgia and the Carolinas deserve to be viewed as the founders of camp meetings because they held such activities before 1800. Yet camp meeting spirituality did not emerge in camp meetings because emotional worship was already reported in the early years of American Methodism by Francis Asbury and other chroniclers. Nonetheless, camp meetings encapsulated the Methodist ethos and kept it alive.[16]

Typically, a camp meeting was an outdoor service whose attendees camped on the grounds throughout the time—ranging from days to weeks—that services were held. Liturgical exercises involved singing, prayer meetings, preaching, and testimonials on salvation, sanctification, and repentance, and the sacraments. The peculiar ethos of camp meetings centred on the altar service, in which sinners and backsliders were asked to come forward and kneel at the mourner's bench, usually after sermons on hell or heaven. Services were punctuated by sighs, groans, moans, weeping, and shouting of 'Hallelujah,' 'Amen,' 'Praise God,' and the like. The physicality of the worship was demonstrated by people falling down, having convulsions, sobbing, prostrating themselves, and clapping hands. By 1820 Methodists had founded about 1,000 annual encampments and the widespread use of camp meetings accounted for the growth of the MEC to one million members before the Civil War. After the hostilities between the Union and the Confederacy subsided, the National Camp Meeting Association for the Promotion of Holiness (NAPH) revived camp meetings. Between 1870 and 1894 the NAPH conducted fifty-two camp meetings and was supported by the following bishops: Randolph Foster (1820–1903), Isaac Joyce (1836–1905), Willard Mallalieu (1828–1911), James Fitzgerald (1837–1907), and Joseph Berry (1856–1931).[17]

Despite the continuing work of the NAPH and the continuing use of campgrounds well into the twentieth century, old-fashioned

---

[16] Wood, *The Meaning of Pentecost in Early Methodism*.

[17] See Sweet, *Methodism in American History*; Johnson, *The Frontier Camp Meeting*; Jones, *Perfectionist Persuasion*; Brown, *Holy Ground*. The National Camp Meeting Association for the Promotion of Holiness (NAPH) was founded by northern Methodist preachers in 1867. But the NAPH did not create the Holiness movement; Phoebe Palmer of New York is generally considered the holiness pioneer in the MEC before the Civil War. In this paper I take the Holiness movement to be inclusive of anyone to whom one, some, or all the following situations apply: supports the idea that the believer needs to be sanctified; personally goes through a specific experience of sanctification after conversion; or makes holiness a lifestyle. After the Civil War some American Methodists supported a lifestyle of holiness without asking for a specific experience of sanctification after conversion.

spirituality was dying off in turn of the century Methodism. However, Holiness Methodists yearned for the camp meeting spirituality that they had enjoyed so much. In 1903 James M. Buckley, editor of the *New York Christian Advocate*, said that he had not heard "a real sermon" on the new birth in twenty years.[18] Bishop Foster also regretted the disappearance of holy enthusiasm: "Formerly every Methodist attended class and gave testimony of experimental religion. Now the class-meeting is attended by very few, and in many churches abandoned.... Formerly nearly every Methodist prayed, testified, or exhorted in prayer-meeting. Now but very few are heard. Formerly shouts and praises were heard; now such demonstrations of holy enthusiasm and joy are regarded as fanaticism."[19]

In cities where McPherson was later to preach, ministers and laypeople also decried the dearth of spiritual vitality. In Philadelphia, Leander W. Munhall, an outstanding evangelist, complained that people were admitted to membership without a declared experience of conversion and another parishioner confessed that he had not seen six penitents at the altar of his local church in fourteen years. In St. Louis, MECS Pastor Morse Markley complained that the old-fashioned altar revival was almost a thing of the past.[20] Holiness leaders used literature in an attempt to reverse the declining interest in traditional spirituality. Bishop Berry published several revival songbooks between 1894 and 1914 and Bishop Mallalieu released *Why, When, and How of Revivals* (1901) and *The Fullness of the Blessing of the Gospel of Christ* (1903), which shouted clarion calls for revival. In addition to asking for a return to traditional spirituality, the Holiness movement welcomed female preachers and thus prepared Methodism for the future Pentecostal ministry of McPherson.[21]

Aimee did not build campgrounds, but she brought to the fore a spirituality that used to be celebrated in the woods and recreated that atmosphere in sanctuaries of brick and mortar in urban America. In so doing, this daughter of a Methodist choirmaster acted with careful intent because she perceived that American Methodists were nostalgic

---

[18] Munhall, *Breakers! Methodism Adrift*, 41.

[19] Munhall, 38–39.

[20] For Leander W. Munhall's stand on sanctification see his work, *The Convert and His Relations*. Also see, Munhall, *Breakers*; McPherson, "Methodism and Pentecost;" Blumhofer, "St Louis Host to 1921 Salvation-Healing Meetings."

[21] Brasher, *The Sanctified South*.

about their loss of power.[22] McPherson promoted experiential religion by making altar calls for salvation, spiritual restoration, and Spirit baptism. Holiness pastors, such as Shreve and others, welcomed Pentecostalism because they themselves had gone through experiential conversion and sanctification.[23] Emotional conversion was evidenced by tears of repentance or of joy. Aimee's own conversion in Ontario had been experiential, and therefore she asked no less from her converts.[24] In both San Diego and St. Louis (1921) Methodists served as altar workers who prayed for those seeking salvation. At times, Sister Aimee asked nominal church members who did not recall to have been through a process of conversion to commit their lives to Christ. During the Hancock revival in Philadelphia, Pastor Amos Crowell noted that "folks were weeping their way through to conscious salvation."[25] McPherson's support in Philadelphia and Baltimore, and probably elsewhere was strengthened by the fundamentalist leanings existing within Methodism. Her call for salvation assumed the depravity of mankind through the Fall of Adam and her healing ministry, based on the fact that the historical Jesus performed miracles, pushed for a literal reading of the Gospels.[26] The fundamentalists, which included people like Munhall, refused to accommodate themselves to the incipient modernism spreading among liberals and in the seminaries. By supporting McPherson, Methodists stood for fundamentalism and rejected modernism.[27]

Worship in McPherson's meetings was demonstrative and the audience felt free to shout. In several instances, those who were supernaturally healed released shouts of joy. At other times, miracles led the crowds to burst out in spontaneous praise to God.[28] In one occasion, after observing the healing of a twenty-five-year-old man who had

---

[22] McPherson, *This is That*, 1919.

[23] Shreve, "Jesus the Same Yesterday, Today, and Forever;" Lautz, "How I Received the Baptism of the Holy Ghost." John Wesley and Methodism made the doctrine and experience of sanctification, also sometimes called 'the baptism of the Holy Spirit', the distinctive of their religion. McPherson, who vigorously called people to secure the baptism of the Spirit, also asked seekers to forsake worldly behaviors such as smoking tobacco, playing cards, and theater going, and the like. This kind of preaching was viewed by holiness Methodists to be in agreement with Methodist discipline. See Downey.

[24] McPherson, "The Bible Baptism in the Bible Way," 19.

[25] McPherson, *This is That*, 1923, 229.

[26] Sweet, *Methodism in American History*.

[27] Sutton, "'Between the Refrigerator and the Wildfire.'"

[28] McPherson, "News Paper Clippings."

been deaf, dumb, and lame since age two, the spectators expressed their admiration by saying 'Hallelujah.'[29] In Denver 12,000 observers shouted, clapped, and cheered after a man was healed from blindness after being saved and praying to God by himself. Aimee also conversed with the people, especially after individual healings, when she would ask them to identify the source of the healing, to which the audience responded with the classic praise expressions, 'Hallelujah,' 'Jesus,' or 'Glory to God!' 'Praise Jesus.'

The physicality of worship was also demonstrated by the unusual phenomenon of 'falling,' which was linked to receiving the Spirit baptism. Aimee fell down when she was baptized in the Spirit in her home country, and in her first Methodist revival in Corona, three people were 'slain under the power.' Throughout her campaigns it was common for seekers to be 'slain in the Spirit.' It is possible that those Methodists who had been familiar with camp meeting spirituality, were preconditioned to fall while seeking the Pentecostal baptism. During the Hancock revival, Aimee noted that most seekers "seemed to go down in good old-fashioned John Wesley Methodist fashion," unlike others she had observed before that time.[30] In Baltimore, ministers praying with and for people seeking Spirit baptism viewed the falling of seekers as similar to what they had seen in past American Methodism.

In addition to emotional conversions and worship, McPherson established prayer meetings and public testimonies, thanks to her Salvationist training. She called her prayer sessions 'tarrying meetings' whose purpose was for people to seek out and wait for the baptism of the Spirit. In such meetings, often held in small rooms, seekers would pray and sing until they began to speak in tongues. Other special prayer meetings sought the healing of sick bodies. Aimee reinvented public testifying by scheduling testimony meetings in her campaigns. These meetings, held both inside and outside church auditoriums, provided space for people to share in public how they were saved, healed, or had received the Pentecostal baptism. As people testified to the miracles accomplished in their lives or those of their family members, the audience often responded with handclapping, which of course contributed to making the service more demonstrative. To older Holiness Methodists, the young female evangelist acted like an exhorter, her

---

[29] McPherson, *This is That*, 308–309.
[30] McPherson, *This is That*, 224.

testimony meeting resembled the disappearing traditional class meeting, and her services were good old camp meeting services, which were needed to revive Methodism.

McPherson's revivalism was in harmony with the emerging call for new converts within the MEC. She interfaced with a Methodism that needed to increase the denomination's membership. Calls for a strong evangelistic push led the General Conference to establish the Commission on Aggressive Evangelism (COE) in 1904. Bishops Mallalieu, Joyce, and Henry Spellmeyer were chosen to lead this very important venture. Again the Holiness movement, through Mallalieu and Joyce, contributed the manpower needed to revitalize the denomination. The COE's vision was to win a large number of converts and its objective sought the holding of tent and open-air meetings and special revival services through the cooperation of pastors and presiding elders.[31]

During 1908–1912 the Commission on Evangelism (CE) encouraged pastors to preach holiness and urged them to be the main evangelists in the Methodist system—i.e., they were to serve as the main channel through which evangelism should take place.[32] A worldwide prayer league was organized with 20,000 Methodists committing to pray for the harvest of souls. Thanks to the CE, a net annual increase in membership between 1905 and 1912 ranged from 64,000 to 78,000. In 1913 the annual growth in membership reached more than 150,000, although this declined to 100,000 by 1915. In all, Methodism gained more than 400,000 members from 1913 to 1915. The MEC looked for a net annual increase of 250,000 new converts for 1916, the year Aimee preached in the MEC in Corona.[33] At the General Conference of 1916, the episcopate called for the period 1918–1919 to be called "a time of Jubilee for Missions" and urged "pastors and people to give themselves to the bringing of lost men to God and their development in Christian life and service." Every layperson was encouraged to preach without

[31] Hingeley, *Journal of the Twenty-Fourth Delegated General Conference of the Methodist Episcopal Church*, 1904; Hingeley, *Journal of the Twenty-Fifth Delegated General Conference of the Methodist Episcopal Church*, 1908.

[32] The figures given are for the worldwide Methodist Episcopal Church because the mandate of the CE was to increase the MEC both at home and abroad. In 1908 the Commission on Aggressive Evangelism became the Commission on Evangelism. See Hingeley, 1908.

[33] Hingeley, *Journal of the Twenty-Sixth Delegated General Conference of the Methodist Episcopal Church*, 1912; Locke, *Journal of the Twenty-Seventh Delegated General Conference of the Methodist Episcopal Church*.

waiting for ordination.[34] In 1916 the MEC set a goal of one million new converts for the next four years, converted the CE into the Department of Evangelism integrated into the Board of Home Missions and Church Extension.[35]

By the end of 1916, the MEC had developed a stronger missionary orientation and expected that pastors and lay leaders, presiding elders, and lay people work with an evangelistic mind for the mass harvest of souls. Coincidentally, some of the people who were involved with the CE would assist McPherson's work within the MEC. Of course, the first to be mentioned is Bishop Berry born in Ontario, Canada. In Ontario Berry grew up in the Primitive Methodist Church which had been founded to promote camp meetings. He later served the resident-bishop of the Philadelphia Conference before and after Aimee preached there. Berry created a climate that made district superintendents and ministers receptive to Pentecostalism in the City of Brotherly Love.[36]

Superintendent John G. Wilson, also a member of the CE, welcomed a McPherson campaign within his district. After observing her charismatic ministry in the Hancock revival, Wilson supported the Mt. Airy meeting, transferred the Canadian evangelist into the American MEC, and made her into an evangelist of the worldwide Methodist communion by granting her an exhorter certificate. In Washington the presiding elder supported McPherson's and Shreve's continuing Pentecostal services in McKendree. District superintendents were required to give official approval for revival meetings by evangelists from outside their conferences, and their approval freed local ministers to support any local church hosting the evangelist. The support given by presiding elders opened the door for McPherson's meetings to be publicized throughout America and overseas through Methodist papers such as the *New York Christian Advocate*, the *Eastern Methodist*, and the *Central Christian Advocate*.[37] The pastor of Mt. Airy MEC so identified with Sister Aimee that he welcomed her to preach the regular Sunday morning sermon.[38]

---

[34] Locke, *Journal of the Twenty-Seventh Delegated General Conference of the Methodist Episcopal Church*, 199, 203, 204.

[35] Locke, *Journal of the Twenty-Seventh Delegated General Conference of the Methodist Episcopal Church*.

[36] Harmon, *The Encyclopedia of World Methodism*.

[37] Carter, "Days of Miracles Not Passed."

[38] See Hingeley, *Journal of the Twenty-Sixth Delegated General Conference of the Methodist Episcopal Church*, 1912; Downey, *Doctrines and Discipline of the Methodist Episcopal Church*, 1916; Gehrett, "Mount Airy Revival Meetings" McPherson,

It is important to note that McPherson did not rent Methodist church buildings in order to preach her crusades. Rather, pastors invited her to come and revitalize their congregations. In many cases she found herself preaching in congregations that claimed more seats than members. McKendree had a capacity of 800, but the membership was 246 in 1920. Shreve complained that McKendree did not have a revival for ten years and was praying for one when she first met McPherson. Her McKendree campaign increased the membership by 300.[39] Similarly, Hancock seated 900, but the number of parishioners was only 600 in 1920. During the Hancock meetings, Sister Aimee won 500 converts, of which 100 joined the church. Lay leaders, such as Sunday school superintendents and councilmen, also challenged by the CE, sought and received the baptism of the Spirit during McPherson's meetings. McPherson identified herself as a preacher of Pentecost, encouraged her converts to join the church of their choice, and did not turn her AG membership into an icon. In other words, she was preaching Pentecost and not Pentecostal denominationalism and sectarianism.[40]

The second contribution of McPherson was offering an alternative way of being Methodist, which involved preaching and living with power, the baptism of the Spirit, and faith healing. A revisionist understanding of the baptism of the Spirit, which was circulating within Methodist circles, prepared the way for the new Pentecostal message. We know that before McPherson left Canada, Mallalieu had promoted the idea that the baptism of the Holy Ghost was given for the purpose of soul winning. By 1920 B.F. Atkinson, an MECS elder, reached the conclusion that the baptism of the Holy Ghost was still available today and granted power to the believer.[41] Bishop Berry took a similar line by

---

"Methodism and Pentecost;" Reiff, "Another Methodist Church Receives Pentecost." McPherson referred to the official welcome by Methodist leaders in the Mt. Airy MEC as "an American renewal of church fellowship," which suggests that she was perceived as a Methodist from Canada by the leaders of the Philadelphia Conference. See McPherson, "Methodism and Pentecost." "Presiding elder" and "district superintendent" refer to the same position, a leader put over a group of churches in a district. The full name of the Philadelphia district superintendent is sometimes misspelled as "John J. Wilson" in This Is That, 1923; the correct spelling is given in the same book in page 230 and corroborated by the Minutes of the Annual Conferences.

[39] See Reiff, "Another Methodist Church Receives Pentecost;" Shreve, "'Lord, Go Among Us,' The Coming of the Spirit to a Washington, D.C." "Methodist Church" (reprinted, 2000).

[40] Sutton, "'Between the Refrigerator and the Wildfire.'"

[41] Mallalieu, "The Need for An Evangelistic Ministry;" Atkinson, "What is 'Bible Holiness.'"

claiming that every revival started with Pentecost and only those who had been filled with the Holy Ghost should be engaged in revivals. Berry went as far as calling for people to 'tarry until the tongues appear.' In this, the holiness faction was getting close to glossolalic Pentecostalism.[42] McPherson was in agreement with Berry whom she called our "beloved bishop." McPherson and Berry, who perhaps met each other, were two Canadian ministers pushing for a revival in Methodism, based on the Wesleyan upbringing acquired in their home country.[43] Obviously McPherson's theological creativity was demonstrated in linking the baptism of the Spirit to Wesley by implying that the Spirit was responsible for the phenomenon of people falling down both in Wesley's meetings and her services. She quoted widely from Wesley in her sermons, and if the quotations originated from the later Wesley who had affirmed the importance of the gifts of the Spirit, then educated Methodist ministers would have found it difficult to reject her message. McPherson insinuated that Wesley would have endorsed Pentecostalism and thus was able to convince Methodist leaders of the respectability of the Pentecostal religion.[44]

Aimee's charismatic and intelligent leadership led many ministers to seek and receive the Pentecostal baptism during her revivals; those who did not receive Spirit baptism then determined to seek it after the departure of the Canadian evangelist. L.S. Shires, a MECS elder from Virginia, surprisingly reported himself cured of an "unwillingness to speak out boldly for Christ" after receiving the Pentecostal baptism during the 1920 Dayton meeting.[45] Someone who observed Shreve's preaching after he had received the Pentecostal baptism described him as "a cyclone of divine power."[46] Edward C. Fintel, a MEC minister from Nebraska, found himself preaching with "mighty power" in his home church the Sunday after attending the Denver campaign in 1922.[47]

---

[42] Berry, "First Steps in a Revival."

[43] McPherson refers to Bishop Berry as "our beloved Bishop Berry," which suggests she may have met him, in Philadelphia perhaps. See *This Is That* 1923, 234.

[44] See McPherson, "Methodism and Pentecost;" Wood, *The Meaning of Pentecost in Early Methodism*. The Wesley citations were not recorded; however, A.B. Cox's article in the *Bridal Call*, 1920 rightly reported that Wesley noted that people in the Valley of Dauphiny spoke in tongues in late seventeenth-century France. If Aimee had access to this Wesley source, perhaps she used it in preaching.

[45] McPherson, *This is That*, 1923, 209.

[46] Reiff, "Another Methodist Church Receives Pentecost."

[47] McPherson, *This is That*, 1923, 443.

Lay believers were eligible to benefit from the alternative Methodist spirituality offered by McPherson. Her doctrine of Spirit baptism (Acts 1–2), which she derived from her first husband, claimed that salvation and Spirit baptism should be preached side by side and that being baptized in the Spirit was a normal way of being Christian. McPherson understood her job was to educate the church universal about the availability of Spirit baptism with speaking in tongues. According to the female evangelist, the baptism of the Spirit endues the believer with power, equips the soul for service, and provides power to pray, testify, and overcome. Many Christians, especially, lay leaders working in Sunday school and church administration, received the baptism in McPherson's meetings.[48]

Aimee promoted the practice of faith healing, which Methodists endorsed without renouncing their denominational connections. Overall, Methodist denominations did not teach faith healing, though regional holiness associations held healing services in their camp meetings. By the early-twentieth century, faith healing had already won the support of MEC pastors such as D.N.F. Blakeney and Frank Thompson of New York. McPherson's evangelistic work contributed to a larger acceptance of divine healing among Methodists. She first observed cases of faith healing during her first husband's ministry in London, Ontario. Her own experience of divine healing occurred in Chicago, where Durham successfully prayed for her broken ankle. She prayed for the sick for the first time at the Free Gospel Church in Corona in 1916 and three years later reported healings in a Methodist church for the first time in Baltimore.[49]

McPherson's usual procedure in a healing service was to first ask the afflicted to get saved, and then prod them to believe that Jesus could heal, and finally command the sickness to leave 'in the name of Jesus.' She also anointed the sick with oil while praying for them. Upon request, she applied holy oil to handkerchiefs that were sent by sick people unable to attend her services. Many claimed to have been healed by being prayed for, anointed with oil, or using anointed handkerchiefs.[50] By healing the sick, Sister Aimee forced lay observers to believe

---

[48] McPherson, *This is That*, 1919.

[49] McPherson, *This is That*, 1919; *The Story of My Life, 1951* Leech, "Personal Testimony;" Blakeney, "Methodist Minister Prays for the Sick;" Jones, *Perfectionist Persuasion*; Dayton, *Theological Roots of Pentecostalism*.

[50] McPherson, "The Bible Baptism in the Bible Way."

that God could perform miracles on or through them. For example, in Washington McKendree parishioners successfully prayed for the healing of a mute while Aimee was out. Aimee was instrumental in leading MEC ministers to endorse faith healing during her local campaigns. In San Diego, Lincoln Ferris, pastor of First MEC, prayed and anointed the sick. E.V. Bronson, a California pastor, accepted the doctrine of faith after attending the 1922 Oakland meeting. During the 1922 Denver campaign, Fintel prayed and anointed the sick with tangible results.[51]

The last contribution of McPherson to Methodism was the Pentecostalization of congregational liturgy. She influenced reluctant ministers, not only to accept faith healing and Spirit baptism for themselves, but also to preach these doctrines as they did the death and resurrection of Christ. Shreve had believed that God could heal but did not feel confident that he could obtain definite results if he prayed for others; as a result he never preached divine healing. After attending a McPherson meeting in the Lyric Theater in Baltimore, he started successful healing services in McKendree.[52] The Pentecostalization of Methodism also involved the continuous holding of tarrying meetings for those seeking the Pentecostal baptism. At the end of the Hancock revival, Pastor Crowell said, "A new day has dawned for our church. It can never be what it was before."[53] Likewise, Shreve, who later became the most aggressive Methodist follower of McPherson, led weekly tarrying services in McKendree after hosting a McPherson revival there.

McPherson's impact on congregational liturgy was amplified by the revivalists who disseminated the Pentecostal message throughout the Methodist world and the denominational itinerant system. Shreve attended the Hancock revival in Philadelphia where he prayed for those seeking the baptism of the Spirit. Sometime between 1920 and early 1922, he convinced Markley to pray for the sick in McKendree. In May 1922 Shreve preached a revival in St. Louis' Scruggs Memorial MECS, during which Pastor Markley, his family, and fifty other people received the Pentecostal baptism. After Shreve's departure Markley continued the tarrying services. Through Shreve, McPherson was

---

[51] Bronson, "A Methodist Minister's Impression."
[52] Reiff, "How Pentecost came to McKendree."
[53] McPherson, *This is That*, 1923, 270.

instrumental in introducing Pentecostal spirituality to a large number of ministers.[54]

The Methodist itinerant system transferred pastors periodically, and so those pastors who had endorsed or hosted McPherson's meetings found themselves in the position to spread the Pentecostal far beyond the congregations in which they had hosted McPherson revivals. A good many ministers continued to function as Methodist pastors even after speaking in tongues through McPherson's direct or indirect influence. In this group are found Shreve, Bronson, Shires and Markley. J.W. Tindall and Crowell remained in the MEC long after the McPherson revivals in their Philadelphia pastorates. Arthur C. Peck, who sponsored the two Denver campaigns retired from the Methodist ministry in 1928, while Markley took over five other churches after the St. Louis meeting and was serving as MECS pastor as late as 1952.[55]

Before concluding with the implications of the findings of this study, we must summarize the Methodist response to early Pentecostalism and the significance of McPherson's work among Wesleyans for the larger Pentecostal movement. McPherson reshaped Methodism by incarnating a camp meeting spirituality involving experiential religion, emotional worship, prayer meetings, and revivalism and by presenting faith healing and Pentecostal baptism as useful practices. In this, she was helped by the holiness sector that nurtured nostalgia for experiential religion, welcomed women preachers and faith healing, while developing and promoting a revisionist understanding of the baptism of the Spirit. McPherson's Wesleyan heritage and her skilful use of that heritage convinced many that her version of Pentecostalism was a more developed form of Methodism. Furthermore, lay and clerical Methodists sought those Pentecostal potentialities that could help them further their personal, professional, and denominational objectives. Presiding elders and pastors perceived that a Spirit baptism that granted empowerment for witnessing was exactly what they needed to

---

[54] Shreve, "Jesus the Same Yesterday, Today, and Forever;" Reiff, "How Pentecost came to McKendree" and "Another Methodist Church Receives Pentecost;" Markley, "Holy Ghost at Scruggs Memorial M.E."

[55] See Bronson, "A Methodist Minister's Impression;" Smith, *Minutes of the Annual Conferences of the Methodist Episcopal Church*, 1930; Clark, *Who's Who in Methodism*; Templin, *The Methodist Evangelical Churches and United Brethren Churches in the Rockies*. The last name of the pastor of the Mt. Airy MEC is misspelled as "Tindell" in *This Is That*, 1923. The correct spelling, Tindall, was verified in the *Minutes of the Annual Conferences*.

revive their ministry and pursue the CE mandate. The vision of the CE to have every layperson engaged in evangelism resonated well with the McPhersonian position that Spirit baptism was available to all for the purpose of evangelizing. McPherson's impact on Methodism doubled as a contribution to Pentecostalism because she offered to the world a version of Pentecostalism that was more nuanced and more focused on Christ than on human personalities and denominationalism.

The above findings call for the linkages between Methodism, the Holiness movement, Fundamentalism, and Pentecostalism to be re-examined. The conventional thesis that mainline churches rejected early Pentecostals, who were poor and uneducated, does not resonate with the fact that the MEC, largely a middle class organization, welcomed a Pentecostal woman evangelist.[56] Furthermore, a closer investigation of the Holiness response to Pentecostalism is called for, because the MEC, the mother holiness group, did not proscribe Pentecostalism, unlike other holiness denominations.[57] McPherson found a ready, fundamentalist group, which like its holiness counterpart, supported biblical literalism though it did not cause major splits in the Methodist denominations. Contra Sutton, I found that McPherson's impact on fundamentalism involved more than her alliances (with Lyman Stewart, William Jennings Bryan, Munhall, and Paul Rader) and her work through her Bible school and *The Bridal Call*.[58] By accepting McPherson's salvation message and healing miracles, pockets of Methodists clearly showed that they endorsed her popular version of fundamentalism and implicitly rejected the academic form of modernism promoted in many Methodist colleges, seminaries, and pulpits.

Finally, this chapter shows that early twentieth-century American Pentecostalism was much influenced by Canada. Recent scholarship tends to stress the global impact of American Pentecostalism and how several Canadians (Samuel Black, R.E. McAlister, and A.H. Argue) went to Los Angeles or Chicago to secure the Pentecostal baptism and how Alice Garrigus from Connecticut established the Pentecostal Assemblies of Newfoundland.[59] However, little attention has been devoted to the impact of Canadian Pentecostals on American

---

[56] Sweet, *Methodism in American History*.
[57] See Anderson, *Vision of the Disinherited*.
[58] See Sutton, "'Between the Refrigerator and the Wildfire.'"
[59] See Rudd, *When the Spirit Came upon Them*; Robeck, *The Azusa Street Mission and Revival*.

Pentecostalism. McPherson from Canada offered a non-sectarian version of Pentecostalism that intentionally reclaimed the Methodist heritage, engaged mainline Christians, and encouraged converts to join any Christian church not just a Pentecostal one. In this, she was ahead of the AG and the larger American Pentecostal movement.

BIBLIOGRAPHY

Atkinson, Rev. B.F. "What is 'Bible Holiness?'" *Methodist Quarterly Review* (1920): 438–51.

Anderson, Robert M. *Vision of the Disinherited*. New York: Oxford University Press, 1979.

Berry, Joseph. "First Steps in a Revival." *The Bridal Call* April 1920, 3. Reprint of *Christian Advocate*, Philadelphia.

Blakeney, D.N.F. "Methodist Minister Prays for the Sick." *The Pentecostal Evangel* October 1921, 9.

Blumhofer, Edith L. *Aimee Semple McPherson: Everybody's Sister*. Grand Rapids, Michigan: Eerdmans, 1990.

——. "St Louis Host to 1921 Salvation-Healing Meetings." *Assemblies of God Heritage* (1995): 5–7.

Brasher, J. Lawrence. *The Sanctified South: John Lakin Brasher and the Holiness Movement*. Urbana and Chicago: University of Holiness Press, 1994.

Bronson, E.V. "A Methodist Minister's Impression." *The Bridal Call* March 1923, 15–16.

Brown, Kenneth O. *Holy Ground: A Study of the American Camp Meeting*. New York and London: Garland Publishing, 1992.

Carter, Louis. "Days of Miracles Not Passed." *The Pentecostal Evangel* 17 September 1921, 8–9.

Clark, Elmer. *Who's Who in Methodism*. Chicago: The A.N. Marquis Company, 1952.

Cox, A.B. "The Baptism of the Holy Spirit. *The Bridal Call* March 1920, 17–18.

Dayton, Donald W. *Theological Roots of Pentecostalism*. Metuchen, NJ: Scarecrow Press, 1987.

Downey, David. *Doctrines and Discipline of the Methodist Episcopal Church*. New York: The Methodist Book Concern, 1916.

Feidler, James E. "Mrs. McPherson's Meetings in Baltimore, MD." *The Pentecostal Evangel* 7 February 1920, 11.

Gehrett, S.W. "Mount Airy Revival Meetings." *The Bridal Call* February 1921, 10–11.

Harmon, Nolan. *The Encyclopaedia of World Methodism*. Nashville: The United Methodist Publishing House, 1974.

Hingeley, Joseph. B. *Journal of the Twenty-Fourth Delegated General Conference of the Methodist Episcopal Church*. New York: Eaton and Mains, 1904.

——. *Journal of the Twenty-Fifth Delegated General Conference of the Methodist Episcopal Church*. New York. Eaton and Mains, 1908.

——. *Journal of the Twenty-Sixth Delegated General Conference of the Methodist Episcopal Church*. New York: The Methodist Book Concern, 1912.

Johnson, Charles A. *The Frontier Camp Meeting: Religion's Harvest Time*. Dallas: Southern Methodist University Press, 1955.

Jones, Charles Edwin. *Perfectionist Persuasion: The Holiness Movement and American Methodism, 1867–1936*. Metuchen, NJ: The Scarecrow Press, 1974.

Lautz, J.F. "How I Received the Baptism of the Holy Ghost." *The Bridal Call* March 1923, 13–14.

Leech, E.W. "Personal Testimony." *The Bridal Call* March 1920, 5–7.

Locke, Edwin. *Journal of the Twenty-Seventh Delegated General Conference of the Methodist Episcopal Church.* New York: The Methodist Book Concern, 1916.

Mallalieu, W. "The Need for An Evangelistic Ministry." *Methodist Review* (November 1895): 849–860.

McPherson, Aimee Semple. "In the John Street Methodist Episcopal Church." *The Bridal Call* September 1919, 16–17.

——. *This is That: Personal Experiences, Sermons, and Writings of Aimee Semple McPherson* Los Angeles: The Bridal Call Publishing, 1919.

——. "The Bible Baptism in the Bible Way." *The Bridal Call* May 1920, 19.

——. 'Reports." *The Bridal Call* May 1920, 13–18.

——. "News Paper Clippings." *The Bridal Call* August 1920, 13–15.

——. "Methodism and Pentecost." *The Pentecostal Evangel* 8 January 1921, 1–3.

——. *This Is That: Personal Experiences, Sermons, and Writings of Aimee Semple McPherson.* Los Angeles: The Bridal Call Publishing House, 1921.

——. *This Is That: Personal Experiences, Sermons, and Writings of Aimee Semple McPherson.* Los Angeles: Echo Park Evangelistic Association, 1923.

——. *The Story of My Life.* Waco, Texas: Word Books, 1951.

Markley, Morse H. "Holy Ghost at Scruggs Memorial M.E." *The Bridal Call* July 1922, 34.

Miller, Thomas William. "The Canadian 'Azusa': The Hebden Mission in Toronto." *Pneuma* (1986): 5–30.

Mills, Edmund. *Journal of the Twenty-Eight Delegated General Conference of the Methodist Episcopal Church.* New York: The Methodist Book Concern, 1920.

Munhall, L.W. *The Convert and His Relations.* Philadelphia, PA: LW Munhall, 1901.

——. *Breakers! Methodism Adrift.* New York: Charles C. Cook, 1913.

Reiff, Anna C. "How Pentecost came to McKendree." *The Latter Rain Evangel* July 1922, 13–15.

——. "Another Methodist Church Receives Pentecost." *The Latter Rain Evangel* August 1922, 16–17.

Robeck, Jr. Cecil. *The Azusa Street Mission and Revival: The Birth of the Global Pentecostal Movement.* Nashville: Thomas Nelson, 2006.

Rudd, Douglas. *When the Spirit Came upon Them: Highlights from the Early Years of the Pentecostal Movement in Canada.* Burlington, Ontario: Antioch Books, 2002.

Semple, Neil. *The Lord's Dominion: The History of Canadian Methodism.* Montreal and Kingston: McGill-Queen's University Press, 1996.

Shreve, Charles. "Jesus the Same Yesterday, Today, and Forever." *The Bridal Call* December 1921, 8–13.

——. "'Lord, Go Among Us', The Coming of the Spirit to a Washington, D.C. Methodist Church." *Assemblies of God Heritage* (2000): 24–25. Reprint of *The Bridal Call* December 1930.

Smith, Frank. *Minutes of the Annual Conferences of the Methodist Episcopal Church (Spring Conferences).* New York: The Methodist Book Concern, 1930.

Sutton, Matthew Avery. "'Between the Refrigerator and the Wildfire': Aimee Semple McPherson, Pentecostalism, and the Fundamentalist-Modernist Controversy." *Church History* (2003):159–88.

——. *Aimee Semple McPherson and the Resurrection of Christian America.* Cambridge, MA: Harvard University Press, 2007.

Sweet, William Warren. *Methodism in American History.* Nashville: Abingdon, 1953.

Templin, J. Alton, ed. *The Methodist Evangelical Churches and United Brethren Churches in the Rockies,* (1850–1976). Denver: Rocky Mountain Conference of the United Methodist Church, 1977.

Wood, Lawrence. *The Meaning of Pentecost in Early Methodism.* Lanham, MD: The Scarecrow Press, 2002.

Controversy

CHAPTER NINE

ONENESS SEED ON CANADIAN SOIL: EARLY DEVELOPMENTS OF ONENESS PENTECOSTALISM

David A. Reed

INTRODUCTION

The physical boundaries between Canada and United States have always been porous. Everything from contraband to intellectual property has been transported from one country to the other. The early Pentecostal movement was no exception. Pioneers of the new revival crossed the border, north and south, for conventions and campaigns, sometimes living for months or years in one country before returning home. Some, like Aimee Semple McPherson (1890–1944) and J. Roswell Flower (1888–1970), were born in Canada and made their home in the United States.[1] Frank Ewart (1876–1947) entered Canada from Australia, but finally settled in California. Sometimes they served in one country while holding ministerial credentials in another.[2] Howard Goss (1883–1964), converted under the ministry of Charles Parham (1873–1929) and an original signatory of the Assemblies of God, pastored in Ontario from 1919 to 1945, before returning to the United States as first General Superintendent of the United Pentecostal Church.[3] During his first years in the Oneness movement, Andrew Urshan reported on Canadian mission efforts in his magazine, *The Witness of God*, including his own itinerary to Canada.[4]

---

[1] McPherson, born in Ingersoll, ON, was a celebrated evangelist and founding pastor of Angelus Temple in Los Angeles. Flower was born in Belleville, ON, and an early leader in the Assemblies of God. He evangelized, pastored and held a variety of administrative posts with the organization.

[2] This is particularly true for many Oneness organizations and independent Pentecostal ministers.

[3] Goss was pastor of Danforth Gospel Temple in Toronto where he served until 1937, after which he moved to Brockville, ON, until he returned to the U.S. in 1945. During the time he was affiliated with the Pentecostal Assemblies of Canada, Goss was also the first chair of the Pentecostal Ministerial Alliance, 1925–32, and later the general superintendent of the Pentecostal Church, Incorporated, 1939–45.

[4] See especially his 1921 Canadian evangelistic trip. The itinerary included Toronto, Hamilton, and Montreal, as well as a host of small towns in Ontario—Alliston, Athens,

Doctrines and practices were likewise oblivious to national borders. But their human carriers were a spiritual and intellectual source for internationally cross-pollinating the revival. Sometimes they transported beliefs and practices from one country to another. In other cases, they made their distinctive contribution on their own soil. This chapter will examine the early Oneness movement and the distinctive role played by Canadian leaders in that emerging tradition. As we shall see, some aspects were conventional and predictable on either side of the border. But other contributions were distinctive and unique, if not controversial. Canadians are written into the early Oneness story in a variety of ways—personally, theologically, and institutionally.

THE CATALYST: R.E. MCALISTER

A human catalyst by nature rarely inherits the mantle of patriarch. This is the case with the birth of the Oneness movement—first labelled the 'New Issue'—within the early Pentecostal revival. Robert E. McAlister (1880–1953), a young Canadian convert to the new spiritual movement, became the catalyst for what soon became the occasion for the second schism within a decade of the Azusa Street Revival in Los Angeles. More significantly, this schism was closely bound to the first; and, as I have argued elsewhere, it was a radicalized outcome of the momentum propelling the first schism.[5] McAlister's public role as catalyst for the New Issue occurred in April 1913, but the forces that brought him to that point began three years earlier.

Specifically, by 1910 the Pentecostal revival had not only plateaued but was experiencing the strain of unresolved tensions—race, organization and doctrine. The two avowed Pentecostal patriarchs were waning in influence. Charles Parham had failed to take command of Alexander Dowie's crumbling ministry in Zion City, Illinois, and was disgraced over an alleged moral indiscretion in Texas.[6] William Seymour, African-American leader of the Azusa Street Revival, was

---

Barrie, Collingwood, Dresden, Hamilton, Lansdowne, Markham, Picton, and Stratford—working with local evangelists; see Andrew Urshan, "Canadian Evangelistic Trip."

[5] See chapters 4 and 5 in Reed, *In Jesus' Name*.

[6] For an account of Parham's indiscretion, see Goff, *Fields White unto Harvest*, 128–146.

losing influence due to racial fragmentation.[7] Ellen Hebden refused to participate in any meetings that attempted to organize the early movement. Appeals for unity became frequent, but the restlessness could not be contained.

The mantle fell upon William Durham (1873–1912), a fiery young evangelist from Chicago, to embody the discontent. A former Holiness preacher and Pentecostal since 1907, by 1910 he had become convinced that the Holiness teaching of two works of grace—justification and complete sanctification—was not scripturally defensible. Instead, Durham called for a return to the 'Finished Work of Calvary.'[8] In other words, all the benefits of salvation are bound up in the atoning work of Christ on the cross. This theological move was in effect a major recalibration in the revival from a more pneumatological to a christocentric direction. Durham was determined to set the record straight and set the Pentecostal movement right. From his inaugural address before a convention at Stone Church in Chicago on 10 May 1910, until his untimely death on 7 July 1912, Durham was as successful as he was indefatigable in shifting the centre of gravity of the movement to the new teaching.

His message swept through the central States into Texas, west to the Pacific coast and north into Canada. It was when he conducted a convention in Winnipeg in November 1911 that the Finished Work of Calvary teaching gained a foothold in Canada. Due in part to geographical proximity, key Canadian players in the early years were deeply influenced by Durham and the new teaching—A.H. Argue (1868–1959) and Franklin Small (1873–1961) in the Prairies and R.E. McAlister in the east.[9] Argue was already an influential evangelist, editor of *The Apostolic Messenger*, and leader throughout the region. Small eventually embraced the Oneness doctrine and formed his own organization, and McAlister championed the Finished Work teaching across Canada through his publication, *The Good Report*.[10]

Reared in a Scottish Presbyterian home, by the time McAlister was exposed to the Pentecostal revival, his family had become part of the

---

[7] See MacRobert, *The Black Roots and White Racism of Early Pentecostalism in the USA*, 58–62.

[8] See William Durham, "Sanctification," 15–16. For an account of Durham's early life and ministry, including influences of Finished Work of Calvary teaching, see Blumhofer, "William H. Durham."

[9] Durham, "The Winnipeg Convention," 11–12.

[10] See Faupel, *The Everlasting Gospel*.

Holiness movement. He was a spiritually hungry young man who, upon hearing of the Azusa Street Revival, immediately embarked on a trip to Los Angeles in 1906, where he received Spirit baptism. But it was when he attended Durham's convention in Winnipeg in 1911 that McAlister was to embrace wholeheartedly the Finished Work of Calvary teaching. *The Good Report* immediately became his platform for propagating the new doctrine.[11] That same year he devoted a four-page special edition titled, "The Finished Work of Calvary." As these introductory remarks indicate, the Finished Work teaching spiritually stirred him deeply and fixed his mind and passion on Jesus:

> No truth in the past ever gripped my soul like this … or brought such floods of divine glory to my soul. In the light of it Calvary filled my whole vision, almost to the exclusion of everything else. Jesus became more precious, and the Gospel message swelled to the very full of my soul.[12]

It is precisely this intense concentration on Jesus that within two years gave birth to a new trajectory within the Pentecostal revival.[13]

The moment that provided the spark for the new movement occurred at what had been advertised as a 'World-Wide Pentecostal Camp Meeting' in Arroyo Seco on the outskirts of Los Angeles, in April 1913. Healing evangelist Maria Woodworth-Etter was invited to conduct the meetings in hopes of healing the divisions created by Durham's new teaching.

Ironically, it was a Canadian evangelist who planted the seed of the revival's second schism. McAlister was asked to preach at a scheduled baptismal service. During the sermon, he engaged in a moment of speculation regarding the apparent discrepancy between Jesus' command to baptize in the name of the Father, Son and Holy Spirit and the practice by the Apostles of baptizing in the name of the Lord Jesus Christ, as recorded in the Acts of the Apostles. His exegetical digression produced an immediate reaction from the hearers. A missionary, Frank Denny, leapt to the makeshift platform, took McAlister aside and warned him that such teaching was being practiced by a local Dr. Sykes who, by accounts of some, was considered unorthodox. McAlister

---

[11] James Craig states that McAlister published the first issue of *The Good Report* in May 1911. Cited in Rudd, *When the Spirit Came Upon Them*, 9.

[12] McAlister, "The Finished Work of Calvary."

[13] Durham initiated a number of themes that provided raw material for the emerging New Issue, especially his christocentric focus and choice of Acts 2.38 as soteriological paradigm for the believer's identification with Christ.

then resumed the pulpit to clarify that he did not consider trinitarian baptism to be in error.[14]

The eyewitness account of this otherwise minor incident is provided by Frank Ewart, a leading architect of the New Issue doctrine. By this time he and McAlister were friends. Ewart reports that, in a later conversation, McAlister explained his reasoning for harmonizing the two scriptural texts: "Lord, Jesus, Christ, being the counterpart of Father, Son, and Holy Ghost, which made Jesus' words in Matt. 28:19, one of those parabolic statements of truth, which was interpreted in Acts 2:38 and other scriptures." Equally important for our purpose is that Ewart reports McAlister's last admonition on the matter before leaving for Canada, "Before he went he deplored anyone causing a split in the movement over this issue."[15]

McAlister's fleeting reflection on this biblical conundrum was surely not serendipitous. For more than two years his heart and mind had been saturated with the fresh insights of Durham's teaching. Three themes in particular that guided his future ministry and policies seem to have made their way into his teaching and practice: the magnetic attraction of the centrality of Jesus Christ, the validity of—and at one time, preference for—water baptism in the name of Jesus Christ according to Acts 2.38, and his unwavering distaste for dividing the Pentecostal fellowship over the issue.

The following year was one of incubation as Ewart continued to study the topic of water baptism. He became convinced that baptism in the name of the Lord Jesus Christ was not only valid but necessary if the power of Pentecost is to be fully realized in the church. On 15 April 1914, Ewart left his position as associate at Victoria Hall, erected a tent in the Belvedere suburb of Los Angeles, and preached his first public sermon on Acts 2.38.[16] At this opening service, he and his associate, Glenn Cook, rebaptized each other.

---

[14] Ewart, *The Phenomenon of Pentecost*, 76–77.

[15] Ewart, 77. Other accounts report that a relatively unknown listener, John G. Schaepe (1870–1939), was inspired by McAlister's insight and ran through the camp early the following morning claiming that God had revealed to him the truth of baptism in the name of Jesus Christ. No details, however, of this revelation were ever forthcoming; see Brumback *Suddenly from Heaven*, 191; and Clanton, *United We Stand*, 15. Ewart and McAlister eventually joined forces as co-editors of *The Good Report* until it ceased publication in 1914.

[16] Ewart, *Phenomenon of Pentecost*, 51. Glenn Cook was a Pentecostal pioneer evangelist and former minister with the Christian and Missionary Alliance.

By the summer of 1915 two developments had occurred. One was theological. Ewart had formulated the doctrinal underpinnings for what he came to consider the exclusive formula to be invoked in baptism; namely, the revealed 'name' of Jesus and the radical oneness of God. As he recounted in 1916, the theological framework, beginning with Acts 2.38, developed this way: "We saw that if the name of the Father, Son and Holy Spirit was Jesus Christ, then in some mysterious way the Father, Son and Holy Ghost were made one in the person of Jesus Christ. We saw from this premise that the old trinity theory was unscriptural."[17]

The second development was the rapid spread of the new teaching. By the summer of 1915 it had threatened to take over the newly organized Assemblies of God fellowship, especially with the rebaptism of E.N. Bell, influential editor of the organization's publication, *Word and Witness*.[18] It had captured two leaders who would become pioneer formulators of the new theology, Garfield T. Haywood and Franklin Small. Haywood was an influential African-American pastor in Indianapolis who had already become a convert to the Finished Work teaching and was an occasional contributor to *The Good Report*. Small was an emerging Canadian leader in Winnipeg.[19]

Small and McAlister were apparently both studying the matter of the baptismal formula following the Arroyo Seco Camp Meeting, even though neither one had been rebaptized. Small was also struggling with the desire for a revival in Winnipeg. As early as the 8th Annual Pentecostal Convention in Winnipeg, November 1913, Small reported that McAlister was the guest preacher and delivered "the first message on the exclusive rite of water baptism in Jesus' Name only." He went on to acknowledge that (undoubtedly influenced by McAlister's teaching), though he personally had not yet been rebaptized, he "baptized thirty candidates in the name of Jesus Christ only."[20]

---

[17] Ewart, "The Unity of God," 1.

[18] For an account of the stormy years, 1914–16, see Reed, chapter 7.

[19] While Ewart is the one who initiated the New Issue as a movement and the first to lay out the basics of Oneness theology—'Jesus' as the revealed name of God and a non-trinitarian view of the oneness of the Godhead—he was not the only formulator of early Oneness theology. Haywood and Small were soon to make their contributions, and by 1919 another prominent Pentecostal evangelist and a Persian immigrant, Andrew Urshan, joined the ranks; see chapters 8 and 9 in Reed, *In Jesus' Name*.

[20] Small, "Historical and Valedictory Account of the Origin of Water Baptism in Jesus' Name Only, and the Doctrine of the Fulness of God in Christ, in Pentecostal Circles in Canada."

Both Small and McAlister were eventually rebaptized at the same convention in the Twin Cities, Minnesota, hosted by Bert Scott, on 15 December 1915. Small reported that he experienced an intensified awareness of the presence and power of God: "I have been baptized in the name of the Lord Jesus and I have never felt more of His power and presence in my life, than since I obeyed His Word (Acts 2:38).... God has been talking to my heart for some time regarding tent meetings for Winnipeg.... We feel sure God is coming forth in a Revival for Winnipeg."[21] The revival began the following summer and continued unabated for a decade.[22]

According to a report by Haywood, who was in Minneapolis at the time, McAlister was baptized at the same convention, along with his brother, Harvey, and their wives. McAlister promptly wrote a letter to Ewart, reflecting on Ewart's apparently new understanding of the threefold nature of God as 'manifestations' instead of 'persons.' Note particularly the effect this spiritual insight produced in him, almost identical to Small's response: "Well, we are coming along the line somewhere. I have had a revelation to my soul of the one God in threefold manifestation. How my heart melted in His presence! I could only weep and cry."[23] This is the only clue we have that McAlister was giving serious consideration to Ewart's new doctrinal framework for the practice of baptism in the name of Jesus Christ. And there is no indication that he ever implemented his preference for the Acts formula as a requirement for all true believers.

While most or all the ministers of the Canadian Eastern District had been baptized in the name of Jesus Christ and practised it prior to the formation of the Pentecostal Assemblies of Canada in 1919, it appears that most did not consider it a matter for dividing the fellowship, as most of the ministers remained when the organization was incorporated. A motion presented by McAlister and accepted by the members at the November 1919 meeting of the General Assembly clearly affirms a Trinitarian faith, freedom in the matter of the formula for baptism, and an abiding concern for the unity of the church:

> Whereas much contention and confusion has been caused over the issue
> of One God and Trinitarian (sic) views, also the Baptismal formula, be it

---

[21] Reported in Ewart, *Phenomenon of Pentecost*, 98.
[22] Wegner, *Streams of Grace*, 34–37.
[23] Published in Ewart, *Meat in Due Season and Phenomenon of Pentecost*, 99.

> resolved, that we as a body go on record as disapproving not only of the above issues, but of all other issues that divide and confuse God's people to no profit, and that aggressive evangelism be our motto.
>
> Whereas we recognize the three-fold relationship of Father, Son, and Holy Ghost being clearly taught in the New Testament, Be it resolved, that we express ourselves in harmony with this truth as expressed in the Word of God.

As to baptism, we feel like leaving the matter of formula with the individual.[24] The following year, McAlister wrote a brief article in *The Pentecostal Testimony*, stating the unity of God "is a compound unity and not a simple unity."[25]

McAlister is an example of confusion that frequently occurs when attempting to determine Oneness theological identity. Except for his reference to the 'threefold manifestation' in 1915, McAlister gave no indication that he fully embraced the Oneness doctrine of God, though prior to 1918 it appears that he gave serious consideration to aspects of the New Issue teaching, especially the Name. Second, though for a brief period he taught and practised baptism in the name of the Lord Jesus Christ, he was reluctant, and finally resistant, to following his Oneness colleagues in making rebaptism a requirement.[26]

The drawing of organizational lines exacted the price of fellowship and unity in the early movement. But McAlister's commitment to showing charity toward those with Oneness beliefs or inclination within the ministerial was demonstrated in the tolerance he extended to at least one person, Howard Goss. Goss was a Oneness leader since 1916 who pastored within the PAOC fellowship from 1919 to 1937 without restriction or recrimination. It was only when he resigned his position at Danforth Gospel Temple that the issue emerged as members prepared to call a new pastor. McAlister attended a congregational

---

[24] Pentecostal Assemblies of Canada, General Assembly Minutes, November 1919; cited in James Craig, "Robert Edward McAlister: Canadian Pentecostal Pioneer," 18–19.

[25] McAlister, "The Unity of God;" Also cited in Craig, "McAlister," 19.

[26] Small reported that, prior to 1920, the presbyters in the Eastern District of PAOC regularly baptized in the name of Jesus Christ; see Small, "Historical and Valedictory Account," 2. McAlister's experience was similar to E.N. Bell's rebaptism in 1915, in which both expressed great spiritual benefit to being baptized in the name of Jesus Christ, but never adopted the more comprehensive Oneness theological framework developed by Ewart and others. For a helpful analysis of Bell's 'conversion,' see Fudge, "Did E.N. Bell Convert to the New Issue?"

meeting at which he clarified the PAOC's official doctrinal position as Trinitarian.

In sum, McAlister was not only the catalyst for the New Issue but represented the link between the first schism begun by Durham and the second schism initiated by Ewart. It was the first schism that fuelled the singular passion for Jesus and the Finished Work, and the second schism that drew on that christocentric vision for a wholly distinct doctrine and practice, albeit landing just outside the limits of established orthodoxy. McAlister's position was unique. He befriended the new movement, but finally did not render his allegiance.

THEOLOGICAL CONTRIBUTION: FRANKLIN SMALL
AND JOHN PATERSON

The rudiments of the Oneness doctrine developed rather quickly between 1914 and 1916. By 1915 Haywood and Small had converted to the new movement, and were making their own contribution. Urshan, the fourth Oneness pioneer, joined in 1919 and immediately began to teach and publish his theological ideas.[27] It was on the Canadian scene that Small and another lesser known writer, John Paterson, were making important contributions to the emerging Oneness theology in its first decade. But Small, a staunch Oneness proponent until his death, stands apart from all the others in two ways: his lifelong promotion of Durham's Finished Work of Calvary, and his founding of a Canadian Oneness organization. Paterson was a lesser known pastor in Montreal who wrote an article in 1920 for Haywood's magazine, *Voice in the Wilderness*, that a year later, by his account, was distributed widely as a booklet and used as a "textbook" in some early Pentecostal Bible Schools.[28] In 1941, he published a second booklet, *The Real Truth about Baptism in Jesus' Name.*[29]

---

[27] The four primary architects of the Oneness theology as it emerged within the first five years, 1914–19, are Ewart, Haywood, Small and Urshan; see chapters 8 and 9 in Reed, *In Jesus' Name*. There is some evidence that Urshan had been considering aspects of what developed later as a Oneness view of God as early as 1908, and was baptizing in the name of Jesus Christ in 1910. Research on Urshan's early beliefs and influences is currently being conducted by a Oneness scholar, Daniel Segraves; see personal electronic correspondence with Daniel Segraves, dated 21 March 2009.

[28] See the forward in Paterson, *God in Christ Jesus*. The original article was published under the title, "Revelation of Jesus Christ." The final publication was considerably larger but, in his words, "the basic view is unchanged."

[29] Paterson, *The Real Truth about Baptism in Jesus' Name.*

But first we examine Small's distinctive theological contribution—the Finished Work of Calvary and eternal security. He was reared by Methodist parents in Ontario and experienced Spirit baptism in Winnipeg in 1907. In 1911 he became A.H. Argue's assistant in a Winnipeg store-front mission, which positioned him well to come under Durham's influence, when Durham preached at the Winnipeg Convention that November.

In brief, Durham's bold theological move was his attack on the Holiness Pentecostal doctrine of two works of grace, in which justification is effected by Christ and sanctification accomplished by the Holy Spirit.[30] Durham called for a return to what he called the Finished Work of Calvary, one act of grace in Christ which grants full salvation, including our sanctification. At the same time, Durham rejected the Reformed doctrine with its overemphasis on imputed or legal righteousness. Rather, at the very inception of the Christian life we are justified and sanctified, and our salvation is both "a state and an experience."[31] While he insisted that he believed in *entire* sanctification, he distinguished his view from the Wesleyan Holiness that taught the root of inbred sin is removed.[32] Rather, we still have the capacity to sin, even though our inherited sin nature from Adam and our actual sins are removed *entirely*. For acts of sin, our one and only recourse is repentance and return to the cross of Christ.

The believer's appropriation of the Finished Work is by identification with Christ in his death, burial and resurrection. The paradigmatic text for Durham was Romans 6.6. But he eventually preferred Acts 2.38, since it taught identification but specified it in a way that would address the Pentecostal reality more clearly—repentance, water baptism, and the Holy Spirit.[33] It is this convergence of Durham's doctrine of identification with Christ and a paradigmatic text that laid the foundation for what followed in the wake of his untimely death with young leaders like Ewart and Small.

Most of the Pentecostal movement that initially followed Durham, primarily the fellowship that became the Assemblies of God, drew

---

[30] For a brief summary of Durham's teaching on the Finished Work of Calvary, see Reed, *In Jesus' Name*, 87–94.

[31] Durham, "Sanctification," 1.

[32] Durham, "Identification with Christ," 10.

[33] By 1912, Durham had replaced Romans 6.6 with Acts 2.38 on the masthead of his magazine, *Pentecostal Testimony*.

inspiration from his forceful leadership and embraced a theology of progressive sanctification. Beyond that, there was little understanding of or commitment to his teaching, which admittedly was underdeveloped due to his untimely death. But it was Small who was initially most influenced directly by Durham's teaching, maintained it as a defining mark of his own ministry, and developed it in a direction that is rare among Pentecostals anywhere in the world.

Small's abiding interest throughout his ministry was, in his words, "the Finished Work of Calvary, including the Deity of the Lord Jesus Christ."[34] Details aside, this statement is more than a hint that Durham's doctrine of the Finished Work and the later Oneness development were closely linked in Small's mind, one growing logically from the other. A further clue to the link is Small's ordering of his book, *Living Waters—A Sure Guide for Your Faith* (an undated publication of select writings)—Part I is devoted to the Finished Work of Calvary and Part III gives attention to the Oneness of God and Christology.

The theological framework for these two distinctive doctrines is captured in two other theological terms—restoration and progressive truth. Small was a staunch believer in the popular 'restorationist' view that God was bypassing the "old denominations" and restoring the pure apostolic truth and practice to the church in the last days before the return of Christ. The means by which God is restoring the church is by progressive illumination or revelation. While 'progressive' is the watchword for Enlightenment modernism, Small was clear about his own meaning: "We are wending our way out of the philosophical timbers of the dark age territories, in other words, we are in the Holy Ghost School of progressive truth which is associated with doctrinal perfection for God's people in the restoration of the faith before the Lord returns to earth again."[35]

Small's theology of the Finished Work of Christ was both an appropriation of Durham's theology and a step beyond it. First, he appropriated Durham's notion that in the new birth one is made righteous positionally and experimentally. On one hand, he used the positional language of Federal theology, in which both Adam and Christ acted representatively, as Federal heads, of the human race. But both Durham and Small expropriated the classical Protestant doctrine for their

---

[34] Small, *Living Waters*, 7. The phrase, 'Deity of the Lord Jesus Christ' is a shorthand reference to the Oneness doctrine of God and Christ.

[35] Small, *Living Waters*, 82.

Pentecostal purposes by adding that the new birth also carries an *experiential* dimension to it. Small attacked not only the modernists but also the fundamentalists who focused almost exclusively on the juridical aspect of the atonement. In his words: "Why will Spirit-filled preachers today persist in a message that casts reflection upon the Blood of Christ, as a mere make believe to free God's people positionally, and not experimentally?"[36]

A corollary to Small's 'experiential' new birth is that, with Durham, he positioned the Finished Work against both the Wesleyan eradicationists who taught that the root of sin is totally removed in entire sanctification and the fundamentalists who believed that the Adamic inherited sin is still present in a Christian's life, that one is saved only positionally. For Small, this new positioning is a direct result of the Pentecostal revival. He pointed to the 'experiential experience' of Acts 2.4 and its application to today. The other teachings were prominent prior to 1900 but were singularly "foreign teachings to the original Latter Rain movement." In other words, "some of these doctrines are outdated, referred to by experimental confirmation and illumination of the Word of God during this twentieth century by the outpoured Spirit. The Spirit—power—and the Word of God agree."[37]

He even criticized fellow Pentecostals for preaching the 'suppression theory,' a probable reference to the Keswick movement which taught that the original Adamic nature was still active but could be 'suppressed' by the power of Christ.[38] For this reason, Small detested the phrase common among preachers, "keeping the old man under."[39] He compared this teaching to "keeping a hog pen at the front gate—the odor is obnoxious."[40]

Small not only appropriated Durham's Finished Work teaching but also used it as a platform for formulating his own doctrine of eternal security. Here he argued his case from the positional or juridical aspect of salvation. The believer's status is eternally changed as a result of Christ's atoning work. Therefore, even if believers sin, they are not judged according to the old life but by their new status in Christ: "The believer is no longer reckoned a child of first Adam, but is now a child

[36] Small, *Living Waters*, 41.
[37] Small, 25–26.
[38] Small, 24.
[39] Small, "The Fallen Nature," 6.
[40] Small, "Editorial," 4.

of God under second Adam his New Federal Head, Christ Jesus.... They are now called 'little children,' and admonished not to sin, but if they do, they have an Advocate—lawyer—to handle the case."[41]

Small began to address the topic of eternal security in his paper, *Living Waters*, at least by 1937, but did not write extensively on the subject until the 1940's and later.[42] Earlier editorials and articles, beginning in 1918, were devoted to the doctrines of God, Christ and Spirit baptism, and baptism in the name of the Lord Jesus Christ. However, in 1945 he acknowledged that he had embraced the doctrine of 'eternal life' as early as 1919, speculating that his credibility with the leaders in the east may have been damaged more by this doctrine than with the 'New Issue.'[43]

Both Small and Paterson propagated the new doctrine through their teaching and writings. They shared a common affinity for rational thinking—and sometimes bluntness—even when they misunderstood the position of their opponents. Both dabbled in analyzing the early doctrinal heresies. But for both, their attention was given primarily to defending the oneness of God, the centrality of Jesus Christ, and the necessity of baptism in the name of the Lord Jesus Christ.

The classical doctrine of the Trinity was consistently misunderstood by both Small and Paterson. Small repeatedly accused Trinitarians of believing in 'separate' persons in the Godhead.[44] His alternative was to explain the threefold nature of God in terms of the threefold human nature as the image of God—body, soul and spirit, yet one person. Paterson likewise accused Trinitarians of at least "jumping to the conclusion that Father and Son are 'separate' Persons."[45] He explained the reason: a "person" (including persons of the Godhead) possesses "conscious intelligence and sensibilities, moral attributes, and perceptions, and a will capable of independent decision.... *It is in exactly this sense that Trinitarians use the expression 'Three Persons'*" [emphasis in text].[46]

But the underlying reason for rejecting the classical formulation of the Trinity is found in the christocentric shift begun with Durham—the Trinity diminishes the high view that Scripture accords Jesus Christ

---

[41] Small, "'Ye Must be Born Again' *versus* The Probation Tangle," 7.
[42] See Small, "Ye Must be Born Again;" "The Sin Question," 2; "The Fallen Nature."
[43] Small, "Historical and Valedictory Account," 2.
[44] For example, see Small, *Living Waters*, 76, 88, 91.
[45] Paterson, *God in Christ Jesus*, 6.
[46] Paterson, 38.

in his deity. Small cleverly stated that Trinitarians had given Christ an "inferiority complex in the eyes of the world" by separating "Christ from his Fatherhood…. Any teaching that minimizes the Lord Jesus Christ to second place in the Godhead in authority or power, is to be laid at the door of the enemy." All this occurred because of the church's "pluralizing of persons" in the Godhead.[47]

For Small and others, two relevant themes emerge. First, Jesus in his deity is none other than Yahweh, and nothing less. This explains the occasional language of 'supreme' or 'absolute' deity of Jesus Christ.[48] Second, the only way to know God aright is through Christ. Whatever 'Trinity' exists in God can only be grasped christologically. This explains the appeal to both Small and Paterson of Trinitarian writers like J. Monro Gibson and Roach Stratton. Small quoted Stratton, a leading Baptist pastor in New York, "The God of the first verse of Genesis is none other than the Lord Jesus Christ of the New Testament." He then quoted Gibson in like manner:

> The Father, Son and Holy Ghost are all in Christ…. The reason some people get into difficulty is their perverse determination … to seek a separate knowledge of the Father, Son and Holy Spirit…. They gaze into the infinite unknown instead of looking at the face of Jesus.[49]

Paterson likewise quoted Gibson: "If we think of the Father, there is Christ … if we think of the Son, union to Christ is the practical thought … if we think of the Holy Spirit, the practical thought is Christ in us."[50] In other words, the real offense in the doctrine of the Trinity for the early Oneness theologians, including Small and Paterson, was that it did not give a proper credit to the centrality of Christ in his deity. The problem with the Trinity for them was, therefore, a christological one.

An interesting observation, however, is that Paterson designed his first book, *God in Christ Jesus*, following the pattern of the Trinity,

---

[47] Small, *Living Waters*, 90.
[48] Traditional Trinitarian thought affirms the unity of the Godhead and the equality of the Persons. The Oneness movement emerged within a larger stream of evangelical reaction to encroaching liberalism in North American Protestantism. The battle was not being fought over the eternal distinctions between the Father and the Son, but the full deity of Jesus Christ, his very identity being that of the God of Israel, and in some cases, Yahweh; for a brief summary of this broader movement, see chapter 3 in Reed, *In Jesus' Name*.
[49] Cited in Small, *Living Waters*, 85.
[50] Paterson, *Real Truth*, 19. Paterson identified Gibson as one time Principal of the Presbyterian Theological College in Montreal and subsequently Moderator of the Presbyterian Church in England.

addressing first the Father, followed by the Word, and finishing with the Holy Spirit, the Comforter. His goal was to demonstrate that Jesus Christ in his deity is the Father and in his humanity the Son, and that the Holy Spirit in the New Covenant, as the Filioque affirms, "proceeds from the Father and the Son." Christ is the cohering centre of the Trinity: "Jesus is Father in His Godhead, Son in His humanity, and Comforter in the body of the Elect." In scripture, God the Father is the spirit of power, the Son is our high priest, and the Holy Spirit is the abiding Comforter.[51] This nuanced attention to the Trinitarian shape of salvation history suggests that, while his arguments were mostly conventional Oneness, one Oneness leader who knew him well suggests that his theology was "classical Trinitarianism with a few word shifts."[52]

Early Oneness writers could not agree on whether or not the historical heresy of Sabellianism, of which they were accused, fairly represented their own view—though it is clear that neither proponents nor opponents grasped the issue. Small and Paterson, likewise, did not agree. Small tended to accept the label since he preferred the term 'manifestations' to 'persons': "Sabellianism appears to be more logical on the Godhead. It resolves the Godhead into Three Manifestations of God to man."[53] Paterson, on the other hand, was convinced that Sabellianism was one of a number of ancient heresies that in the end devolved into some form of Patripassionism.[54]

For both Small and Paterson, the Name was central to their doctrine of baptism. The difference, a subtle one, is that for Paterson the name is Jesus while Small tended to prefer the full name, Lord Jesus Christ. Paterson followed the conventional Oneness exegesis of harmonizing Matthew 28.19 and Acts 2.38; namely, that the word 'name' in Matthew is singular and therefore refers to 'Jesus' in Acts 2.38. However, he engaged in an extended discussion of the various Synoptic versions of the Great Commission, arguing against the traditional preference for the Matthean account. He also taught that 'Jehovah' was the special name of God in the Old Testament that is embodied in the name 'Jesus' ('Jehovah the Saviour').

Small was accustomed to using the names 'Jesus,' 'Jesus Christ,' and 'Lord Jesus Christ' interchangeably, but preferred the full name when

---

[51] Paterson, *God in Christ Jesus*, 33–37.
[52] This is the opinion of Scott, cited in Fudge, *Christianity without the Cross*, 67.
[53] Small, "The Godhead," 7; also, "Historical and Valedictory Account," 6.
[54] See his comment in Fudge, *Christianity without the Cross*, 65.

referring to water baptism. Commenting on the two baptismal formulas, he argued that, "in Matt. 28:19 the name is singular, which is the name of the Lord Jesus Christ."[55] Elsewhere he used the same method of correlation as McAlister, which is likely the reason for his use of the full name: "'Go ye, therefore, baptizing them in the Name (singular) of the Father (which is the LORD), and the Son (Jesus), and of the Holy Ghost (Christ the Anointed),' which said is LORD JESUS CHRIST. "[56] Both Small and Paterson agreed, however, that 'Lord' and 'Christ' designate and differentiate this Jesus from the common human name. Paterson stated that, "JESUS is His Name, and the titles merely distinguish Him from all others."[57]

Finally, there is no indication that either Small or Paterson embraced the baptismal theology of Haywood and Urshan that Acts 2.38 constitutes the new birth mentioned by Jesus in John 3.5. Throughout his writings, Small followed Durham's Finished Work theology of one act of grace that is made effective for the penitent in conversion. As he stated, "The Christian is saved through faith by a second birth, by grace."[58] Paterson likewise rejected the 'new birth' teaching of many in the Oneness movement, as it often led to an exclusive doctrine of salvation. That is, if Acts 2.38 constitutes the new birth, then eternal salvation is at best jeopardized for those who have not repented, been baptized in the name of Jesus Christ and received Spirit baptism. Paterson spoke directly of his disdain for what he called the "Holy Ghost or Hell" preaching of many in the Oneness movement.[59]

In summary, Small and Paterson made their theological contribution to the emerging Oneness movement in two ways. First, they added their voices and enriched the wider theological discussion south of the Canadian border. More importantly, Small marked out a singularly distinct course with his single-minded commitment to Durham's Finished Work of Calvary, and his readiness to extend that theology into the otherwise uncharted territory for Pentecostals of the doctrine of eternal security. This stand undoubtedly affected his relationships within the wider Oneness movement. But Small's distinctive articulation of Finished Work theology, though somewhat

---

55 Small, *Living Waters*, 92.
56 Small, *A Synopsis of the Name and Deity of Christ*.
57 Paterson, *God in Christ Jesus*, 59. See Small, *Living Waters*, 97–98.
58 Small, 15.
59 Quoted in Fudge, *Christianity without the Cross*, 118, 165.

underdeveloped, demonstrates the theological potential within that tradition for future mining.

INSTITUTIONAL CONTRIBUTION: APOSTOLIC CHURCH OF PENTECOST

The New Issue became an unsettling factor within the early Pentecostal fellowship that followed Durham's Finished Work teaching, primarily the newly organized Assemblies of God. In the United States the disruption occurred simultaneously with the birth of the organization in April 1914, and it was resolved with a painful rupture at the Fourth General Council meeting in 1916. The resolution in Canada was similar except that it occurred later, and with a somewhat less volatile separation of ways.

Not unlike other calls in the early Pentecostal movement for an organizational structure to coordinate missions support and protect the faithful, the Canadian movement was growing but still small in number and scattered across a vast territory. By the time the Canadians were ready to organize, the split in the AG had already occurred and lines had been drawn. As already noted, many leaders in the eastern region were either supportive of or sympathetic to the Oneness teaching.

Two prominent Oneness leaders, Goss and Small, were initially positioned well within the leadership circle. The first exploratory meeting was held in May 1917 in Montreal, with Small present. By that summer, Goss had apparently arrived and was present for conversations held at Lansdowne Camp in Ontario. PAOC historian Thomas Miller reports that Goss pressed hard for adoption of Oneness doctrine in its doctrinal statement, but failed in the end.[60] Another meeting was held in Ottawa on 7 June 1918, at which those present decided to ask Goss to assist in forming an 'association' to be called "'Pentecostal Assemblies of Canada,' working in conjunction with the Pentecostal Assemblies of the World." Albeit exploratory, the status of this meeting is unclear since it was not mentioned in Miller's history but appears in Small's paper, *Living Waters*, in the form of the Minutes of the meeting and signed by the Secretary, William Draffin. Also, McAlister's name is conspicuously absent from the list of those attending the meeting, perhaps an early warning signal that he would not support the proposal

---

[60] Miller, *Canadian Pentecostals*, 115.

put forth by Goss and Small.[61] It is clear, however, that at least those present were prepared to align the Canadian fellowship with the American Oneness movement.

A theological sifting began to occur during this period, according to Miller. A further exploratory meeting was held in November 1918 followed by two meetings during the winter of 1919, during which Goss and Small urged for the adoption of the name, Pentecostal Assemblies of the World in Canada. Though it was rejected, the name finally chosen was an adaptation, the Pentecostal Assemblies of Canada.[62]

On 17 May 1919, a dominion charter was granted, with McAlister and Small included among the signatories. But the Minute Book of the meeting on 25–28 November 1919 reveals that the mood had shifted toward Trinitarian orthodoxy. As noted above, the meeting went on record as affirming the "three-fold relationship of Father, Son and Holy Ghost being clearly taught in the New Testament," but leaving the formula in baptism to the discretion of the individual.[63] That same year the western churches affiliated with the Assemblies of God, followed in 1920 by the eastern region. By 1922, however, PAOC became independent of the American organization due to differences in mission policy and the desire for a national identity.[64]

This shift caused a dilemma for Goss and Small. Goss seems to have made peace with the decision and continued without interference as pastor of Danforth Gospel Temple until his departure in 1937. Small, on the other hand, felt betrayed and formed an organization on Oneness principles. His account of the division suggests that he was willing, though disappointed, to remain in the PAOC fellowship so long as he was granted freedom of his own convictions without interference. In a letter dated 1 January 1920, to the PAOC leadership, he stated,

---

[61] Draffin, "To the Pentecostal Assemblies of Canada," 2. It should be noted that the Pentecostal Assemblies of the World had just been constituted as a Oneness organization on January 22, 1918; see Tyson, *The Early Pentecostal Revival*, 191. Small later expressed his suspicion that McAlister's absence was related to his withdrawal of support; see Small, "Historical and Valedictory Account," 2.

[62] Miller is imprecise regarding the timing of these discussions. He makes reference to the urgings by Goss and Small when he is discussing the 1917 meeting. However, the Pentecostal Assemblies of the World was not reconstituted as the Oneness organization until January 1918. It is likely, therefore, that the name proposal occurred during the 1918 and 1919 exploratory discussions.

[63] Cited in Miller, *Canadian Pentecostals*, 117.

[64] Miller, 118.

> If you feel that I am unworthy of your further fellowship owing to my doctrinal stand, I shall leave my further fellowship to your judgment as to whether I am recognized as one of you. Otherwise, I feel I must be free to obey my personal convictions as specified in our preamble adopted under our charter.[65]

Receiving no reply and observing his name missing in the next publishing of the ministerial list, he set out to form an organization that would embody his Oneness convictions. In 1921 he was granted a charter for the formation of the Apostolic Church of Pentecost (ACOP).

Small immediately turned his attention to evangelism and the founding of a Bible School. While the strength of ACOP was in the western provinces, Small traveled east in 1928 to make connections with Oneness churches in the Maritimes, especially New Brunswick (see Chapter 10 on Wynn Stairs). While there was a gracious reception, concerns regarding affiliation with ACOP continued throughout the 1930's. Distance, strength of numbers in the west, and concerns over Small's doctrine of eternal security eventually militated against affiliation. In 1946, the Maritimes fellowship, the Full Gospel Pentecostal Church, finally joined the United Pentecostal Church. But due to doctrinal disagreements in the ensuing years, a split in 1973 led a number of ministers to seek out affiliation with ACOP.[66]

Small's vision of ACOP as an identifiable Oneness organization was tested when the leaders began merger conversations in 1950 with the Evangelical Churches of Pentecost, a small but mostly Trinitarian fellowship (including some ministers who held an amillennialist view in eschatology). Following six years of inter-organizational fellowship and discussion, a merger was finally realized in 1956.[67]

It will be no surprise to learn that Small, the patriarch of an organization that represented the breach of fellowship with many of his early

---

[65] Cited in Larden, *Our Apostolic Heritage*, 90; Wegner, *Streams of Grace*, p. 50. Small's reference to his personal convictions refers to the freedom of conscience clause in the PAOC charter, "allowing liberty of conscience in matters of personal conviction;" printed in Small, "Historical and Valedictory Account," 2. Small's analysis was that his "disfellowship" was due to both his Oneness stand and his belief in eternal security; see Larden, *Apostolic Heritage*, 90.

[66] As of December 2005, there were only four congregations affiliated with ACOP, though the ministerial is considerably larger; see Wegner, *Streams of Grace*, 318. For an account of Small's trip to the Maritime Provinces and the ensuing conversations, see 211–32.

[67] For a detailed account of the merger and discussions that led to it, see chapters 3 and 4 in Wegner, *Streams of Grace*.

fellow-workers, was disturbed at the prospect of what he perceived to
be a dangerous doctrinal compromise. As ACOP historian Linda
Wegner observed, "The Merger of ECP and ACOP brought heartache
to Frank Small." [68] He feared that his two most cherished beliefs—the
Finished Work and Oneness—would be seriously undermined, and he
viewed the present organizational negotiation a hindrance to the principles of gospel truth. In sharper terms than this, his allusion to the
merger could not be mistaken, referring to "teachings that have been
borrowed from the bookshelf with beliefs that are high treason against
the blood of the Lord Jesus Christ."[69]

The reconstituted ACOP, however, moved forward and made theological adjustments that illustrate a way in which the theological divide
between Oneness and Trinitarians can be bridged. Two statements in
particular from its Statement of Faith demonstrate this accommoda-
tion. First, water baptism is to be administered in the name of the Lord
Jesus Christ, a practice that has been acceptable in the Canadian
Pentecostal movement from the beginning. Second, its statement
forged a unity on the doctrine of God by omission—that is, by avoiding the problematic terms of 'persons' or 'manifestations.' It reads: "We
believe in ... the eternal existence of one true God who is Father, Son,
and Holy Spirit."[70]

In order to reflect its broader spectrum of belief, ACOP leadership
generally avoids the 'Oneness' label because of its association with the
United Pentecostal Church and other groups that represent the exclu-
sive non-Trinitarian doctrine. One preferred term of description for
God is 'Tri-unity,' a less exclusive term and one that both Andrew
Urshan and Goss considered acceptable.[71]

In sum, the organizational beginnings of the fellowship that followed in the wake of Durham's Finished Work sweep of the early
revival were deeply impacted by the New Issue on both sides of the
border. While the larger Canadian Oneness constituency remains
under the umbrella of an American organization, Small must be

---

[68] Wegner, 150.

[69] Wegner, 157.

[70] Taken from the current ACOP Statement of Faith, http://www.acop.ca/AboutUs/
faith_statement.asp (accessed March 21, 2009).

[71] Personal telephone interview with former Moderator, Gil Killam, 19 April 2001.
See Urshan, "The Doctrine of the Trinity and the Divinity of Jesus Christ," 1–2; and
Goss, "Godhead," 7. It is therefore surprising that Small was critical of the term,
"Tri-Unity," since for him it means "Trinitarian;" see Wegner, *Streams of Grace*, 151.

credited with forging the only enduring Canadian organization borne out of the New Issue, and one that continues distinct among Pentecostals for its adherence to the doctrines of the Finished Work and eternal security.

Conclusion

Beginnings can be messy, and beginnings with controversy embedded in them are particularly untidy. This discord characterizes the story of the early years for both the AG and the PAOC. But the Canadian story unfolded differently. It was a Canadian who inadvertently set off a chain of events that resulted in a schism within the early Pentecostal revival, but more importantly who personified the hidden intrinsic relationship between Durham's Finished Work doctrine and the radical New Issue. Small and Paterson contributed to the growing body of Oneness literature in both countries. But it was Small who stands alone among early Pentecostal leaders for his undivided commitment to Durham's Finished Work teaching and the doctrine of eternal security which he developed from it.

Finally, Small was a signatory to the first Pentecostal organization, the PAOC, but with the doctrinal break in fellowship, he founded an organization that for many years endured as the only native Canadian Oneness organization. In reading the histories of both groups, it is evident in the language and attitude of the writers that knowledge of and interest in the other have long since passed. But a vestige of an earlier fellowship remains, like a fossil, in the name of the largest Canadian Pentecostal denomination—'Pentecostal Assemblies of Canada' was an intentional adaptation of the first Oneness organization, Pentecostal Assemblies of the World; a reminder of an early aspiration, now a forgotten fellowship.

Bibliography

Blumhofer, Edith. "William H. Durham: Years of Creativity, Years of Dissent," in *Portraits of a Generation: Early Pentecostal Leaders*, edited by James R. Goff, Jr., and Grant Wacker, 123–42. Fayetteville, AR: The University of Arkansas Press, 2002.

Brumback, Carl. *Suddenly from Heaven: A History of the Assemblies of God*. Springfield, MO: Gospel Publishing House, 1961.

Clanton, Arthur L. *United We Stand: A History of Oneness Organizations*. St. Louis, MO: Pentecostal Publishing House, 1970.

Craig, James. "Robert Edward McAlister: Canadian Pentecostal Pioneer." Unpublished paper, 1987.
Draffin, William. "To the Pentecostal Assemblies of Canada." *Living Waters* June 1918.
Durham, William. "Sanctification: Is It a Definite, Second, Instantaneous Work of Grace?" *Articles Written by Pastor W.H. Durham, Taken from Pentecostal Testimony.* Springfield, MO: Assemblies of God Archives, n.d.
——. "Sanctification: The Bible Does Not Teach That It Is a Second Definite Work of Grace." *Articles Written by Pastor W.H. Durham, Taken from Pentecostal Testimony.* Springfield, MO: Assemblies of God Archives, n.d.
——. "Identification with Christ." *Articles Written by Pastor W.H. Durham, Taken from Pentecostal Testimony.* Springfield, MO: Assemblies of God Archives, n.d.
——. "The Winnipeg Convention." *Pentecostal Testimony* January 1912.
——. "Some Other Phases of Sanctification." *Pentecostal Testimony* July 1912.
Ewart, Frank. "The Unity of God." *Meat in Due Season* June 1916, 1.
——. *The Phenomenon of Pentecost: A History of the "Latter Rain".* St. Louis, MO: Pentecostal Publishing House, 1947.
Faupel, D. William. *The Everlasting Gospel: The Significance of Eschatology in the Development of Pentecostal Thought.* Sheffield, UK: Sheffield Academic Press, 1996.
Fudge, Thomas A. "Did E.N. Bell Convert to the New Issue?" *Journal of Pentecostal Theology* 18 (2001): 122–140.
——. *Christianity without the Cross: A History of Salvation in Oneness Pentecostalism.* Parkland, FL: Universal Publishers, 2003.
Goff, James R. Jr. *Fields White unto Harvest: Charles F. Parham and the Missionary Origins of Pentecostalism.* Fayetteville, AR: The University of Arkansas Press, 1988.
Goss, Howard. "Godhead," *Pentecostal Herald* 23 December 23 1948.
Larden, Robert A. *Our Apostolic Heritage.* Calgary, AB: Kyle Printing and Stationery, Co., 1971.
MacRobert, Ian. *The Black Roots and White Racism of Early Pentecostalism in the USA.* London: Macmillan, 1988.
McAlister, R.E. "The Finished Work of Calvary." *Supplement to the Good Report,* nd.
——. "The Unity of God," *Pentecostal Testimony* 1 December 1920.
Miller, Thomas W. *Canadian Pentecostals: A History of the Pentecostal Assemblies of Canada.* Edited by William A. Griffin. Mississauga, ON: Full Gospel Publishing House, 1994.
Paterson, John. *The Real Truth about Baptism in Jesus' Name.* Hazelwood, MO: Pentecostal Publishing House, 1953.
——. *God in Christ Jesus.* Montreal: Privately published, 1966.
Reed, David A. *'In Jesus' Name' – The History and Beliefs of Oneness Pentecostals.* Blandford, UK: Deo Publishing, 2008.
Rudd, Douglas. *When the Spirit Came Upon Them: Highlights from the Early Years of the Pentecostal Movement in Canada.* Burlington, ON: Antioch Books, 2002.
Small, Franklin. *A Synopsis of the Name and Deity of Christ.* Winnipeg: Zion Apostolic Church, n.d.
——. *Living Waters: A Sure Guide for Your Faith.* Winnipeg: Columbia Press, Ltd., nd.
——. "'Ye Must be Born Again' *versus* The Probation Tangle." *Living Waters* May 1937.
——. "Historical and Valedictory Account of the Origin of Water Baptism in Jesus' Name Only." *Living Waters* April 1941.
——. "The Doctrine of the Fulness of God in Christ, in Pentecostal Circles in Canada." *Living Waters* April 1941.
——. "The Sin Question." *Living Waters* February 1944.
——. "Editorial." *Living Waters* September 1946.
——. "The Godhead: Questions and Answers." *Living Waters* September 1946.

——. "The Fallen Nature: Total Moral Depravity of the Human Heart." *Living Waters* March 1951.

Tyson, James L. *The Early Pentecostal Revival: History of Twentieth-Century Pentecostals and The Pentecostal Assemblies of the World, 1901–30.* Hazelwood, MO: Word Aflame Press, 1992.

Urshan, Andrew. "Canadian Evangelistic Trip." *Witness of God* January 1922.

——. "The Doctrine of the Trinity and the Divinity of Jesus Christ." *Pentecostal Witness* 3 December 1926.

Wegner, Linda. *Streams of Grace: A History of The Apostolic Church of Pentecost of Canada.* Edmonton, AB: New Leaf Works, 2006.

CHAPTER TEN

WYNN T. STAIRS: ATLANTIC CANADIAN FULL GOSPEL PENTECOSTAL LEADER

Shane Flanagan

I was serving the devil then but now I am serving the Lord.[1]

INTRODUCTION

Dramatic life transformation was the result for many who joined the early Full Gospel-Pentecostal community in New Brunswick, Canada. This reorientation not only affected the intellect and the emotions of the individual but also significantly changed his or her actions as well. The opening statement noted above was penned by Wynn Stairs within a few months of his own conversion to Christ in a revival meeting. It is a summary statement of personal conversion which underscored the change in spiritual allegiance shared by many early Full Gospel-Pentecostal Christians. Conviction of sin changed the way people lived and it revolutionized their relationships with others.

The life and ministry of Wynn Stairs serves as a case study of an early Full Gospel-Pentecostal leader in Atlantic Canada. Stairs is an example of the indigenization and development of a Full Gospel-Pentecostal identity in the Atlantic Northeast. This broader geographic area includes the Maritime Provinces of Canada especially New Brunswick and Nova Scotia but also includes the state of Maine. His ministry legacy impacted the Atlantic Northeast in Canada and the United States, Quebec, the American mid-west and internationally on several different mission fields.

During his ministry career he belonged to several different, and in some cases, overlapping organizations and ministerial fellowships. Originally receiving ministerial credentials with the Apostolic Church of Pentecost of Canada (ACOP), Stairs would later hold credentials,

---

[1] Stairs, letter written to the CPR, 2 February 2 1921.

with several other Pentecostal organizations. He established several pioneer churches, pastored or gave oversight to a local church in St. Stephen, New Brunswick for several decades, was asked to be missions secretary by three different organizations, was active in the Full Gospel Ministerial Fellowship, established the Full Gospel Pentecostal Church denomination in New Brunswick, and participated in the merger of the New Brunswick based denomination with the American based United Pentecostal Church. His conversion and ministry career in this region is representative of the character displayed by many early converts to the Pentecostal tradition and how their influence shaped its later development.

EARLY YEARS

Wynn Theodore Stairs (1901–1982) was born on the family farm in Temperance Vale, New Brunswick. He was the son of Theodore and Annie Stairs.[2] He grew up in this area and his family attended the United Baptist Church located in Temperance Vale. He did not profess any faith commitment while growing up. His mother and aunt were active lay leaders organizing a large Baptist Sunday school. In time, his mother was nicknamed "Annie Be Saved" and her sister-in-law Liz Sharp was called "Lizzie Divine".[3] The Stairs family was exposed to the Pentecostal movement by Wynn's uncle, a Primitive Baptist minister, who had attended a convention at Mars Hill, Maine. Upon returning home he related his experience and observations to the Stairs family. At the time, Wynn Stairs was not interested in religion or his uncle's stories, however. Occasionally he felt compelled to listen at a distance.

Beginning with the original tent revival meeting conducted in 1917 by Aimee Semple McPherson, several Pentecostal mission centres were established in Caribou, Ashland, Presque Isle, Monticello, Mars Hill, Easton, and Summerville, Maine. Edgar Grant, who was baptized in the Spirit in the McPherson meeting, established Pentecostal missions in Summerville (commonly called the "Tin Church"), Clearview, and River du Chute, New Brunswick.[4] During the winter of

---

[2] Theodore and Annie (nee Sharp) Stairs had five children: Wynn, Roy, Quincy, Bernice and Lena. See: Peters, *Prevailing Westerlies*, 60.

[3] Type written manuscript of Stairs interview with Anne Stairs, "Growth and Dates," c. May 1982.

[4] Stairs, "How and When the Oneness message came to N.B."

1918–1919 Grant arrived in Woodstock, New Brunswick and pitched a tent. Using tents to conduct revival meetings was a common method used by many Full Gospel-Pentecostal evangelists and pioneer ministers. During Grant's tent meetings Wynn Stairs reported that the "power fell like rain."[5] Woodstock was deeply impacted and several "drunkards and respectable citizens were converted."[6]

In 1920, Grant was asked to go to the Lower Southampton-Nackawic area to conduct a funeral for a baby. While he was there, he arranged to use the 'Old Round Top Church' that had formerly belonged to the United Baptists and was used occasionally by the Primitive Baptists. These special meetings led to the 'Round Top Revival' in which several people, including Wynn Stairs, were converted. Stairs noted the impact this revival had on his family and friends. "Ten young people got saved including Bros. Milford Stairs, Leonard Parent, Wynn and Quincy Stairs. The entire country was moved toward God."[7] These specific individuals became significant leaders in the Jesus Name Pentecostal[8] movement in New Brunswick. Stairs highlighted the results of the conversions from this revival. "Conviction seized the people, they began getting right with each other and with God. Husbands and wives made things right with each other. Brothers that had not spoken to each other in years got right with each other and with God. 'Horse traders' (horse-trading was a way of life then, many made their living by 'trading' horses) went and paid money to those they had cheated in the trade. Men carried back tools they had stolen from Penders Mill, and men made restitution to the C.P. Railway."[9]

Conviction of sin, repentance of sin and restitution of known sins were important elements in the development of a Full Gospel-Pentecostal popular piety. Promotion of this rubric was supported, especially among Baptistic-Pentecostals[10] such as the Full Gospel-Pentecostals,

---

[5] The 'power' referred to in this statement is a common shorthand way to express the power of the Holy Spirit.

[6] Stairs, *How and When*.

[7] Stairs, *Brief history*, 1.

[8] Jesus Name is a common label used by Oneness Pentecostals to describe their movement.

[9] Stairs, *How and When*.

[10] Baptistic-Pentecostal is a term that functions as a label for the Keswick Holiness influenced Pentecostals in contrast to the Wesleyan Holiness influenced Pentecostals. Baptistic-Pentecostal denominations include the Assemblies of God, the Pentecostal Assemblies of Canada and the United Pentecostal Church.

due to the general understanding that conversion-sanctification[11] and
Spirit baptism was a two step process. After this initial experience of
conversion-sanctification it was necessary to make the appropriate
apologies and to return stolen goods or property. These actions continued the sanctification process begun at salvation until all things were
'made right.' Once this occurred, it was believed that the individual
was in a position to receive the subsequent baptism in the Holy Spirit
accompanied by speaking in tongues.

Water baptism in the name of the Lord Jesus Christ was a central
practice and an important experiential milestone for Jesus Name
Pentecostals. During the summer of 1922, two years after his conversion in the revival meetings, Stairs was working at the Smith Mill in
Deer Lake. He prayed and studied his Bible often throughout this
period. Although there is no evidence of a previous profession of faith
in the United Baptist Church, nonetheless, he may have been water
baptized in the Trinitarian formula of Father, Son and Holy Spirit some
time prior to 1920. This would appear to be the case based on his assertion "that God spoke to my heart and told me to be baptised in Jesus
Name. At that time no one had been 're-baptized.'" Stairs was baptized
in Jesus Name by John Deering along with several others Sunday
evening 1 October 1922.[12]

Shortly after his conversion, Stairs was one of a group of men who
offered to make restitution with Canadian Pacific Railway in New
Brunswick. He felt that it was necessary to write a restitution letter
which itemized certain areas of misconduct and asked pardon for his
lack of stewardship while working for the company. He described how
he had stolen candy and fruit when he worked in the freight shed, and
other company resources such as a lantern. He also asked forgiveness
for doing things on company time such as cashing a pay check or for
stealing rides from the trains without a pass. Stairs was clear in his
purpose for writing the letter. "I am writing this morning to ask forgiveness and to make some wrong right." He gave witness to his conversion and what that meant to him stating that he had taken "… Jesus
as my Saviour and I mean to live an honest Christian life before this

---

[11] Support for a combined conversion-sanctification experience called the 'Finished
Work of Calvary' was introduced to the early Pentecostal community in the United
States by William Durham in 1910. It led to controversy with the Holiness Pentecostal
position that advocated separate experiences for conversion and sanctification. See
Riss, "Finished Work Controversy."
[12] "Down Memory Lane," 2.

world and I want to make every wrong right."[13] There is indication of a reply from the Canadian Pacific Railway but it would appear that nothing was pursued and criminal charges were not laid against Stairs. The Superintendent simply asked Stairs to return the lantern that he had mentioned in the letter and assured Stairs that the company "will forgive and forget about all the other matters mentioned in your letter."[14] Honesty and integrity in all things and seeking to make amends was central to the commitment to a life of holiness for Full Gospel-Pentecostal adherents. This was one of the primary methods of witness to the transforming power of the gospel of Jesus Christ.

Sharing the new found 'full gospel' of Jesus Christ with others was soon to become a life long obsession for Stairs. On a Saturday evening in June 1923, Stairs was reading *On Mule Back Thru Central America with the Gospel*[15] by Mattie Crawford.[16] It was the writing of Crawford that inspired Stairs immediate interest in foreign missions. At this time he was a stationary engineer at a saw mill located in Canterbury, New Brunswick. One evening he was sleeping in a small building located behind the mill. While he was sleeping he had a dream that was to focus his developing missionary interest. "I had a visitation from God … I have never called it a vision but rather a dream – I suppose it could be called a night vision. In my night vision I saw South America; I saw the need; I saw that country as plain as could be; I heard the call from God. The next morning I came out of that little shack with the love of God burning in my heart; I went to the Baptist[17] church because we had no Pentecostal Church at that time."[18] The dream that he experienced that night and the rising passion for missions was something that he wanted to share with other Christians. His cousin Pearly Quigg pastored the Primitive Baptist Church which Stairs attended in Canterbury. During a testimony meeting Stairs shared his experience with the congregation: "… we gave our few words and told them the heathen were lost and could not help it. It seemed to touch many in the church that morning as well as my own heart. The yearning and

---

[13] Stairs, to unidentified CPR representative.

[14] Signature unclear, Superintendent, Canadian National Railway, to Wynn T. Stairs, Lower Southampton, New Brunswick.

[15] See Crawford, *On Mule Back Thru Central America with the Gospel*.

[16] Stairs, interview by Anne Stairs. Crawford was a Baptist evangelist who later became a Full Gospel-Pentecostal healing evangelist.

[17] Hand written insertion indicates that it was a Primitive Baptist Church.

[18] Stairs, "I Was Not Disobedient To The Heavenly Vision."

longing for the souls of South America was terrific...."[19] Stairs also developed an interest in missions in other countries such as India, China, Japan and the continent of Africa. "So, from that day we started to work for South America and the whole world."[20]

Although Stairs kept attending the Primitive Baptist church, he started to transition into Full Gospel-Pentecostal ministry. His calling into full-time Christian service was influenced in part through Lillian Jacques who identified herself as his 'Mother in Christ.' Her motherly counsel is noted in a letter to Stairs where she stated: "... you are dinging your time out in those old mills and other things and young people are going to Hell every day in the name of our great God who is Jesus get alone with him and tarry until the Holy Spirit comes in and awake out of your sleep that the enemy has tried to keep you in and get out in the great field for I know that God is calling you for I just spoke in tongues and got the message that why stand you idol [sic] all the day when God hath need of thee oh Wynn the message is for you."[21] Around this time, Stairs offered to assist Mrs. Jacques' son Earl, as well as Harvey and Margaret Flewelling in their tent revival ministry. He was directly involved in the tent meetings conducted in Zealand Station and Fredericton. This evangelistic team was eventually augmented with the ministry of Carro Davis, Susie Davis[22] and later by Clifford Crabtree. The Davises had just left John Deering[23] in charge of the Bangor mission in Maine. Carro Davis wanted to move the tent from Zealand Station and set it up in Fredericton. There was opposition from the people including the mayor of Fredericton who printed an article in the *Daily Gleaner* asserting: "the Holy Rollers cannot roll in Fredericton!"[24] After seven attempts, a lot was secured on Woodstock Road and the tent was set up. During one of the services a young boy 'fell under the power of God.' This was cause for concern for a woman who attended the meeting and she called in the police. The police subsequently arrived and ordered Crabtree to close the meeting down.

---

[19] Stairs, "I Was Not Disobedient To The Heavenly Vision."
[20] Stairs, "I Was Not Disobedient To The Heavenly Vision."
[21] Jacques to Stairs, 25 June 1924. 1 & 2. Personal files of Anne Stairs.
[22] Jacques to Stairs, 25 June 1924. 1 & 2. Personal files of Anne Stairs, 4.
[23] Deering was an influential mentor to many early Full Gospel-Pentecostals in Maine and New Brunswick beginning in the 1920s and lasting for about two decades. He was the minister who introduced Oneness theology and water baptism in the name of the Lord Jesus Christ to the Atlantic Northeast region.
[24] Peters, *Prevailing Westerlies*, 122.

Crabtree then asked the congregation: "Who is on the Lord's side?" In response the congregation "arose to their feet as one, cheering and shouting and praising God." The police left and while they were leaving Stairs offered them tracts. The officers suggested he mind his own business. Stairs replied: "This is my business."[25]

FULL GOSPEL ASSEMBLY

The first Full Gospel-Pentecostal tent meeting held in the St. Stephen area was conducted on 25 July 1926.[26] Earl Jacques brought the tent from Fredericton in an effort to pioneer a new church in the community. He continued holding evangelistic services throughout the summer and was assisted by Wynn Stairs, C.W. Hyde and Rev. and Mrs. E.C. Joyall. The crowds were never large and the tent was never filled but a few individuals did make professions of faith. Among these early converts were Nelson Getchell and Burton Eastman.[27] In September the services moved to the Johnston Hall and the following month to a small hall in the Douglas building. At the end of September, Jacques returned to his pastoral duties in Fredericton. For the next year, Erwin Joyall became pastor of the small group. It was during this time of consolidation for the pioneer church in St. Stephen that Stairs experienced the baptism in the Holy Spirit on 26 October 1926. When Pastor Joyall left in July 1927, Wynn Stairs became the pastor of Full Gospel Church.[28]

Many of the independent Full Gospel-Pentecostal churches, such as the assembly in St. Stephen, New Brunswick had ministers who were credentialed by the ACOP including Hubert Perkins, Milford Stairs, Earl Jacques,[29] Wynn Stairs, Harvey Flewelling and George Croft. In 1928, the year after Stairs became the pastor in St. Stephen, Franklin Small, Moderator of the fellowship, visited the Maritime Provinces. The ACOP historian Robert Larden noted that the Full Gospel churches in the region "were in common fellowship with Apostolic Church of Pentecost."[30] In essence, these churches cooperated with the

---

[25] Peters, 123.

[26] Stairs, "Brief history of the Saint Stephen Pentecostal Church," 1.

[27] Stairs, "Brief history of the Saint Stephen Pentecostal Church," 1.

[28] Stairs, "Brief history of the Saint Stephen Pentecostal Church," 1.

[29] Jacques was the Apostolic Church of Pentecost of Canada's District Presbyter in the Maritimes at the time of Small's visit in 1928.

[30] Larden, *Our Apostolic*, 159.

denominational fellowship and were loosely affiliated with the organization. While in the Maritime Provinces, Franklin Small held special services at several established Full Gospel assemblies including St. Stephen, Windsor, Yarmouth, Fredericton, Millville, Woodstock, Tilley and Saint John.[31] In St. Stephen, after the meetings had ended there were several who professed faith in Christ and about "thirty-five candidates were buried in the Name of the Lord Jesus Christ amid floating ice upon the waters."[32] While Small was in Tilley, several were baptized in the Holy Spirit at the church and in homes. Larden states: "When it was time for the altar call there wasn't kneeling room. Oh such prayer … young men and older people with uplifted hands crying to God for the latter rain. They began falling under the power almost in all directions, and came through speaking in other languages until ten or twelve received the baptism. During our four nights there so crowded became the space for altar work it seemed impossible to continue in the church. Then the power broke upon many during the day in their homes where numbers received the Holy Ghost."[33] These experiences were the goal of a Full Gospel-Pentecostal revival service: conversions, water baptisms in Jesus' Name and Spirit baptisms evidenced by speaking in tongues. 'Receiving the Holy Ghost' was a shorthand term to describe the experience of Spirit baptism. During this year, Stairs was ordained by Earl Jacques and Milford Stairs, the two original Apostolic Church of Pentecost of Canada ordained ministers in New Brunswick.

Throughout the 1930s, Full Gospel Church in St. Stephen continued to grow as Stairs emerged as an influential leader in the borderland region of Maine and New Brunswick. During the depression years, he was active in home missions, preaching, and establishing new missions and churches in communities such as Honeydale, McAdam and St. Andrews in New Brunswick as well as Princeton and Milltown, Maine.[34] Clifton McCarthy assisted Stairs with the pioneer work in Honeydale and later pioneered a church in Alexander, Maine.[35]

---

[31] Larden, 160. The pastors of the Full Gospel churches were as follows: St. Stephen: Wynn Stairs; Windsor: H.T. Adams; Yarmouth: Harvey Flewelling and George E. Croft; Fredericton: Earl Jacques; Millville: Andy Mowatt; Woodstock: 'Brother' McAffee; Tilley: William Rolston; Saint John: Carro Davis and Susie Davis.

[32] Larden, 159. It was common for Jesus Name Full Gospel-Pentecostals to conduct outdoor water baptisms in rivers and lakes in all four seasons.

[33] Larden, 160.

[34] Stairs, *Growth and Dates*, 1.

[35] Stairs, *Growth and Dates*, 1.

Foreign Missions Advocate

Home mission opportunities were not the only outlet for Stairs' pioneering spirit. Although he enjoyed sharing the gospel with others in missions and preaching points in New Brunswick and Maine his primary interest was the promotion of foreign mission opportunities. Initially, he could not go himself but he was tireless in his organization of financial support for those who felt called to go. Stairs' passion for foreign missions was responsible for creating awareness about the need to evangelize in foreign lands. Due to his influence many individuals as well as several congregations financially supported Full Gospel-Pentecostal missionaries. The financial resources were important but Stairs also stressed the necessity of prayer for the various missionary pioneer projects. Lastly, he inspired several Jesus Name Full Gospel-Pentecostal adherents to respond to the call of life service in foreign missions. The stanza noted below was written by Burton Eastman one of Stairs original converts at Full Gospel Assembly. The poem is illustrative of the missionary zeal that characterized Stairs ministry for several decades.

> Thank God for the church whose preacher is on fire,
> That refuses to be led by deacon or choir.
> That preaches the Word regardless of cost,
> To redeem from sin the man that is lost.
> Thank God for the church with the missionary vision,
> Like Paul of old, has made his decision;
> That will preach the Word in every clime,
> And be ready to go in God's appointed time.[36]

With the passion of foreign missions in his mind, Stairs attended the Mars Hill Annual Convention in 1931 where he had the first opportunity to meet missionaries working in South America. Charles Berchtold had recently returned from a short-term assignment to Bolivia with the Indian Bolivian Mission and his wife had been baptized in the Holy Spirit and spoke in tongues while in Bolivia. After this brief encounter, Stairs believed that his 'dream' was beginning to be realized with the arrival of the Berchtolds. He invited them to attend his church in St. Stephen and to share their passion for South America.

---

[36] Stairs, *Brief History*, 3.

Soon Stairs had arranged opportunities for them to speak in other Full Gospel assemblies in the surrounding region.[37] Berchtold was subsequently baptized in the Holy Spirit at Full Gospel Assembly in Saint John.[38] In 1933, the same year that the Berchtolds were going to leave for Colombia, a special meeting of gospel workers had convened at Full Gospel Assembly. William Booth-Clibborn[39] was preaching for the Davis sisters. During these special services, a missionary board was established at the assembly consisting of Carro Davis, William Rolston and Wynn Stairs as chairman.[40]

The Berchtolds stayed in New Brunswick and toured the region promoting missions for Columbia. In several churches, individuals responded to the challenge and embraced a personal call to return with the Berchtolds to Colombia to pioneer in that country. They confidently asserted: "Colombia is where we want to go; Colombia has never been touched; Colombia has eleven million people; Colombia must hear this… Colombia must hear the Word of the Lord; We're ready to go to Colombia… Who will go to Colombia?"[41] Among those who responded were: A. Verner Larsen, Abbie Staples, Bill Drost, Sanford Johnston and eventually Charles Berchtold's sister Eleanor.[42] Stairs went to the Full Gospel Pentecostal Church in Newcastle Bridge on Missionary Day and made an appeal for the support of the Berchtolds in their Colombian mission. The congregation responded with an offering of cash and pledges of $400 and with this the Berchtolds went to Colombia.[43] Larsen and Staples were later married and after the birth of their first child joined the Berchtolds.

Through this encounter between Stairs and the Berchtolds, a missionary partnership was forged between Full Gospel churches in New Brunswick with missions in Colombia that lasted for several decades. In summarizing this new relationship Stairs happily noted concerning the ministry of the Berchtolds in Sogomosa: "They laboured there and in other parts of Colombia presenting the wonderful name of Jesus; here was a happy privilege to back and support them."[44]

---

[37] Stairs, *Brief History* 2.
[38] Stairs, *Brief History* 3.
[39] Grandson of William Booth founder of the Salvation Army.
[40] Stairs, *My Thirteenth Visit to Columbia*.
[41] Stairs, *My Thirteenth Visit to Columbia*, 2.
[42] Stairs, *My Thirteenth Visit to Columbia*, 2.
[43] Stairs, *My Thirteenth Visit to Columbia*, 2.
[44] Stairs, *My Thirteenth Visit to Columbia*, 2.

As the missionary partnerships were being forged Stairs attended a
funeral for an influential minister from Maine commonly known as
Mother Clark. At the funeral he happened to meet a widow named
Margaret Delano.[45] Stairs and Delano were later married on 10 October
1934. She would become his partner in life and in ministry. Together
they committed themselves to Full Gospel-Pentecostal ministry. His
new wife had one ten year old daughter from the marriage to her first
husband Reuben Delano. The Stairs would have an additional five children together.[46] The Stairs family were among the early Full Gospel-
Pentecostal pioneers in New Brunswick. Through their ministry efforts
several new churches were pioneered in Canada as well as around the
world.

DENOMINATIONAL ORGANIZER

Although there was a concentration of Jesus Name Full Gospel-
Pentecostal churches pioneered in New Brunswick and Nova Scotia
the distance between the Western Conference and the Eastern
Conference of the ACOP was geographically significant. The majority
of the churches in the Western Conference were established in the
Prairie Provinces with the national headquarters located in Winnipeg,
Manitoba. The Eastern Conference was primarily composed of
churches in the Maritime Provinces with a few located in Ontario. The
result was that meaningful relationships and connections were chal-
lenging due to the distance and limited means of travel especially during the 1920s–1930s. The relationship between the Western Conference
and the Eastern Conference leaders remained cordial but in New
Brunswick there was a shift towards greater organizational autonomy.
This was due in part to the development of a missionary program
that was separate from the other areas of ACOP denominational mission involvement. The indigenization of Jesus' Name Pentecostal leadership in the Maritime region and the development of an unrelated
missionary support program with South American missionaries meant
the seeds for independence were beginning to germinate.

---

[45] Margaret Stairs was the daughter of Solomon and Catherine Drost.
[46] The children included Robena Delano the eldest and the Stairs siblings Earl,
Philip, Rolfe, Joan and Anne. See "Pentecostal Missionary Fellowship," 3.

The Full Gospel Pentecostal Church continued supporting missionary work in Colombia. Sanford Johnston was involved in mission work
in Bucaramanga, Colombia beginning in 1937 which had progressed
so that nine years later it had a solid base of converts and had constructed a church and a house. This happened at an opportune moment
because they were no longer able to rent. Priests were putting pressure
on the people not to assist the Full Gospel missionaries.[47] Stairs wrote
and circulated an article in December 1946 titled "No More Rent to
Pay." The money for the purchase of the land came primarily from the
former Pentecostal Assemblies of Jesus Christ and 'undesignated missionary money' from Full Gospel churches in New Brunswick.[48]

In 1938, Wynn Stairs, Milford Stairs, and Willard Willson (sic)
attended the Pentecostal Assemblies of Jesus Christ General Conference
in Columbus, Ohio.[49] While there they were encouraged to join the
denomination, they declined to do so. It would appear that this was an
investigative journey related to affiliation with another organization.
The continued relationship with the ACOP was proving inadequate on
a number of levels.

The ACOP network of churches had grown considerably in New
Brunswick by 1939. Three important issues had surfaced, however, and
were discussed by the ministers in the Eastern Conference of the fellowship. The primary matter related to the deeds of church properties.
Wynn Stairs was in communication with Franklin Small in Winnipeg
as well as Raymond Storie in Regina.[50] Stairs was trying to ascertain the
correct procedure for holding property, not only in New Brunswick
but also in the missionary effort in Colombia, South America. Storie
told him the majority of church properties in Saskatchewan belonged
to the ACOP and that the churches were likewise affiliated with the
organization.[51]

The second issue of concern was the teaching of 'eternal security' also called 'eternal life' in the ACOP. This belief promoted the
idea that once a person was converted that individual remained
a Christian for eternity. While J. Eustace Purdie taught and practiced

---

[47] Letter from Stairs, Secretary-Treasurer, Full Gospel Pentecostal Church, St.
Stephen, 1946.
[48] Letter from Stairs, Secretary-Treasurer, Full Gospel Pentecostal Church, St.
Stephen, 1946.
[49] Stairs, *Interview 6*.
[50] Letter to Raymond Storie from Wynn Stairs 3 July 1939, St. Stephen, NB, 1.
[51] Letter to Wynn Stairs from Raymond Storie 6 June 1939, Regina, SK, 1.

a moderate Calvinism in the Pentecostal Assemblies of Canada, his influence extended primarily to the leaders trained through the Bible school in Winnipeg. The pastoral leaders did not make this belief into a significant issue with the denomination at large. In contrast, the ACOP became even more Calvinistic through the influence and ministry of men such as Walter Smith. This move affected many leaders and their churches in western Canada. Storie wrote to Stairs:

> When we first started teaching Eternal life we did not find it caused slack living. It did the very opposite. Before we seen [sic] the complete rapture there was a lot of judging one another among the saints. One would say the other would not go up in the rapture if they did so and so, but they did not see themselves as others seen [sic] them. I quit preaching a partial rapture before I seen [sic] Eternal life because of the judging of one another caused division instead of unity. After we started teaching Eternal life that judging disappeared and they became fishers of men instead of judges sitting on the fence watching others [sic] mistakes. The revival spirit came into the Assembly and the Lord has blessed ever since.[52]

The main issue for Stairs and the other eastern Canadian ministers concerning this teaching seemed to be rooted in the belief that the promotion of eternal security teaching would lead to lax living by Christians and might actually encourage Christians to sin because they were not in jeopardy of being damned. Storie encouraged Stairs saying that he believed that all, including Stairs, had eternal life whether they enjoyed it or not.[53] Lastly, Storie assured Stairs that his concern was not warranted. "You need have no fears as far as the brethren are concerned. We fellowship with those who do not believe in the Eternal life teachings.[54] We do not believe in force. The Holy Spirit is the only one that reveals the word to any one."[55] Storie asserted "I am not so interested in teaching Eternal life as I am in seeing the unsaved get eternal life."

The third point of increasing concern was the inability to cultivate meaningful spiritual relationships between the ministers in the Western and Eastern Conferences of the fellowship. The ACOP was a western Canadian based organization with its administrative base in Winnipeg.

---

[52] Letter to Wynn Stairs from Raymond Storie 6 June 1939, Regina, SK, 3.

[53] Letter to Wynn Stairs from Raymond Storie 6 June 1939, Regina, SK, 3.

[54] This sentence is an example of popular Pentecostal phraseology in use at the time. The meaning of the phrase could be restated as follows: We extend fellowship to those who do not believe in the Eternal life teachings.

[55] Letter to Wynn Stairs from Raymond Storie 6 June 1939, 2.

It was perhaps difficult to justify travelling to Winnipeg from New Brunswick especially during the Great Depression.

In the end, the Eastern Conference ministers decided to apply for a New Brunswick provincial charter, to the dismay of Storie, in order to settle the matters relating to the ownership of property, the concerns they expressed over Calvinistic doctrine and to satisfactorily resolve the distance issue with the Western Conference. After the Full Gospel Pentecostal Church society was set up, the properties could become part of the new organization. In practical terms, the Eastern Conference ministers continued their relationship with the ACOP but many applied for credentials with the new organization as well. In this way, credibility was maintained by belonging to the older fellowship while the benefits of membership in a local fellowship were developed.

The first meeting of the Organization Committee of the Full Gospel Pentecostal Church, consisting of Wynn Stairs, Quincy R. Stairs, Earl L. Jacques and E.C. Joyal, convened on 15 March 1939.[56] In his opening remarks as chairman, Wynn Stairs reassured the assembled ministers:[57] "In the Full Gospel Pentecostal Church you have the same liberty as in the Apostolic Church of Pentecost; and have extra privilege of holding property in the name of the Full Gospel Pentecostal Church if the individual Assembly chooses to do so."[58] The preamble of the provincial charter outlined the purpose and the parameters of the new local organization:

> WHEREAS certain Ministers of the Gospel resident in the Province of New Brunswick and State of Maine, in the United States of America, holding the Full Gospel Pentecostal Faith, have organized as a religious, charitable and benevolent body under the name "Full Gospel Pentecostal Church," and are desirous of becoming incorporated for the purpose of

---

[56] *Minutes of the Full Gospel Pentecostal Church* 15 March 1939, 2.

[57] *Minutes*, 2 List of ministers who are noted as 'applicants' who wished to join the Full Gospel Pentecostal Church: E.A. Cole, Alton Stewart, Orval Lyons, Henry Crocker, Dow Estey, Geo. Stanley, Stanley McConaghy, Samuel Steeves, Mrs. Milford Stairs, Verner Larson, Clement Hyde, Walter Norris, David Crabtree, 5. Credential applications were received for the following on 23 August 1939: Clement W. Hyde, Stanley McConaghy, G.W. Stanley, Milford Stairs, Harvey M. Howe. For license: Ellary M. Cady, J.C. Lyons, A.W. Post. 24 August 1939 further credential applications: W.H. Ring, B.A. McQuarrie and probationary license: A.B. Copeland, C.B. Dudley. Others mentioned: Peter Cosman, William Rolston, C.H. McCarty,

[58] This statement about holding property with the Full Gospel Pentecostal Church suggests that many of these churches, although probably pastored by an Apostolic Church of Pentecost of Canada minister, nonetheless, were independent local Full Gospel churches.

better enabling them to acquire, hold and manage property and administer their affairs.[59]

At this meeting, Earl Jacques was elected to serve as chairman and E.C. Joyal as secretary until the annual meeting was held at the Newcastle Bridge Convention.[60] Jacques was a respected early leader among the Jesus Name Full Gospel-Pentecostal community and he was already serving in the capacity of District Presbyter for the ACOP.

The first annual meeting was held 24 August 1939 just prior to the Second World War. At this meeting several important decisions were made that would secure the by-laws of the organization. First, it was decided that there should be seven trustees. Second, Wynn Stairs' church, located in St. Stephen, was chosen as the headquarters of the new organization. Third, the following motion was put forward by Quincy Stairs and seconded by Orval Lyons, "that we require all members of F.G.P.C. be Baptized in Jesus' name."[61] This latter provision ensured that the membership would be drawn from Jesus Name Pentecostals, in the tradition of the ACOP. The result of this action excluded Trinitarian Full Gospel-Pentecostals from joining the organization unless they had been baptized in Jesus' name.[62] In 1940, the Full Gospel Pentecostal Church conducted its first ordination service.[63]

The process towards greater autonomy for the Eastern Conference gained momentum during the war years. Under the capable leadership of men such as Wynn Stairs, Samuel Steeves and Earl Jacques, the Full Gospel Pentecostal Church continued to grow as many more churches

---

[59] Full Gospel Pentecostal Church Charter, Province of New Brunswick, 1939.

[60] This church was one of the leading independent Full Gospel churches in New Brunswick pastored by Samuel Steeves. It sponsored an annual camp meeting convention and later founded Emmanuel Bible School a Jesus' Name Full Gospel Bible training school. Steeves is noted among the early leaders present at the establishment of the Full Gospel Pentecostal Church. Like his involvement in the Full Gospel Ministerial Fellowship, possible involvement in the Apostolic Church of Pentecost of Canada, this present church association would not be the last for Steeves or others like him in the New Brunswick and Maine borderland region.

[61] Full Gospel Pentecostal Church Minutes, 1939, 6.

[62] Full Gospel Pentecostal Church Minutes, 1939, 10. Note: Full Gospel Assembly in Saint John, New Brunswick was one church that did baptize in Jesus' Name however the congregation was made up of both Oneness and Trinitarian members. The Davis sisters at Full Gospel Assembly although remaining organizationally aloof were nonetheless held in high regard by the Full Gospel Pentecostal community in New Brunswick. A.W. Lewis asked to be considered for credentials with the Full Gospel Pentecostal Church but was declined due to working with Fred Clark in a Saint John mission that was in opposition to the Davis sister's church.

[63] Full Gospel Pentecostal Church Minutes, 1939, 2.

were established, ministers were credentialed or ordained[64] and missionaries commissioned. The experiment of local administration and
supervision proved to be successful. The organizing behaviours of the
Full Gospel Pentecostal Church was not inconsistent with the affiliation concept held by the ACOP and other early Pentecostal groups. It
was common for organizations to work closely together, allow multiple
concurrent credential papers for ministers and missionaries and to
freely fellowship with one another without much concern for doctrinal
views preferring unity and charity to division.

During the 1940s Stairs continued to develop as a leader in the promotion and support of missionaries. His ability at raising awareness
and funds for financial support was recognized by the Full Gospel
Ministerial Fellowship based in Mars Hill, Maine. On 22 October 1942,
at the annual business meeting, Stairs was appointed Missionary
Secretary along with Corinne Reed also from St. Stephen.[65] Two years
later in 1944 he succeeded W.T. Witherspoon as Missionary Chairman
with the Pentecostal Assemblies of Jesus Christ.[66] In 1945, Stairs
was also asked to be Missionary Secretary with the Full Gospel
Pentecostal Church.[67] When the Pentecostal Assemblies of Jesus Christ
and the Pentecostal Church Incorporated merged to form the United
Pentecostal Church in 1945, Stairs continued in the capacity as
Missionary Secretary with the new organization.[68]

DENOMINATIONS AND DOCTRINAL DIVERGENCE

The journey that had begun in 1939 by the Full Gospel Pentecostal
Church led to the last step of organic dissolution six years later between

---

[64] *Full Gospel Pentecostal Church Minutes*, 1939, 10. Note: J.O. Lyons was the first
person to be ordained by the Full Gospel Pentecostal Church on 8 February 1940 in
Bangor, ME and two other ordinations took place for Allison Post and Bernard
Cromwell the following month on 4 March 1940 in Fredericton, NB.

[65] Bickford. *Letter of introduction re: Wynn Stairs and Corinne Reed.*, Mars Hill, ME
22 October 1942.

[66] Clanton, *United We Stand*, 78. It is interesting that Stairs became associated with
this denomination due to the radical position that it promoted. In this organization,
'salvation' was equated to repentance, Jesus' name water baptism and Spirit baptism.
Conversion did not happen until the last of the three had occurred. Stairs did not
believe this doctrine and believed conversion occurred at repentance. See: Fudge,
History, 86.

[67] Unsigned *Letter of introduction re: Wynn Stairs and Quincy Stairs* 21 December
1945.

[68] *Manual United Pentecostal Church*, n.d., c. 1947.

the Western and Eastern Conferences of the ACOP. Although, initially
a secondary concern, nonetheless, the Eastern Conference ministers
were still not completely comfortable with the Calvinistic direction of
the ACOP and its ministers. Robert Larden described the reasons for
the distinct development of the Full Gospel churches in the east during
the 1940s that led to separation.

> This eastern group of ministers, on the most part, did not see eye to eye
> on the message of the finished work of Calvary or the grace of God as it
> is more commonly identified today. But this was not the reason for their
> early interests in fellowship with the United Pentecostal Church of the
> U.S.A. The predominant strength of Apostolic was in Western Canada.
> Fellowship was lean. The three thousand mile span made meaningful
> fellowship very difficult in those early years of limited travel. Necessary
> requested leadership and aid was not provided. The close proximity of
> the U.S.A. organization with its strength on the eastern seaboard seemed
> to be an answer to their need.[69]

Proximity may have been one concern but the more probable reason
for the discussion of a merger was the perceived similarity of doctrine
between the Full Gospel Pentecostal Church and the United Pentecostal
Church. The successful merger between the two organizations ensured
a measure of doctrinal certainty for the Full Gospel Pentecostal Church
ministers and this was believed to be essential to the future of the
group. By exchanging allegiances, they would rid themselves of the
Calvinistic influence on the one hand but on the other hand they
exposed themselves to the radical element in the newly merged United
Pentecostal Church.

The United Pentecostal Church was founded the year before in 1945
between the Pentecostal Church Incorporated and the Pentecostal
Assemblies of Jesus Christ. These two American Oneness organizations were Jesus Name Pentecostal groups with similar doctrine and
practice. They differed doctrinally and experientially, however, in one
important area. The issue centred on the interpretation of Christian

---

[69] Larden, *Our Apostolic*, 161–162. Note: Ministers such as Stairs would have made
requests for Western Conference ministers to visit the Eastern Conference for assistance and direction in Eastern Conference business as well as strengthening personal
relationships and enjoying spiritual fellowship together. Franklin Small, Moderator of
the fellowship, was based in Winnipeg, Manitoba and this was in effect the national
office of the organization. The two contributing factors of the Great Depression and
the geographical distance between Manitoba and New Brunswick meant that it was
difficult for meaningful exchange to occur. Relationships were maintained primarily
by correspondence.

conversion and initiation into the body of Christ. Both organizations
believed in the cardinal Oneness doctrines summarized by Acts 2.38.
But they differed on the timing of salvation.

The interpretation promoted by the Pentecostal Church Incorporated
maintained the traditional evangelical position that conversion followed repentance. Subsequent to conversion the individual was encouraged to be water baptized in the name of Jesus and to be further
baptized in the Holy Ghost. In contrast, the Pentecostal Assemblies of
Jesus Christ advocates promoted a radical position summarized by the
phrase "born of the water and the Spirit". Essentially, "water baptism in
Jesus' name remitted sins, and was the birth of the water ... [and] baptism of the Holy Ghost was the birth of the Spirit."[70] Ultimately, conversion was conditional and completed only after repentance, Jesus' name
water baptism and Spirit baptism had occurred.

This issue threatened to undermine the whole process of the original
merger. A satisfactory resolution to this belief needed to be found. W.T.
Witherspoon, a Pentecostal Assemblies of Jesus Christ minister wrote
a statement that became known as the 'Fundamental Doctrine' of the
organization. This diplomatic statement sealed the merger for the two
groups:

> The basic and fundamental doctrine of this organization shall be the
> bible standard of full salvation, which is repentance, baptism in water by
> immersion in the name of the Lord Jesus Christ, and the baptism of the
> Holy Ghost with the initial sign of speaking with other tongues as the
> Spirit gives utterance. We shall endeavor to keep the unity of the Spirit
> until we all come into the unity of the faith, at the same time admonish-
> ing all brethren that they shall not contend for their different views to the
> disunity of the body.[71]

Stairs had personally joined the Pentecostal Assemblies of Jesus Christ
some time after 1938, perhaps at the time of the foundation of the Full
Gospel Pentecostal Church. Since joining, he had been active on the

---

[70] Clanton, *United We Stand*, 120. This doctrine is based on John 3.5.
[71] Manual, United Pentecostal Church, 1969, 24. Presently the UPC is involved in
revisionist history about the merger. Since 1992, with the drafting of the Westburg
Resolution, the leadership of the denomination has downplayed the position of the
PCI element in the church at the time of the merger as well as throughout the development of the denomination in subsequent years. The new understanding is that the
majority of both organizations in 1945 originally supported the 'full salvation' model
of fulfilling all three steps before salvation actually occurred. For further reading in
this regard see Fudge, *Christianity Without the Cross*, 200 ff. Also see Reed, *"In Jesus'
Name."*

missionary board of the denomination and took over the role upon the retirement of Witherspoon as noted earlier. Stairs attended another Pentecostal Assemblies of Jesus Christ General Conference in 1945. He was involved in working with the denomination to secure the merger with the Pentecostal Church Incorporated. In the newly combined denomination, he was elected to serve as Missionary Secretary with the United Pentecostal Church in 1945.

The next two years were fairly busy for him traveling between St. Louis, Missouri and St. Stephen, New Brunswick. He encouraged the merger between the United Pentecostal Church and the Full Gospel Pentecostal Church in 1946. This move seemed like a natural progression from the former Canadian Jesus Name denomination, to establishing a regional Jesus Name denomination, to a new Canadian-American Jesus Name denomination. The latter became the largest Oneness denomination in North America. By establishing districts in Canada it would offer other Jesus Name churches an option between remaining independent congregations and belonging to the ACOP. The merger proposal involved the following six conditions: That we drop the words 'Full Gospel' from our charter and add 'United' in their place, and make any other changes in the charter that may be necessary; that the property now held by the Full Gospel Pentecostal Church Inc. become the property of the Maritime District of the United Pentecostal Church; that the United Pentecostal Church receive our ministerial list as they are without filing a new application form; that there always be one member of the Missionary Board residing in Canada; we ask that we be permitted to pay only six dollars budget fee to Headquarters, the remaing [sic] twelve dollars be held in the district for extension work; that in the event the Canadian brethren or members felt their desire to withdraw that they may withdraw upon a two-third-majority vote. Also that the charter of the Full Gospel Pentecostal Church present and accumulated property become the property of the Canadian brethren without any formal vote on the part of the General board of the General Conference.[72]

On 15 May 1946 these merger stipulations were approved with thirty-five yes votes and two no votes. The following day was the first session of the newly merged organization. S.G. Steeves was elected District Superintendent and Quincy Stairs was elected District

---

[72] *Maritime District of the United Pentecostal Church Minutes*, 1946.

Secretary Treasurer. In a board meeting held on 27 August a proposal was approved to ask Wynn Stairs, General Missionary Secretary, to appoint Quincy Stairs his assistant secretary in the Maritime District.[73]

Beginning in 1933 with an appointment to be Chairman of the Missionary Board at Full Gospel Assembly, Saint John and lasting until the 1960s, Stairs continued to develop as a leader in the promotion and support of missionaries. His ability at raising awareness and funds for financial support was recognized by the Full Gospel Ministerial Fellowship based in Mars Hill, Maine. On 22 October 1942, at the annual business meeting Stairs was appointed Missionary Secretary along with Corinne Reed also from St. Stephen. Two years later in 1944 he succeeded W.T. Witherspoon as Missionary Chairman with the Pentecostal Assemblies of Jesus Christ.[74] When the Pentecostal Assemblies of Jesus Christ and the Pentecostal Church Incorporated merged to form the United Pentecostal Church 1945, Stairs was elected Missionary Secretary with the new organization.[75]

During the next decade Stairs was consumed with promoting and fundraising for various foreign mission projects. He noted that two of the primary motivating factors in the merger of the two American denominations were first to promote 'harmony in the US' and second to 'promote foreign missions.' His first journey abroad to mission destinations occurred in 1947 with his trip to Colombia and Jamaica. Later that year, after the close of the morning service on 14 December 1947, Stairs suggested a discussion and a vote on whether his wife "Sister Margaret Stairs should be left as assistant or supply Pastor while Brother Stairs was away."[76] But Stairs assured the church that approving this action did not affect or change his status as the Pastor and Overseer of the church. His reasons were threefold. First he was concerned about who could be secured as a Pastor as many were only instructors and costly and in some cases detrimental to the spiritual welfare of the church. Second, Canadian supply Pastors would have no place to stay in St. Stephen. He was not sure where he was going to live as moving his family to St. Louis was financially impossible. Third, perhaps the most compelling reason was that Margaret felt called to preach in the church.

---

[73] *Maritime District of the United Pentecostal Church Minutes*, 1946.
[74] Clanton, *United We Stand*, 78.
[75] Stairs interview 6 with Anne Stairs, c. May, 1982. See also: Manual United Pentecostal Church, nd, c. 1947.
[76] *Minutes of the Full Gospel Pentecostal Church*, St. Stephen, 1947, 67–68.

In the past my Wife has had some indications as though God wanted her to carry on the work while I was away doing Missionary work. These feelings or indications was [sic] some years ago before I ever went away. Also it seems she did very good lately with your help. So I thought it might be good to let her supply for the time being, which would be for one year or less.[77]

In response to Stairs proposal, a vote was taken by secret ballot and was passed eighteen in favour and five against. Margaret Stairs, although technically the assistant pastor responsible for preaching, was essentially co-pastor with her absent husband, for the next ten years. This arrangement allowed Wynn Stairs to devote his energies to mission projects and to travel to the various countries around the world.

The missionary legacy of Wynn Stairs is represented especially by the Full Gospel church movements that were planted and founded in Columbia and Spain in 1937 and 1967 respectively. Bill and Ruth Drost began as missionaries in Colombia and eventually moved to Malaga, Spain and began to plant churches there as well. In 1988, anecdotal evidence suggests there may have been approximately 600 churches in Colombia and 15 churches in Spain as a result of Stairs ongoing mission promotion, financial support and multiple trips directly on the field for personal short term ministry.[78] Today in Colombia the Iglesia Pentecostal Unida de Colombia[79] is one of the largest and fastest growing non-Catholic churches in the country. Beginning with a handful of converts in 1937 it has grown to such an extent that in 2007 it had approximately 23,500 constituents, 561 ministers, and 976 churches and preaching points.[80] The Federation of Apostolic Churches in Spain does not have current statistics available for the church development in that area.

Stairs original missionary call, which began with a dream in 1923, was the motivating force during his entire ministry. His personal call inspired other Full Gospel missionaries from New Brunswick to consider giving their lives in full-time Christian service to spread the Full Gospel-Pentecostal message to new frontiers. The call to missions for Stairs was not bound to any one organization. The mission field in

---

[77] *Minutes of Full Gospel Assembly* 14 December 1947, 67.
[78] Peters, *Prevailing Westerlies*, 397.
[79] Translated: The United Pentecostal Church of Colombia.
[80] These statistics offered by the American based parent organization the United Pentecostal Church International may be significantly dated. See http://www.foreign-missions.com/missionaries/missionaryInfo.asp?MID=16297.

Colombia developed into a United Pentecostal Church International organization. Whereas, the mission field in Spain developed into an Apostolic Church fellowship that was separate from the Apostolic Church of Pentecost of Canada organization.

Towards the end of his ministry career Stairs was no longer involved in either of the two Canadian based denominations noted above. Instead he founded Pentecostal Missionary Fellowship and continued to support missions through the long standing personal relationships he had developed throughout the decades with missionaries who originated from New Brunswick. The purpose of the fellowship was to "[p]romote Christian fellowship based on Love and Integrity," "[s]upport our missionaries in their various fields of labour in Quebec, Europe and Spain" and "[m]aintain a close and active fellowship with our brethren in Colombia, South America."[81]

The development of Stairs' ministry career demonstrates the maturation of the Full-Gospel Pentecostal movement in New Brunswick and the Atlantic Northeast. The Full-Gospel Pentecostal piety expressed by Stairs was direct and personal. He believed the result of what the Holy Spirit did in his life at conversion demanded his complete devotion personally and restitution for wrongs he may have committed against others. As he matured in his faith, the motivating force in Stairs' life was his commitment to evangelism through the promotion and support of foreign missions. His personal influence, character and commitment to Christ impacted the lives of many Full Gospel-Pentecostal adherents in Atlantic Canada and beyond.

Bibliography

Bickford, F. Harold. Letter of introduction re: Wynn Stairs and Corinne Reed. Mars Hill, ME. 22 October 1942. Anne Stairs Collection.

Clanton, Arthur L. *United We Stand: A History of Oneness Organizations.* Hazelwood, MO: The Pentecostal Publishing House, 1970.

Crawford, Mattie. *On Mule Back Thru Central America with the Gospel.* Los Angeles: n.p., 1922.

Crabtree, Clifford. Letter to undesignated recipient. 11 July 1977. Patricia Pickard Collection.

Deering, John, Bradford, ME. Letter to Anna Miller, August 29, 1921. See: Patricia Pickard, *Voices of Pentecost in Bangor Maine,* a booklet for the 70th Anniversary of Glad Tidings Church 1923–1993, privately published, 1993.

---

[81] "Pentecostal Missionary Fellowship," 2.

"Down Memory Lane." typewritten manuscript for U.P.C. Home Mission News. n.d., c. 1964.

Fudge, Thomas A. *Christianity without the Cross: A History of Salvation in Oneness Pentecostalism*. Parkland, Florida: Universal Publishers, 2001.

Larden, Robert. *Our Apostolic Heritage*. Calgary: Kyle Printing & Stationary Ltd., 1971.

Minutes of Full Gospel Assembly, St. Stephen.

Minutes of the Full Gospel Pentecostal Church.

Minutes of the Maritime District Conference of the Pentecostal Assemblies of Canada.

Minutes of the Maritime District of the United Pentecostal Church.

McLellan, Kitty M. Winterport, ME. Letter to Anna Miller, c. 1920. Patricia Pickard, *Voices of Pentecost in Bangor Maine*, a booklet for the 70th Anniversary of Glad Tidings Church 1923–1993, privately published, 1993.

Paynter, Matilda, Saint John, NB. Letter to Patricia Pickard. 17 June 17 1988. Patricia Pickard Collection.

"Pentecostal Missionary Fellowship." *Contact* Spring 1983, 2.

Peters, James. *Prevailing Westerlies: The Pentecostal Heritage of Maine*. Shippensburg, Pennsylvania: Destiny Image, 1988.

Reed, David A. *"In Jesus' Name": The History and Beliefs of Oneness Pentecostals*. Blandford Forum, Dorset, UK: Deo Publishing, 2008.

Riss, R.M. "Finished Work Controversy," in *Dictionary of Pentecostal and Charismatic Movements*, edited by Stanley M. Burgess and Eduard M. Van Der Maas, 306–309. Grand Rapids: Zondervan, 2002.

Saxton, A.C. Letter to J.H. Dearing, Grangeville, Idaho. 9 January 1913. Patricia Pickard, *Voices of Pentecost in Bangor Maine*, a booklet for the 70th Anniversary of Glad Tidings Church 1923–1993, privately published, 1993.

Stairs, Wynn T., Lower Southampton, NB. Letter to unidentified CPR representative. 3 February 1921. Anne Stairs Collection.

——. Letter to Raymond Storie. 3 July 1939. Anne Stairs Collection.

——. Brief History of Pentecost in New Brunswick and Maine, manuscript, c. 1981.

——. Growth and Dates. Interview 2 with Anne Stairs, manuscript, c. May 1982.

——. Interview 6 with Anne Stairs, manuscript, c. May 1982.

——. I Was Not Disobedient to the Heavenly Vision, manuscript, c. 1962.

——. How and When the Oneness message came to N.B., manuscript, n.d., c. 1982.

——. My Thirteenth Visit to Colombia, Foreign Missionary Department, c. 1970.

——. Untitled manuscript outlining holiness rules for Pentecostal Full Gospel Assembly, St. Stephen, N.B., c. July 1, 1935.

——. "Brief history of the Saint Stephen Pentecostal Church," c. 1981, 1.

Storie, Raymond. Letter to Wynn Stairs 6 June 1939. Anne Stairs Collection.

Unsigned, Letter of introduction re: Wynn Stairs and Quincy Stairs. 21 December 1945. Anne Stairs Collection.

United Pentecostal Church Handbook. n.d., c. 1947, 1969.

Woodstock, N.B. Letter to John Deering, Bradford, ME. 20 July 1921. Anne Stairs Collection.

CHAPTER ELEVEN

THE NEW ORDER OF THE LATTER RAIN: RESTORATION OR RENEWAL?

D. William Faupel

INTRODUCTION

When Pentecostalism burst upon the world stage at the turn of the twentieth century, its leadership was convinced that the movement was participating in a revival that would renew the entire church.[1] Sustained criticism from historic churches soon caused Pentecostals to abandon this ecumenical vision and establish their own denominations.[2] Between the two world wars Pentecostalism gained grudging acceptance by other denominations. Simultaneously a desire for fellowship with mainline churches led the movement to mute its distinctive charismatic manifestations which resulted in a sense of dryness.[3] With first generation leaders passing away,[4] the second generation who had risen through the ranks left many feeling something to be desired. Calls for renewal were heard. A.G. Ward, a first generation leader in the Pentecostal Assemblies of Canada (PAOC), flatly declared that a new kind of leadership was necessary:

> Such a revival as we have in mind will require a new order of leadership. Many of our present leaders are men of God and, we believe, men who are ably filling their respective positions, but the church must be presented with a more challenging program than the one she has before her at this hour—a program which only the most daring leaders will venture to advance. ... Leaders who will dare to be reckless adventurers in God ... leaders who will be strategists rather than tacticians.[5]

---

[1] For a full articulation of early Pentecostal ecumenical expectations see Robeck, "Pentecostals and the Apostolic Faith," 61–84.

[2] For one account of this process see Faupel, *The Everlasting Gospel*, 228–306.

[3] Synan, *The Holiness Pentecostal Tradition*, 212.

[4] The movement was forced to note the passing of its first generational leadership in 1947 when three of its most prominent leaders died: Charles Price, Smith Wigglesworth, and Dan Williams. Gee, *Wind and Flame*, 218–219.

[5] Ward, "A Postwar Revival," 3.

When revival came in 1948, the closing words of David DuPlessis, general secretary of the First World Pentecostal Conference held in Zurich Switzerland the previous year became prophetic. "Let us pray for a greater outpouring than ever. … and remember when the floods come it will not keep to our well prepared channels but it will overflow and most probably cause chaos in our regular programs."[6] The revival became known as the New Order of the Latter Rain.

Unlike the initial Pentecostal outpouring, the leadership did not understand this to be a renewal movement. Rather they believed God was starting over, calling his saints to come forth from existing denominations.[7] This chapter will briefly describe the developments of this revival and set forth its major teachings before assessing whether the leadership accomplished its goal of restoring the New Testament church.

THE REVIVAL

The Latter Rain Revival was born in February 1948 in North Battleford, Saskatchewan. Herrick Holt, a pastor of a church affiliated with the International Church of the Foursquare Gospel purchased a 1,000 acre farm nearby to establish Sharon Orphanage in the mid-1940s.[8] In the fall of 1947 he invited George Hawtin to found Sharon Bible College. Hawtin, a PAOC minister, had been Principal of Bethel Bible Institute in Saskatoon, Saskatchewan. Pioneering Bethel as an independent school in 1935, he turned the school over to his denomination in 1942. Breaking with the PAOC over a policy dispute in 1947, Hawtin resigned and left the denomination.[9]

Hawtin opened Sharon in October 1947 by calling the student body to fasting and prayer.[10] The following month, he journeyed to Vancouver, British Columbia to hear healing evangelist, William Branham.[11] Upon returning he confessed: "Never in my life have I ever seen anything to equal what I saw in Vancouver. … I saw the deaf receive their hearing. I heard the dumb speak. … I saw a goiter vanish. I saw sick people get

---

[6] DuPlessis, "Chaff, Fire, Wheat," 6.
[7] Blumhofer, *Restoring the Faith*, 204.
[8] Riss, "The Latter Rain Movement of 1948," 202.
[9] Holdcroft, "The New Order of the Latter Rain," 47.
[10] Hawtin, "How It Started," 1.
[11] Riss, "The Latter Rain Movement of 1948," 80.

up from their beds ... To my best knowledge I did not see one person who was not healed."[12]

He called the community to renew their fasting and prayer hoping revival would come to Sharon. The visitation arrived the following year. On 11 February 1948, a student prophesied that Sharon was "on the very verge of a great revival." All they had to do was "open the door" and "enter in." Hawtin responded: "Father, we do not know where the door is, neither do we know how to enter it."[13] Further instructions came though Hawtin's younger brother, Ernest: "The gifts of the spirit will be restored to my church. ... They shall be received by prophecy and the laying on of hands of the presbytery."[14] George Hawtin continues the narrative: "I can never begin to describe the things that happened on that day. It seemed that all Heaven broke loose upon our souls, and Heaven came down to greet us. The power and the glory were indescribable.[15]

By the time the 'Feast of Pentecost' camp was held 30 March 1948, news of the revival had spread far and wide. Milford Kirkpatrick remembered: "We never saw such a variety of cars and license plates before, from many provinces in Canada and from so many states across the border."[16] They did not leave disappointed. The Sharon Star reported: "People hungry to meet God had come many hundreds of miles, and God met them. ... the sick are being healed; the Devils are being cast out; Saints are being edified; sinners are being saved."[17]

A second camp meeting was held in July. This time "thousands of people throughout the continent who had heard of awakening" were reported in attendance.[18] People had come from as far north as Peace River, Alberta; as far west as Vancouver, British Columbia; as far east as Prince Edward Island; and from twenty states south of the Canadian border.[19] Phyllis Spiers, wrote: "How long we have desired to see the signs following the preaching of the Word! With this hunger, and also mingled feelings, we landed at the North Battleford camp. Although we saw things that we had never seen before, we sensed that the place

---

[12] Hawtin, "Editorial," 2–3.
[13] Hawtin, "How It Started," 1.
[14] E. Hawtin, "How This Revival Began," 3.
[15] Hawtin, "How It Started," 2.
[16] Kirkpatrick, The 1948 Revival and Now, 9.
[17] Hawtin, "Local Church Government," 2–4.
[18] McNeill, "As of a Rushing Mighty Wind," 27.
[19] Hawtin, "Editorial," 2.

whereupon we stood was Jehovah's holy ground, and that place was vibrating and pulsing with the dynamic power of God."[20]

THE REVIVAL SPREADS ACROSS THE CONTINENT

After Feast of Pentecost concluded, the brothers were invited to Full Gospel Assembly in Saskatoon. George exalted: "To be in one of these meetings is like living in another Chapter of the Acts of the Apostles." The May 1948 issue of *The Sharon Star* reported that "Mighty outpourings are taking place among the saints in Prince Albert and McDowall."[21] Following the July meeting local revivals broke out in several Saskatchewan communities.[22] A.W. Rasmussen left to take the message to the Eastern United States.[23] Jim and Phyllis Spiers traveled to Minnesota.[24] George Hawtin went to Calgary, Alberta in October. He reported that the meetings were a great success.[25]

Leaving Calgary, Hawtin accepted A.W. Rasmussen's invitation to speak at the Independent Assemblies of God national convention in Edmonton, Alberta on 24–31 October 1948.[26] One of the persons present, J. Mattson Boze, editor of *The Herald of Faith*, returned transformed to his church in Chicago, Illinois. His church would become a strategic centre for the movement and his magazine a leading voice for the revival.[27] Following the Edmonton Convention, George Hawtin and James Watt returned with E.H. Blomberg to Hibbing, Minnesota, for a series of meetings in November.[28] Hawtin returned to Glad Tidings in Vancouver, BC pastored by Reg Layzell to hold services 14–28 November 1948.[29]

By this time the Hawtins were swamped with invitations. In the 1 February 1949 issue of *The Sharon Star*, George Hawtin reported: "Calls are coming in daily from all over the continent."[30] When he

---

[20] Spiers, "Marvelous Support for Call to Chinese Missions," 3.
[21] Hawtin, "Editorial," 2.
[22] *The Sharon Star* 1 September 1948, 2.
[23] *The Sharon Star* 1 October 1948, 2.
[24] Rasmussen, "Report from Northern Minnesota," 16.
[25] Hawtin, "Editorial," 2.
[26] *The Sharon Star* 1 October 1948, 4.
[27] *The Sharon Star* 1 December 1948, 2–3.
[28] Watt, "Progress with God," 1; Hawtin, "Report from Hibbing, Minnesota," 3; and Rasmussen, "Report from Northern Minnesota," 16.
[29] Watt, "Progress with God," 3.
[30] Hawtin, "Editorial," 1.

arrived at Wings of Healing Temple pastored by Thomas Wyatt on 24 February 1949 he found ninety ministers awaiting him, from Montana, Iowa, Kansas, Texas, California, Utah, Idaho, Colorado, Washington, and Canada.[31] His four day meeting turned into three weeks. Wyatt's radio program broadcast on sixty-four stations saturated the country with news of the revival.[32] Enroute home, Hawtin stopped for a series of meetings in Tacoma, Washington before returning to Sharon to prepare for the upcoming camp meeting.[33]

The meetings were conducted 15–17 July 1949. The local newspaper, *The North Battleford News*, took note. "Hundreds of visitors from every part of the prairie provinces, from the North West Territories, and from many of the United States, including as far south as Alabama … are arriving daily. … North Battleford hotels and cafes are crowded … with visitors," It concluded that close to 3,000 attended the meetings, returning "to their various places refreshed and ready to go on with their work with new vigor."[34]

By the end of 1949, centres for the revival had been established in major cities throughout the continent. Among those were Bethesda Missionary Temple, pastored by Myrtle Beall in Detroit, Michigan; Faith Temple, pastored by Paul and Laura Grubb in Memphis, Tennessee; Glad Tidings Temple, pastored by Omar Johnson in St. Louis, Missouri; Immanuel Temple pastored by Earl Lee in Los Angles California; Elim Missionary Association and Bible College led by Ivan Spencer in Lima, New York; Faith Temple, pastored by Fred Poole in Philadelphia, Pennsylvania; The Latter Rain Baptist Church, pastored by William Kitchen in Oklahoma City, Oklahoma; and Christian Faith Temple, pastored by Lawrence O. McKinney in Cleveland, Ohio. Other centres were pastored by Bill Britton in Springfield, Missouri; Cecil Cousen in Hamilton, Ontario and B.G. Evans in Toronto, Ontario. As new centres were established they assumed responsibility for providing leadership and instruction to dozens of churches being swept into the movement from the surrounding communities.[35] Upon investigating the revival, E.L. Moore

---

[31] "Heaven's Great Spiritual Offensive," *The Sharon Star* 1 May 1949, 1, 3.

[32] Hawtin, "Editorial," 1.

[33] Hawtin, "Editorial," 1.

[34] "Large Group Now in Attendance at Sharon Camp," *North Battleford News* 7 July 1949, 1; "Large Crowds at Annual Sharon Summer Camp," *North Battleford News* 13 July 1949, 1; and "Successful Camp Held by Sharon Group Now Over," *North Battleford News* 21 July 1949, 1.

[35] Beall, Interview with Faupel.

concluded: "Thousands of ministers and laymen ... received the spiritual blessing for which they had been seeking ... [and] ... began to proclaim the message of the Latter Rain throughout the country."[36]

AND AROUND THE WORLD ...

In December 1948 George Hawtin wrote that since the revival began the Sharon group had "received requests from China, India and Norway." The previous month, the revival's first missionaries, Brother and Sister Swaan, set sail for the Fiji Islands.[37] In April 1949 two couples left for Liberia, Africa; another went to India. By June, Global Missions had started a shortwave broadcast to communicate the latest news of the revival to their missionaries.[38] *The North Battleford News* reported July 1949 that a minister from New Zealand had attended, and planned to take the message with him.[39] He returned a year later to report that he had succeeded "in bringing the truths of this revival into working knowledge among the churches."[40]

Lewi Pethrus, pastor of the Filadelfia Church in Stockholm, Sweden came to investigate the revival in 1949. Meeting with the principal leaders, Pethrus accepted the revival returning to commend it to his Swedish homeland.[41] The following January, Mattsson Boze, together with William Freeman, returned Pethrus' visit, holding meetings in Stockholm and then traveling to Norway, Finland, and England.[42] In March, 1950, *The Pattern*, the official organ of The Bible-Pattern Church Fellowship reprinted Lewi Pethrus' report thereby endorsing the revival to the Free Pentecostal Churches throughout the British Isles.[43]

It was not until 1951, however, that the Latter Rain leadership systematically sought to spread the message globally. Thomas Wyatt brought the climaxing message at the first "National Latter Rain

---

[36] Moore, "Handbook of Pentecostal Denominations in the United States," 318.
[37] Hawtin, "Editorial," 2.
[38] "Global Mission News," 2.
[39] "Successful Camp Held by Sharon Group Now Over," *North Battleford News* 21 July 1949, 1.
[40] "Camp Meeting News," *The Sharon Star* 1 August 1950, 2.
[41] Pethrus, "The Revival in Canada," 10–11.
[42] "To Europe," *The Herald of Faith* December 1949, 11.
[43] Pethrus, "The Revival in Canada," 3–4.

Convention" in St. Louis on 15 November 1950. He disclosed that God had revealed His desire to bring this Latter Rain outpouring to the ends of the earth.[44] Wyatt's message stirred the audience. Teams of the revival's leaders made plans for missionary crusades to the Holy Land, India, Japan, and Latin America.[45]

Wyatt led the first team to Jamaica in January 1951 accompanied by his associate, Raymond Hoekstra; Harry Hodge, pastor in Beaumont, Texas; Theodore Fitch, pastor in Council Bluffs, Iowa; Cecil Cousen, Fred Poole, Arnold Washborn and Roscoe Davies. Meetings were held in Kingston and Christiania.[46] Omar Johnson together with Ivan Spencer and Donald Murphy, spent three months in India traveling to Madras, Bangalore, Calcutta, Hyderabad, Bombay, and New Delhi in 1951. They reported that they were overwhelmed with demands speaking several times daily with thousands in attendance. Enroute home, Ivan Spencer spent April traveling throughout Kenya and Ethiopia.[47] Milford Kirkpatrick left for Japan, arriving 4 January 1951. After ministering for four months, he returned at the end of April to prepare a group to return the following year.[48]

From January 1951 the periodicals are filled with reports of teams going throughout the world. Earl Lee led a party to Australia and New Zealand in February 1951. Fred Poole took a party to the British Isles in April, going on to the European continent.[49] Other tours of note included the John Owen team that went to Switzerland and France;[50] Reg Layzell to Sweden; Richard Iverson and Adam McKeown to Ireland;[51] and Harry Hodge to the Philippines.[52] Like the Pentecostal movement before it, the Latter Rain Revival spread rapidly across the continent and around the world.

---

[44] Spencer, "Spiritual Advance at St. Louis," 6.

[45] Mulford," Sons of God March Forward," 7.

[46] Poole, "Rain Falls on Sunny Jamaica," 1.

[47] "Flash," *The Voice of Faith* February 1951, 3 and Spencer, "Our Editor Returns," 2–3.

[48] Kirkpatrick, "Missionary News and Reports," 31; and "Kirkpatrick Returns to Japan," 14.

[49] "Schedules of Missionary Tours," 8.

[50] "Mitchell and Owens in Europe," 14.

[51] Riss, "The Latter Rain Movement of 1948" 132 citing Interview with Cecil Cousen,Scarborough, Yorkshire, England 20 March 1977, tape cassette.

[52] *The Elim Pentecostal Herald* November–December 1951, 15.

THE MESSAGE OF THE REVIVAL

The message of the Revival was complex. The doctrines were a new emphasis on existing Pentecostal teaching or a belief that had been briefly considered but subsequently rejected. Built upon the Pentecostal world-view, Latter Rain theology soon developed its own coherent whole.

When Herrick Holt established his orphanage, he taught that God was about to do a 'new thing.' Just what is not clear, but it soon was subsumed in George Hawtin's vision.[53] From his writings in *The Sharon Star*, it is clear Hawtin had a definite perception of what God was about to do. However, he seemed content to allow this plan to unfold, step by step. In general terms he believed that God was sending a world-wide revival. As in previous moves he also believed that the revival would bring the restoration of new truth. Returning from the Branham campaign in November 1947 he gave full expression to this theme. "All great outpourings of the past have had their outstanding truths. Luther's truth was Justification by faith. Wesley's was Sanctification. The Baptists taught the premillennial coming of Christ. The Missionary Alliance taught Divine Healing. The Pentecostal outpouring has restored the Baptism of the Holy Ghost to its rightful place. But the next great outpouring is going to be marked by ... a demonstration of the nine gifts of the Spirit as the world ... has ever witnessed before."[54]

When the revival came, 'gifts of the Spirit' were restored, and other 'new truths' followed. Hawtin exulted: "To be in one of these meetings is like living in another Chapter of the Acts of the Apostles."[55] As adherents reflected on their experience, they realized that internal coherence of the revival's message could be summarized in one word – restoration.[56] Primarily, this restoration focused on one major doctrine, the church. The message concerned four aspects: its nature, mission, worship, and authority.

THE NATURE OF THE CHURCH

A surface reading of the primary literature suggests that instead of a coherent unifying doctrine, the revival 'restored' a series of unrelated

---

[53] Jaenen, "The Pentecostal Movement," 87.
[54] Hawtin, "Editorial," 3.
[55] Hawtin, 2.
[56] Grubb. Interview with Faupel.

truths. Only as they are analyzed does the internal coherent structure unfold. What follows are the essential features in roughly the order they emerged.

Fasting and Prayer

The first mark of the revival was that it was preceded by several months of fasting and prayer. Ernest Hawtin attributes this as the great factor initiating the revival. He records that Sharon was called to fasting through Franklin Hall's book.[57] Hall asserted: "The truth of fasting is being revealed to us now that we ... may receive the 'Gifts of the Spirit,' and that a mighty world-wide revival of spiritual power will sweep over the world."[58] The implication was clear. If Sharon fasted and prayed, revival would come.

The Laying on of Hands

The second restoration was 'the laying on of hands.' George Hawtin believed that the coming revival would be accompanied by the restoration of the gifts of the Spirit, but had confessed that he did not know how to implement it.[59] His brother's prophetic words on 14 February 1948, "They shall be received by ... the laying on of hands," proved to be the catalyst.[60] A.W. Rasmussen reports that Ernest Hawtin had been mulling the idea over in his mind for several days.[61] Furthermore, Cornelius Jaenen contends the aspect of the Branham meetings which impressed George Hawtin most was that the spectacular healings came as Branham laid hands upon people.[62] Finally, James Watt remembers the school had been deeply influenced by Episcopalian, J.E. Stiles' book, *The Gift of the Holy Spirit.*[63]

---

[57] E. Hawtin, "How the Revival Began," 3–4.
[58] Hall, *Atomic Power with God with Fasting and Prayer*, 9.
[59] Hawtin, "How It Got Started," 1.
[60] E. Hawtin, "How the Revival Began," 3.
[61] Rasmussen, *The Last Chapter*, 138–144.
[62] Jaenen, "The Pentecostal Movement," 86.
[63] Stiles attacked the then common Pentecostal practice of 'tarrying' for the baptism of the Holy Spirit which was modeled on the disciples' experience in the Upper Room. He argued that the disciples had to wait until Pentecost, because the Spirit had not yet been given dispensationally. Stiles' analysis of other New Testament evidence led him to conclude that the Holy Spirit was conferred subsequently through the laying on of hands. Stiles, *The Gift of the Holy Spirit*, 79–89; it is quite probable the Hawtins were influenced by Stiles prior to the revival. Stiles was at Gordon Lindsay's church in Oregon holding meetings in March 1947, when Lindsay received his call to become

The Gifts of the Spirit

The 1948 revival was accompanied by the 'gifts of the Spirit' as George Hawtin had anticipated. In his first account of the revival in the April 1948 edition of *The Sharon Star*, Hawtin noted: "the Gifts of the Spirit are definitely being restored to the Church."[64] Later, he elaborated in more detail: "I can never begin to describe the things that happened on that day … Men and woman [sic] received the gift of healing, and immediately began to heal the sick. Discernment of spirits was given, and the influence of evil spirits was discerned, and the evil spirits were cast out. Some received the gift of faith. …"[65]

While the manifestation of all nine gifts was claimed, the gift of prophecy became the focus. Ernest Hawtin declared: "The Gift of Prophecy is in particular prominence."[66] The seminal understanding for this emphasis was rooted in the events which took place at the outset of the revival as they were later remembered. While Ernest Hawtin struggled on 12 February 1948, trying to decide whether he should act on his impression to lay hands on the young man, a young woman went to him "saying the same words, and naming the identical student he was to pray for."[67]

The prophecies usually contained a 'word of knowledge' of past events in the person's life unknown to the person speaking, and a 'word of wisdom' revealing events of future ministry. This became standard practice and known as the act of 'Impartation' and/or the act of 'Confirmation.' As Raymond Hoekstra asserted, "By the laying on of hands and prophecy, gifts are imparted, and ministries are confirmed."[68] The leadership found support throughout Scripture. A key passage was I Timothy 4.14: "Do not neglect the gift you have, which was given you by prophetic utterance when the council of elders laid their hands upon you."

William Branham's crusade manager. Lindsay, *William Branham*, 115. Stiles followed the Braham campaign to Vancouver, remaining in Canada for eight months. He held meetings throughout the western Provinces, including a meeting at Bethel Bible Institute, Hawtin's former school. Stiles, *The Gift of the Holy Spirit*, 175–192.

[64] Hawtin, "Revival at Sharon," 2.
[65] Hawtin, "How It Started," 3.
[66] E. Hawtin, "The Other Side of the Picture," 3.
[67] E. Hawtin, "How the Revival Began," 3.
[68] Hoekstra, *The Ascension Gift Ministries*, 39.

The Ascension Gift Ministries

The revival was barely under way when the leadership began to claim that the Ascension Gift Ministries were being re-established. Paul N. Grubb reflected the representative view: "The revival is also a restoration to the church of the five ministries mentioned in Ephesians 4."[69] Adherents recognized that evangelists, pastors, and teachers had been operative in the church, the focus of their attention, therefore, was directed to the offices of apostle and prophet.[70] They took issue with those who claimed that the ministry of the apostle had ceased. They pointed out that many in the New Testament had held the title and noted that in the Ephesians passage this ministry was included among those who were to "build up the body of Christ until we attain the unity of the faith."[71]

The leadership understood the work of an apostle to be that of the missionary in its broadest sense, that is, one who establishes churches and is responsible to convey the faith to them. Paul was seen as the exemplar. "His ministry was apostolic, which necessitated governing churches, establishing and confirming churches. He was able to preach, teach, minister to the sick, discern and cast out demons, heal the sick and even work special miracles as God's gifts and graces operated through him."[72]

Prophetic ministry was seen as second in importance to that of an apostle, proclaiming the 'mysteries of God' making them plain to the church. "It is not their voice that is heard, but it is THE VOICE OF GOD."[73] In the service of Confirmation, the Prophet speaks for God in separating persons to specific ministries.[74] Three levels of prophecy were recognized. First, there were those who had 'the gift of prophecy' that functioned in the local church. Second, there were prophets who, like the apostles, were given authority to minister to the church at large. Finally, there were "a few prophets … whose ministry will be in the extraordinary use of the term. These are 'raised-up' for special purposes. They shall enter a phase of ministry such as Samuel, Elijah, Moses, and Ezekiel. There will be unusual manifestations of 'the word

---

[69] Grubb, *The End Time Revival*, 34–35.
[70] Stewart and Franzen, *Confirmation*, 79.
[71] Hoekstra, *The Ascension Gift Ministries*, 14.
[72] Hoekstra, 30.
[73] Urgren, "The Prophet, His Ministry and Office," 5.
[74] Hoekstra, *The Ascension Gift Ministries*, 48.

of knowledge' and the 'word of wisdom' in their ministry. They will not be limited in scope of ministry to just the church, but they are sent as witnesses for special purposes to the world as well."[75]

Evangelists, pastors and teachers had ministries that were much the same as those bearing similar titles in Protestant denominations. In all cases, however, they were to function under the authority of the apostles and prophets.[76] The five ascension gift ministries combined to form the Presbytery, as the leadership of the church. Once a local church was established, it was through them that local ministries were confirmed.[77]

Elders and Deacons

Other ministries, such as elders and deacons, were recognized. Like the ascension gift ministries, these were confirmed by the Presbytery through the laying on of hands, accompanied by prophecy.[78] Local churches were under their authority. Every member of the local church was to have a ministry. These were confirmed through the laying on of hands with prophecy.[79]

The Body of Christ

In June 1948, Hawtin took up the issue of 'church organization.' In an article entitled, "Local Church Government," he wrote: "No church exercises or has any right to exercise authority or jurisdiction over another church, its pastors or members."[80] The tone of the article suggested a congregational church government. In this respect it sounded very much like the pattern practiced by the Independent Assemblies of God. Indeed, the January and February 1948 issues of *The Sharon Star* carried a two-part article by A.W. Rasmussen, entitled, "Scriptural or Unscriptural Church Order," setting forth the principles of his denomination's governance.[81]

---

[75] Urgren, "The Prophet, His Ministry and Office, 10.
[76] Hawtin, "Ministries in the Body of Christ," 3.
[77] Stewart and Franzen, *Confirmation*, 76–77.
[78] Hawtin, "Restoration of Elders and Deacons," 4.
[79] Hawtin, "Ministries in the Body of Christ," 3. Other ministries that Hawtin suggest includes such things as the ministry of tongues, the ministry of helps and the ministry of giving.
[80] Hawtin, "Local Church Government," 1.
[81] Rasmussen, "Scriptural or Unscriptural Church Order," 3.

In August 1949 Hawtin and his brother co-authored a book entitled, *Church Government*, their definitive thinking on the matter. They wrote: "The Church is the most democratic of all institutions. ... The believers themselves accept new members into the church, and when a member is excommunicated, the believers are the final voice in the matter." Large churches would be established in the major population centres. These 'mother churches' would take responsibility for shepherding the clusters of smaller churches springing up nearby. These churches would be under the direct oversight of persons trained by the mother church. Local churches would send missionaries to establish churches in non-Christian lands. The training and support would come from the local church.[82]

In the months that followed, Hawtin gave more attention to 'the Divine Pattern.' As 1950 closed it was clear that he did not understand the church to be congregational at all, but rather believed it was hierarchical. Although elders and deacons had jurisdiction over local affairs, they were under authority to those called to the 'Ascension Gift Ministries.'[83]

The Mission of the Church

As the theology of the revival unfolded, the mission of the church received increased attention. Its mission can be brought together into four categories: world evangelization, church unity, perfecting the saints, and restoring all things.

World Evangelization

Concern for world mission was evident at Sharon from the outset. Milford Kirkpatrick recalled: "As a result of the visitation there was a tremendous emphasis on world wide vision."[84] In actuality, concern for world mission preceded the revival. Shortly after the Hawtins arrived in North Battleford, they established a board of Global Missions.[85] The first real impetus as a direct result of the revival occurred in the meetings at Vancouver held in November 1948. Messages in tongues were

---

[82] Hawtin and E. Hawtin, *Church Government*, 19, 26–29.
[83] Hawtin, "Ministries in the Body of Christ," 3–4.
[84] Kirkpatrick, Milford E. *The 1948 Revival and Now*, 15.
[85] *The Sharon Star* 1 April 1948, 1.

given that were understood as human languages. "Those who attended
these meetings went away thoroughly convinced by experience that
the Gift of Tongues is actually the gift of languages. Those possessing
this marvelous [sic] gift can actually preach the gospel in foreign languages without any foreign accent."[86]

The claim had an immediate effect. Following the meeting, the
Swaans left for the Fiji Islands. Shortly thereafter, others were sent to
Africa, China and India.[87] Despite this, however, world evangelization
did not come to the fore until the National Latter Rain Convention in
St. Louis in November 1950. Thomas Wyatt brought the climaxing
message disclosing that God had revealed to him that it was the Lord's
plan to "... speedily dispatch apostolic and prophetic ministries to the
key-cities of all foreign lands. Thousands will have hands laid upon
them with a confirmation of their ministry in the Body by prophecy,
and the impartation of gifts of the Spirit. ... These will in turn go
through the length and breadth of their own lands confirming others,
and thereby, in a few short months, every nation on earth shall have
received the last day message."[88] His message sparked a ready fire. The
movement's leadership immediately began forming teams to tour overseas. Wyatt's vision became the method of world evangelization until
the revival subsided.

Church Unity

In 1965 Reg Layzell, pastor of Glad Tidings Temple in Vancouver,
recalled: "Bro. George Hawtin taught under the anointing. ... how it
would be one church in one great building in each center. No longer
would the church be called by its divisive names but The Church of
Vancouver, The Church of Detroit or The Church of Portland."[89]

Layzell was reflecting on the July 1948, Sharon camp-meeting, when
Hawtin suggested that a major purpose for the revival was to bring the
church together.[90] In *The Body of Christ*, the authors took an oblique

---

[86] Watt, "Progress with God," 3.
[87] Watt, "Progress with God," 3, and Hawtin, "Editorial," 2. In each instance the
person or couple sent to a particular field went having received a word of prophecy
directing them to go. In several cases, further confirmation had come in the form that
the 'tongues' they spoke was the actual language spoken by the people of the country
to whom they were sent.
[88] "Revelation of World Evangelization Given at St. Louis Convention," 8.
[89] Gaglardi, *The Pastor's Pen*, 65.
[90] Hawtin, "Editorial," 2.

shot at the recently formed World Council of Churches.[91] Adherents concurred with the World Council and the Roman Catholic Church that the one universal church must have visible expression. They were convinced, however, that unity would come by the truths being restored through the revival. Christians everywhere would leave their denominations to join the emerging church. George Warnock noted: "At the beginning it was hoped that Christians everywhere would catch the vision, and that before long the whole Body of saints would become one vital, living organism, united together in the bonds of the Spirit unto one common purpose." As the revival progressed, it became obvious most would remain content to ignore the revival. Warnock lamented: "it is becoming apparent that only a remnant are returning to Jerusalem."[92]

Manifested Sons of God

As hope for the unity of the church narrowed to the concept of 'faithful remnant,' the third mission came into focus. The revival would prepare 'overcomers' equipped to prepare the church and the world for Christ's second coming. The concept took on a cloak of elitism. Contrasting the revival's faithful with the universal church, Warnock suggested: "If men choose to remain where they are in their Christian experience, then this message is not for them. Thank God that they may eat of the manna that falls from Heaven, and drink of the water that flows out of the rock, and receive healing and strength for their journey. But sorry to say, they shall die in the wilderness."[93]

On the other hand, those who chose to "arise and cross over Jordan" would join the 'true church,' 'the Body of Christ,' 'The Overcomers,' 'The Bride,' 'The Sons of God.' The terms that would become most popular were 'The Manchild' and 'Manifested Sons of God.'[94] Whereas, adherents of the revival first understood these terms to be identical with the church, they came to understand them to refer to a special group who would play a critical end-time role. "God is manifesting Himself to man in a new way... As sure as Christ ushered out the Dispensation of Mosaic Law, by a manifestation of himself in an individual 'Body prepared by the Holy Ghost' (the Son of man) an

---

[91] Stewart and Franzen, *The Body of Christ*, 5.
[92] Warnock, *The Feast of Tabernacles*, 90.
[93] Warnock, 121.
[94] Warnock, 119–121.

offspring of the virgin Mary, even so, He is ushering out the Dispensation of Grace by a manifestation of Himself again in a corporate 'Body, prepared of the Holy Ghost' (composed of many Sons of men), an offspring of the visible Church."[95]

The theme was introduced by George Hawtin. In an article entitled: "The Great Manifestation," published near the end of 1950, Hawtin argued that not only is it possible to experience justification and sanctification in this life, but immortality as well. Basing his understanding on Romans, he confessed:

> With shame of face I wish to make this confession: For years I taught and preached that we could never be free from the carnal nature in this life. My argument was this, though some preached such an experience, I had never seen one who possessed it, and therefore it could not be so. ... This, however, does not alter the Word of God. ... whether or not Paul ever attained this experience does not matter. This is the experience he sought with all his might: to be rid of the carnal nature and to gain perfection, sinless perfection, to be delivered from THIS BODY OF DEATH ... and to experimentally reach the glories of the eighth chapter of Romans.[96]

The Restoration of All Things

This doctrine, tied to the 'Manifested Sons of God,' followed closely on its heels. The phrase is taken from St. Peter's sermon following the Day of Pentecost. The doctrine conformed closely to the premillennial understanding of the millennium. Hawtin introduced the teaching to his constituency in the November-December 1951 issue of *The Sharon Star* in an article entitled: "Thy Kingdom Come." He opened by declaring: "The Kingdom of Heaven, the seventh dispensation, is at hand." After giving a summary of the previous six dispensations, he continued:

> And she brought forth a man-child who was to rule all nations with a rod of iron, and her child was caught up unto God and throne. (Rev. 12:5) The man-child is the body of Overcomers that keeps his works. They are the manifested sons of God for which the whole creation groaneth and travaileth. (Rom. 8:22). ... This glorious reigning-company does not include all the church. It is the Body of Christ that is being formed in this present revival; not the body of the bride, but the body of Christ who is

---

[95] Grubb, *The End-Time Revival*, 5.
[96] Hawtin, "The Great Manifestation," 1.

the HEAD, the firstborn among many brothers. ... It was this same glorious MAN whom Daniel, the prophet, saw: I saw in the night visions and behold, one like the SON OF MAN came with clouds of heaven.[97]

Abandoning the pre-tribulation he declared that these Overcomers would undergo much suffering to bring in the new dispensation. "The possessing of Kingdom of Heaven by the saints of the most high is not going to be a mere 'push-over' but through MUCH TRIBULATION we will enter it."[98] All things would be restored to the pre-fallen state, and they, the Overcomers, would rule and reign with Christ with a rod of iron.

THE WORSHIP OF THE CHURCH

Restoration of worship is also traced to the outset of the revival. The concept was two-fold: worship as sacred space and worship as praise.

Worship as Sacred Space

The 11 February 1948 prophecy uttered by a young woman at Sharon declared that they "were on the very verge of a great revival" and that all they had to do was 'open the door' and 'enter in.'[99] This image of a 'closed door' with a great revival on the other side became the key to their understanding of worship. The community was waiting for renewal of the 'latter rain' that had fallen at the beginning of the century with the Pentecostal revival. The 'closed door' epitomized their conviction that the rain had ceased. George Hawtin responded by saying, "We don't know where the 'door' is neither do we know how to 'enter it'".[100] His brother Ernest provided the key. Accepting 'laying on of hands' as the key that opened the door adherents believed they crossed the threshold and entered sacred space. Ernest's prophesy continued: "I would have you to be reverent before Me as never before. Take the shoes off thy feet for the ground on which thou standest is holy."[101] The very place where they had gathered became hallowed. Like Moses they were to take off their shoes.

---

[97] Hawtin, "They Kingdom Come," 1.
[98] Hawtin, 2–4.
[99] Hawtin, "How It Got Started," 1.
[100] Hawtin, 1.
[101] Hawtin, "The Great Restoration," 3.

At the Camp Meeting in July 1948, James Watt was teaching on the meaning of the Old Testament Feasts for the church. He noted that the Feast of Passover had been fulfilled in the Cross, the Feast of Pentecost had been fulfilled with the coming of the Holy Spirit, but the Feast of Tabernacles had not yet been fulfilled. The observation struck a responsive cord in George Warnock who subsequently published a book in July 1951. In the Introduction, Warnock transferred 'the door' image to the exodus account, and Israel's call to 'possess the land.'

> The first generation that came out of Egypt by Moses failed to enter in because of unbelief, and God decreed that they should die in the wilderness. … The early generation of Spirit-filled people at the turn of the century took their journey from the blighting wilderness of denominationalism and encamped at their Kadesh-Barnea on the very door-step of Canaan—but they too failed to enter in because of unbelief. … [T]he Lord [is] now raising up a new generation who shall be empowered to take the promised land.[102]

Using typology, Warnock developed the thesis that this revival is the dispensational move of God. The Tabernacle became the type of the place of God's presence. The metaphor of tabernacle was merged with 'body of Christ,' and 'heart.' The Old Testament tabernacle in the wilderness was transformed into the true church and into the hearts of true believers. The 'door' which Hawtin discovered, came to represent a limited access to the latter rain which was falling. Now they possessed the corresponding 'key' for entry into God's overflowing presence – the Tabernacle, the dwelling place of God.[103]

Worship as Praise

The leadership of the revival believed that the dwelling place of God was a 'felt' presence to be experienced in worship. Fasting and prayer followed by the laying on of hands of the Presbytery became the initiation rite of entry by the individual. For the gathered community the point of entry lay elsewhere. James Watt reflecting on the events of 1948 concluded: "Jerusalem is about to be made a praise in the earth. … Prepare ye your hearts."[104] 'Jerusalem,' for Watt, meant the restored church which was about to be made 'praise' in the earth.

---

[102] Warnock, *The Feast of Tabernacles*, 6–7.
[103] Darrand and Shupe. *Metaphors of Social Control in a Pentecostal Sect*, 125, 128.
[104] Watt, "Progress with God," 3.

Early literature abounds with such references as 'Praise is the door-opener.' Such scriptures as Psalm 22.3: "Thou art Holy, O Thou that inhabits the praises of Israel," were also cited repeatedly. Praise, was the 'key' enabling the gathered community to 'enter in' the Holy of Holies.[105] Reg Layzell claimed God revealed this truth to him in January 1946, two years before the revival began. At the time, Layzell was a sales manager for a large office furniture firm serving as a lay preacher on the side. He was called to hold a week of meetings at a small church in Abbotsford, British Columbia. The meetings did not go well. He started a fast and begged God for a breakthrough. The verse from Psalm 22 burst in upon his memory. It dawned on him: "God actually lives in the praises of His people."[106]

Acting on this 'revelation from God' he praised the Lord silently as he announced the opening hymn, "There is Power in the Blood." At the end of the second verse, a young lady threw up her hands and began to speak in tongues. Then another, and still another received the baptism of the Holy Spirit. He interpreted this response to be confirmation to the insight he had received that afternoon.[107] Layzell shared his revelation with the Sharon brethren. They readily accepted his message.[108]

Praise became the basis for the Latter Rain understanding of worship. What had first come forth in a somewhat spontaneous manner became institutionalized. Reflection on these experiences led to the conviction that "'praise' produces the divine presence – an 'atmosphere' in which 'supernatural' manifestations can take place."[109]

THE AUTHORITY OF THE CHURCH

The final aspect of the revival's message is divine authority. This claim to authority has three implications: authority to understand divine history, to interpret Scripture, and to require absolute obedience.

Authority to Understand History

For adherents, Ernest Hawtin's prophecy on 12 February 1948 marked the beginning of the Latter Rain dispensation. With the keys of 'the

---

[105] Darrand, *Metaphors of Social Control*, 120–122.
[106] Gaglardi, *The Pastor's Pen*, 9–11.
[107] Layzell, *"Into Perfection*, 1.
[108] Watt, *Progress with God*, 4.
[109] Gaglardi, *The Pastor's Pen*, 152.

laying of hands' and 'praise' revealed, the church was given the authority to carry out God's end-time program. Before the revival was a year old, adherents began recording the founding events of the movement. These recitals were presented in such a manner that the meaning of Latter Rain history pre-empted and often distorted the factuality of that history. They served to establish the authority of the particular leader seeking to win the allegiance of converts.[110]

Authority to Interpret Scripture

Converts to the revival often were heard to say that for the first time in their lives the Bible really came alive for them. Part of the reason for this was that the Old Testament was applied to the Latter Rain movement by means of typology. The exodus of the Jews from Egypt and the return of the Jews from Babylon were seen as types of their call to "come out from the bondage of apostate man-made organizations."[111] The tabernacle in the wilderness during the exodus became the type of dwelling place of God that is now found in the gathered Body of Christ, the true church.[112]

The justification for the Latter Rain hermeneutic was set forth by George Warnock in 1951. "It is essential therefore, that the saints know for a certainty that the Old Testament was written for us." Its truths once applied only to natural Israel but are now "applicable to a heavenly and spiritual Israel." Since "God's hour of revelation" has struck, "the Spirit of God is gloriously present to remove the veil from God's secrets and initiate His people in the mysteries of God."[113] Warnock maintained his interpretative method came from the Apostles. "The most conclusive evidence of all is the fact that the apostles, in their writings, refer constantly to the Old Testament to prove the truths they are declaring to the Church, and make innumerable quotations from all portions of the Law and the Prophets to confirm their doctrines of Christ and the Church. Nor do they make any apologies whatsoever, or even intimate that they are taking an Old Testament Scripture out of its context."[114]

---

[110] See my doctoral dissertation, "The Everlasting Gospel," 465–472, where I illustrate how, over the passage of time, this was done.

[111] See, for example, Stewart and Franzen, "The Spirit of Babylon," 95.

[112] Layzell, *Into Perfection*, 22.

[113] Warnock, *The Feast of Tabernacles*, 5.

[114] Warnock, 10–11.

Authority through Submission

When adherents thought about authority in the church, their minds were directed towards Christ, the elder brother, who in obedience to the Father "made Himself of no reputation." They were reminded that self must be crucified before being used of God.[115]

> The Church is not perfected by prayer, by the reading of the Word, nor the many other ways we have been taught. But God has set in the Church … apostles, prophets, evangelists, pastors, teachers for the PERFECTING OF THE SAINTS for the WORK OF THE MINISTRY for the BUILDING UP of the body of Christ, till we all come in the unity of the faith and the knowledge of the Son of God unto a perfect man.[116]

To submit to Christ meant to submit to those whom God has set in authority over them. Beginning in North Battleford in February 1948, adherents believed the church had been established on the foundation of apostles and prophets. Readers of *The Sharon Star* were constantly urged to follow the pattern that had been laid down by the Word of God.[117] Adherents came to understand this as a "theocratic chain of command" that came "from Christ down, not from people up."[118] Authority came from the Father to the Son to those whom the Holy Spirit had revealed to be apostles and prophets. These divinely appointed leaders then were given the wisdom and knowledge to appoint pastors, evangelists, and teachers and to confirm them through the laying on of hands. Together, as the Ascension Gift ministers, they appointed first elders and then deacons in the local church. Finally, there came the 'congregational ministries.' Each rank stood in a descending order, not only having less authority, but also less direct access to God.[119]

THE SIGNIFICANCE OF THE NEW ORDER OF THE LATTER RAIN

From the perspective of the stated aims of its leadership the revival needs to be judged a complete failure. Far from 'restoring the church,' and achieving the unity of the body of Christ, it only served to bring

---

[115] Beall, "At the Cross," 6.
[116] Hawtin, "Submission," 7.
[117] Hawtin, "Submission," 8; and Hawtin, "A Letter to the Ecclesia," 6.
[118] Iverson, *Present Day Truths*, 71.
[119] Iverson, 71.

further fragmentation and controversy. Within a few years virtually every Pentecostal denomination had rejected the revival. Repeated warnings of doom failed to materialize. Classical Pentecostalism would go on to experience the greatest period of sustained growth in the years that followed. Internally the new movement soon began to fragment. New centres of influence emerged that refused to submit to the chain of command linked to North Battleford. The short term missionary strategy proposed by Wyatt failed to sustain a growing network of global churches. By 1955 the New Order of the Latter Rain had ceased to function as a movement.

On the other hand, the assessment of Classical Pentecostal historians, typified by Carl Brumback's classic comment that by the mid-fifties "The new Order had practically come to naught," is clearly incorrect.[120] Walter Hollenweger is accurate when judging this appraisal to be an example of "the same wishful thinking that led the traditional churches to ignore the beginnings of the Pentecostal movement."[121] As an agent of renewal, the New Order of the Latter Rain has proven to be successful. First of all, a quick check on the internet reveals hundreds of congregations in North America and thousands globally that identify directly with the revival.[122] More significantly, when the Charismatic Movement burst into prominence in the late 1960's it was Latter Rain leaders rather than Classical Pentecostalism that had the major influence. Richard Riss, the most prominent historian of the New Order, identified nineteen ministries that brought Latter Rain teaching and practices in the Charismatic movement. The Charismatic movement in turn has had much impact on worship patterns of mainline denominations in the last decades of the twentieth century. Its teachings and practices are clearly evident in the flood of independent churches that have sprung into existence both in North America and worldwide during the same period. Riss correctly concludes: "Traditional Pentecostal denominations have been, to a large extent, unaware of the lasting effects of the Latter Rain Movement. However the Latter Rain was one of several important influences upon the Charismatic Renewal of the

---

[120] Brumback, *Suddenly ... from Heaven*, 333.

[121] Hollenweger, "Handbuch der Pfingstbewegung," 758.

[122] Ten years ago, one of my student assistants identified over 2,000 Latter Rain Church's websites in North America and hundreds more globally. I am not aware of any published statistics that has sought to identify such churches separately from Pentecostalism.

1960's and 1970's. Its significance in the context of World Protestantism, therefore, lies in its effects upon a growing influence in most Protestant denominations."[123]

BIBLIOGRAPHY

Beall, James L. Interview with D. William Faupel. 4 August 1976, tape cassette. D. William Faupel papers, David DuPlessis Center, Pasadena, California.
Beall, Myrtle D. "At the Cross." *The Latter Rain Evangel* [Detroit] March 1952.
Blumhofer, Edith L. *Restoring the Faith: The Assemblies of God, Pentecostalism and American Culture.* Urbana, IL: University of Illinois Press, 1993.
Brumback, Carl. *Suddenly … from Heaven: A History of the Assemblies of God.* Springfield, MO: Gospel Publishing House, 1961.
"Camp Meeting News." *The Sharon Star* 1 August 1950.
Darrand, Tom Craig and Anson Shupe. *Metaphors of Social Control in a Pentecostal Sect.* New York, NY: Edwin Mellen Press, 1983.
DuPlessis, David H. "Chaff, Fire, Wheat." *The Elim Pentecostal Herald* March 1950.
"Flash." *The Voice of Faith* February 1951.
Faupel, D. William. "The Everlasting Gospel: The Significance of Eschatology in the Development of Pentecostal Thought." Ph.D. Dissertation, University of Birmingham, England, 1989.
——. *The Everlasting Gospel: The Significance of Eschatology in the Development of Pentecostal Thought.* Sheffield: Sheffield Academic Press, 1996.
Gaglardi, Maureen. *The Pastor's Pen: Early Revival Writings of Pastor Reg Layzell.* Vancouver, BC: New West Press, 1965.
Gee, Donald. *Wind and Flame.* Croydon, Eng: Heath Press, 1967.
"Global Mission News." *The Sharon Star* 1 June 1949.
Grubb, Paul N. Interview with D. William Faupel. 1 July 1976, tape cassette. D. William Faupel papers, David DuPlessis Center, Pasadena, California.
——. *The End Time Revival.* Memphis, TN: The Author, n.d.
Hall, Franklin Hall. *Atomic Power with God with Fasting and Prayer.* San Diego, CA: The Author, 1946.
Hollenweger, Walter J. Hollenweger. "Handbuch der Pfingstbewegung." Th.D. Dissertation, University of Zurich, 1965.
Hawtin, Ernest. "The Other Side of the Picture." *The Sharon Star* 1 November 1948.
——. "How This Revival Began." *The Sharon Star* 1 August 1949.
Hawtin, George R. "Editorial." *The Sharon Star* 1 January 1948.
——. "Revival at Sharon." *The Sharon Star* 1 April 1948.
——. "Local Church Government." *The Sharon Star* 1 May 1948.
——. "Editorial." *The Sharon Star* 1 August 1948.
——. "Report from Hibbing, Minnesota." *The Sharon Star* 1 February 1949.
——. "How It Started." *The Sharon Star* 1 March 1950.
——. "The Great Manifestation." *The Sharon Star* 1 November 1950.
——. "The Great Manifestation." *The Sharon Star* 1 December 1950.
——. "Ministries in the Body of Christ." *The Sharon Star* 1 January 1951.
——. "The Great Restoration." *The Sharon Star* May 1951.
——. "Thy Kingdom Come." *The Sharon Star* November-December 1951.
——. "Restoration of Elders and Deacons." *The Sharon Star* May 1952.

---

[123] Richard Riss, "The Latter Rain Movement of 1948," 45.

_____. "Submission." *The Sharon Star* May 1952.

_____. "Submission." *The Sharon Star* June-July 1952.

_____. "A Letter to the Ecclesia." *The Sharon Star* November-December 1952.

Hawtin, George R. and Ernest H. Hawtin. *Church Government*. North Battleford, SK: Sharon College, 1949.

"Heaven's Great Spiritual Offensive." *The Sharon Star* 1 May 1949.

Hoekstra, Raymond G. *The Ascension Gift Ministries*. Portland, OR: Wings of Healing, 1950.

Holdcroft, L. Thomas. "The New Order of the Latter Rain." *Pneuma* (1980): 46–60.

Iverson, Richard. *Present Day Truths*. Portland, OR: Bible Press, 1975.

Jaenen, Cornelius J. "The Pentecostal Movement." M.A. Thesis, University of Manitoba, 1950.

Kirkpatrick, Milford E. *The 1948 Revival and Now*. Dallas, TX: The Author, n.d.

_____. "Missionary News and Reports." *The Elim Pentecostal Herald* January 1951.

"Large Group Now in Attendance at Sharon Camp." *North Battleford News* 7 July 1949.

"Large Crowds at Annual Sharon Summer Camp." *North Battleford News* 13 July 1949.

Layzell, Reg. *Into Perfection: The Truth about the Present Restoration Revival*. Mountlake Terrace, BC: The King's Temple, 1979.

Lindsay, Gordon. *William Branham: A Man Sent from God*. W. Branham, 1950.

McNeill, Noel. "As of a Rushing Mighty Wind: An Assessment of North America's Pentecostal Movement." Unpublished manuscript. Haliburton, Ont: 1964.

"Mitchell and Owens in Europe." *The Elim Pentecostal Herald* November-December 1951.

Moore, Everett L. "Handbook of Pentecostal Denominations in the United States." M.A. Thesis, Pasadena College, 1954.

Mulford, William A. "Sons of God March Forward." *The Elim Pentecostal Herald* November-December 1950.

Rasmussen, George. "Report from Northern Minnesota." *The Pentecostal Evangel* 18 December 1948.

Rasmussen, A.W. "Scriptural or Unscriptural Church Order." *The Sharon Star* 1 February 1948.

Riss, Richard. "The Latter Rain Movement of 1948 and the Mid-Twentieth Century Evangelical Awakening." M.C.S. Thesis, Regent College, 1979.

_____. "The Latter Rain Movement of 1948." 4 *Pneuma* (1982): 32–45.

Robeck, Cecil M., Jr. "Pentecostals and the Apostolic Faith: Implications for Ecumenism." *Pneuma* 8 (1986): 61–84.

Synan, Vinson. *The Holiness Pentecostal Tradition: Charismatic Movements in the Twentieth Century*. Grand Rapids, MI: Eerdmans Publishing Company 1997.

Spiers, Phyllis. "Marvelous Support for Call to Chinese Missions." *The Sharon Star* 1 August 1948.

"Successful Camp Held by Sharon Group Now Over." *North Battleford News* 21 July 1949.

Pethrus, Lewi. "The Revival in Canada." *The Herald of Faith* December 1949.

_____. "The Revival in Canada." *The Pattern* March 1950.

Poole, Fred C. "Rain Falls on Sunny Jamaica." *The Elim Pentecostal Herald* March 1951.

"Revelation of World Evangelization Given at St. Louis Convention." *The Voice of Faith* February 1951.

"Schedules of Missionary Tours." *The Voice of Faith* February 1951.

Spencer, Ivan. "Spiritual Advance at St. Louis." *The Elim Pentecostal Herald* November–December 1950.

_____. "Our Editor Returns." *The Elim Pentecostal Herald* April–May 1951.

Stiles, J.E. *The Gift of the Holy Spirit*. Glendale, CA: The Church Press, n.d.

Stewart, Paul W. and Barbara Franzen, *Confirmation*. Book 2. Harvest Rain Series Detroit, MI: Evangel Press, 1954.

_____. *The Body of Christ*. Book 3. Harvest Rain Series Detroit, MI: The Evangel Press, 1954.

"To Europe." *The Herald of Faith* December 1949.

Warnock, George H. *The Feast of Tabernacles*. Springfield, MO: Bill Britton, 1951.

Ward, A.G. "A Postwar Revival." *The Pentecostal Evangel* 10 May 1941.

Watt, James. "Progress with God." *The Sharon Star* 1 December 1948.

CHAPTER TWELVE

THE LATTER RAIN MOVEMENT AND THE PHENOMENON OF GLOBAL RETURN

Mark Hutchinson

INTRODUCTION

History, as David Martin has noted, is volatile.[1] Just when the world seems to be irrevocably secular, religion pushed off the world stage by the events of the 1960s, its comes bounding back again through another door. As some scholars were watching France for a lead in the way that modernization treated religion, the Middle East brought religion back to everybody else's attention. The flashpoints of the world seemed to be increasingly aligned along the frontiers of religious and cultural difference. This has led to a renewed concentration on the movement of ideas and cultural influences on a global scale. For both scholars of religion and for sociologists interested in global emergence, Pentecostalism has thus been a particularly important subject. The fact that Pentecostalism has proven to be inveterately fissiparous, mobile and adaptive raises the possibility that for the first time there is a form of Christianity which cannot be studied solely in the local, regional, and/or national frames. Indeed, the effect of the new scholarship is to suggest that perhaps Christianity was always part of a universalist project, and that it needs to be studied as part of a process of worldwide reticulation, feedback and reinforcement.[2] It is this latter which, in this chapter, will be called the phenomenon of 'global return.'

ORIGINS OF THE LATTER RAIN MOVEMENT

This is nowhere more visible than in the remarkable case of the Latter Rain revival which emerged in Canada in 1948. The local course of this

---

[1] This is a standing argument of Martin's, present in almost all his works since his contributions to the secularization debates in the 1960s – for his most substantial recent piece on this, see *On secularization*.

[2] See Walls, *The Cross-cultural Process in Christian History*.

revival has been traced elsewhere and does not need repeating here except in the barest details.[3] Emerging from institutional confrontation within the Pentecostal Assemblies of Canada centred on the Sharon Orphanage and Schools in North Battleford, Saskatchewan, this tiny sectarian revivalist movement quickly realized its internal ideology of 'global missions' by following the lines of post-war reconstructionism around the world. Building on widespread dissatisfaction amongst Pentecostals about institutionalization of their tradition among the major denominations, the effect of the revival quickly reached out to Vancouver, Detroit, and New York, finding champions in Elim Bible Institute, Bethesda Missionary Temple and a wide network of independent revivalist churches.

Highly typological, the movement drew upon Old Testament prophetic fulfillment (particularly with regard to the Feast of Tabernacles) and 'the foundational truths' of Hebrews 6: 1–2 to shape its particular appropriation of early Pentecostal practices such as laying on of hands, singing in the Spirit, prostrations, etc. The 'foundational truths,' in particular, gave a sense of dispensational certainty and inevitability to the restorationism which had been basic to Pentecostalism right from its origins.[4] Indeed, one might typify it as the *realization* of restoration – so much of its teachings and practice related to visible manifestation that, in its particular appropriation of the language of the Spirit, it held within it the potential to become the ideological basis for some of North America's more materialist exports. The 'manifest sons of God,' the emphasis on restoration *now*, on evidences, signs and wonders, its mobile convention form (a variation on nineteenth-century brush arbours, 'tabernacles in the wilderness' which appropriated to themselves the sense of the wandering people of Israel), and particularly physical healing, all made this the natural interpretive framework for a renewed Pentecostalism emerging as a missiological program in the context of post-war, global consumerism.

The Latter Rain movement rapidly fused with the North American healing revival and its global extensions, influencing and being influenced by the work of William Marion Branham, Oral Roberts, and T.L. Osborne (among others).[5] While not originally identified with Word

[3] See, for example the following by Riss: *A Survey of 20th-century Revival Movements in North America; Latter Rain;* and "The Latter Rain Movement of 1948."
[4] For these roots, see Blumhofer, *Restoring the Faith.*
[5] See Harrell, *Oral Roberts* and *All Things are Possible.* Also, Weaver, *The Healer-prophet, William Marrion Branham.*

Faith teaching, Latter Rain teachings came to inhabit many of the same circles among the denominationally dispossessed and the ever-growing crowds of mobile convention-goers, particularly after the Classical Pentecostal denominations rejected its teachings in the early 1950s, and the charismatic movement gave it its own platform from the latter end of that decade. The Latter Rain was pushed out – but nothing in the 'space of flows' which was the emerging global society of the post-war period can remain out forever.[6]

THE LATTER RAIN IN AUSTRALIA AND NEW ZEALAND

This 'global return' of the Latter Rain can be demonstrated through a case study – in the case of this chapter, the case relates to the percola-tion of Latter Rain teachings through Pentecostal networks in South-east Asia and Australia. The bombing of Pearl Harbor and the rapid Japanese engagement with American interests in the Pacific had the remarkable outcome of focusing American attention on the part of the world which to some degree was still a new frontier. The new empire was still to some extent stymied by the remnants of old empires in Southeast Asia – the French in Indochina, the Dutch in Indonesia and the Malay Archipelago, the British in New Guinea and the Pacific Islands. This was something that American predominance after the war would set about adjusting. Japanese invasion of Indonesia led to the displacement of missionaries associated with numbers of American Pentecostal agencies, among them those attached to W.H. Offiler's Bethel Temple in Seattle, Washington.

Offiler was an Englishman who had migrated to Seattle via Canada, and into Pentecostalism (as so many did) via the Salvation Army. The church maintained a consistent presence in Surabaya until they were expelled by the Japanese.[7] Several missionaries – including Ray Jackson,

---

[6] Appadurai posits the existence in the global setting of "imagined worlds" where "imagination is no longer mere fantasy, escape, pastime nor contemplation, but is the structured ground, both as work and negotiation, in which the localised individuals envisage global possibilities. Imagination is no longer a talent of only the creative indi-viduals – such as designers – but of the population in general, who imagine and design their own worlds, which can be far from their immediate realities." Paula Bello, "Places of Flows: [Re]framing design." Appadurai's idea of the space of flows was first men-tioned in his article, "Disjuncture and Difference in the Global Culture Economy," 295–310. Also see Wilkinson, "Religion and Global Flows" for a discussion related to Pentecostalism.

[7] www.bethelfellowshipinternational.com/history.htm, accessed 4 August 2008.

John Banks and Al Edmondson - instead of returning to North America, spent some of the war years in Auckland, New Zealand, where their revivalism and novel teachings about the Tabernacle of Moses made them at first welcome.[8] When they returned in 1945, division over their teaching of 'Baptism in the Name of Jesus' made them suspect, and then sectarian as they pulled three churches (Auckland, Wellington and Blenheim) out of the fledgling Assemblies of God in New Zealand. Their early success depended, in New Zealand as it was in Canada, on Salvation Army revivalism, and the preceding independent healing networks established by J.A. Dowie, Aimee Semple McPherson, and Smith Wigglesworth.[9]

Among the most important of these was the Revival Fire Fellowship, founded by A.H. Dallimore – a wandering English Methodist with connections both in Canada and New Zealand, and with such people as Charles S. Price and John G. Lake.[10] Dallimore established a significant healing mission in Auckland through the 1930s, and it was out of this connection that people such as Rob Wheeler would arise. New Zealand thus provided a confluence of personalities and institutions which established a base for what would become a movement with remarkable global reach. There is nothing to suggest, however, that this small collection of three churches would necessarily have become more influential if it had not been for the outbreak of the Latter Rain Revival in Canada in 1948. Jackson's style was powerful and dramatic,[11] and concentrated on a teaching ministry inspired by Offiler's millennial, dispensational and illuminist typological approach.[12] As is often the case with churches founded around charismatic individuals, however, the tendency of the churches in Jackson's absence was to fall back into legalism and sectarianism. They were isolated from a Pentecostal mainstream, which had been heavily influenced by Wigglesworth and A.C. Valdez Sr., and which was reliant upon the norms provided by the Anglican influenced Sunderland circles, and the anti-oneness emphases emerging from Azusa Street. (Interestingly, the oneness emphasis emerging from the original Pentecostal upsurge was also the result of the cross pollination of Pentecostal thought between

---

[8] Knowles, "History of the New Life Churches in New Zealand," 76.
[9] Hutchinson, "Adams, John Archibald Duncan (1844–1936)."
[10] Guy, "One of a Kind."
[11] Wheeler, Interview with Wilkinson.
[12] Knowles, "History of the New Life Churches in New Zealand," 78.

Canadian R.E. McAlister and Australian Frank Ewart at the Arroyo Seco camp meetings.)[13]

Jackson's pre-Latter Rain church itself did not have a model for leadership multiplication or a consistent theology which could be adapted to the circumstances. In the mass movement of soldiers around the world with the cessation of war, travel was comparatively difficult and mass communications between New Zealand and North America not yet as free as they would become. The global reflexivity that Pentecostals had depended upon since their foundation – the ability to bring in the big-name evangelist/healer and so overcome local resistance to religious innovation – was neither organized nor available. The return of Jackson and Edmondson to the United States in 1947 was not in response to incipient revival – they were after all missionaries, and returned to the United States on furlough. While there, however, they became involved in the Latter Rain Revival, a movement which shared many of the millennial, dispensational and illuminist aspects that Offiler had already established among them. Jackson was appointed 'Apostle of New Zealand' with the laying on of hands.[14]

The impact on the local churches in New Zealand was dramatic. Rob Wheeler (who, with Kevin Conner, Peter Morrow, Paul Collins, and Ron Coady, would become one of the key members of the first generation of New Zealand Latter Rain activists) notes that: "When the people heard [from Ruth Jackson] what was happening in Canada, the Spirit of the Lord fell on that meeting, and we had in that service what they had in Canada. It was incredible."[15] The new influence combined with the older Bethel teaching, and fused the long standing emphases on healing and spiritual gifts with those of the laying on of hands, fasting, prayer, prophecy, allegiance to the five-fold ministry, the importance of the Jewish feast of Pentecost and Tabernacles, distrust of denominations, the manifestations of the sons of God, and the returning of Jesus Christ as signified by the outpouring of God's Spirit. The lines quickly established themselves – Wheeler (who had grown up in the Auckland church and considered Ray Jackson a father figure) was ejected from his associations with evangelical organizations (e.g. Youth for Christ, the Sydney Bible Training Institute), and, after six months of labouring work, traveled with Ray Jackson to Australia (Sydney,

---

[13] Reed, "Oneness Pentecostalism," 937.
[14] Knowles, "History of the New Life Churches in New Zealand," 80.
[15] Wheeler, interview.

Melbourne and Bendigo) as his song leader in a campaign aimed at starting new churches. With Jackson having to return to Sydney in order to care for the new but troubled work there, his son (David Jackson) and Wheeler (then only nineteen years of age) found themselves pastoring the Melbourne church. The coming of another Salvation Army convert, Kevin Conner (who, though only a few years older than Wheeler, already had pastoral experience in the Assemblies of God Church in Bendigo) helped significantly. Years later, Conner would still remember Wheeler's sermon on Gideon, "Where be all these miracles if God be with us?" which he preached the night they met. Their common experience of rejection over the issue of 'the Name,' and their youthful pioneering in the face of rejection, taught them the necessity of training, something that they adopted readily out of the short-term Bible Institute approach which was already widely established in Latter Rain circles.[16]

So it was that with Ron Coady, Kevin Conner, Peter Morrow and others, Wheeler attended Ray Jackson's three month 'Bible school' in Sydney, in 1951. "They called it Bible school, but really it wasn't. We had only two lectures in three months. It was virtually just waiting on the Lord."[17] Students in the Sydney School "would meet together for prayer at nine [a.m.]; we might still be 'singing in the Spirit' at one o'clock in the afternoon."[18] The intensity of the spiritual formation, however, would model for them the short term Bible school as a means for formation, and entrench in them the Latter Rain experientialism brought back by Jackson. It was sealed by the prophetic visit of David Schoch, Omar Bradley and Jack Opie: the twenty-one students at the school then went out and began looking for openings for church planting and ministry. Wheeler, Morrow and David Jackson hitchhiked up the Australian east coast attempting to engage in itinerant preaching, but 'nothing was flowing.' The Bible Institute model had overcome the problem of leadership multiplication – the emerging movement now had to solve the problems of isolation (both geographical and ecclesiological) and the need for a consistent 'world building' theology.

In the United States, geographical isolation had been overcome through the emergence of high-profile, media oriented itinerant ministry, particularly that associated with international missions and

---

[16] Conner, interview.
[17] Wheeler, interview.
[18] Knowles, "History of the New Life Churches in New Zealand," 83.

healing evangelism. This solution was imported into New Zealand with the visit of Tommy Hicks in 1957: "that was our first exposure to an evangelist, really. ... Ron Coady and myself got fired up on evangelism."[19] Following the trajectory of the Latter Rain movement as it moved from Branham's leadership to the broader charismatic evangelism of Oral Roberts, in late 1957 Wheeler took up itinerant tent-crusade evangelism under the name 'Word of Faith Ministry.' Early discouragement and opposition from the Assemblies of God in both Australia and New Zealand ('lifeless churches' as Wheeler referred to them), turned into success through engagement with pre-existing healing movements amongst east coast Maori, and an increasingly nuanced use of the media: "We finished up with three big tents, three big trucks, a team of about fifteen workers, and our own magazine, radio programs, the lot."[20]

A real 'breakthrough' came in the South Island, with a highly successful campaign conducted in Timaru by an independent American evangelist standing in for Hicks, A.S. Worley,[31] in June and July 1960. Avoiding Pentecostal distinctives such as baptism in the Spirit the campaigns emphasized healing and salvation – a mechanism sidestepping the denominational barriers that had structured most postcolonial Western countries at that time. This interdenominationalism worked for some time, but the objectives of the mainline churches and the revivalists were so far apart that friction around key points of denominational distinctive – such as the sacraments – was inevitable. The Latter Rain practice of baptizing in Jesus name thus became the centre for criticism – first, on the suspicion that the teaching was Unitarian or Oneness Pentecostalism, and secondly, on the general belief among traditional churches that the sacrament of baptism could not be repeated. This opposition grew as Wheeler and others targeted the traditional churches in their preaching and publications as manifestations of the 'Harlot Church' predicted in the book of the Revelation, a metaphor that they associated in their endtimes thinking with the emerging ecumenical movement. In time it would not only build the New Life Churches, but would continue to divide the more mainstream Assemblies of God for years to come.

The other influence of Jackson's Sydney Bible School was that it passed on the typical Latter Rain, Bethel Temple emphases on Bible

---

[19] Wheeler, interview.
[20] Wheeler, interview.

teaching: "It generated a characteristic style of Pentecostal Bible teaching, and provided the movement with an hermeneutical methodology
which gave full rein to the imaginative use of allegory and typology.
Consequently, many of the New Life Churches' characteristic doctrines, such as their emphasis on the Tabernacle of Moses, came directly
from their Bethel Temple antecedents."[21] The evangelist and allegoriz-
ing Bible teacher were fused categories in the New Life movement, in
ways not seen in other movements. This made the Bible school a basis
for expansion rather than a potential by-way or subcultural point of
resistance. Using the Tauranga fellowship as a base, Wheeler and Coady
had formed an evening school which between 1959 and 1966 became
the training ground for pastors, who would supply the churches being
founded on Worley's coattails.

After Jackson's model, Wheeler would run many short term Bible
training schools which prepared people for practical charismatic ministry. The emphasis was on experience and narrative rather than scho-
lastics and content. Ironically, given the imported nature of theology
and practice, and its reliance on visiting ministry, these churches came
to be called the 'Indigenous Churches of New Zealand.' By 1965, as
Knowles notes, its early sawdust trail approach was giving way to a
church planting approach,[22] but by then the effectiveness of the
approach had been demonstrated, causing a resurgence of similar
activities in other Pentecostal traditions.

No doubt, given the Latter Rain movement's role as a renewer of
renewal, the resultant culture shift in the Assemblies of God under
Frank Houston at Lower Hutt was gratifying to Ray Jackson and others. Another former Salvationist, Houston would take Latter Rain
influence into the largest Pentecostal movement in New Zealand. In
part, the issue was one of cultural identity: "the Assemblies were in the
hands of British pastors, stiff and formal as could be." [23] The younger
pastors on the other hand wanted something that was their own, and
were attracted both to the idea of 'indigeneity' and power distinct from
tradition. While Houston and Ray Bloomfield began revivalist meetings among rural Maori at Waiomio, near Kawakawa in Northland in
1955–1956,[24] it was the broader impact of New Life Churches which

---

[21] Knowles, "History of the New Life Churches in New Zealand," 78.
[22] Knowles, "History of the New Life Churches in New Zealand," 158.
[23] Clark, *Pentecost at the Ends of the Earth*, 56.
[24] Clark, *Pentecost at the Ends of the Earth*, 57.

helped make Houston's 'new model' acceptable to a fairly traditional Assemblies of God culture. As the early indigenous church revivals overlapped significantly with the work of the 'National Revival Crusades' in which Leo Harris and his family participated, the foundation of the Commonwealth (later Christian) Revival Crusade movement in South Australia was another way in which Latter Rain influence seeped back into Australia. Moreover, Wheeler's short but impacting campaign in Queensland in 1960 impacted four students at Commonwealth Bible College in Brisbane in a way they did not easily forget: classmates Andrew Evans, David Cartledge and Philip Hills and their near Contemporary Reg Klimionok would go on to have a substantial impact on the Assemblies of God in Australia. For them, Wheeler was a representative of the trend they already admired in the ministry of Oral Roberts, made visible to them through film, newspapers and finally by the evangelist's visit to Australia in 1956.[25] Not surprisingly, the church based 'Bible college' – part of the ecclesiological reorientation which took place under David Cartledge and Andrew Evans – became a major contributor to church growth in Australia in ways which had escaped more centralized institutions in previous years.

To some degree, the choice of itinerant ministry was forced by the lack of access to broader means of communication. The emergence of the Latter Rain churches coincided with the postwar breakup of traditional relationships between mainline churches and the state, and so in a sense the emergence of Wheeler and others in the New Zealand secular and religious media is a marker of the progress of de-institutionalization. As Knowles points out, radio in New Zealand largely remained closed to the Latter Rain churches until at least 1967, forcing them to seek alternative media. Most leaders published their own newsletters and papers – Wheeler's emerging under the name 'Bible Deliverance' between April 1959 and March 1966.

In 1961 the National Revival Crusade Convention run by Rob and Beryl Wheeler became a site for conflict and controversy and later that year the indigenous church pastors found themselves rejected by the Pentecostal pastorate in Christchurch. Wheeler, deeply alienated by Assemblies of God traditionalism and denominationalism, took on a more combative stance resulting in growth – through outright

---

[25] See Harrell, "Introduction," *Oral Roberts*, 73; Hutchinson, "Cartledge, David Frederick (1940–2005)."

opposition to the larger Assemblies of God movement in particular – in both South Island and in the North. "We'd go into a town and (I say this with shame now) we'd pitch the tent right opposite the Assembly of God and preach 'Come Out.'"[26] Wheeler observed that as a result of this, "at one stage, between Ron Coady and myself, we were opening a new church every two weeks."[27] A series of national conferences saw the gradual emergence of a new denomination, which combined Wheeler's *Bible Deliverance* magazine with Ray Necklen's *Church Bells* in June 1966 to form a new national journal.

From 1964, Wheeler became pastor of the Auckland Christian Fellowship in Epsom. It was a good time, the Charismatic movement and the advance of the New Life Churches feeding into the church's growth. In August 1964, Wheeler participated with Trevor Chandler and Frank Houston in a Massey University Conference, which became a foundation stone for the rising charismatic movement in the mainstream churches. Wheeler shared his testimony of how he had been baptized in the Holy Spirit. It was the beginning of a flow of people from traditional churches into the rising Pentecostal churches – a movement which Wheeler's own church also enjoyed.

As key educational centres for the post-war period of reconstruction and the emergence of new nation states, the influence of Australia and New Zealand extended throughout Southeast Asia and the Pacific. Along these lines of influence Latter Rain evangelists and missionaries moved out from the new churches and movements. Paul and Bunty Collins worked extensively in Thailand and Hong Kong, Graham Truscott worked in India, and missionaries such as Michael Baré and David Young worked out of communitarian missions support groups in the Philippines and Indonesia. At one stage, Collins' important 'Christian Faith Centre,' the largest Pentecostal church in Sydney at the time, supported up to 50 missionaries in the field.[28] Kevin Conner's Church in Waverley, Victoria, became a particular centre for visiting Asian students studying at Melbourne's leading universities, often under the Colombo Plan. Numbers of these students (including Kriengsak Chareonwongsak) became important in the founding of the influential 'Hope of Bangkok' Church, which was the basis for the international "Hope of God' network. Conner had become a major

---

[26] Wheeler, interview.
[27] Knowles, "History of the New Life Churches in New Zealand," 81.
[28] Hutchinson, "Collins, Paul (1936-)."

proponent of Jackson's Bethel theology, and gained a name as 'the teacher' in Latter Rain circles, influencing major churches such as Peter Morrow's growing charismatic centre in Christchurch, and Clark Taylor's Christian Outreach Centres based in Brisbane.

In 1967 Conner was invited to return to Seattle, out of which he traveled up and down the west coast of the United States for some eighteen months.[29] During that time he met Dick Iverson, from Bible Temple in Portland, Oregon and spent time in Canada, connections which would see him work with Ern Baxter in the Pacific Northwest. In 1972, he returned to Portland and became dean of the Bible School at Iverson's Bible Temple, a post he held for a decade. During that time, his books and study guides circulated throughout Latter Rain circles around the world, establishing structure around the early prophetic illuminism which enabled many churches to make the transition from sectarian revival centres to megachurch status. One of his students, Frank Damazio, would succeed Dick Iversen as pastor of Bible Temple (now renamed as City Bible Church), and marry Conner's daughter. This last connection has maintained into the second generation strong connections between the Pacific Northwest and Melbourne, and through that connection Damazio's regular preaching in major conventions such as Hillsong Conference.

In retrospect, the 1970s were the heyday, and also swansong, for direct Latter Rain influence in Australian churches. Christian Faith Centre in North Sydney did well until 1975, when its founder's mission orientation left the church in the hands of leaders (including David Jackson) who were increasingly influenced by the Shepherding movement. In the absence of a charismatic teacher, like Ray Jackson, this movement dissolved into legalism and control. Another New Zealander, Howard Carter, who had brought over the Logos Institute, took over Faith Centre and fused it with his own group in the Blue Mountains, a Christian community that became increasingly sectarian, influenced by American reconstructionist theology, and divorced from reality over the years. Logos demonstrated in a more fully blown form the fascination with political realization of Kingdom Now principles which would, to a lesser degree, be reflected in the emphases of Australian megachurches on 'influence' in later years. Logos conferences continued to have significance up until the end of the 1980s, but collapsed

---

[29] Conner, interview with Wilkinson.

with the founder's admitted moral lapse in 1991. Latter Rain churches (among which one would have to include at this time Clark Taylor's Christian Outreach Centre at Mansfield, Trevor Chandler's Christian Life Centre in Brisbane, and Frank Houston's Christian Life Centre in Darlinghurst) were also increasingly tempered by the inrush of charismatic Christians, who enjoyed manifestations but did not share the subtending theology.

Perhaps the most significant ongoing influence has been through second generation leaders such as Phil Pringle and Frank Houston's son, Brian, whose huge Hillsong church grew to national and then to international prominence over the next two decades. In all of these churches, contemporary worship music, a theology of Presence, and liturgical acts such as the laying on of hands, provide clues for those who know where to look for the historical influence of the Latter Rain. By the early 1990s, however, the collapse of membership in traditional denominations, and the increasing regional dominance of megachurches produced a situation whereby 'corporate church' models began to replace the earlier influence of the free movement of the Spirit. The same sense of theocratic control which was typical of Latter Rain churches still remains, but the justifications for it shift from the inevitable return of Christ or the dispensational 'Now,' to the imported Word of Faith sense of obedience acting as the gateway to blessing. The implicit materialism of Latter Rain 'manifest sons' theology has been fully elicited with the decline of pneumatic practice under the pressure of public prominence and media scrutiny. The sense of the imminent return of Christ no longer motivated or held the now much broader constituency. The nationalism which had driven the early indigenous churches in New Zealand by the 1990s was also not an issue – churches now were looking for influence on regional and global missions fronts, and interaction with other 'churches of significance' in the global megachurch networks. Ironically, the movement which began as an indigenous revival in Canada, and took on the same role in New Zealand in the 1950s, was bypassed by the necessary filtering which went on as it crossed cultural borders. As Sam Hey has noted with regard to the Christian Outreach Centres:

> The COC did not uncritically adopt overseas models. It adapted, modified and indigenised them. By merging socially conservative Christian beliefs with creative overseas and local responses to social and religious change, the COC was able to grow one of Australia's larger megachurches, and a sizeable national and international religious movement. The COC's

religious beliefs and their organisational practices gave their attendees greater choice that was appropriate to advancing suburbanisation, deinstitutionalisation, and modernity, the development of new technologies and increasing consumer diversity. ...[30]

In the end, the attempt to revive revival through access to spiritual power in 1948 was, within forty years, swamped by restorationism's terminal lack of 'coolness' and relevance.

Apart from those influenced by the Latter Rain movement, the continuing lineal descendants of the movement gathered by Ray Jackson under the title of Associated Mission Churches of Australasia (AMCA) – have had a difficult time in a period of rising concern over the infringement of individual rights and spiritual abuse. In the face of the increasing visibility of Pentecostalism in Australia as a social and political force, AMCA churches have proved themselves incapable of sufficient change. The reported antagonism between Brisbane Christian Fellowship and Christian Outreach Centres,[31] for instance, lies in the fact that while the latter have shown "a capacity for self correction, institutional redevelopment, and interaction with the wider society," resulting in growth, the former have remained inwardly turned and stagnant.[32] Their anti-institutionalism divorced them from the corporatizing movement, and made organization and growth difficult.[33] The departure of Kevin Conner in joining Richard Holland's Waverley Christian Fellowship in the early 1970s demonstrated the difficulty of claiming either perfectionism or apostolic authority over an area.

The intense concentration on 'manifestation' and externalities also played havoc with interior lives. Looking back on the events of the outbreak of the Latter Rain revival in New Zealand, Paul Collins described himself as 'last man standing' – he could not think of anybody who had emphasized the apostolic nature of the movement without suffering from a moral or psychological collapse of some sort.[34] By way of contrast, Waverley Christian Fellowship in time passed to 'the teacher' Kevin Conner, and is now pastored (under the name Citylife Church) by Kevin's son, Mark Conner – it remains one of the largest

---

[30] Hey, "Independent Charismatic Churches in a Period of Post-modernization – A Case Study of the Christian Outreach Centre movement," 9.
[31] Holden, at http://defenceofthefaith.org/BCF2ed.pdf (accessed 1 August 2008).
[32] Hey, "Independent Charismatic Churches," 9.
[33] Hey, 3.
[34] Collins, interview with Hutchinson.

churches in Melbourne. In Collins' own case, he too ended up more as
a teacher than an apostle, basing his Internet-based Bible College out
of a property in Newcastle, NSW. The survivors were those who adapted
and embedded their 'revival of revival' into other movements, into the
space of flows. Those who took the Latter Rain to be an absolute, on the
other hand, grew increasingly shrill and distant.

In 2008, the leading Australian investigative journalism program,
Four Corners, aired on national television a thoroughgoing denunciation of the mind control, emotional blackmail and elitism which
allegedly typified remaining AMCA churches (particularly Brisbane
Christian Fellowship and Toowoomba Christian Fellowship). Fundamental to the criticisms was the perfectionism and the element of
apostolic oversight (the combination of which led to incessant interference in personal and family affairs) which flows out of the fusion of
Latter Rain teachings and Offiler's Wesleyan Salvation Army roots.[35]
There must be some doubt as to whether, with shifting definitions of
family and community, and the disappearance of the private, such ava-
tars of the 1948 revival can continue to exist under the social pressure
which is being exerted on them.[36]

THE GLOBAL RETURN

There is a sense in which the Latter Rain movement was both the end
and the beginning of early Pentecostalism. Early Pentecostalism
embodied within it the aspirations and language of the Latter Rain outpouring. Many of those who joined the movement which emerged in
Canada from 1948, and many of those influenced by it, certainly thought
that what they were involved in was more reflective of early Pentecostalism; more so, they insisted, than many of the first generation
Pentecostal denominations which had become institutionalized across
the years. The particular movement, as is the case with many revival
movements, had its oddities. This is only natural – after all, revival is
by definition a change from 'the norm' (or, at least from the revivalist

---

[35] "God of Broken Hearts," http://www.abc.net.au/4corners/special_eds/20080623/
bcf/default.htm, accessed 1 August, 2008; See Holden, *Who are the Brisbane Christian
Fellowship?*
[36] Note the 'exodus' of members since the running of the program: http://safehouse
.forumup.com.au/about52-safehouse.html, accessed 1 August 2008.

perspective, a re-normalization of Christian communities that had become badly out of skew).

In assessing the long-run impact of the Latter Rain, however, one needs to look not at its oddities but in its continuing effects. By any measure, these effects have been significant. If one thinks of, for instance, the largest church in the world (Yoido Full Gospel Church, Korea), and maps the areas of its major influence – which are mostly in the Asia-Pacific and along the American West Coast – there is a significant overlap with the areas of continuing Latter Rain influence. It will take further research, but on the surface it would appear that there is an important reflexive conditioning effect on the rise of the Asian mega-church and the influence of the Latter Rain through its missionary impulse from Seattle, Portland, and parts of California. It is the position of this chapter that a significant role in that reflex was played by Australia and New Zealand, where the Latter Rain found a home amongst a less bureaucratic, less culturally normed, more missionary oriented Pentecostal culture.

Other more subtle effects are observable. In 2007, for example, a youth band by the name of 'United Live' toured Canada, playing to sell-out crowds in Vancouver, Edmonton, Montreal, and Toronto.[37] The band's music was the number one Christian bestselling album in both Canada and the United States. The reception reflected the adoption of more charismatic forms of contemporary worship in Canadian and other churches, a trend which was being fought out in typical form in the United States (at least among those with enough theology to care) under the rubric of 'the worship wars.'[38] Interestingly, the debate quickly took on the typical tensions between Arminian and Calvinist camps, thereby missing a key element. Much of the contemporary music was in fact emerging from Australia and New Zealand. As Brett Knowles has pointed out, both the Scripture in Song phenomenon which helped fuel the charismatic movement of the 1970s, and the music of Hillsong which has made Australia the third largest exporter of Christian music on the planet, have their roots in the free worship traditions of the Latter Rain movement.[39] The band that acted as the focus for the worship of Canadian youth in 2007 was in fact the youth

---

[37] http://christianmusic.about.com/od/tournews/a/hillsongtour.htm.
[38] E.g. Towns, *Putting an End to Worship Wars*; Byars, *The Future of Protestant Worship*.
[39] Knowles, "From the Ends of the Earth We Hear Songs."

band of Hillsong, and so represented a third generation of developments on the Latter Rain theme.

Such examples (and there are many others) demonstrate that the
Latter Rain provided key elements to the rise of a global charismatic
culture that sidestepped the denominational forms emerging from the
first generation of Pentecostal churches.[40] Its highly symbolic, ener-
getic nature, its embrace of liturgical confirmations (such as laying on
of hands) which fitted church cultures to the 'search for authority' in
churches around the world, and its use of a hermeneutic which freed
the reader of the need to interpret the world from any other source
apart from the Bible, made the Latter Rain eminently transportable. By
the third generation, the Latter Rain's 'Kingdom Now' emphasis on
presence and manifestation was heavily evident in the contemporary
worship music which was the language of the global charismatic movement. The Latter Rain movement, which had been expelled from North
America in the 1950s, was seeping back through the search for cultural
relevance and engagement with youth culture.

From being on the receiving end of the 'international credibility
exchange' which helped build Latter Rain influence in Australasia in the
1940s and 1950s, there is now no doubt that the flow is mutual, if not
slightly in the other direction. In the process of adaptation and transfer,
to be sure, the Latter Rain was not unchanged. In the strictest sense,
Poewe is right when she says that, "Unlike their forerunners, British
Puritanism and Methodism, German Pietism, American Holiness, and
Canadian Latter Rain, Pentecostalism and charismatic Christianity are
still growing."[41] When one drills down to the local case study, however,
one quickly discovers that the process is not one of 'end on' transfer of
a metaphorical historical baton. The charismatic movement, at least in
Australia, depended heavily on support and teaching from Latter Rain
exponents. The process is thus more one of a fusing of influences in
'the space of flows' then of subjugation and extinction. Second generation Australian founders directly influenced by the Latter Rain in New
Zealand, for example, included Frank Houston (Christian Life Centres,
Australia and New Zealand), David Cartledge (and, so, by connection,

---

[40] viz. Poewe, *Charismatic Christianity as a Global Culture*. Charismatic Christianity
"has become a global culture or way of life based on perceptions and identities that are
transmitted worldwide through high-tech media; international conferences, fellowships, and prayer links; and megachurches," xi.

[41] Poewe, *Charismatic Christianity as a Global Culture*, 1.

Andrew Evans) (Assemblies of God in Australia), Leo Harris (Christian Revival Crusade), Bob Midgely (Assemblies of God in Australia and New Zealand), and Clark Taylor (Christian Outreach Centres), while third generation leaders directly influenced included Phil Pringle (Christian City Churches), Phil Baker (Riverview Church), and Brian Houston (Hillsong Church, and Assemblies of God in Australia).

Australian readers will recognize that these were the founders of most of the largest churches in Australia, and a significant proportion of the founders of post-charismatic Pentecostalism in Australasia. The use of laying on of hands, the rise of the idea of 'gifted' as opposed to office related leadership (central to the push for an 'Apostolic Revolution' in many parts of the world), the idea of a progressive restoration of truths embedded in cultural renovation, relevance, and typological preaching, the emphasis on praise and worship in church services, and an aversion to wider structural organization beyond that of the local church, are mainstays of what is now the contemporary church movement in Australasia. While the Latter Rain movement as such no longer continues, its influence has been very significant in fusing with charismatic, healing revival, corporate church and cultural relevance influences to produce some of the more dynamic contemporary charismatic movements in the world today. While the direct lineal descendants seem to be withering on the vine, 'the vine' itself (a metaphor widely used in the Latter Rain movement) seems to be flourishing in many other parts of the world, and flowing back into those places where extinction seemed to be a given.

Conclusion

What is of interest to the scholar of modern Pentecostalism in this phenomenon is the implication of the Latter Rain for the effects of globalization. The assumption in most of the literature, even that which takes as its subject a global framework, is that the Latter Rain movement floundered in the 1970s. Such an assessment, while technically true, misses the point of mobile global societies – movements change shape, names, and pass themselves on through institutional renovation, generational succession, and cultural innovation. By playing the margins and flows of an increasingly interconnected world, Latter Rain influences have become entrenched in Pentecostalism as one of its formal, if disavowable, renewal techniques. In this space of imagined communities, the only real is the imagined, and so this most spiritual of movements baptized technology, materialism and the seemingly objective world of modernity in such a way as to create a self-sustaining (though not enclosed) community of mutual reference.

If Pentecostalism in North America could claim to be part of a rapidly growing movement elsewhere in the world, therefore, it could do so only along the global networks which also carried the Latter Rain movement. The inevitable turf-wars, over what Americans call 'the gospel' and others read as spiritual colonialism, are a reflection of the controversial and contested meanings in this shared imaginative space managed through conferences, CD sales, internet presences etc. If Pentecostalism elsewhere in the world could draw upon American influence to consolidate its position, it also had to do so (at least partially) because of the connective influence of Latter Rain forerunners. The result was that the theological/liturgical approaches which were so energetically expelled in the 1950s from North America were, by the 1990s, the emerging orthodoxy of Pentecostal self-renewal. In a global society, the road out through the front door always leads (through migration, communications, community connections etc) eventually to re-entry through the back door. This is the phenomenon of 'global return' and the Latter Rain movement demonstrates its potency.

Bibliography

Appadurai, A. "Disjuncture and Difference in the Global Culture Economy." *Theory, Culture, and Society* 7 (1990): 295–310.
Australian Broadcasting Commission. "God of Broken Hearts." http://www.abc.net .au/4corners/special_eds/20080623/bcf/default.htm.
Bello, Paula. "Places of Flows: [Re]framing Design." *Locating Design Conference*, International Design History Society, London, UK. https://www.taik.fi/designresearch/img/publib/PlacesFlows_PBello.pdf.
Blumhofer, Edith. *Restoring the Faith: the Assemblies of God, Pentecostalism, and American Culture*, Urbana: University of Illinois Press, 1993.
Byars, Ronald P. *The Future of Protestant Worship: Beyond the Worship Wars*. Louisville, KY: Westminster John Knox Press, 2002.
Clark, I.G. *Pentecost at the Ends of the Earth: The Assemblies of God in New Zealand, 1927–1933*. New Zealand: Christian Road Ministries, 2007.
Collins, P. Interview with Mark Hutchinson 14 February 2003. Pentecostal Heritage Centre Sound Archives, Alphacrucis College, Sydney, Australia.
Conner, K. Interview with J. Wilkinson 29 October 1987. TSS held at Pentecostal Heritage Centre, Alphacrucis College, Sydney, Australia.
Guy, L. "One of a Kind: The Auckland Ministry of A.H. Dallimore." *Australasian Pentecostal Studies*. http://aps.webjournals.org/articles/1/07/2004/5016.htm.
Harrell, Jr., David E. *All things Are Possible: The Healing & Charismatic Revivals in Modern America*. Bloomington: Indiana University Press, 1975.

——. *Oral Roberts: An American Life*. San Francisco, CA: Harper & Row, 1987.
Hey, S. "Independent Charismatic Churches in a Period of Post-modernization – A Case Study of the Christian Outreach Centre movement." Social Change in the 21st-century Conference. Centre for Social Change Research, Queensland University of Technology 27 October 2006. http://eprints.qut.edu.au/archive/00006298/01/6298.pdf.
Holden, D. *Who Are the Brisbane Christian Fellowship?* Albany Cree, Q: Aletheia Press, 1993.
Hutchinson, M. "Adams, John Archibald Duncan (1844–1936)." *Australasian Dictionary of Pentecostal and Charismatic Movements*, http://adpcm.webjournals.org/articles/30/10/2002/6701.htm.
——. "Cartledge, David Frederick (1940–2005)." http://adpcm.webjournals.org/articles/28/10/2002/6649.htm.
——. "Collins, Paul (1936-)." *Australasian Dictionary of Pentecostal and Charismatic Movements*, ttp://adpcm.webjournals.org/articles/ 28/10/2002/6798.htm.
Knowles, B. "History of the New Life Churches in New Zealand." University of Otago, Ph.D. diss., 2003.
——. "'From the Ends of the Earth We Hear Songs': Music as an Indicator of New Zealand Pentecostal Spirituality and Theology." *Australasian Pentecostal Studies*, 5–6 (April 2002). http://aps.webjournals.org/articles/1/04/2002/2984.htm.
Martin, David. *On Secularization: Towards a Revised General Theory*. Burlington, VT: Ashgate, 2005.
Poewe, Karla, ed. *Charismatic Christianity as a Global Culture*. Columbia, SC: University of South Carolina Press, 1994.
Reed, D.A. "Oneness Pentecostalism," in *New International Dictionary of Pentecostal and Charismatic Movements*, edited by Burgess and Van der Maas, 936–44. Grand Rapids: Zondervan, 2002.
Riss, Richard M. "The Latter Rain Movement of 1948." *Pneuma* 4 (1982): 32–45.
——. *Latter Rain: The Latter Rain Movement of 1948 and the Mid-Twentieth Century Evangelical Awakening*. Mississauga, ON.: Honeycomb Visual Productions, 1987.
——. *A Survey of 20th-century Revival Movements in North America*. Peabody, MA: Hendrickson, 1988.
Towns, E. *Putting an End to Worship Wars*. Nashville, TN: Broadman and Holman, 1996.
Walls, Andrew. *The Cross-cultural Process in Christian History: Studies in the Transmission and Appropriation of Faith*. Maryknoll, N.Y.: Orbis Books, 2002.
Weaver, C. Douglas. *The Healer-prophet, William Marrion Branham: A Study of the Prophetic in American Pentecostalism*. Macon, GA: Mercer University Press, 1987.
Wheeler, Rob. Interview with Jerry Wilkinson. 21 July 1980. TSS held at the Pentecostal Heritage Centre, Southern Cross College.
Wilkinson, Michael. "Religion and Global Flows," in *Globalization, Religion, and Culture*, edited by Peter Beyer and Lori Beaman, 375–89. Leiden, Netherlands: Brill Academic Publishers, 2007.

INDEX

Lightning Source UK Ltd.
Milton Keynes UK
UKOW06f0143250317
297459UK00001BA/37/P